# Contested identities

MANCHESTER
1824
Manchester University Press

# Contested identities

## Catholic women religious in nineteenth-century England and Wales

CARMEN M. MANGION

Manchester University Press
Manchester and New York

distributed exclusively in the USA by Palgrave Macmillan

*Published by* Manchester University Press
Oxford Road, Manchester M13 9NR, UK
*and* Room 400, 175 Fifth Avenue, New York, NY 10010, USA
www.manchesteruniversitypress.co.uk

*Distributed exclusively in the USA by*
Palgrave, 175 Fifth Avenue, New York,
NY 10010, USA

*Distributed exclusively in Canada by*
UBC Press, University of British Columbia, 2029 West Mall,
Vancouver, BC, Canada V6T 1Z2

*British Library Cataloguing-in-Publication Data*
A catalogue record for this book is available from the British Library

*Library of Congress Cataloging-in-Publication Data applied for*

ISBN    978 0 7190 7627 5  *hardback*

First published 2008

17  16  15  14  13  12  11  10  09  08        10  9  8  7  6  5  4  3  2  1

*For Rich*

# Contents

# List of figures and tables

## Figures

## Tables

# Preface and acknowledgments

When I decided to become a historian, I imagined it would be solitary work – that I would be shut up in archives and libraries wading through texts, manuscripts and correspondence. Little did I realise that academic life would be so full of camaraderie and collaboration and would create for me not only a new set of work colleagues, but also new friendships with scholars near and far. New friends and old proved invaluable as I expressed my many insecurities about this new venture. I had spent most of my working life in front of spreadsheets and financial statements and anything I wrote needed to be concise, to the point and short! Now I found myself again in front of my laptop, but this time learning to write in an entirely new manner, and it was not a smooth process as I wrote and rewrote (mostly rewriting it seemed!) essays, my thesis and finally this book. Therefore, it is with great pleasure that I recognise the many wonderful friends and colleagues who deserve much more praise and thanks than I can possibly give. They have all played a part in sustaining and lifting my spirits when it seemed (to me at least) that I was attempting an impossible task.

First and foremost, special thanks to my supervisor, Professor Joanna Bourke, who supported me despite so many very 'rough' drafts of chapters and half-thought-through ideas. She has always been supportive, honest with her feedback and accessible even in the midst of her own very heavy teaching and writing commitments. I kept waiting for her to give up on me – but instead, she continued to push and to prod me to think, assuring me that I was capable of finishing. My examiners, Professor Maria Luddy and Dr Anna Davin, were very thorough and fair in their critique of this work, and have proved very supportive throughout the rewriting process. A very special group of congregation archivists have been vital to this project; it wouldn't exist without them. They have allowed me access to private archives, listened to my ramblings and fed me copious quantities of tea and biscuits (and sometimes lunch and dinner too!). They have answered all sorts of questions during and after my research visits: Marion Mc Carthy RSM, Barbara Jeffery RSM, Stephen Christon RSM, Magdalen Reilly RSM, Maria Goretti RSM, Sister Bernadette RSM, Sister Joan RSM, Anne Cunningham SCSP, Judith Greville DC, Joan Conroy DC, Anne Burke SND (RIP), Mary Rooney SND, Mary Campion McCarren FCJ, Denise Mulcahy FCJ, Helen Forshaw SHCJ, Paul Shaw, Patricia Vaulk DHM, Marie de Montfort Parry SSJ, Bridgetta Rooney CSJP, Margaret Lonergan LSA, Pauline Mahoney RLR, and Clare Veronica Wyman RA. Diocesan archivists also contributed their valuable time to assisting me with this project: I am grateful for the support of Fr David Lannon, Robert Finnegan, Dr Meg Whittle, Mrs Osborne, Canon Anthony Dolan, Dr Graham Foster and Fr Ian Dickie.

I am indebted as well to those who have given so generously of their time in reading and commenting on parts of this book. Anne Murphy SHCJ and Mary Sullivan RSM read the manuscript in draft form, and their feedback was very important when I couldn't possibly see the forest for the trees. Dr Rosa MacGinley's copious (and most welcome!) feedback and our subsequent e-mail discussions were very important in helping me understand the ins and outs of canon law. Dr Rebecca Rogers, Dr Stephanie Spencer, Dr Camilla Leach and Annemarie Woodward all read various chapters and commented upon them. There were many family members, friends and colleagues who were held captive (much to their dismay I think!) by my rambling on and on about nuns, who heard me moan about my writing difficulties and who still continued to encourage me. They are too numerous to name, but they know who they are. I am very grateful for their encouragement. Dr Caroline Bowden, Dr Sean Brady, Dr Amanda Capern, Dr Judith Lancaster, Dr Ruth Manning and Dr Susan O'Brien deserve special mention as they received the brunt of my exhortations. Two other groups merit mention. The members of the Historians of Women Religious of Britain and Ireland (H-WRBI) and the Catholic Archives Society also deserve special recognition; these scholars and archivists were quick to answer my strange and somewhat pedantic queries! I cannot thank vigorously enough this generous community of archivists and scholars. They were an essential part of this book, although it goes without saying that they are responsible only for sharing their knowledge and sources; any errors are my own.

The financial support for this research was very important. I am thankful to the institutions that funded my visits to many far-flung archives and specialist conferences. My own institution, Birkbeck College, was financially supportive as was the Royal Historical Society. I also gratefully acknowledge research support from the University of London Central Research Fund.

Lastly, but most importantly, my thanks go to my husband Rich Wagner, who believed in the importance of this work. We have been on an incredible journey together, but the journey of the past five years has been all the more incredible because of his stalwart support as I transformed myself into a historian. It was not an easy transition for me, and therefore not an easy transition for him. Yet through it all, he unswervingly and enthusiastically believed in my ability to make this change, despite my arguments to the contrary. To him this work is dedicated.

# List of abbreviations

CSJP   Congregation of St Joseph of Peace
DC   Daughters of Charity of St Vincent de Paul
DHM   Daughters of the Heart of Mary
FCJ   Faithful Companions of Jesus
LSA   Little Sisters of the Assumption
RLR   Religious of La Retraite
RSM   Religious Sisters of Mercy
SCSP   Sisters of Charity of St Paul the Apostle
SHCJ   Society of the Holy Child Jesus
SMG   Poor Servants of the Mother of God
SND   Sisters of Notre Dame de Namur
SSJ   Sisters of St Joseph of Annecy

# Introduction

Roman Catholic women's congregations are an enigma of nineteenth-century social history. Over 10,000 women,[1] establishing and managing significant Catholic educational, health care and social welfare institutions in England and Wales, have virtually disappeared from history. Despite their exclusion from historical texts, these women featured prominently in the public and the private sphere. By examining the lives of women religious within a historical context and assessing their contribution to the growth of Catholicism, the influence of their religious activism becomes visible. The significance of women religious goes beyond the Catholic boundaries that circumscribed them. Their functioning in society has much to say about women's spirituality as a source of self-definition and the fluid boundaries of femininity. Their independence, though ambiguous and circumscribed within a rigid, hierarchical structure, contributed to the changing landscape of nineteenth-century femininity. This text places women religious in the centre of nineteenth-century social history and reveals how religious activism shaped the identity of Catholic women religious.

In nineteenth-century England, representations of women religious were ambiguous and contested from both within and without the convent. The nun was often the centre of controversy in the Protestant press: sometimes as a scheming mother superior, other times as a young nun incarcerated against her will and now and again as an innocent led astray by the manipulative schemes of the Catholic clergy. The Catholic

---

1 Francesca M. Steele, *The Convents of Great Britain* (London: Sands, and Dublin: M.H. Gill, 1902), p. xi. This figure is based on Steele's calculation of 600 convents with an average of seventeen professed sisters in each convent. There has been no comprehensive work done to calculate the number of women who entered religious life in nineteenth-century England, although various studies exist, including this one, which include a calculation of the number of women religious who entered specific congregations.

press and internal convent documents offered a different depiction of women religious. The Catholic press represented nuns as pious, obedient, subordinate and self-effacing. Convent documents offered similar descriptions but added to the image of the 'good nun' the more practical qualities of intelligence, perseverance and strength. These images of the 'perfect nun' were continually being formed and reframed throughout the nineteenth century. To understand these representations better, this book will focus on the identity of women religious – how it was formed, maintained and modified during the course of the nineteenth century.

The identity of women religious was linked specifically to nineteenth-century ideas of gender, class and ethnicity. Gender was a prime determiner of social positioning in the Roman Catholic Church. Although not members of the ecclesiastical hierarchy, women religious, as church workers, held a special place in the church and were a dynamic, authoritative and pervasive influence. Gender had an assumed authority which was constructed both publicly and privately. This authority was constantly changing during the course of the nineteenth century as women's congregations developed from small conventual establishments to large, national or multinational institutions. Ethnicity was also an important aspect of identity for women religious of England and Wales. The relationship between English and Irish-born sisters added another complex layer to the dimensions of convent life. Intertwined with the issues of ethnicity was the notion of class. No history of the nineteenth century can avoid the complexities of class, and it is no different for this history of women religious. Class was relevant to the congregation that a woman entered, the work that women religious performed and the path to leadership.

Women religious accepted contemporary beliefs about women's 'place' in nineteenth-century society, yet transcended these beliefs by using religious ideology to expand their authority into the public sphere. Their representation of a 'good nun' was as a woman of prayer and action and revolved around their conviction of her ability to change the world through her evangelicalism; this representation informed their actions and united their efforts. As such, women religious were commanding role models in nineteenth-century England and Wales. Prescriptive literature offered one model of womanhood, that of married life, with a second model, that of single life, which was often regarded as an inauspicious alternative. This book argues that women religious provided a third model of womanhood, one that embraced the influence of unmarried, consecrated women. This exemplar of womanhood had its own language, customs and shared history that extended round the world.

## Terminology

Catholic women interested in entering religious life in the nineteenth century had two options: they could lead a contemplative life of prayer in an enclosed community or they could pursue an active life performing philanthropic activities typically outside the cloister.[2] Women who entered contemplative life were called nuns, took solemn vows and lived in religious institutes called orders. The active religious life was also one of prayer but included philanthropic and evangelical work such as teaching, nursing and parish visiting; these activities typically occurred outside the convent walls. These women, called sisters, took simple vows and lived in religious institutes called congregations.[3] Nuns and sisters are now typically referred to by the generic term of 'women religious'. While it is commonly accepted that all women religious are referred to as nuns, it is canonically correct to refer to women who took solemn vows as nuns and women who took simple vows as sisters. This book will use the terms 'nuns', 'sisters' and 'women religious' interchangeably. While this does not conform strictly to canon law, it does agree with popular usage within and without the Roman Catholic Church.[4]

This book examines the identity of active, simple-vowed women religious who entered congregations and whose philanthropic and evangelical

2  Some solemn-vowed, enclosed orders did perform philanthropic work, often teaching, from inside the cloister. However, in this book 'active' institutes are defined as those that perform their activities outside the cloister.

3  The terms 'communities' and 'institutes' will be used interchangeably throughout this book to denote both solemn and simple-vowed groupings of women religious. 'Congregation' as used in this book refers to a community of women who take simple vows. The term 'mother house' or 'provincial house' refers to the convent that is the administrative and oftentimes spiritual centre of centralised communities of women religious.

4  The terminology used to refer to women religious is defined by canon law, a series of pronouncements circulated through the centuries in the form of Holy Writs, decrees of Roman pontiffs and canons of councils. These laws and regulations of the Roman Catholic Church were summarised in 1917 into a comprehensive text that provided 'order and clearness' by removing obsolete laws, adapting laws to current practices and enacting new laws. P. Chas. Augustine OSB, DD, *A Commentary on the New Code of Canon Law*, 8 vols (London: B. Herder Book Co., 1918), III, pp. 60 and 315–21.

5  This book does not examine the identity of nineteenth-century solemn-vowed nuns as this would have broadened the scope of this project to an unmanageable level. This is another facet of nineteenth-century religious life that is currently under-researched.

activities took place outside convent walls.[5] In the early nineteenth century, these 'modern orders' were still a relatively new form of religious life. The emergence of a great number of simple-vowed groups of women religious such as the Ursulines, the Visitation Sisters, the English Ladies and the Daughters of Charity occurred despite the threat of enclosure. Some groups were forcibly enclosed; others existed surreptitiously and some denied their religious status in order to exist within the Roman Catholic Church. Despite the numerous papal edicts outlawing their activities outside the cloister, support from a local bishop could safeguard their existence.[6] Only enclosed religious orders were canonically recognised. Despite this lack of canonical legitimation, simple-vowed congregations grew dramatically from the late eighteenth century onwards.[7]

While the time span of this book is a wide-ranging one and includes the entire nineteenth century, the primary focus will be from the middle to the end of the century. As will be explained in the next chapter, this was the period of the greatest growth and change. The end-point selected, 1900, was chosen because of two important events. Simple-vowed women religious were fully and formally recognised as 'religious' in 1900 with Pope Leo XIII's *Conditae a Christo*, which clearly defined the juridical nature of both pontifical and diocesan approved religious congregations.[8] The second event, yet another bout of anticlericalism in France, resulted in an influx of French women religious into England in the early 1900s. This development influenced further changes in religious life in England and is beyond the remit of this book.[9] The use of 1900 as the end date of this book provides a logical and manageable space of time in which to discuss simple-vowed women's congregations.

6  M.R. MacGinley, PBVM, *A Dynamic of Hope: Institutes of Women Religious in Australia* (Darlinghurst, New South Wales, Australia: Crossing Press, 2002), pp. 1–64.

7  Over time, Rome became more tolerant of simple-vowed women religious, and in *Quamvis justo* (1749) congregations were given legitimate and juridical authority although their members were not considered 'true nuns'.

8  Catherine C. Darcy RSM, *The Institute of the Sisters of Mercy of the Americas: The Canonical Development of the Proposed Governance Model* (Lanham: University Press of America, 1993), p. 23.

9  Nicholas Atkin, 'The Politics of Legality: The Religious Orders in France, 1901–45', in Frank Tallett and Nicholas Atkin, eds, *Religion, Society and Politics in France since 1789* (London: The Hambledon Press, 1991), pp. 149–66; Sarah A. Curtis, 'Lay Habits: Religious Teachers and the Secularization Crisis of 1901–1904', *French History*, 9 (1995), 478–98; Caroline Ford, 'Religion and the Politics of Cultural Change in Provincial

## Methodology

The publication of the *Decree on the Adaptation and Renewal of Religious Life, Perfectae caritatis*, issued on 28 October 1965, emphasised that a key factor of renewal was a 'return to the sources of Christian life' and a return to the 'original spirit of the institutes and their adaptation to the changed conditions of our time'.[10] This emphasis on the 'spirit of the institutes' stressed the importance of historical records and encouraged religious institutes to initiate a deeper, more critical assessment of their history. The result has been a dramatic increase in published histories of congregations, founders and the establishments they built and managed. This development has also led to the opening of congregation archives to social and religious historians. Congregational archives contain valuable sources documenting the history, works and life of a congregation and are also a rich source for social historians researching topics as varied as piety and prostitution, poverty and philanthropy. It is these archives that have provided the rich collection of sources that inform this book. In addition, census reports, diocesan records, periodicals and contemporary texts have been examined to corroborate and fill in the gaps in the congregation records.

These documents serve as the basis for a prosopographical analysis within which precise historical questions about a collective group can be posed. Prosopography is often called a 'biography of a community'[11] as it suggests relationships and connections between a group of individuals and the social, political and religious environment of their time.[12] Lawrence Stone, an early patron of prosopography, used this methodology in his work on the family to 'make sense of political action, to help explain ideological or cultural change, to identify social

France: The Resistance of 1902 in Lower Brittany', *Journal of Modern History*, 62 (1990), 1–33; Judith F. Stone, 'Anticlericals and Bonnes Soeurs: The Rhetoric of the 1901 Law of Associations', *French Historical Studies*, 23 (2000), 103–28.

10 *Decree on the Adaptation and Renewal of Religious Life, Perfectae caritatis* (28 October 1965), www.vatican.va/archive/hist_councils/ii_vatican_council/ [accessed 29 August 2006]. The Pontifical Commission for the Cultural Heritage of the Church issued *The Pastoral Function of Church Archives* on 2 February 1997, which emphasised that the creation and maintenance of church archives was imperative for congregations, orders and dioceses.

11 Lawrence Stone, *The Past and the Present Revisited* (London: Routledge & Kegan Paul, 1981), p. 45.

12 K.S.B. Keats Rohan, 'Prosopography and Computing: A Marriage made in Heaven?', *History and Computing*, 12 (2000), 1–13 (p. 2).

reality, and to describe and analyze with precision the structure of society and the degree and nature of movements within it'.[13] Prosopography is also a useful tool with which to investigate both collective and individual identity. Identities are formed through interactions between individuals and groups, and this prosopographical analysis of women religious will reveal some of the personal and behavioural attributes of women who entered religious life. In this work, prosopography is used to explore both the group and the individual identities of women in selected congregations to reveal commonality and difference. The connection to the group, in this case women's religious congregations, has many implications for understanding the identity of women religious. A prosopographical analysis allows us to see the ways in which this affiliation both created and constrained the identity of individual women religious.

Historians employ such concepts as social identities, gendered identities, cultural identities, public identities and private identities in order to explain facets of culture and society. Despite the ubiquity of this type of enquiry, identity as a historical concept exists in a haze of ambiguity. How it is defined and used to explain historical change in particular areas is important. The creation of identity is a process shaped by myriad forces, including gender, ethnicity and class, and formal and informal social groupings which include family, friends, social clubs, work, religion and the state.[14] This shaping of identity can be both conscious and unconscious, imposed and selected.[15] Identity is not singular and fixed, but contains many facets and is malleable, contested and changeable.[16] Identity is pivotal to understanding class, as the construction of identity has been important in defining and maintaining social divisions. Notions

13 Stone, 1981, p. 46.
14 Stephanie Adams, 'Women Returners and Fractured Identities', in Nickie Charles and Felicia Hughes-Freeland, eds, *Practising Feminism: Identity, Difference, Power* (London: Routledge, 1996), 202–22 (pp. 203–4).
15 Megan Matchinske, *Writing, Gender and State in Early Modern England: Identity Formation and the Female Subject* (Cambridge: Cambridge University Press, 1998), p. 12.
16 Kath Woodward, 'Concepts of Identity and Difference', in Kath Woodward, ed., *Identity and Difference* (London: Sage, 1997), p. 15; Alan Kidd and David Nicholls, 'Introduction: History, Culture and the Middle Classes', in Alan Kidd and David Nicholls, eds, *Gender, Civic Culture and Consumerism: Middle-Class Identity in Britain, 1800–1940* (Manchester: Manchester University Press, 1999), p. 6; Adams, 1996, pp. 203–4; Neville Kirk, *Northern Identities: Historical Interpretations of 'The North' and 'Northernness'* (Aldershot: Ashgate, 2000), p. xii.

of femininity and masculinity, which are culturally derived and constantly shifting, influence the identity of individuals.[17] Here again, examining the construction of identity provides a means of understanding the gendering of individuals.

The sociologist Nickie Charles maintains that identity formation is contingent upon culture, and within any one culture a diversity of subcultures exists. From this, we can posit that within the metaculture of Victorian life, Catholic women's religious congregations formed one of many subcultures. An analysis of this subculture provides us with the tool for understanding the identity of women religious.[18] The interaction between the individual nuns and the congregation, and the influence of the dominant culture in which they lived, shaped how their identity was created and maintained as well as how it shifted over time. Identities were reworked through individual agency, but a tension existed between social structures and this agency.[19] This tension is the centre of this book. Women religious negotiated multiple identities, at the core of which was their religious identity. Women's religious congregations mobilised women to define themselves and their actions through this religious identity. Their identity was constructed through specific historical, social, cultural, religious and economic conditions in place in nineteenth-century Britain and Ireland. This, in itself, says much about their relationship with those inside and outside the religious community, within the institution of the Roman Catholic Church and within the wider Victorian culture.

This book examines the identities of women religious through the lens of gender, ethnicity and class in three main parts. The first part, 'Developing identities', begins in Chapter 1 with the evolution of religious life in England, paying particular attention to early monastic life, and then continues with an analysis of the growth of women's religious congregations in England. The dramatic growth of nineteenth-century

17  Craig Young, 'Middle-Class "Culture", Law and Gender Identity: Married Women's Property Legislation in Scotland, c. 1850–1920', in Alan Kidd and David Nicholls, eds, *Gender, Civic Culture and Consumerism: Middle-Class Identity in Britain, 1800–1940* (Manchester: Manchester University Press, 1999), 133–45 (p. 134).
18  Nickie Charles, 'Feminist Practices: Identity, Difference, Power', in Charles and Hughes-Freeland, 1996, p. 4.
19  Jennifer Gove and Stuart Watt, 'Identity and Gender', in Kath Woodward, ed., *Questioning Identity: Gender, Class, Nation* (London: Open University Press, 2000), 43–78 (p. 47). In this instance, agency is defined as the amount of control exercised over identity.

women's congregations says much about the dynamism of religious life and the attraction this subculture held for many women. Chapter 2 seeks to unravel what drove or attracted women to religious life. This was not a passive choice. Catholic women were not pushed into becoming women religious; they were attracted by what they considered the advantages of religious life. On the basis of their available options, they chose a path that best suited their personal, spiritual, economic and vocational needs. Chapter 3 considers how the training for religious life shaped the identity of women religious. The postulancy and novitiate period formed a rite of passage that tested the vocation of each aspirant. The second part, 'Working identities', explores the religious activism of women religious first, in Chapter 4, through their missionary identity. The labour of women religious in the fields of education and health care and in the provision of social services was intricately linked to their role as evangelisers. Another related factor was their professional identity as educators and health care professionals; this is discussed in Chapter 5. The final part, 'Corporate identities', begins in Chapter 6 with the development of a congregation's corporate identity which brought together a disparate group of women under the banner of religious life. Chapter 7 looks specifically at class and ethnicity and the women who entered religious life. The entry of a diverse group of women into simple-vowed congregations had many implications for the status of religious congregations and the identity of women religious. Chapter 8 concludes this part by identifying the source of authority for the congregation and the individual sister. Chapter by chapter, the study expands our understanding of women religious and Catholicism in nineteenth-century England and Wales. Significantly, it also extends our knowledge of the role of women in the public and private sphere. It is part of the larger story of the agency of nineteenth-century women and the broader transformation of English society.

## Historiography

Religion is rarely seen as a factor in histories of social change, owing in part to what Jeffrey Cox describes as the master narrative of secularisation.[20] Industrialisation, science and technology can provide logical and rational explanations used to explain economic, political and cultural change. However, religion, judged as irrational and not part of modernity, has been marginalised as a reason for social change in

20 Jeffrey Cox, 'Audience and Exclusion at the Margins of Imperial History', *Women's History Review*, 3 (1994), 501–14 (pp. 501–2).

the modern world. The standard association between religion and hierarchical religious institutions is also problematic as it ignores an entire facet of religious engagement which is not tied to an institutional structure. Another issue is that women are frequently seen as oppressed by religious institutions; for some historians, their lives have come to represent another unwelcome symbol of patriarchy. In looking at the beliefs and lives of women religious in the nineteenth-century context, a less static interpretation will be suggested. This study of women and religion will challenge some prevailing conventions by analysing religion as an empowering belief system. The ambiguity that existed in the relationship between women and the institutional church is recognised. Women's involvement within any religious hierarchy is a problematic paradigm in the nineteenth century.

Apologetic and promotional church histories are an intrinsic part of the chronicles of ecclesiastical scholarship, particularly in the early part of the twentieth century. Their partisan content and lack of self-criticism have made it difficult to assess critically the contribution of religious institutions to the life of the laity. In addition, ecclesiastical historians have long focused on institutional or hierarchical history and ignored the contribution of lay women and men to culture, religious life, philanthropy and spirituality. Nevertheless, some ecclesiastical historians have used gender as a tool of analysis. *Gender and Christian Religion* (1998), published by the Ecclesiastical History Society, contained thirty-two essays focused on gender and Christianity, including such topics as the origins and development of Christian thinking about gender, misogyny and the patriarchal church order, gender stereotyping in the clerical profession and feminine expressions of religious commitment. This gendered approach to appraising the influence of religion on social change will, it is hoped, foster a less partisan attitude in ecclesiastical history.

Social historians have, in the last few decades, become more attentive to the historical significance of women and religion. Well-known scholars such as Gail Malmgreen and Patricia Crawford have explored women's agency in institutional church structures in early modern England and found women's spirituality a source of strength, accomplishment and self-definition.[21] Historians of the nineteenth century have begun to pay more attention to women's religious experience, recognising the significance of religious belief as an ideological influence in the

---

21 Gail Malmgreen, *Religion in the Lives of English Women, 1760–1930* (London: Croom Helm, 1986), p. 9; Patricia Crawford, *Women and Religion in England 1500–1720* (London: Routledge, 1993), p. 1.

lives of nineteenth-century women.[22] Leonore Davidoff and Catherine Hall's *Family Fortunes: Men and Women of the English Middle Class, 1780–1850* (1987) placed religion in the centre of middle-class lives, recognising that middle-class identity and community were based on religious affiliations.[23] Frank Prochaska's *Women and Philanthropy in Nineteenth-Century England* (1980) recognised philanthropic activity, often affiliated with religious institutions, as the 'lever' which women used to gain experience that was relevant to their entry into the professions in England.[24] In 2002, Sue Morgan brought together a collection of essays in *Women, Religion and Feminism in Britain, 1750–1900* that assesses the influence of religion on the lives of eighteenth- and nineteenth-century feminist activists. Julie Melnyk, editor of *Women's Theology in Nineteenth-Century Britain: Transfiguring the Faith of their Fathers* (1998), argued that women's theological writing, often disguised as letters, fiction and devotional manuals, began to transform Victorian spirituality.[25]

Important histories defining women's roles within specific religious institutions have also been published. Sean Gill's *Women in the Church of England from the Eighteenth Century to the Present* (1994) examined the relationship between Anglican teachings and women's gendered roles. His findings reflect an ambiguity that is unsurprising: women's lives were both liberated and constricted by Anglican theology.[26] Susan Mumm's *Stolen Daughters, Virgin Mothers: Anglican Sisterhoods in Victorian Britain* (1998) considered Anglican sisterhoods a 'powerful example of feminist practice'.[27] Katharine Gleadle's *The Early Feminists:*

22  Susan Morgan, 'Faith, Sex and Purity: The Religio-Feminist Theory of Ellice Hopkins', *Women's History Review*, 9 (2000), 13–34 (p. 13); Kerri Allen, 'Representation and Self-Representation: Hannah Whitall Smith as Family Woman and Religious Guide', *Women's History Review*, 7 (1998), 227–39 (p. 235); Sandra Stanley Holton, Alison Mackinnon and Margaret Allen, 'Introduction', *Women's History Review*, 7 (1998), 163–9 (p. 164).
23  Leonore Davidoff and Catherine Hall, *Family Fortunes: Men and Women of the English Middle Class, 1780–1850* (London: Hutchinson, 1987), p. 77.
24  F.K. Prochaska, *Women and Philanthropy in Nineteenth-Century England* (Oxford: Clarendon Press, 1980), p. 227.
25  Julie Melnyk, *Women's Theology in Nineteenth-Century Britain: Transfiguring the Faith of their Fathers* (London: Garland Publishing, 1998), p. xii.
26  Sean Gill, *Women in the Church of England from the Eighteenth Century to the Present* (London: Society for Promoting Christian Knowledge, 1994), p. 4.
27  Susan Mumm, *Stolen Daughters, Virgin Mothers: Anglican Sisterhoods in Victorian Britain* (London: Leicester University Press, 1998), p. 210.

*Radical Unitarians and the Emergence of the Women's Rights Movement, 1831–1851* (1995) investigated Unitarian women's contribution to the women's rights movement.[28] Linda Wilson's *Constrained by Zeal: Female Spirituality amongst Nonconformists, 1825–1875* (2000) explored the relationship between contemporary ideologies and the spirituality of nonconformist women.[29] Martha Vicinus's *Independent Women: Work and Community for Single Women, 1850–1920* (1985) argued that nineteenth-century Anglican sisterhoods and deaconesses used Victorian myths of womanhood and the concomitant rhetoric of duty and obedience to forge a 'narrow path of self-fulfilment'.[30]

The historiography of women religious is both national and international in scope; it is wide-ranging and extends from the early days of the church to the aftermath of Vatican II. Since the 1980s, there has been an upsurge in the historiography of women religious, due in part to the opening of religious archives to academic scholars as well as the scholarly interest of women religious themselves. One of the most ambitious additions to this historiography is Jo Ann Kay McNamara's *Sisters in Arms: Catholic Nuns through Two Millennia* (1996). This comprehensive reference synthesises 2,000 years of the history of Catholic women's religious life in congregations and orders. McNamara begins in the years of the early church by linking chastity with female identity, explaining how virginity 'wiped out gender differences' and gave women religious the 'independence and the authority to pursue a lofty spiritual calling'.[31] From here, McNamara charts the steady gendering of religious life: by the early modern era, strict claustration was the norm for

28 Katherine Gleadle, *The Early Feminists: Radical Unitarians and the Emergence of the Women's Rights Movement, 1831–1851* (London: Routledge, 1995), p. 4.
29 Linda Wilson, *Constrained by Zeal: Female Spirituality amongst Nonconformists, 1825–1875* (Carlisle, England: Paternoster Publishing, 2000), pp. 12–13.
30 Martha Vicinus, *Independent Women: Work and Community for Single Women, 1850–1920* (London: Virago Press, 1985), p. 47.
31 Jo Ann Kay McNamara, *Sisters in Arms: Catholic Nuns through Two Millennia* (London: Harvard University Press, 1996), pp. 3–6. Other important texts that examine women's religious life and the early church are Gillian Cloke, *This Female Man of God: Women and Spiritual Power in the Patristic Age 350–459* (New York: Routledge, 1995); Kate Cooper, *The Virgin and the Bride* (Cambridge, Massachusetts, USA: Harvard University Press, 1999); Joyce E. Salisbury, *Church Fathers, Independent Virgins* (New York: Verso, 1992).

women religious. The nineteenth century brought further changes, as simple-vowed women religious became the driving force that built 'an unparalleled network of educational and care-giving institutions'.[32] Her broad scope provides an excellent overview of Catholic women's religious life.

Gaps exist in the history of women and religion in nineteenth-century England, and in particular scholarship on Catholic women is virtually non-existent. Frank Prochaska's seminal work *Women and Philanthropy in Nineteenth-Century England* (1980) acknowledges the existence of women religious by stating that 'Sisters of Charity, Sisters of Mercy, and Sisters of Nazareth were active in various parts of the city'; but after this comment, women religious are barely mentioned again.[33] The references to the activities of women religious in Catholic histories are often equally brief; women religious are typically dismissed with a one-sentence plaudit acknowledging their existence and contribution.[34] However, here too there have been some positive changes. V. Alan McClelland and Michael Hodgetts's *From without the Flaminian Gate: 150 Years of Roman Catholicism in England and Wales 1850–2000* (1999) contains an entire chapter on religious life for women.[35] Even so, given religion's significance in the lives of women[36] and the widespread growth of religious life in the nineteenth century, such treatment seriously understates the influence of Catholic women's congregations. The lives of women religious shaped and moulded the society in which they lived. The development of the depth and breadth of their philanthropic and evangelical endeavours was instrumental in strengthening the Roman Catholic Church. By deconstructing the lives of the women themselves and by examining the construction of their identities, what appears is a religious discourse that both enabled and disabled women religious. Using the lens

32  McNamara, 1996, p. 574.
33  Brief, general references to women religious exist on pp. 109, 147 and 189.
34  John Bossy, *The English Catholic Community, 1570–1850* (London: Darton, Longman & Todd, 1975); Denis Gwynn, *A Hundred Years of Catholic Emancipation (1829–1929)* (London: Longmans Green and Co., 1929); J. Derek Holmes, *More Roman than Rome: English Catholicism in the Nineteenth Century* (London: Burns and Oates, 1978); E.E. Reynolds, *The Roman Catholic Church in England and Wales: A Short History* (Wheathampstead, Hertfordshire: Anthony Clarke Books, 1973).
35  Susan O'Brien, 'Religious Life for Women', in V. Alan McClelland and Michael Hodgetts, eds, *From without the Flaminian Gate: 150 Years of Roman Catholicism in England and Wales 1850–2000* (London: Darton Longman + Todd, 1999), pp. 108–41.
36  Holton, Mackinnon and Allen, 1998, p. 163.

of religion as an interpretive framework can shed new light on the significance of Catholic women religious.

In England, the scholarship on women religious is in its embryonic stage. This is in part due to challenges of accessing primary sources, but perhaps also to the difficulties of 'rescuing' the image of veiled women willingly implicated in a patriarchal church. Research on medieval and early modern women religious is much more developed despite fewer extant primary sources; Claire Cross, Roberta Gilchrist, Eileen Power, Sally Thompson, Bruce Venarde and Claire Walker are notable historians of English medieval and early modern women religious.[37] Scholarship pertaining to nineteenth- and twentieth-century women religious exists only in journal articles and a handful of texts, most of which are biographies. Much of the early historiography for nineteenth-century women's congregations of England consists of hagiographical works on congregation founders or notable nuns and broad-based histories of congregations. These works are unlikely to provide a critical analysis of issues regarding the role of women in the institutional church. A frank exploration of women's congregations and their members, including an investigation of the difficulties they faced because of rapid growth, the repercussions of defections and the disagreements between individuals with authority, is necessary.

Susan O'Brien, the leading historian of nineteenth-century Catholic women's religious congregations in England, provides this academic rigour.[38] Her pioneering work on women religious is probing and insightful; she argues that women religious had a 'greater control of the direction of their congregation, the use of its resources and the employment of their sisters' than is generally acknowledged.[39] As centralised entities, congregations could, and did, develop and manage new types

---

37 Claire Cross and Noreen Vickers, *Monks, Friars and Nuns in Sixteenth Century Yorkshire* (Leeds: Yorkshire Archaeology Society, 1995); Roberta Gilchrist, *Contemplation and Action: The Other Monasticism* (London: Leicester University Press, 1995); Roberta Gilchrist, *Gender and Material Culture: the Archaeology of Religious Women* (London: Routledge, 1994); Eileen Power, *Medieval English Nunneries: 1275–1535* (Cambridge: Cambridge University Press, 1922); Sally Thompson, *Women Religious: The Founding of English Nunneries after the Norman Conquest* (Oxford: Oxford University Press, 1991); Bruce L. Venarde, *Women's Monasticism and Medieval Society: Nunneries in France and England, 890–1215* (London: Cornell University Press, 1997).
38 See the Bibliography for a complete list of publications.
39 O'Brien, 1999, p. 109.

of institutions that met the needs of the people they served. They were innovative and flexible. But with growth and stability came the institutionalisation of women's religious life.[40] Barbara Walsh's *Roman Catholic Nuns in England and Wales, 1800–1937: A Social History* (2002) also provides important insights into religious communities in England and Wales from 1800 to 1937. Walsh's geographic analysis of Catholic convents develops significant conclusions pertaining to the geographical spread of Catholic convents. Since the 1990s, the publication of biographies of congregation founders such as Cornelia Connelly, Mary Potter and Elizabeth Prout, and histories of individual convents such as Maria McClelland's *The Sisters of Mercy, Popular Politics and the Growth of the Roman Catholic Community in Hull, 1855–1930* (2000) provide critical and contextual analysis of women religious and the communities they led.[41]

Despite this developing literature on women religious in England, the depth of the scholarship pales by comparison with Irish and French scholarship of the same period. Margaret MacCurtain's influence on Irish early modern history and her inclusion of women religious in her work have proved inspirational to the advancement of scholarship on women religious.[42] Caitriona Clear's meticulously researched text, *Nuns in Nineteenth-Century Ireland* (1987), as well as her subsequent journal

---

40  Ibid, p. 124.
41  Radegunde Flaxman, *A Woman Styled Bold: The Life of Cornelia Connelly, 1809–1879* (London: Darton Longman and Todd, 1991); Edna Hamer, *Elizabeth Prout, 1820–1864: A Religious Life for Industrial England* (Bath, England: Downside Abbey, 1994); Judith Lancaster, *Cornelia Connelly and her Interpreters* (Oxford: The Way, 2004); Elizabeth A. West, *One Woman's Journey: Mary Potter: Founder – Little Company of Mary* (Richmond, Victoria, Australia: Spectrum Publications, 2000).
42  Suellen Hoy and Margaret MacCurtain, *From Dublin to New Orleans: The Journey of Nora and Alice* (Dublin: Attic Press, 1994); Margaret MacCurtain, 'Godly Burdens: The Catholic Sisterhoods in Twentieth Century Ireland', in Anthony Bradley and Maryann Gialanella Valiulis, eds, *Gender and Sexuality in Modern Ireland* (Amherst: University of Massachusetts Press, 1997), pp. 245–56; Margaret MacCurtain, 'Late in the Field: Catholic Sisters in Twentieth-Century Ireland and the New Religious History', in Mary O'Dowd and Sabine Wichert, eds, *Chattel, Servant or Citizen: Women's Status in Church, State and Society* (Belfast: The Institute of Irish Studies, 1995), pp. 34–44; Margaret MacCurtain, 'Women, Education and Learning in Early Modern Ireland', in Margaret MacCurtain and Mary O'Dowd, eds, *Women in Early Modern Ireland* (Edinburgh: Edinburgh University Press, 1991), pp. 160–78.

articles, broke new ground regarding Ireland's nineteenth-century women religious. Some of Clear's arguments have been challenged by subsequent scholars of Irish women religious such as Mary Peckham Magray in *The Transforming Power of the Nuns: Women, Religion, and Cultural Change in Ireland, 1750–1900* (1998) and Marie O'Connell in her chapter on Ulster women religious in Janice Holmes and Diane Urquhart's *Coming into the Light: The Work, Politics and Religion of Women in Ulster 1840–1940* (1994).[43] Maria Luddy's numerous contributions to Irish history have been crucial to integrating women religious into the history of Irish social and political organisations.[44] She argues that women religious in Ireland were 'the most significant of charitable

43 Other texts about Irish women religious include Tony Fahey, 'Nuns in the Catholic Church in Ireland in the Nineteenth Century', in Mary Cullen, ed., *Girls Don't Do Honours: Irish Women in Education in the 19th and 20th Centuries* (Dublin: Women's Education Bureau, 1987), pp. 7–30; J. Lee, 'Women and the Church since the Famine' in Margaret MacCurtain and Doncha O'Corrain, eds, *Women in Irish Society: The Historical Dimension* (Dublin: Arlen House, 1978), pp. 37–45; Janet A. Nolan, *Ourselves Alone: Women's Emigration from Ireland, 1885–1920* (Lexington, Kentucky: University Press of Kentucky, 1989); Marie O'Connell, 'The Genesis of Convent Foundations and their Institutions in Ulster, 1840–1920', in Janice Holmes and Diane Urquhart, eds, *Coming into the Light: The Works Politics and Religion of Women in Ulster 1840–1940* (Belfast: The Institute of Irish Studies, 1994), pp. 149–201.
44 Maria Luddy, 'Women and Charitable Organisations in Nineteenth Century Ireland', *Women's Studies International Forum*, 11 (1988), 301–5; Maria Luddy, 'An Agenda for Women's History in Ireland: 1800–1900', *Irish Historical Studies*, 28 (1992), 19–37; Maria Luddy, 'An Outcast Community: The "Wrens" of the Curragh', *Women's History Review*, 1 (1992), 341–84; Maria Luddy, 'Presentation Convents in County Tipperary, 1803–1900', *Tipperary Historical Journal* (1992); Mary Cullen and Maria Luddy, eds, *Women, Power and Consciousness in 19th Century Ireland* (Dublin: Attic Press, 1995); Maria Luddy, *Women in Ireland, 1800–1918: A Documentary History* (Cork: Cork University Press, 1995); Maria Luddy, *Hanna Sheehy Skeffington* (Dundalk: Irish Historical Association, 1995); Maria Luddy, '"Abandoned Women and Bad Characters": Prostitution in Nineteenth-Century Ireland', *Women's History Review*, 6 (1997), 485–505; Maria Luddy, 'Religion, Philanthropy and the State in Late Eighteenth- and Early Nineteenth-Century Ireland', in Hugh Cunningham and Joanna Innes, eds, *Charity, philanthropy and reform: from the 1690s to 1850* (Basingstoke: Macmillan Press, Ltd, 1998), pp. 148–67; Maria Luddy, 'Religion, Philanthropy and the State in Eighteenth- and Early Nineteenth-Century Ireland', in Cunningham and Innes, 1998, pp. 148–67; Maria Luddy,

providers of the nineteenth century' and that they 'played a vital role in extending the power of the Catholic Church'.[45] Importantly, Luddy's *The Crimean Journals of the Sisters of Mercy, 1854–6* (2004) and the researcher Mary C. Sullivan's *The Correspondence of Catherine McAuley, 1818–1841* (2004), *The Friendship of Florence Nightingale and Mary Clare Moore* (1999) and *Catherine McAuley and the Tradition of Mercy* (1995) provide scholars accessible transcriptions of original diaries and correspondence written by nineteenth-century women religious.

The study of French women religious is also a prominent field of enquiry, perhaps because of the many documents from women's religious houses that reside in the Archives Nationales.[46] Historians have been able to research and publish on women of Languedoc of the thirteenth and fourteenth centuries, contemplative nuns of the seventeenth and eighteenth centuries and education and vocation in seventeenth- and eighteenth-century France.[47] The rich historiography of nineteenth-century women religious begins with Claude Langlois's seminal *Le catholicisme au féminin: les congrégations françaises à supérieure générale au XIX siècle* (1984) and is followed by Odile Arnold's *Le corps et l'âme: la vie des religieuses au xixᵉ siècle* (1984) and Yvonne Turin's

Catherine Cox, Leeanne Lane and Diane Urquhart with Jean Agnew, Sarah Costley and Rosemary Raughter, eds, *A Directory of Sources for Women's History in Ireland* (Dublin: Women's History Project/Irish Manuscripts Commission, 1999); Maria Luddy and Mary Cullen, eds, *Female Activists: Irish Women and Change, 1900–1960* (Dublin: Woodfield Press, 2001).

45 Luddy, 1998, p. 149.

46 After monasticism was legally terminated in France in 1790, the French National Assembly sent municipal officers to religious houses to record their assets. They confiscated many of the internal documents including annals, registers, chapter meeting records, etc. These records are now housed at the Archives Nationales.

47 Daniel Hickey, *Hospitals in Ancien Regime France: Rationalization, Resistance, Renewal 1530–1789* (Montreal: McGill-Queen's University Press, 1997); Édouard Privat and Centre National de la Recherche Scientifique, *La femme dans la vie religieuse du Languedoc (XIIIe–XIVe s)* (Toulouse: Privat, 1988); Elizabeth Rapley, *A Social History of the Cloisters: Daily life in the Teaching Monasteries of the Old Regime* (Montreal: McGill-Queen's University Press, 2001); Elizabeth Rapley, *The Dévotes: Women and the Church in Seventeenth-Century France* (London: McGill-Queen's University Press, 1990); Elizabeth Rapley, 'Women and the Religious Vocation in Seventeenth-Century France', *French Historical Studies*, 18 (1994), 613–31.

*Femmes et religieuses au XIXème siècle: le féminisme 'en religion'* (1989). More recently, targeted studies such as Sarah Curtis's *Educating the Faithful: Religion, Schooling, and Society in Nineteenth-Century France* (2000) have argued that the initiative and organisation of women's congregations were critical to the growth of French primary education.[48] In addition, historians the Ralph Gibson, Hazel Mills and Rebecca Rogers have explored other aspects of nineteenth-century French religious life in more general texts, journal articles and edited collections.[49]

Since the 1990s, the Australian historiography of women religious has expanded significantly. Stephanie Burley argues in her historiographical review of this genre that 'where initially religious, social, women's and feminist histories influenced the writing of the history of women religious, the latter is now influencing and penetrating the original fields'. Historians of Australian women religious are exploring various methodologies and 'benefiting from an interdisciplinary approach'.[50] North American historiography of women religious revolves around the

48 Sarah A. Curtis, *Educating the Faithful: Religion, Schooling, and Society in Nineteenth-Century France* (Dekalb, Illinois: Northern Illinois Press, 2000), pp. 4–5. This initiative is particularly significant because of the socio-economic turbulence of the time and the state's attempts to circumscribe the educational efforts of women religious.

49 Ralph Gibson, *A Social History of French Catholicism, 1789–1914* (London: Routledge, 1989); Ralph Gibson, 'Female Religious Orders in Nineteenth-Century France', in Frank Tallett and Nicholas Atkin, eds, *Catholicism in Britain and France since 1789* (London: The Hambledon Press, 1996), pp. 105–13; Hazel Mills, 'Negotiating the Divide: Women, Philanthropy and the "Public Sphere" in Nineteenth-Century France', in Frank Tallett and Nicholas Atkin, eds, *Religion, Society and Politics in France since 1789* (London: The Hambledon Press, 1991), pp. 29–54; Rebecca Rogers, 'Boarding Schools, Women Teachers and Domesticity: Reforming Girls' Secondary Education in the First Half of the Nineteenth Century', *French Historical Studies*, 19 (1995), 153–81; Rebecca Rogers, 'Retrograde or Modern? Unveiling the Teaching Nun in Nineteenth-Century France', *Social History*, 23 (1998), 146–64; Rebecca Rogers, 'Schools, Discipline, and Community: Diary-Writing and Schoolgirl Culture in Late Nineteenth-Century France', *Women's History Review*, 4 (1995), 525–54.

50 Stephanie Burley, 'An Overview of the Historiography of Women Religious in Australia', *Journal of the Australian Catholic Historical Society*, 26 (2005), 43–60. Burley gives a much more thorough bibliography of Australian historiography than this brief paragraph represents. Some of the important work mentioned includes Anne McLay, *Women out of their Sphere: A History of the Sisters of Mercy in Western Australia* (Western Australia: Vanguard Press, 1992); MacGinley, 1996; Madeleine Sophie

traditional themes of authority, agency and ministry but also contends with issues of nation building, indigenous peoples and the integration of immigrants into national and Catholic life.[51] This added nuance to nationalism introduces a unique dimension to the historiography of nineteenth-century women religious. Congregations entering the 'New World' sought dispensations to eliminate 'Old World' rules and customs that were difficult to observe in a new environment.[52] Maintaining connections with the European Mother House became difficult as convents were pressured by American bishops to become independent. This European cultural connection, particularly in the United States context, became problematic, and some communities reconfigured themselves as 'American' congregations.

This brief historiography of women religious is, of necessity, summarised in a broad manner. Much of the work in the chapters that follow will compare and contrast women religious of England and Wales with Irish, French, North American and Australian women religious to provide an understanding of the similarities and differences in religious life. Some of these differences in religious life, as discussed in the next chapter, stem from the unique history of Catholicism in England and from the social, political and religious environment that Catholicism influenced and was influenced by in the nineteenth century.

---

McGrath, *These Women? Women Religious in the History of Australia – The Sisters of Mercy Parramatta 1888–1988* (Kersington, New South Wales: New South Wales University Press, 1992); Janet West, *Daughters of Freedom: A History of Women in the Australian Church* (Sydney: Albatross Books, 1997).

51  A more thorough review of the historiography of North American women religious can be found in Carol K. Coburn, 'An Overview of the Historiography of Women Religious: A Twenty-Five-Year Retrospective', *U.S. Catholic Historian*, 22 (winter 2004), 1–26, and Elizabeth M. Smyth, 'Writing the History of Women Religious in Canada (1996–2001)', *International Journal of Canadian Studies*, 23 (spring 2001), 205–12.

52  Mary Ewans, *The Role of the Nun in Nineteenth Century America* (New York: Arno, 1987), p. 70.

# Part I

# Developing identities

# 1

# Becoming visible

I see plainly that they are not what we want, and that they have half our idea, but only half. I do not regret stopping for I learnt a great deal in my visit. It is curious how many people have had the same idea at the same time.[1]

Frances Taylor's comment, written to Lady Georgiana Fullerton after her 1869 visit to the religious congregation of the Maids of Christ, was an astute one: it suggests that the expansion of women's congregations in the nineteenth century was dynamic, not only in England, but also in parts of Europe.[2] There were many women who had 'the same idea at the same time'. Yet this idea was not new; it had been evolving over the past eighteen hundred years.[3] Women's pursuit of religious life was not static despite Rome's attempts to rigidly define monastic life for women. Women tested the boundaries of their enclosed existence. Sometimes they were thrust back into the cloister; at other times they found a space that allowed them to modify the prescribed monastic model. By the nineteenth century, the dominance of simple-vowed congregations and religious life outside the cloister became the norm. This new way of leading religious life shifted the gendered identity of women religious and slowly redefined the understanding of femininity and religious life.

In England, this expansion of religious life was developing just after the initial dismantling of repressive penal laws against Catholicism.[4] The

---

1 F.C. Devas SJ, *Mother Mary Magdalen of the Sacred Heart (Fanny Margaret Taylor): Foundress of the Poor Servants of the Mother of God 1832–1900* (London: Burns, Oates & Washbourne, 1927), p. 96.
2 Comprehensive, comparative studies of women religious of the nineteenth century have yet to be written.
3 Jo Ann Kay McNamara, *Sisters in Arms: Catholic Nuns through Two Millennia* (London: Harvard University Press, 1996).
4 The penal laws were a series of legislation issued after the English Reformation and directed against Roman Catholics that penalised, both politically and economically, those who practised the Catholic faith.

threat of the penal laws was not so easily forgotten by Catholics, and Protestant attitudes towards Catholics and Catholicism were not easily altered. The migration of great numbers of Irish Catholics and the influx of new converts to Catholicism also influenced the cultural mix of Catholic England. Within this melange of Catholicism, the developments in women's religious life flourished. As congregations were founded in England, the number of convents and the number of women religious grew exponentially. This was not a unique trend, but one that coincided with the moral and devotional culture that flourished in nineteenth-century England.

## Catholic England

Catholic Emancipation in 1829 was highly contested in Protestant England. The fiery cry of 'No popery' may appear to be more connected to the evangelical eighteenth century than to the more 'liberal' nineteenth century. Yet bursts of anti-Catholic vitriol, often incited by the rancorous rhetoric of the anti-papal English press, reintroduced old fears and intolerances. Indignation at papal activities or Irish intransigence would erupt at various intervals: at the time of Catholic Emancipation in 1829, the expansion of the Catholic episcopacy in 1840, the Maynooth controversy in 1845, the restoration of the hierarchy in 1850, the pronouncement of Papal Infallibility in 1870 and the furore in 1872 over the inspection of convents.[5] Every Guy Fawkes Day brought a reminder of the 'other' within England. Anti-Catholic rhetoric was vociferous. While there is no complete summary of the anti-Catholic works published during each crisis, Robert J. Klaus has calculated that in the two-week period just after the restoration of the hierarchy in 1850, seventy-five anti-Catholic works were published.[6] The following year, 1,673 petitions and 260,078 signatures remonstrated against the so-called 'Papal Aggression'.[7]

5  Edward R. Norman, *The English Catholic Church in the Nineteenth Century* (Oxford: Oxford University Press, 1984), p. 2.
6  Robert J. Klaus, *The Pope, the Protestants, and the Irish: Papal Aggression and Anti-Catholicism in Mid-Nineteenth Century England* (London: Garland Publishing, 1987), p. 228. On 29 September 1850, Pope Pius IX reestablished the English Catholic hierarchy, a canonical form of church government which included a hierarchy of bishops who had episcopal authority over clergy and laity.
7  Frank H. Wallis, *Popular Anti-Catholicism in Mid-Victorian Britain* (Lewiston, New York: The Edwin Mellen Press, 1993), p. 58. The restoration of the hierarchy was termed the 'Papal Aggression' by the English press.

English fears stemmed from a variety of sources. Catholics were judged to be disloyal to England as a consequence of their fidelity to the papacy in Rome. Catholic rites offended Protestant religious beliefs. The sacerdotal nature of the priesthood, prayers to saints and the cult of the Virgin Mary affronted Protestant sensibilities. This so-called idolatry and the primacy of saints and priests ran counter to Protestant claims that salvation was attained through the individual's direct relationship with God. Dispensations available through priests and the Pope incensed non-Catholics. Celibacy was anathema. Priestly celibacy could be ignored as a personal choice, but a woman's celibacy was a radical concept, quite contrary to the gendered ideal of a domesticated womanhood and the cult of the family. Religious congregations of women, in particular, with their vows of poverty, celibacy and obedience, enraged many Protestants.[8]

Women's congregations were seen as a curiosity as well as a threat. The *Tablet* commented in 1850 that 'Religious ladies' were welcomed in late eighteenth-century England, but their acceptance was tinged with inquisitiveness:

> When the French Revolution drove hither some Religious ladies, they were absolutely mobbed in some parts and towns, and every one were regarded by persons with more surprise and wonder, and superstitious fear, than with pity or respect. They were creature of a new species, very proper objects of curiosity, but without any claim to sympathy or administration; and even after the settlement in England of the olden conventual establishments, the Nuns were shunned and feared by the common people, except only those who came within the scope of their charity.[9]

This curiosity created what Philip Ingram refers to as a 'professional leisure industry'[10] which fed the insatiable desires of Protestants: plays, fiction, biographies, poetry, tracts and public lectures titillated the inquisitiveness and fears of the public.[11] This curiosity could lead to situations

8 Carmen M. Mangion, 'Centre of a Maelstrom: Anglican Sisterhoods in Victorian England', master's thesis, Birkbeck College, University of London, 2000.

9 *The Tablet* (23 February 1850), p. 123.

10 Philip Ingram, 'Protestant Patriarchy and the Catholic Priesthood in Nineteenth Century England', *Journal of Social History*, 24 (1991), 783–97 (p. 783).

11 Diana Peschier, *Nineteenth-Century Anti-Catholic Discourses: The Case of Charlotte Brontë* (Houndmills: Palgrave, 2005); Katherine DeMartini Barrus, '"Putting Her Hand to the Plough": Nuns and Sisters in Nineteenth-Century England' (doctoral thesis, University of Albany, State University of New York, 1999). Barrus looks at how women religious were represented in nineteenth-century high art and popular culture.

that proved dangerous to women religious. Allessandro Gavassi, Edith O'Gorman and William Murphy lectured quite frequently on the nature of religious life: they recounted stories of depraved nuns, tormented nuns, trapped nuns and escaped nuns. William Murphy's visit to Handsworth alarmed the Catholic community at St Mary's:

> A deputation of the clergy waited upon the Superintendent of Police, who received them with great courtesy and promised to lend his assistance. One night several gentleman belonging to the congregation of St Mary's volunteered to remain in the Convent all night, while some of our humbler friends tried to protect the Sisters by walking about outside.[12]

The Sisters of Mercy in Handsworth were not directly threatened, but they, and other congregations, remained vigilant when anti-Catholic or anti-nun sentiment became public. The founder of the Sisters of Charity of St Paul the Apostle, Geneviève Dupuis, wrote, 'In this heretical country they speak against us. They say we do not eat enough or that we sleep on straw; that the Superior kills her Sisters; in fact all sorts of detractions of this kind.'[13] Catholics attempted to counter these calumnies. The Catholic Truth Society published many histories of women religious and religious institutes in the nineteenth century. John Nicholas Murphy, a Protestant, in his *Terra incognita: or, The Convents of the United Kingdom* (1873) attempted to correct the 'ignorance and misconception' about nuns.[14] Tracts were written by bishops and clergy and editorials written by members of the laity. These rejoinders seemed only to fuel the controversy.[15] The debate over the inspection of convents re-emerged several times from the 1850s to

12  RSM Handsworth: 1/200/9/1 'Handsworth Annals', 1868, pp. 74–5.
13  SCSP: Box 1, 30, letter dated 19 August 1863 from Geneviève Dupuis to Mère Elie Jarret.
14  John Nicholas Murphy, *Terra Incognita: or, The Convents of the United Kingdom* (London: Longmans, Green & Co., 1873), p. vii.
15  Father Gallwey SJ, *Convent Life and England in the 19th Century: Two Sermons Preached in the Church of the Immaculate Conception, Farm Street, Mid-Lent, March 7th 1869, On Occasion of an Appeal on Behalf of the Little Sisters of the Poor* (London: Burns, Oates & Co., 1869); Father Gallwey SJ, *The Committee on Convents. The Nun's Choice: Newgate or Newdegate. A Letter to a Barrister* (London: Burns, Oates, and Company, 1870); Rev. M. Hobart Seymour, *Convents or Nunneries. A Lecture in Reply to Cardinal Wiseman, delivered at the Assembly Rooms, Bath, on Monday, June 7, 1852* (Bath: R.E. Peach, 1852); Bishop Ullathorne, *A Plea for the Rights and Liberties of Religious Women, with reference to the Bill proposed by Mr. Lacy* (London: Thomas Richardson and Son, 1851); Right Reverend Bishop Ullathorne, *A Letter Addressed to Lord Edward Howard, on the Proposed Committee of Enquiry into Religious Communities* (London:

the early twentieth century.[16] Women religious remained a contentious and visible symbol of catholicity in England in the nineteenth century.

In addition, nineteenth-century Roman Catholicism was regarded as foreign. Irish Catholics were vehemently not English, and ultramontane Catholics espoused a continental view of Catholicism.[17] Some of the land-owning classes and clergy, notably regular clergy, did not want a formal relationship with the Roman Catholic Church; they favoured a relationship that corresponded with French Gallicanism, which advocated a degree of independence from papal control of the Roman Catholic Church in France.[18] The English men who were pivotal in the passing of the Relief Acts of 1789 and 1791 were a part of the Cisalpine movement, and while they did not question papal supremacy, they maintained that English church matters should be decided in England.[19]

England was designated a missionary country after the English Reformation and the English Roman Catholic Church came under the auspices of the Sacred Congregation for the Propagation of the Faith, commonly referred to as Propaganda or *Propaganda Fide*. Vicars

Thomas Richardson and Son, 1854); Bishop Ullathorne, *Three Lectures on the Conventual Life* (London: Burns, Oates & Co., 1868).

16 Walter L. Arnstein, *Protestant versus Catholic in Mid-Victorian England: Mr. Newdegate and the Nuns* (London: University of Missouri Press, 1982).

17 John P. Rossi, 'Lord Ripon's Resumption of Political Activity 1878–1880', *Recusant History*, 11 (1971–72), 61–74 (p. 61); G.A. Cahill, 'British Nationalism and Nativism, 1829–1848: "No-Popery" and British Popular Culture', *Journal of Popular Culture*, 3 (1969), 480–91 (p. 486); Anthony F. Denholm, 'The Conversion of Lord Ripon in 1874', *Recusant History*, 10 (1969–70), 111–18 (p. 114).

18 Jack Kitching, 'Roman Catholic Education from 1700–1870: A Study of Roman Catholic Educational Endeavour from the Early Eighteenth Century to the Elementary Education Act of 1870' (doctoral thesis, University of Leeds, 1966), p. 125; J. Derek Holmes, *More Roman than Rome: English Catholicism in the Nineteenth Century* (London: Burns and Oates, 1978).

19 E.E. Reynolds, *The Roman Catholic Church in England and Wales: A Short History* (Wheathampstead, Hertfordshire: Anthony Clarke Books, 1973), p. 317. The Cisalpine movement embraced the decentralisation of the national church in matters of episcopal organisation and control, but did not question papal supremacy in spiritual affairs. Vicars apostolic who belonged to the Cisalpine movement did not want English affairs controlled from Rome. Gallicanism was the French version of the Cisalpine movement and was quite strong in France. The ultramontane movement was opposed to the Cisalpine movement and embraced the centralisation of English church authority by papal authority rather than national and diocesan independence.

apostolic, appointed by Rome to manage the English Catholic Church, exercised their authority on behalf of the Cardinal Prefect of Propaganda but they lacked the full judicial power of bishops. Given the additional difficulties of English penal legislation, vicars apostolic often led a peripatetic life, surreptitiously moving from house to house, one step ahead of the long arm of the law. The result was a church administrative hierarchy that was, by most accounts, loosely structured, and from the standpoint of the authority of the vicars apostolic, ineffective. Bishop Richard Smith, vicar apostolic in 1631, wrote to the cardinals in Rome from his hiding place complaining that 'I am at the mercy of the plots of the heretics and of the harassing Regulars'.[20]

Bishop Smith's mention of 'harassing Regulars' identifies an additional challenge to episcopal authority from within the Roman Catholic Church. The rivalry between the regular priests, those who belonged to a religious order, and diocesan secular priests, those who reported (at least nominally) directly to the vicars apostolic, was increasingly problematic and divisive. This rivalry was due in large part to the independence of the orders of regular priests. One of the more powerful religious congregations, the Jesuits, had been fervent missionary priests in England since the sixteenth century and had formed, according to the Catholic historian Aiden Bellenger, 'a church within a church'.[21] In the years prior to the restoration of the hierarchy, Rosminians, Passionists and Redemptorists flourished in England. Each of these religious institutes had its own internal hierarchy and constitutions which defined the scope of its activities.[22] These orders did not owe an allegiance to the vicars apostolic. Vicars apostolic, managing the needs of their growing missions, found that their requests for regular priests to perform certain functions or to relocate to remote missions were sometimes ignored or refused.[23] This threat to their authority virtually disappeared by the end of the nineteenth century.

20 M.D.R. Leys, *Catholics in England 1559–1829: A Social History* (London: Longmans, 1961), p. 80.
21 Aidan D. Bellenger, 'Religious Life for Men', in V. Alan McClelland and Michael Hodgetts, eds, *From without the Flaminian Gate: 150 Years of Roman Catholicism in England and Wales 1850–2000* (London: Darton Longman & Todd, 1999), pp. 142–66 (p. 143).
22 Rosminians preached, gave retreats and missions, taught, managed prisons and hospitals and wrote literary works. Redemptorists and Passionists held retreats and missions. Jesuits preached and taught.
23 Denis Gwynn, 'Growth of the Catholic Community', in George Andrew Beck, ed., *The English Catholics, 1850–1950* (London: Burns Oates, 1950), pp. 410–42 (p. 414).

A third challenge to the vicars apostolic was the relationship between the Catholic land-owning classes and the clergy. After the Reformation, it was the land-owning classes who financially supported the priesthood in England: they provided funds for churches, chapels and priests' living expenses. This trend continued through to the nineteenth century. Given the financial support of prominent benefactors or lay organisations, it was the laity who dominated parish life. The vicar apostolic, a distant figure, was not directly involved in the growth of the mission. In addition, a bond existed between regular priests and the laity; according to John Bossy, 'religious orders had stood out as defenders of the ecclesiastical rights of laity'.[24] These relationships were a threat to the authority of the vicars apostolic.

After Pope Pius IX's apostolic letter of September 1850, *Universalis ecclesiae*, which restored the English episcopal hierarchy, a series of events took place that altered English Catholicism. The restoration of the hierarchy created a diocesan organisational structure under the authority of bishops. The politically astute Nicholas Wiseman became the newly designated Cardinal Archbishop of Westminster. Wiseman was convinced that the creation of the diocesan hierarchy, sanctioned by Rome, would enable the newly established bishops to bring 'law and order' to the independent clergy and laity.[25] In the latter half of the nineteenth century, political manoeuvring and personal feuds led to divisive factions within the nascent Roman Catholic hierarchy,[26] but this church hierarchy firmly established and secured its authority over the next fifty years. The independence of male religious orders with regard to diocesan authority was addressed in 1881 when the Papal Bull *Romanos pontifices* removed the freedoms of the largest religious orders to attend to their own corporate interests first.[27] By the 1890s, the Cisalpine movement was dead and the laity had lost most of its vestiges of authority and power. Bishops had become the undisputed leaders of the Roman Catholic Church in England and Wales.[28]

24 John Bossy, *The English Catholic Community, 1570–1850* (London: Darton, Longman & Todd, 1975), p. 354.
25 Ibid, p. 361.
26 Norman, 1984, p. 2; V. Alan McClelland, 'From without the Flaminian Gate', in McClelland and Hodgetts, eds, 1999, pp. 1–20 (p. 6); Klaus, 1987, pp. 28–9.
27 Edward Cruise, 'Development of Religious Orders' in Beck, ed., 1950, pp. 442–74 (p. 454).
28 Sheridan Gilley, 'The Years of Equipoise, 1892–1943', in McClelland and Hodgetts, eds, pp. 21–61 (p. 22).

The restoration of the Catholic hierarchy in 1850 treated England and Wales as one unit; it is doubtful that the Holy See was aware of Wales as a separate entity.[29] Yet in many ways the Welsh version of indigenous Catholicism was different from the English. Even as late as 1895, Bishop John Cuthbert Hedley wrote of Wales as a missionary country: 'It was more sparsely inhabited, Catholicism was more feeble, and the Welsh people had a peculiar national character of their own'.[30] At the beginning of the nineteenth century, Welsh missions existed in Holywell, Abergavenny, Perthir, Monmouth, Brecon, Chepstow and Usk, with domestic chapels at Talacre, Llanarth and Courtfield. These missions and chapels serviced probably not more than 1,000 Catholics.[31] By 1850, the Catholic population in Wales reached 9,000.[32] By this time, large ironworks, coal mining and railway development dominated the economy and employed many working-class Welsh and Irish men and women.[33] Welsh Catholics were few, and Catholicism was dominated by the immigrant Irish population who worked in industrial towns of South Wales.[34]

Ultra-Protestant vitriol represented Catholics as a concordant body, united in its efforts to proselytise Protestant England and return it to the papal fold. Yet this solidarity of the English Catholic laity was a mirage; there were unequivocal, tangible divisions between Catholics in England. Three distinct groups of Catholics existed; they were divided by class barriers, ethnic prejudice and forms of religious fervour.[35] To a great extent, the two groups on the extreme ends of the spectrum, the 'Old Catholics' and the 'Irish Catholics', seemed worlds apart. At a dinner party in 1860, the 'Old Catholic' Barbara Charlton retorted after hearing disparaging ref-

---

29  Daniel J. Mullins, 'The Catholic Church in Wales', in McClelland and Hodgetts, eds, 1999, pp. 272–94 (p. 272). See Appendix for an explanation of this study's focus on Wales.
30  J. Anselm Wilson, *The Life of Bishop Hedley* (London: Burns Oates and Washbourne, 1930), p. 137.
31  Donald Attwater, *The Catholic Church in Modern Wales: A Record of the Past History* (London: Burns Oates & Washbourne, 1935), p. 66. Little research has been done on the Catholic Church in nineteenth-century Wales. Attwater's text, published in 1935, is still the most current text on the subject.
32  *Catholic Directory* (1850), 70–4.
33  Joseph Gross, *A Brief History of Merthyr Tydfil* (Newport: The Starling Press, 1980), pp. 40–7.
34  Michael Gandy, *Catholic Family History: A Bibliography for Wales* (London: Michael Gandy, 1996), p. 6, and Mullins, 1999, p. 273.
35  This is a simplistic view but serves to illuminate the major differences between Catholics in England.

erences to Irish Roman Catholics that she was an 'English Catholic, not an Irish one which is all the difference in the world'. She explained, 'English Catholics are responsible beings who are taught right from wrong, whereas Irish Catholics, belonging to a yet savage nation, know no better and are perhaps excusable on that account'.[36] The middle group, a mix of converts and ultramontane Catholics, had their own challenges to face. Ultramontanists' insistence on reinstating the authority of the papacy was interpreted by 'Old Catholics' as reducing their liberty.[37] The supremacy of the 'Old Catholics' dwindled towards the end of the nineteenth century.

Sheridan Gilley, in his extensive work on nineteenth-century English Catholics and the Irish poor, describes the 'Old Catholics' as quiet, urban, wealthy families living on landed estates and responsible for the maintenance of the faith of the Catholic poor. Their church and clergy resided on the lands they owned and maintained. To preserve their faith, they educated their children at home or in continental convents and monasteries.[38] Their faith was a kind of latitudinarian Catholicism which rejected ultramontane practices; these 'Old Catholics' embraced a Catholicism that seemed consistent with Gallicanism.[39] Dramatic stories were told and retold by each generation of the hardships suffered by Catholic ancestors for their faith. They banded together as a group, socialising and intermarrying and relying on connections and kinship for advancement. The wealthy elite of these nineteenth-century Catholic families were active in fuelling the growth of Catholic organisations through the poor schools movement, through the support of religious institutes and by subsidising church building.[40] The Howards, Arundels, Jerninghams, Maxwells, Welds, Blundells, Plowdens, Throckmortons, Mostyns, Cliffords, Stourtons, Tichbournes, Vaughans and Petres earnestly promoted their catholicity in the philanthropies they supported.

On the other end of the Catholic spectrum, Irish Catholics had existed in England long before the large influx of poor tenant farmers who

36 Barbara Charlton, *The Recollections of a Northumbrian Lady, 1815–1866, being the Memoirs of Barbara Charlton (nee Tasburgh) Wife of William Henry Charlton of Hesleyside Northumbria*, ed. L.E.O. Charlton (London: Jonathan Cape, 1949), p. 244. Sheridan Gilley argues that Charlton was 'too lively to be taken as the sole gauge of the tone and temper of the English Catholic response to the Irish'. Sheridan Gilley, 'English Catholic Charity and the Irish Poor in London: Part I, 1700–1840', *Recusant History*, 11 (1971–72), 179–95 (p. 182).
37 Bellenger, 1999, p. 143.
38 Gilley, 'English Catholic Charity . . . Part I', 1971–72, pp. 182–3.
39 Klaus, 1987, p. 14.
40 Gilley, 'English Catholic Charity . . . Part 1', 1971–72, pp. 183–4.

Table 1.1 Irish-born population of England and Wales as a percentage of total population of England and Wales, 1841–1901

| Year | Number of Irish-born | Irish-born as a % of total population | % change in Irish-born population |
|------|---------------------|--------------------------------------|-----------------------------------|
| 1841 | 289,404 | 1.8 | – |
| 1851 | 519,959 | 2.9 | 79.7 |
| 1861 | 601,634 | 3.0 | 15.7 |
| 1871 | 566,540 | 2.5 | −5.8 |
| 1881 | 562,374 | 2.2 | −0.7 |
| 1891 | 458,315 | 1.6 | −18.5 |
| 1901 | 426,565 | 1.3 | −6.9 |

*Source*: Census reports, 1841–1901.

arrived after the potato famines of the 1840s. In 1841, the census reported 289,404 Irish-born living in England and Wales.[41] By 1861, this figure had risen to 601,634, more than doubling in twenty years. But as the figures in Table 1.1 indicate, the Irish-born contingent continued to fall during the course of the next forty years.[42] Many of the Irish-born immigrants remained in England and Wales and gave birth to children whose ethnicity would be influenced by their 'Irishness' although their birthplace would be England. Their catholicity was as much a badge of their culture, national identity and separateness as it was of their faith. Yet regular attendance at Mass and the practice of Catholic devotions by Irish Catholics were less than rigorous. John Bossy's research indicates that only half the Irish attended church services, and it was this Irish 'leakage' that worried Catholic clergy in England.[43] By the century's end, Catholics in England and Wales were thought to number 1,300,000; much of this increase was due to Irish immigrants.[44]

It was the third group, converts as well as ultramontane Catholics, who publicly, even flamboyantly, embraced the Roman Catholic faith with vigour and a decidedly continental flavour. Their faith resonated in their architecture, religious devotions and intellectual pursuits. Newly built churches and cathedrals reflected this exuberant passion, in either the neo-classical Italianate structures favoured by Ultramontanists or the gothic displays of munificence designed by Augustus Welby Pugin; they

41  Klaus, 1987, p. 7.
42  Not all the Irish-born population were Roman Catholic, but a great majority would have been.
43  Bossy, 1975, p. 313.
44  Reynolds, 1973, p. 349.

were a triumphant expression of the new confidence of the Roman Catholic Church.[45] The Passionists and Redemptorists, regular orders whose mission was to convert the English, imbued their converts with a continental flavour. Rituals such as the *Quarant'Ore*, devotions to the Virgin Mary, the renewal of baptismal vows, frequent communion and jubilant processions with lights and banners were the outward signs of Catholicism and reflected continental influences that were not favoured by 'Old Catholics'. Men like Henry Manning, John Henry Newman and W.G. Ward, converts from the Anglican Church, enhanced the intellectual capital of English Roman Catholics, whose theological rigour was considered defunct and derelict.[46]

While these are broad categorisations, they are requisite to understanding the character of Catholic life in nineteenth-century England. Mary Heimann, in her examination of the social and intellectual aspects of English Catholic devotion of the second half of the nineteenth century, maintains that it was the revivalist spirit of devotional change, with its extra-liturgical activities, which provided the cohesion to unite these disparate Catholics together.[47] She describes Catholics of different classes, ethnic backgrounds and political persuasions working and worshipping together. We see a microcosm of this played out in women's religious congregations, but this 'cohesion' was not without its tensions.

Ultramontane practices were more than merely continental practices and devotions; they endorsed a strong hierarchical organisation linked closely with Rome and its apostolic authority.[48] V. Alan McClelland writes that the one feature of Ultramontanism which changed the face of English Roman Catholicism was its 'concern for the masses'.[49] This 'concern for the masses' was also intricately linked with the objectives of women's religious congregations. Women's congregations were in the forefront of Catholic philanthropic activities in the nineteenth century despite the rather irregular path of monasticism in England.

## Monasticism in early modern England

Monasticism survived after the Reformation in England but evolved in a unique manner owing to Henry VIII's formation of the *Ecclesia Anglicana*

45  Norman, 1984, p. 9.
46  Klaus, 1987, p. 19.
47  Mary Heimann, *Catholic Devotion in Victorian England* (Oxford: Clarendon Press, 1995), p. 172.
48  Klaus, 1987, p. 18.
49  McClelland, 1999, p. 12.

with himself at its head. The Dissolution of the Monasteries in 1536 and 1539 resulted in the disbanding of over 140 women's monastic communities, and approximately 1,600 nuns were pensioned off. The vast majority of nuns accepted their pensions and returned to their family homes.[50] Some women, with great difficulty, continued their way of life. Elizabeth Shelley, abbess of the Nunnaminster Benedictine monastery, lived with several nuns near the dismantled monastery.[51] A few religious communities were re-established under the auspices of Henry VIII.[52] Some women entered orders on the continent, but, as Claire Walker explains, membership to 'foreign houses' posed logistical and cultural problems.[53] The solution to frustrated conventual aspirations arrived sixty years later: 'English convents' on the continent. Between 1591 and 1710, twenty-five English convents established themselves in France, the Netherlands and Portugal.[54] These communities recruited from the daughters of English Catholic aristocracy and landed gentry. They provided educational institutions for their children and, in return, were funded by English Catholics. Claire Walker argues that English orders remained strongly connected with the English Catholic community and maintained a strong relationship with the English Church, state and people, despite their distance from England. These orders became strong 'symbols of Catholic nonconformity' and 'actively engaged in compatriots' spiritual and political affairs'.[55]

Two hundred years later, these religious orders would again be faced with dissolution, this time on the continent. Supporters of the French

---

50 Patricia Crawford, *Women and Religion in England 1500–1720* (London: Routledge, 1993), p. 29.

51 Aidan Bellenger, 'The Brussels Nuns at Winchester, 1794–1857', paper presented at conference entitled 'English Benedictine Congregation History Commission Symposium', 1999, p. 1, www.catholic-history.org.uk/ebc/1999bellenger.pdf [accessed 1 August 2006].

52 Philip Hughes, *The Reformation in England* (London: Hollis & Carter, 1950), p. 295. Henry VIII granted royal licences to forty-seven houses of men and women who were re-established 'in perpetuity' with new charters. These communities were small and were unable to pay the fees for royal licences. By 1540, they too had disbanded.

53 Claire Walker, *Gender and Politics in Seventeenth-Century English Convents: English Convents in France and the Low Countries* (Basingstoke: Palgrave Macmillan, 2003), p. 2.

54 Derived from Caroline Bowden, 'Community Space and Cultural Transmission: Formation and Schooling in English Enclosed Convents in the Seventeenth Century', *History of Education*, 34 (2005), pp. 365–86 (pp. 385–6).

55 Walker, 2003, pp. 3–5.

Revolution, ardent in their republicanism and anti-clericalism, found religious life antithetical to the state they were building. In February 1790, the National Assembly of France released religious from their vows, declaring that women religious were now free to marry.[56] By 1791, property held by monasteries was seized by the state, and on 4 August 1792 many monasteries were evacuated.[57] English religious communities, as 'foreign' entities and convents, were even more suspect and likely to be disbanded.[58] Many communities felt that a quick departure from France was the only option. The French Benedictine nuns of Montargis were the first to leave for England. In early September 1792, the civil government deposed Madame de Mirepoix, the mother prioress, and ordered the evacuation of the cloister. Twenty-nine nuns, eight lay sisters, two servants and two chaplains left Dieppe, France, on 16 October 1792 aboard the *Prince of Wales*. They remained in temporary quarters in London until they found a suitable residence at Bodney Hall, near Brandon, Norfolk, in March 1793.[59] They were just one of twenty-three communities that fled the continent to England during the period 1792–1800. Nineteen were English communities coming 'home'. Each community had its own story of the difficulties of its harrowing escape, its reliance on the benevolence of English Catholics and its assimilation to (or lack of) a 'home-land' that was not Catholic.[60] The communities faced many challenges as their

56 Lynn Jarrell OSU, 'The Development of Legal Structures for Women Religious between 1500 and 1900: A Study of Selected Institutes of Religious Life for Women', doctoral thesis, Catholic University of America, 1984, p. 302.

57 Elizabeth Rapley, *A Social History of the Cloisters: Daily Life in the Teaching Monasteries of the Old Regime* (Montreal: McGill-Queen's University Press, 2001), pp. 104–5, 258–9. Women religious slowly and surreptitiously regrouped so that by 1806, when teaching congregations were allowed to reopen their schools, they returned to the 'old order of the day'.

58 Bellenger, 1999, p. 3.

59 Diocesan Archives of Northampton: A.3.5 Collins MS; Charlton, 1949, pp. 58–9.

60 Some of these stories are told in Mark Bence-Jones, *The Catholic Families* (London: Constable, 1992); Richard Trappes-Lomax and Joseph Gillow, *The Diary of the 'Blue Nuns' or Order of the Immaculate Conception of Our Lady, at Paris, 1658–1810* (London: Catholic Record Society, 1910); Margaret J. Mason, 'The Blue Nuns of Norwich: 1800–1805', *Recusant History*, 24 (1998), pp. 89–122; M. McCarthy, *A History of the Benedictine Nuns of Dunkirk, now at St Scholastica's Abbey, Teignmouth, Devon* (London: Catholic Book Club, 1957).

contemplative style of religious life was altered to fit the cultural landscape of England.[61] The British government offered financial support to
these exiles; each nun who arrived before November 1794 was given an
annual grant of £10.[62] The irony of this financial support and 'toleration' in a virulently anti-Catholic nation did not go unnoticed. The so-
called tolerance of catholicity may have reflected more an antipathy for
the French government and the revolutions in France than an acceptance for Catholicism or religious life. At the signing of the Concordat
in 1801, some communities returned to France, but most remained in
England.[63]

By 1800, twenty-four religious communities, listed in Table 1.2,
resided in England. All were solemn-vowed orders except the Institute of
Mary at York.[64] As Susan O'Brien has established, this initial migration
of women's orders from the continent marks the beginning of a new
phase in the history of religious life in Britain.[65] Yet this phase began
inauspiciously; the refugee religious communities did not expand into
multiple communities. In fact, they contracted. Two communities

---

61 Some changes to contemplative life are mentioned in Margaret J.
   Mason, 'Nuns of the Jerningham Letters: Elizabeth Jerningham (1727–
   1807) and Frances Henrietta Jerningham (1745–1824), Augustinian
   Caronesses of Bruges', *Recusant History*, 22 (1995), 350–69 (p. 354)
   and Bellenger, 1999, p. 4, but this topic needs to be researched in more
   detail.
62 Kitching, 1966, p. 137.
63 Most communities had lost their convents and all their possessions in
   France. The 1801 Concordat re-established ties between France and the
   Papacy and restored the Catholic Church and Catholic worship in France.
   Only one English community is recorded to have returned to France
   in 1802. Its convent had been spared the destruction of revolutionary
   forces.
64 The Institute of Mary had established a house at Heworth, Yorkshire, in
   1643. In 1650, the sisters left Heworth and entered their convent in Paris. In
   1669, Frances Bedingfield refounded the Institute of Mary temporarily in
   London until permanent accommodation was found in Hammersmith, but
   by 1795 the last member of this community had died. Frances Bedingfield
   founded a second house in Dolebank in 1677; this relocated to York in 1686
   and is still in existence today.
65 Susan O'Brien, 'A Survey of Research and Writing about Roman Catholic
   Women's Congregations in Great Britain and Ireland', in Jan De Maeyer,
   Sophie Leplaie and Joachim Schmiedl, eds, *Religious Institutes in Western
   Europe in the 19th and 20th Centuries*, (Leuven, Belgium: Leuven University
   Press, 2004), pp. 91–116 (p. 93).

Table 1.2  Convents in England, 1800

| Date founded in England | Ethnicity of members | Institute | Founded from |
|---|---|---|---|
| 1686 | English | Institute of Mary | Dolebank, Yorkshire |
| 1792 | French | Benedictines | Montargis |
| 1794 | English | Augustinians | Bruges |
| 1794 | English | Augustinians | Louvain |
| 1794 | English | Benedictines | Ghent |
| 1794 | English | Benedictines | Brussels |
| 1794 | English | Carmelites (Teresians) | Lierre |
| 1794 | English | Carmelites (Teresians) | Antwerp |
| 1794 | English | Dominicans | Brussels |
| 1794 | English | Franciscans, Third Order | Bruges, Princehoff |
| 1794 | English | Holy Sepulchre | Liège |
| 1795 | English | Carmelites (Teresians) | Hoogstraete |
| 1795 | English | Benedictines | Dunkirk |
| 1795 | English | Benedictines | Cambrai |
| 1795 | English | Benedictines | Paris |
| 1795 | French | Bernardines | Douai |
| 1795 | English | Poor Clares | Aire |
| 1795 | English | Poor Clares | Dunkirk |
| 1795 | English | Poor Clares | Gravelines |
| 1795 | English | Poor Clares | Rouen |
| 1799 | English | Conceptionists (Blue Nuns) | Paris |
| 1800 | English | Austin Dames | Bruges |
| Unknown | French | Salesians | |
| Unknown | French | Hospitalières | Cambrai |

*Source*: Of the four French communities, little is known about the Salesians and the Hospitalières. Compiled from Caroline Bowden 'Foundations of English Convents in the Seventeenth Century', http://www.rhul.ac.uk/bedford-centre/history_women_religious/sources/foundations-english-convents.html, accessed 30 December 2007; *Laity's Directory* (1800), 17–22; Ullathorne, 1854 p. 6; Diocesan Archives of Northampton, Collins MS A3.5, p. 2.

returned to the continent in the early nineteenth century, three became 'extinct', and three merged together to form one community.[66]

66  Any further assessment of these religious communities is difficult until more research is done.

## The arrival of the 'modern orders'

The next phase of religious life in England began in 1830, with the arrival of the first of the 'modern orders', the Faithful Companions of Jesus. After 1830, a veritable flood of congregations and orders founded communities in England. Most, unlike the influx at the end of the eighteenth century, were simple-vowed, active religious congregations. These congregations expanded throughout England, spawning new convents and beginning the apostolic work that was so crucial to the development of the English Catholic Church in the nineteenth century. The remainder of this chapter will examine the expansion of these religious institutes, paying special attention to the growth of simple-vowed congregations in England. This expansion will first be examined in aggregate; then a more detailed analysis will focus on the patterns of growth found in a sample of ten congregations.[67]

### Religious institutes

As can be seen in Table 1.3, there was a steady and, for simple-vowed congregations, vigorous growth in the numbers of religious institutes that made their first foundation in England after 1830. By 1860, eight of what would become the ten largest of the nineteenth-century active congregations had already founded convents in England[68] and thirty per cent of the religious institutes settling in England in the nineteenth century had made their first foundation. Of these thirty-four institutes, nearly two-thirds were active, simple-vowed congregations. This trend continued throughout the nineteenth century. In each of the subsequent four decades between eighteen and twenty-two institutes made foundations in England and Wales, and just over two-thirds of the religious institutes founded were congregations. By 1900, seventy per cent of the institutes in England and Wales were active congregations.

### Convents

The dominance of simple-vowed congregations was further reinforced by the proliferation of branch convents established by individual con-

---

67  See the Appendix for more discussion of this sample of ten congregations.
68  These eight were the Sisters of Mercy (1839), the Sisters of Charity of St Paul the Apostle (1847), the Daughters of Charity of St Vincent de Paul (1857), the Poor Sisters of Nazareth (1851), the Sisters of the Most Holy Cross and Passion (1851), the Sisters of Notre Dame de Namur (1845), the Faithful Companions of Jesus (1830) and the Holy Family of Bordeaux (1853). The remaining two, the Little Sisters of the Poor and the Servants of the Sacred Heart of Jesus, were founded in 1861 and 1871 respectively. This ranking is based on the number of convents managed by each congregation.

Table 1.3 Religious institutes founded in England and Wales, 1801–1900

| | Congregations | Orders | Total | % per decade | Cumulative total | % cumulative total |
|---|---|---|---|---|---|---|
| 1801–10 | 0 | 3 | 3 | 2.65 | 3 | 2.65 |
| 1811–20 | 0 | 0 | 0 | – | 3 | 2.65 |
| 1821–30 | 1 | 0 | 1 | 0.88 | 4 | 3.54 |
| 1831–40 | 2 | 1 | 3 | 2.65 | 7 | 6.19 |
| 1841–50 | 7 | 5 | 12 | 10.62 | 19 | 16.81 |
| 1851–60 | 13 | 2 | 15 | 13.27 | 34 | 30.09 |
| 1861–70 | 14 | 5 | 19 | 16.81 | 53 | 46.90 |
| 1871–80 | 14 | 4 | 18 | 15.93 | 71 | 62.83 |
| 1881–90 | 15 | 5 | 20 | 17.70 | 91 | 80.53 |
| 1891–1900 | 14 | 8 | 22 | 19.47 | 113 | 100.00 |
| *Total* | 80 | 33 | 113 | 100.00 | | |
| *% total* | 70.8 | 29.2 | 100.0 | | | |

*Source*: Appendix.

gregations. It is this development that points to the unmistakable vibrancy of this period of religious life. The number of convents, twenty-four in 1800, increased to 596 in 1900. Consistent with the analysis of the religious institutes themselves, approximately eighty-six per cent, or 513, were convents of simple-vowed congregations.[69] To understand this growth better, it is useful to cluster the congregations by size in order to make comparisons between congregations and to examine the institutional nature of nineteenth-century congregations. Table 1.4 shows the results of this tiered analysis. What is immediately conspicuous is that seven congregations were fuelling the bulk of the convent growth. The Tier 1 congregations, the Sisters of Mercy, Sisters of Charity of St Paul the Apostle, Daughters of Charity of St Vincent de Paul, Poor Sisters of Nazareth, Little Sisters of the Poor, Sisters of the Most Holy Cross and Passion and Sisters of Notre Dame de Namur, contributed 269, or just over half of the convents, by the end of the nineteenth century. The middle tier, which contained seventeen congregations, had founded 135 convents or twenty-six per cent of the convents by 1900. The third tier, which included the majority of

69 Barbara Walsh also arrives at a similar figure of seventy-five per cent although she concludes that there were 469 convents in 1897. Barbara Walsh, *Roman Catholic Nuns in England and Wales, 1800–1937: A Social History* (Dublin: Irish Academic Press, 2002), p. 177. This difference in the number of convents is discussed in the Appendix.

Table 1.4 Congregations in England and Wales grouped by number of convents, 1900

|  |  | Number of congregations | % | Number of convents | % |
|---|---|---|---|---|---|
| Tier 1 | >15 convents | 7 | 8.9 | 269 | 52.5 |
| Tier 2 | 5–15 convents | 17 | 21.3 | 135 | 26.3 |
| Tier 3 | <5 convents | 56 | 70.0 | 109 | 21.2 |
| Total |  | 80 | 100.0 | 513 | 100.0 |

*Source*: Appendix.

congregations, seventy per cent, contributed only twenty-one per cent of the number of convents.

Table 1.5 reports on ten congregations, four of which were included in the dominant first tier of congregations, and lists the decade-by-decade change in the number of convents managed by each.[70] This distribution of convents reveals that convent foundations began in earnest in the 1860s. The Sisters of Mercy and the Sisters of Charity of St Paul the Apostle, who arrived in England in 1839 and 1847 respectively, dominated convent expansion in this decade. In the 1860s, the Daughters of Charity of St Vincent de Paul began founding numerous convents. Their great numbers of convents made these three congregations more visible and better known in Catholic communities, and this not only spurred requests for new foundations of convents, but also increased the quantity of potential postulants to fill those convents. After the flurry of convent foundations in the 1860s, thirty-five to forty-seven convents were founded in each decade.

### Geographic expansion

Barbara Walsh has done significant work on the geographic expansion of convents in England and Wales from 1800 to 1937. Her analysis reveals that fifty-nine per cent of initial foundations made prior to 1897 were made in London and the south-east.[71] The first location of a religious institute was critical for future growth. Foundation convents were often placed where funding and potential postulants were available and

70 The figures in this table comprise convents opened and convents closed during the decade. Negative figures result when more convents were closed than opened. See Chapter 8 for a discussion of the reasons behind the closing of convents.
71 Walsh, 2002, p. 171. This dominance of London and the South-East continues through to 1937.

Table 1.5  Net convent foundations in ten congregations by decade, 1801–1900

| | Tier 1 | | | | Tier 2 | | | | Tier 3 | | Total | % |
|---|---|---|---|---|---|---|---|---|---|---|---|---|
| | RSM | SCSP | DC | SND | FCJ | SMG | SHCJ | DHM | CSJP | SSJ | | |
| 1810 | 0 | 0 | 0 | 0 | 0 | 0 | 0 | 0 | 0 | 0 | 0 | – |
| 1820 | 0 | 0 | 0 | 0 | 0 | 0 | 0 | 0 | 0 | 0 | 0 | – |
| 1830 | 0 | 0 | 0 | 0 | 1 | 0 | 0 | 0 | 0 | 0 | 1 | 0.4 |
| 1840 | 1 | 0 | 0 | 0 | 2 | 0 | 0 | 0 | 0 | 0 | 3 | 1.2 |
| 1850 | 16 | 3 | 0 | 2 | 3 | 0 | 1 | 2 | 0 | 0 | 27 | 10.4 |
| 1860 | 23 | 25 | 3 | 8 | 2 | 0 | 6 | 3 | 0 | 0 | 70 | 27.0 |
| 1870 | 10 | 4 | 9 | 7 | 3 | 0 | 2 | 1 | 0 | 1 | 37 | 14.3 |
| 1880 | 6 | 17 | 5 | 0 | 2 | 4 | 0 | 0 | 0 | 1 | 35 | 13.5 |
| 1890 | 16 | 11 | 13 | 2 | 2 | 0 | 0 | 0 | 2 | 1 | 47 | 18.1 |
| 1900 | 25 | 0 | 4 | 3 | 0 | 6 | 0 | 5 | 2 | 0 | 39 | 15.1 |
| Unknown | 4 | –6 | 0 | 0 | 0 | 0 | 0 | 1 | 0 | 1 | 0 | – |
| Total | 101 | 54 | 34 | 16 | 15 | 10 | 9 | 12 | 4 | 4 | 259 | 100.0 |

Source: Appendix.

where there was a need for their services. When the Faithful Companions of Jesus arrived in Somers Town, London, in 1830, they immediately began managing a fee-paying boarding school. The Religious Sisters of Mercy foundation in Bermondsey was cushioned by a ready-made convent plus immediate postulants, one of whom, Lady Barbara Eyre, funded many of its philanthropic efforts.[72] Available sources of funding and postulants were important if convents were to expand their services and evangelise among the working classes. This, after all, was for most congregations their primary responsibility. The Sisters of Notre Dame de Namur founded their first convent in Penryn, where Cornwall's dissident tradition was strong and Catholics numbered a small handful.[73] They opened a boarding school and a poor school in Penryn. Despite the financial support of the Redemptorists, making ends meet proved difficult. They could not maintain a steady attendance of boarding school students, and the number of boarders never exceeded twenty.[74] This, along with recurrent illness, a very slow stream of postulants and the departure of the Redemptorists, encouraged them to relocate to Clapham in 1848. Here, where students and boarders were more plentiful, the community grew and prospered. [75] Within two years, it was able to open a branch convent in Blackburn and in the next decade, eight additional convents were opened.

By 1897, there was a noticeable shift in convent locations as congregations expanded to multiple locations. Congregations did not remain solely in London and the south-east; they begin establishing convents in the north. Although fifty-nine per cent of congregations founded their initial convent in London and the south-east, only thirty-nine per cent of all convents were located there by 1897. The south-west, which received fifteen per cent of all initial foundations, had only nine per cent of all convents by 1897. While the dominance of London and the south is not disputed, congregation expansion was more widespread into the Midlands and the north of England. The north-west received ten per cent of foundation convents, but twenty per cent of all convents by 1897. Similar growth was

---

72 *Trees of Mercy: Sisters of Mercy of Great Britain from 1839* (Essex, England: Sisters of Mercy, 1993), p. 53.
73 SND: BX PRV/1. Cornwall's population numbered 34,000 and an estimated 700 were Catholic.
74 SND: BX PRV/2 in BPND, box marked 'Province History', pp. 65–7.
75 Their location in Clapham also brought them to the attention of the widow Laura Petre Stafford-Jerningham, who entered the Sisters of Notre Dame de Namur in 1850 and used her personal wealth to fund several Notre Dame de Namur foundations and projects.

seen in the Midlands and the north-east.[76] Convent expansion to the Midlands and the north was related to the influx of Irish Catholics in these regions. One of Her Majesty's Inspectors of Schools, E.M. Sneyd-Kynnersley, remarked that in the north-west of England, 'who says Roman Catholic says also "Irish" '.[77] The south-east and south-west, as Walsh has suggested, benefited from the suburbanisation of Catholics. As Catholics relocated outside London to the more spacious suburbs in the south, convents and nearby boarding and day schools were built to educate their daughters. The north saw its share of expansion also; its pattern of growth was one of expanding clusters within neighbouring urban locations. The bulk of Lancashire's convents were based around Liverpool and Manchester, also significant locations of immigrant Irish. Here again, Walsh documents a pattern of urbanisation.[78]

In a survey of only the ten active, simple-vowed congregations, the pattern is markedly similar. Table 1.6 reveals that by 1900, London and the south-east was still the dominant location for convents. However, there was also a strong emergence of convents in the Midlands, where both the Sisters of Mercy and the Sisters of Charity of St Paul the Apostle had a large number. The north-west also pulled convents from all but the smallest two congregations. East Anglia and Wales did not attract many convents, perhaps in part because of the small numbers of Catholics and low levels of industrialisation.[79] A closer look at the five smallest congregations gives evidence of the distinct clustering of convents. The Poor Servants of the Mother of God, the Society of the Holy Child Jesus and the Daughters of the Heart of Mary located over seventy per cent of their convents in London and the south-east. The Congregation of St Joseph of Peace was located entirely in the Midlands. The Sisters of St Joseph of Annecy clustered in the south-west. The five larger convents were more spread out, although Notre Dame de Namur and the Faithful Companions of Jesus both located almost half their convents in the north-west. The focus of the Sisters of Charity of St Paul the Apostle in the Midlands and the north was not surprising as their mother house was located in Selly Park, near Birmingham. The Sisters of Mercy and Daughters of Charity of

76 Walsh, 2002, p. 178.
77 E.M. Sneyd-Kynnersley, *H.M.I. Some Passages in the Life of One of H.M. Inspectors of Schools* (London: Macmillan and Co., 1908), pp. 231–2.
78 Walsh, 2002, pp. 66–87, 108.
79 Ibid, pp. 78–87; David Mathew, 'Old Catholics and Converts', in George Andrew Beck, ed., *The English Catholics, 1850–1950* (London: Burns Oates, 1950), pp. 223–42 (p. 223).

Table 1.6 Regional distributions of ten congregations, 1900

| Region | RSM | SCSP | DC | SND | FCJ | SMG | SHCJ | DHM | CSJP | SSJ | Total | % |
|---|---|---|---|---|---|---|---|---|---|---|---|---|
| London and south-east | 37 | 5 | 9 | 4 | 3 | 7 | 7 | 10 | 0 | 0 | 82 | 31.7 |
| East Anglia | 0 | 1 | 0 | 1 | 0 | 0 | 0 | 0 | 0 | 0 | 2 | 0.8 |
| South-west | 3 | 2 | 4 | 1 | 1 | 0 | 0 | 0 | 0 | 3 | 14 | 5.4 |
| Midlands | 26 | 18 | 4 | 1 | 0 | 0 | 0 | 0 | 4 | 0 | 53 | 20.5 |
| Wales | 0 | 2 | 0 | 0 | 0 | 1 | 0 | 0 | 0 | 1 | 4 | 1.5 |
| North-west | 9 | 10 | 9 | 7 | 7 | 2 | 2 | 2 | 0 | 0 | 48 | 18.5 |
| North-east | 14 | 6 | 3 | 0 | 1 | 0 | 0 | 0 | 0 | 0 | 24 | 9.3 |
| Yorkshire | 11 | 7 | 5 | 2 | 3 | 0 | 0 | 0 | 0 | 0 | 28 | 10.8 |
| Unknown | 1 | 3 | 0 | 0 | 0 | 0 | 0 | 0 | 0 | 0 | 4 | 1.5 |
| Total | 101 | 54 | 34 | 16 | 15 | 10 | 9 | 12 | 4 | 4 | 259 | 100.0 |

Source: Appendix.

St Vincent de Paul were spread throughout England, although both had a strong base in London and the south-east.

The Catholic dioceses were another important factor in the geographic spread of convents. As can be seen in Table 1.7, the Catholic dioceses garnering the most convents were those of Westminster and Southwark, which covered London and the south-east. Another forty-three per cent of the convents were split fairly evenly between the dioceses of Birmingham, Hexham, Beverley and Liverpool. The majority of the convents residing in the north-east of England were found in County Durham and Northumberland. Unfortunately, county-by-county or diocese-by-diocese population figures for numbers of Catholics are not readily available for the nineteenth century.[80] An analysis of the relationship between the Catholic population and the number of convents would doubtless suggest other important explanations for the regional distribution of convents. Another significant factor could be the relationship between individual bishops and women's religious congregations. Unfortunately, historians have not looked at this factor in great detail.[81]

### Sisters

As can be seen in Table 1.8, the numbers of women entering these ten religious congregations increased dramatically from the foundation of the Faithful Companions of Jesus in 1830 through to the end of the century. The 1830s and 1840s saw a small but steady inflow of entrants. By the 1850s, the number of women entering these ten congregations jumped significantly to almost 700 women per decade. By the 1870s, over 1,000 women were entering each decade. The growth continued unabated through to the end of the century, and almost fifty per cent of the women in these ten congregations entered in the last twenty years of the century.

This deluge of religious institutes, convents and women entering religious life in England was dramatic, but perhaps not altogether unexpected, as women's religious institutes were developing rapidly in other countries as well. Rome was overwhelmed by requests for the approbation of new congregations. Forty-two new congregations were approved between

---

80  The 1851 religious census would not be helpful as there were only thirty-two convents in existence in 1851.

81  Research on individual congregations or founders such as Liz West's, *One Woman's Journey: Mary Potter: Founder – Little Company of Mary* (Richmond, Victoria, Australia: Spectrum Publications, 2000) does address the issue of the relationship between Mary Potter and Bishop Edward Gilpin Bagshawe in great detail.

Table 1.7 Regional distributions of ten congregations by diocese, 1900

| Region | RSM | SCSP | DC | SND | FCJ | SMG | SHCJ | DHM | CSJP | SSJ | Total | % |
|---|---|---|---|---|---|---|---|---|---|---|---|---|
| Westminster | 13 | 3 | 8 | 0 | 3 | 4 | 3 | 8 | 0 | 0 | 42 | 16.2 |
| Southwark | 25 | 0 | 1 | 4 | 0 | 3 | 4 | 2 | 0 | 0 | 39 | 15.1 |
| Birmingham | 12 | 15 | 2 | 0 | 0 | 0 | 0 | 0 | 0 | 0 | 29 | 11.2 |
| Hexham | 15 | 10 | 3 | 0 | 1 | 0 | 0 | 0 | 0 | 0 | 29 | 11.2 |
| Beverley | 11 | 7 | 5 | 2 | 3 | 0 | 0 | 0 | 0 | 0 | 28 | 10.8 |
| Liverpool | 3 | 5 | 5 | 5 | 2 | 2 | 2 | 2 | 0 | 0 | 26 | 10.0 |
| Nottingham | 10 | 4 | 0 | 0 | 0 | 0 | 0 | 0 | 4 | 0 | 18 | 6.9 |
| Salford | 5 | 0 | 4 | 2 | 2 | 0 | 0 | 0 | 0 | 0 | 13 | 5.0 |
| Clifton | 3 | 2 | 2 | 0 | 0 | 0 | 0 | 0 | 0 | 3 | 10 | 3.9 |
| Newport & Menevia | 1 | 2 | 2 | 0 | 0 | 0 | 0 | 0 | 0 | 1 | 6 | 2.3 |
| Shrewsbury | 2 | 2 | 0 | 0 | 3 | 1 | 0 | 0 | 0 | 0 | 8 | 3.1 |
| Plymouth | 0 | 0 | 2 | 1 | 1 | 0 | 0 | 0 | 0 | 0 | 4 | 1.5 |
| Northampton | 0 | 1 | 0 | 2 | 0 | 0 | 0 | 0 | 0 | 0 | 3 | 1.2 |
| Unknown | 1 | 3 | 0 | 0 | 0 | 0 | 0 | 0 | 0 | 0 | 4 | 1.5 |
| Total | 101 | 54 | 34 | 16 | 15 | 10 | 9 | 12 | 4 | 4 | 259 | 100.0 |

Source: Appendix.

Table 1.8 Number of entrants (subsequently professed) in ten congregations in each decade, 1801–1900

| | RSM | SCSP | DC | SND | FCJ | SMG | SHCJ | DHM | CSJP | SSJ | TOTALS | % |
|---|---|---|---|---|---|---|---|---|---|---|---|---|
| 1801–10 | 0 | 0 | 0 | 0 | 0 | 0 | 0 | 0 | 0 | 0 | 0 | — |
| 1811–20 | 0 | 0 | 0 | 0 | 0 | 0 | 0 | 0 | 0 | 0 | 0 | — |
| 1821–30 | 0 | 0 | 0 | 0 | 2 | 0 | 0 | 0 | 0 | 0 | 2 | 0.0 |
| 1831–40 | 7 | 0 | 2 | 3 | 22 | 0 | 0 | 2 | 0 | 0 | 36 | 0.7 |
| 1841–50 | 117 | 5 | 10 | 28 | 59 | 0 | 19 | 13 | 0 | 0 | 251 | 4.7 |
| 1851–60 | 180 | 87 | 51 | 148 | 130 | 0 | 64 | 30 | 0 | 3 | 693 | 12.9 |
| 1861–70 | 231 | 84 | 80 | 165 | 155 | 6 | 64 | 18 | 0 | 11 | 814 | 15.2 |
| 1871–80 | 168 | 208 | 114 | 179 | 164 | 97 | 52 | 14 | 0 | 16 | 1,012 | 18.9 |
| 1881–90 | 290 | 165 | 226 | 188 | 171 | 78 | 64 | 25 | 17 | 12 | 1,236 | 23.0 |
| 1891–1900 | 338 | 139 | 231 | 143 | 182 | 94 | 71 | 33 | 22 | 23 | 1,276 | 23.8 |
| Unknown | 9 | 2 | 1 | 0 | 12 | 1 | 14 | 3 | 0 | 3 | 45 | 0.8 |
| Total | 1,340 | 690 | 715 | 854 | 897 | 276 | 348 | 138 | 39 | 68 | 5,365 | 100.0 |

Source: Appendix.

1850 and 1860. From 1862 to 1865, seventy-four additional congregations were approved.[82] As mentioned in the introduction to this chapter,
Frances Taylor remarked after her visit to the Maids of Christ that 'many
people have had the same idea at the same time'.[83] Her comment strikes
at the heart of this dynamic world-wide growth of religious congregations.
Hazel Mills notes the dominance of the numbers of female congregations
in France in comparison to the 'marginalised' contemplative orders.[84]
Congréganistes, simple-vowed women religious, were the dominant form
of religious life in France. They represented eleven per cent of female
women religious at the beginning of eighteenth century and twenty-one
per cent by 1789, and by 1880 they represented a resounding eighty per
cent of all female women religious.[85] Claude Langlois identified 16,172
convents in France by 1901 and 128,315 women in religious life.[86]
According to Langlois, women were at most one third of all church personnel prior to the French Revolution; a century later, this percentage had
increased to fifty-eight per cent.[87] Similar patterns can be found in other
European countries. The number of women religious in Belgium increased
from 1,617 in the beginning of the nineteenth century to 31,355 at the end.
The number of religious communities in Belgium increased from 129 to
2,182.[88] In Spain, the number of convents more than doubled in a century
from 1,076 in 1797 to 2,656 in 1901. The numbers of women religious
increased from 24,007 to 40,030.[89] Religious life in the Netherlands also

---

82  Anthony Fahey, 'Female Asceticism in the Catholic Church: A Case-Study of
    Nuns in Ireland in the Nineteenth Century' (doctoral thesis, University of
    Illinois at Urbana-Champaign, 1982), p. 42.
83  Devas, 1927, p. 96.
84  Hazel Mills, 'Negotiating the Divide: Women, Philanthropy and the "Public
    Sphere" in Nineteenth-Century France', in Frank Tallett and Nicholas Atkin,
    eds, Religion, Society and Politics in France since 1789 (London: The
    Hambledon Press, 1991), pp. 29–54 (p. 45).
85  Ralph Gibson, A Social History of French Catholicism, 1789–1914
    (London: Routledge, 1989), pp. 106–7.
86  Claude Langlois, 'Les effectifs des congrégations féminines au XIXe siècle:
    de l'enquête statistique à l'histoire quantitative', Revue d'Histoire de l'Eglise
    de France, 60 (1974), 39–64 (p. 53).
87  Ibid, pp. 62–3. Langlois's research indicates that women were 41 per cent,
    54.5 per cent and 58 per cent of clergy in the years 1830–31, 1861, and 1878
    respectively.
88  André Tihon, 'Les religieuses en Belgique du XVIIIe au XXe siècle: approche
    statistique', Revue Belge d'Histoire Contemporaine, 7 (1976), 1–54 (p. 32).
89  May P. Edmunds, 'But the Greatest of These is Chastity . . .', (doctoral thesis,
    Australian National University, 1986), p. 71.

proved popular. Seventy-two convents existed in 1850, and by the end of 1900 423 convents were in place. In the decade of the 1850s, 124 women, aged between twenty and twenty-nine, entered the thirteen largest Dutch congregations each year.[90] By the decade of the 1890s, 288 women were entering these same thirteen congregations each year. Across the Atlantic, the story was strikingly similar. In 1840, there were a couple of hundred women religious in Quebec, Canada. Sixty years later, there were thirty congregations with 6,629 women religious.[91] Forty thousand women religious entered 334 congregations in the United States by 1900.[92] Further afield in Australia, women religious totalled 3,150 compared with 1,042 priests and 377 brothers in 1900.[93] Closer to home, Scotland's population of women religious grew from two convents in 1840 to sixty-five in 1914.[94] In Ireland, the number of women religious multiplied eight-fold between 1841 and 1901 despite the fifty per cent decline in Catholic population in the same period. In 1901 Ireland had over 8,000 women religious, residing in 368 convents.[95] This great surge of women religious was an international phenomenon.

90 H.P.M. Goddijn, 'The Sociology of Religious Orders and Congregations', *Social Compass*, 7 (1960), 431–47 (p. 445).
91 Marta Danylewycz, *Taking the Veil: An Alternative to Marriage, Motherhood, and Spinsterhood in Quebec, 1840–1920* (Toronto, Canada: McClelland and Stewart, 1987), p. 17.
92 Rosemary Radford Reuther, 'Catholic Women', in Rosemary Radford Ruether and Rosemary Skinner Keller, eds, *In Our Own Voices: Four Centuries of American Women's Religious Writing* (San Francisco: Harper San Francisco, 1995), pp. 17–60 (p. 21); Carol K. Coburn and Martha Smith, *Spirited Lives: How Nuns Shaped Catholic Culture and American Life, 1836–1920* (Chapel Hill and London: The University of North Carolina Press, 1999), p. 134; Margaret Susan Thompson, '"Charism" or "Deep Story"? Toward a Clearer Understanding of the Growth of Women's Religious Life in Nineteenth-Century America', paper presented at conference entitled 'History of Women Religious', Chicago, June 1998.
93 Sophie McGrath, 'An analysis of the Australasian Catholic Congresses of 1900, 1904 and 1909 in relation to Public Policy from the perspective of Gender', *Australian Religion Studies Review*, 16 (autumn 2003), p. 3. Cited from the *Australian Catholic Directory* (1900), 162–3.
94 O'Brien, 2004, p. 95.
95 Fahey, 1982, p. 56, and Tony Fahey, 'Nuns in the Catholic Church in Ireland in the Nineteenth Century', in Mary Cullen, ed., *Girls Don't Do Honours: Irish Women in Education in the 19th and 20th Centuries* (Dublin: Women's Education Bureau, 1987), pp. 7–30 (p. 7).

## Reasons for the growth of congregations

The growth of the numbers of women entering religious life in England was influenced by a variety of factors, but one was pivotal: women were attracted to religious life. It gave them a spiritual focus, a useful and admirable occupation, companionship and physical security, and, most significantly, they believed it led to their 'salvation' and the salvation of others. For the select few, it gave them an opportunity to exercise their leadership in managing large, sometimes multinational, institutions.[96] Societal factors also influenced this attraction.[97] A moral and devotional culture fired up by Christian evangelism flourished in nineteenth-century England. Women were an integral part of this culture and an important part of this renewed growth of institutional churches. Their evangelical-ism was tangible and extended outside the home. Benevolence became more than just a moral obligation. For many women, it was a mission to spread their own middle-class ideological values of moral fervour, social piety and other virtues associated with womanhood and family life. These women came in many forms: they were members and organisers of the Charity Organisation Society and mothers' clubs.[98] They were Anglican deaconesses, 'Hallelujah lasses' and Bible women. Some, like Josephine Butler, Elizabeth Heyrick and Elizabeth Coltman, were social activists who took their place in the public sphere.

As this suggests, women's roles were changing in the nineteenth century. Despite a prescriptive literature that lauded women as wives and mothers, women were clearly involved in matters outside the home. Louisa Hubbard's survey of philanthropic activity in Great Britain in 1893 provides a rough estimate of 500,000 women 'continuously and semi-professionally' involved in philanthropy.[99] The growth of philan-thropic organisations was extensive. E.C.P. Lascelles reported that 279 charities were founded in the first half of the century, and 144 between 1850 and 1860.[100] Frank Prochaska's magnum opus charted the

96  Chapter 8 will discuss leadership in women's congregations in more detail.
97  The personal circumstances that motivated women to enter religious life will be discussed in more detail in the next chapter.
98  More research is needed to understand the motivations behind lay Catholic women's philanthropy in England and Wales.
99  Louisa M. Hubbard, 'Statistics of Women's Work', in Baroness [Angela] Burdett-Coutts, ed., *Woman's Mission* (London: Sampson Low, Marston & Company, 1893), pp. 361–6 (pp. 361–4).
100  E.C.P. Lascelles, 'Charity', in G.M. Young, ed., *Early Victorian England, 1830–1865*, 2 vols (London: Oxford University Press, 1934), II, pp. 315–48 (pp. 320–1).

'explosion' of charities managed and run by women in the nineteenth century.[101] Philanthropic work was seen as an extension of womanly duties and as such, a natural activity for women.[102] The growth of philanthropy in England was fuelled by a complex set of factors including the pressures of a rapidly industrialising society, the increasing number of public policies regarding education, health care and social welfare and the increasingly visible face of poverty. Women took action in the nineteenth century in order to address and redress this state of affairs in the name of the 'family'.

Catholic lay women in England were also involved in philanthropic work. Although little has been written specifically about these women and philanthropy, the archives of women religious provide ample evidence that lay women were involved in supporting active congregations, financially and through their involvement in confraternities, sodalities and mothers' clubs. Yet it was women's congregations that were at the forefront of this philanthropic mission despite the difficulties of a lifestyle that appeared antithetical to a culture which was pro-family, anti-celibacy and anti-papal. It was this female-centred model of womanhood that took the lead in Catholic philanthropy.

Catholic philanthropy was integral to the resurgence of the Catholic faith in the nineteenth century. In 1850, the newly restored hierarchy of England's Roman Catholic Church acknowledged that in order to build a strong, unified constituency, it needed to instil religious piety and develop religious practice in its ever-growing but ever wayward flock. The first Cardinal Archbishop of Westminster, Nicholas Wiseman, had welcomed male religious congregations to England but was thwarted by their inflexibility. Wiseman poured out his frustration to Fr Frederick Faber in October 1852 and protested that he had 'introduced or greatly encouraged establishment of five religious congregations' but 'I am just (for the great work) where I first began! Not one of them can (for it cannot be want of will) undertake it.'[103] Wiseman's subsequent encouragement of women's religious congregations proved to be more fruitful.

Many clergy were quick to realise the pragmatism of having women religious working in their mission. Clergy could not cope with the

---

101  F.K. Prochaska, *Women and Philanthropy in Nineteenth-Century England* (Oxford: Clarendon Press, 1980).

102  Barbara Caine, 'Beatrice Webb and the "Woman Question"', *History Workshop Journal*, 14 (1983), 23–43 (p. 30); Catherine Hall, 'The Early Formation of Victorian Domestic Ideology', in Sandra Burman, ed., *Fit Work for Women* (London: Croom Helm, 1979), pp. 15–32 (p. 28).

103  Gwynn, 1950, p. 416.

huge volume of work involved in administering to the needs of their parishioners. Annals and correspondence in congregation archives record the persistent letters that clergy and others wrote to superiors requesting foundations in their parishes. The allure of women's congregations is not difficult to understand: they were effective, needed little managing and were a source of cheap labour. This dramatic growth of women's congregations points to both the attractiveness of the life of women religious to women and the effectiveness of women's congregations in the view of the Catholic hierarchy and clergy.

Ultimately, as Susan O'Brien has cogently articulated, women religious created a demand for their services. This demand, in the nineteenth century, centred on the most vital need of a Catholic mission: education. This focus was not unexpected. It reflected the need to address what Sheridan Gilley identified as the English Catholic hierarchy's most pressing difficulty in the 1840s: the Irish.[104] Irish immigration had increased the number of Catholics in England but irregular church attendance was problematic. Education, bishops believed, would transform working-class Irish into loyal English subjects, sober members of the working class and above all, devout Catholics. Equally important, Catholic education would neutralise 'Irishness' by strengthening Catholic identity.[105] But educating the vast numbers of Irish Catholics was problematic for a financially impoverished English Catholic Church. Religious congregations, particularly women's congregations, played an important role in achieving the aims of the Catholic hierarchy. The educational institutions that women's congregations built and managed ranged from orphanages to teacher's colleges, from poor schools to boarding schools, from industrial schools to night schools. The urgent need for Catholic educational institutions far outstripped the resources, human and financial, available in the nineteenth century. Seventy per cent of religious institutes in England and Wales were involved in managing educational institutions.[106]

Yet the popularity of women's congregations was more than simply a need for their services. As will be argued in the next chapter, it was also a response to the needs of women for not only a deeper spiritual life, but also for an active philanthropic life. This life was not idyllic; it had its fair share of difficulties.

104  Sheridan Gilley, 'English Catholic Charity and the Irish Poor in London: Part II, 1840–1870', *Recusant History*, 11 (1971–72), 253–69.
105  Mary J. Hickman, *Religion, Class and Identity: The State, the Catholic Church and the Education of the Irish in Britain* (Aldershot, England: Avebury, 1995), pp. 200–3.
106  Walsh, 2002, p. 172.

## Conclusion

The history of women religious reveals that women pushed the boundaries of religious life to accommodate their needs. These new models of religious life were more evangelical and philanthropic, consistent with the Tridentine reforms but inconsistent with the requirements of religious life within a cloister.[107] The boundaries of religious life were pushed forwards, backwards and sideways by women religious seeking to expand their roles in Catholic life, and by clerical and papal authorities concerned with the boundaries of femininity and the sanctity of religious life. By the nineteenth century, what had clearly been proscribed was now *de facto*. Women's congregations were well ahead of formal legislation; simple-vowed women religious did not canonically obtain the status of 'religious' until Pope Leo XIII's *Conditae a Christo* in 1900.[108]

The needs of the times prevailed over gendered prescriptions of femininity. Supply and demand economics played a role in the growth of women's religious orders. There was a huge demand for the labour performed by religious sisters. Bishops, priests, brothers and the laity were constantly making requests for 'a few sisters' to run a school, for mission work, to teach orphans and so on. These requests have obscured the importance of women's responsibility for 'creating the demand and recognition for their own services'.[109] The rapid growth of simple-vowed congregations illustrates their attractiveness to Catholic women. It was within these congregations that Catholic women religious expanded the parameters of women's identity by edging private religious activity into the public space. Nineteenth-century England provided unprecedented opportunity for these women, and the nineteenth-century English Catholic Church was uncommonly liberal in the freedom it allowed new and existing congregations. It comes as no surprise that women were limited in the roles they could play and in the public action they could take, yet women were empowered to begin the institution building that was the hallmark of their active apostolic work. As the convent network expanded, women religious became a visible presence in mission

107 Tridentine reforms which defined Catholic dogma and reformed the Catholic Church came out of the workings of the Council of Trent (1545–63), an ecumenical council called in response to the Protestant Reformation.

108 Jarrell, 1984, p. 279; M.R. MacGinley, *PBVM, A Dynamic of Hope: Institutes of Women Religious in Australia* (Darlinghurst, New South Wales: Crossing Press, 2002), pp. 59–60.

109 Susan O'Brien, '"Terra Incognita": The Nun in Nineteenth-Century England', *Past and Present*, 121 (1988), 110–40 (p. 112).

functions. This visibility served to build awareness of, and in some cases, an attraction to, active religious life. The next chapter will look in greater detail into individual women's lives and explore this and other factors that encouraged women's entry into religious communities.

# 2

# Choosing religious life

As you go on you will learn to understand religious life, how it means doing God's will and not your own. We don't become nuns because we like it – because the life attracts us – but solely because 'The Master has come and called us'.[1]

The persistent myth of the Victorian woman, idle and innocent, performing domestic duties in the private sphere, protected from and unaware of the political world around her, has been rejected by many historians.[2] Victorian women's activities in the public and the private spheres are the centre of a canon of women's history which questions these myths and advocates a more complicated, often ambiguous rendering of Victorian womanhood.[3] This rendering is made more complex by the abundance of conduct manuals that provided Victorian women

1 F.C. Devas SJ, *Mother Mary Magdalen of the Sacred Heart (Fanny Margaret Taylor): Foundress of the Poor Servants of the Mother of God 1832–1900* (London: Burns, Oates & Washbourne, 1927), p. 305.
2 Patricia Branca, 'Image and Reality: The Myth of the Idle Victorian Woman' in Mary S. Hartman and Lois Banner, eds, *Clio's Consciousness Raised: New Perspectives on the History of Women* (New York: Harper Torchbooks, 1974), pp. 179–91 (p. 179); Duncan Crow, *The Victorian Woman* (New York: Stein and Day, 1971), pp. 13, 26, 28; Elizabeth Langland, *Nobody's Angels: Middle-Class Women and Domestic Ideology in Victorian Culture* (London: Cornell University Press, 1995), p. 14; Harold Perkin, *The Origins of Modern English Society 1780–1880* (London: Routledge and Kegan Paul, 1964), p. 159.
3 Sean Gill, *Women and the Church of England from the Eighteenth Century to the Present* (London: Society for Promoting Christian Knowledge, 1994); Katherine Gleadle, *The Early Feminists: Radical Unitarians and the Emergence of the Women's Rights Movement, 1831–1851* (London: Routledge, 1995); Kathryn Gleadle and Sarah Richardson, eds, *Women in British Politics, 1760–1860* (London: Macmillan, 2000); Leonore Davidoff and Catherine Hall, *Family Fortunes: Men and Women of the English*

with numerous examples of the prescribed nineteenth-century ideal of womanly virtue. In this literature, marriage was the pinnacle of true womanhood; single life was deemed unattractive and a personal failure.[4] There were, of course, some exceptions to this opinion. Mrs William Grey, lecturing on 'Old Maids' in 1875, protested against this widespread view of a single woman as a 'social failure, a social superfluity, or a social laughing-stock' and lectured on the utility of 'old maids'.[5]

Catholic women possessed a third alternative: religious life.[6] This offered a model of womanhood that was, in some circles, highly regarded and provided an opportunity for single Catholic women to find spiritual and professional satisfaction. Catholic women were cognisant of the consequences of religious life. They thoughtfully assessed its benefits and drawbacks, oftentimes basing their evaluation on personal knowledge and experience before taking the first steps towards entering a religious community. As convent networks developed, women religious became a visible presence as educators, nurses and parish visitors. Their visibility served to build awareness of, and in some cases, an attraction to, active religious life. This chapter will look in more detail into individual women's lives and explore the factors that encouraged their entry into religious communities.

The previous chapter explored the dramatic growth of religious life in the nineteenth century, which fuelled not only by the substantial numbers of women entering religious congregations, but also by the increasing number of requests from bishops, clergy and lay Catholics for experienced women religious to develop and manage educational, health care or social welfare institutions. Religious institutions were stamped with the congregation's special spirit of evangelisation and were essential for the growth of Catholic missions in England. These developments in

---

*Middle Class, 1780–1850* (London: Hutchinson, 1987); Linda Wilson, *Constrained by Zeal: Female Spirituality amongst Nonconformists, 1825–1875* (Carlisle, England: Paternoster Publishing, 2000).

4 Joan Perkin, *Women and Marriage in Nineteenth-Century England* (London: Routledge, 1988), p. 226.

5 Mrs William Grey, *Old Maids; A Lecture* (London: William Ridgway, 1875), p. 5. Mrs William (Maria Shirreff) Grey (1816–1906) was an early promoter of women's education.

6 Anglican women entered Anglican religious institutes after the foundation of the first Anglican sisterhood, the Park Village Sisterhood, in 1845. For more on Anglican sisterhoods see Susan Mumm, *Stolen Daughters, Virgin Mothers: Anglican Sisterhoods in Victorian Britain* (London: Leicester University Press, 1998).

Catholic women's religious life mirrored the international trend for women's religious congregations as discussed in the last chapter, and also paralleled the national trend of women's active involvement in philanthropic activities. Catholic women explored suitable outlets for their labours and spiritual yearnings, as did other women in England.[7] Frank Prochaska's extensive research on the explosion of charities managed by women in the nineteenth century gives ample evidence of this.[8] Domestic ideology was reconstructed in such a way that women's moral authority expanded from the private to the public sphere. Inside some churches, women preached and took leadership roles in 'cottage-based' religion.[9] Women journeyed outside their homes to express this expanded domestic and religious ideology. Female soldiers of the Salvation Army, the 'Hallelujah lasses', marched through the streets giving testimony to their faith in Jesus Christ; they preached in crowded halls and played a public role in the conversion of the working classes.[10] As 'moral regenerators', evangelical women applied their 'natural' attributes of piety and morality to 'reform and revive the nation'.[11] These 'angels in the house' were actively participating in more than the usual domestic activities and churchly duties. Jane Rendall and others propose that the feminisation of the church was a vital aspect of religious growth in the nineteenth century.[12] Catholic lay women also contributed to the growth of the

7  Jane Lewis, 'Introduction: Reconstructing Women's Experience of Home and Family', in Jane Lewis, ed., *Labour & Love: Women's Experience of Home and Family 1850–1940* (Oxford: Basil Blackwell, 1986), pp. 1–24 (p. 10).
8  F.K. Prochaska, *Women and Philanthropy in Nineteenth-Century England* (Oxford: Clarendon Press, 1980), p. 32.
9  Olive Anderson, 'Women Preachers in Mid-Victorian Britain: Some Reflexions on Feminism, Popular Religion and Social Change', *The Historical Journal*, 3 (1969), 467–84; Deborah Valenze, *Prophetic Sons and Daughters: Female Preaching and Popular Religion in Industrial England* (Princeton, New Jersey: Princeton University Press, 1985); Wilson, 2000, p. 9.
10  Lynne Marks, 'The "Hallelujah Lasses": Working-Class Women in the Salvation Army in English Canada, 1882–92', in Franca Iacovetta and Mariana Valverde, eds, *Gender Conflicts: New Essays in Women's History* (Toronto: University of Toronto Press, 1992), pp. 67–117 (pp. 68–73).
11  Catherine Hall, 'The Early Formation of Victorian Domestic Ideology', in Sandra Burman, ed., *Fit Work for Women* (London: Croom Helm, 1979), pp. 15–32 (p. 25).
12  Gill, 1994, p. 84; Gail Malmgreen, 'Domestic Discords: Women and the Family in East Cheshire Methodism, 1750–1830', in Jim Okelkevich, Lyndal Roper and Raphael Samuel, eds, *Disciplines of Faith: Studies in Religion, Politics and Patriarchy* (London: Routledge, 1987), pp. 55–70 (p. 56); Sue

Catholic Church, but the predominant form of Catholic female church workers were women religious who devoted themselves full-time to philanthropic work.[13]

Religious sisters as church workers were problematic; their adherence to the vows of poverty, celibacy and obedience incensed many Protestants. Public opinion articulated in the press, published tracts and the pulpit often vilified nuns and 'nunneries'. This reaction was rooted in anti-Catholicism, but also influenced by gendered prescriptions of women's role within the family. The three vows taken by women religious, of poverty, chastity and obedience, appeared to clash with the middle-class family ideology.[14] The vow of chastity was particularly abhorrent in a society which idealised motherhood. Many Victorians could not consider that a woman would freely choose a life of celibacy over what they believed was the one true vocation for women: motherhood.[15] In *Woman's Mission* (1839), Sarah Lewis addressed Protestant parents in her effort to dissuade them from sending their daughters to Catholic convent schools. Her observations revealed predictable Protestant views of Catholic nuns:

---

Morgan, 'Review', *Gender & History*, 14 (2002), 163–5 (p. 163); Jane Rendall, *The Origins of Modern Feminism: Women in Britain, France and the United States 1780–1860* (London: Macmillan, 1985), pp. 73–107. Sue Morgan defines the 'feminisation of religion' as the 'conflation of women's sphere with the affective, moral and spiritual dimensions of Victorian culture'.

13 Scholarship on the activities of lay Catholic women in nineteenth-century England is woefully inadequate. Convent records suggest that lay women were very active in fund-raising and were members of the numerous confraternities and sodalities, many of which were organised by women's religious congregations.

14 Carmen M. Mangion, 'Centre of a Maelstrom: Anglican Sisterhoods in Victorian England' (master's thesis, Birkbeck College, University of London, 2000). While this thesis was written about public attitudes towards Anglican women religious, many of the points discussed, and particularly this one with respect to the vows of poverty, chastity and obedience, would have been applicable to Catholic women religious.

15 Anne Frances Norton, 'The Consolidation and Expansion of the Community of St Mary the Virgin, Wantage, 1857–1907' (doctoral thesis, King's College, London, 1978), p. 197; James Spurrell, *Miss Sellon and the 'Sisters of Mercy': An Exposure of the Constitution, Rules, Religious Views, and Practical Working of their Society; Obtained through a 'Sister,' who has recently Seceded* (London: Thomas Hatchard, 1852), p. 53.

The wisdom of employing those who had renounced the world to form the minds of those who were to mix in it, to be exposed to all its allurements, to share in all its duties, was doubtful indeed; and the danger was enhanced by the fact, that the majority of recluses were anything but indifferent to the world which they had renounced. The convent was too often the refuge of disappointed worldliness, the grave of blasted hopes, or the prison of involuntary victims; a withering atmosphere this in which to place warm young hearts, and expect them to expand and flourish.[16]

Lewis's acquaintance with conventual establishments appeared to be restricted to the persistent mythology of nuns 'immured' behind forbidding convent walls.[17] These misconceptions were in place thirteen years later, when Hobart Seymour lectured on the perils of twelve-year-old postulants and sixteen-year-old nuns being imprisoned inside convents walls and becoming nuns 'against their inclinations'.[18] These medieval imaginings of religious life were in contrast to the lived experience of religious life in England. By 1852, approximately sixty-two of the eighty-one convents in England and Wales were associated with simple-vowed congregations, and convents were firmly established in major conurbations of London, Liverpool and Manchester.[19] Religious sisters were visible in the public sphere and engaged in their philanthropic work outside the cloister. Yet these perceptions of Catholic religious life remained obdurate. At the end of the century, a similar tirade was presented by Mrs Arbuthnot. She passionately challenged her audience: 'Are secluded celibates, themselves estranged from home ties and influences, fit persons to train girls for the position of wives and mothers?'[20]

16 [Sarah Lewis], *Woman's Mission* (London: John W. Parker, 1839), pp. 69–70.
17 Walter L. Arnstein, *Protestant versus Catholic in Mid-Victorian England: Mr. Newdegate and the Nuns* (London: University of Missouri Press, 1982); G.F.A. Best, 'Popular Protestantism in Victorian England', in Robert Robson, ed., *Ideas and Institutions of Victorian Britain* (London: G. Bell & Sons, 1967), pp. 115–42; E.R. Norman, *Anti-Catholicism in Victorian England, Historical Problems: Studies and Documents* (London: Allen and Unwin, 1968); Diana Peschier, *Nineteenth-Century Anti-Catholic Discourses: The Case of Charlotte Bronte* (London: Palgrave Macmillan, 2005).
18 Rev. M. Hobart Seymour, *Convents or Nunneries. A Lecture in Reply to Cardinal Wiseman, delivered at the Assembly Rooms, Bath, on Monday, June 7, 1852* (Bath: R.E. Peach, 1852), pp. 24–7.
19 Compiled from *Catholic Directory* (1852), 133–45 and my own database of convents (see Appendix).
20 Mrs Arbuthnot, 'The Danger of Conventual Education and the Importance of Home Training', in *Romanism and Ritualism in Great Britain and*

She argued that religious life defied the key precept of a family-centred life as the ideal role for women and therefore celibate women religious were not suitable as teachers of young females. Despite the growth of active congregations in the nineteenth century and the visibility of women religious and the institutions they managed, the representations that resurfaced again and again during the nineteenth century were of cloistered nuns imprisoned behind convent walls or disappointed women unable to find marriage partners. [21]

Nineteenth-century Catholic texts tell another story of women religious. Many emphasised the 'higher calling' of religious life. One conduct manual for Catholic women, *The Mirror of True Womanhood* (1883), instructed mothers not to put obstacles in the way of those daughters who felt 'called to the higher, the Virginal Life'. Mothers were reminded that they would be rewarded for their own generosity with 'untold blessings'.[22] The language of this discourse suggests that some parents did not wish their daughters to become religious sisters. In these cases, the notion of being 'called' to religious life was used to dissuade Catholic parents from their objections. William Bernard Ullathorne, Bishop of Birmingham, used the writings of St Paul to argue that 'the state of the nun is holier than the state of the wife'.[23] C.S. Devas in his *Studies of Family Life* (1886) promoted religious life as the:

> state to which many are called, and is a nobler and better state, and the call higher; inasmuch as the lower part of our nature are more completely conquered by the higher, and all the heroic works of Christian charity can be fulfilled unhindered . . . there can be among the unmarried closer union with God, more complete imitation of the Incarnate Word, as their hearts are more undivided, their self-oblation more complete.[24]

---

Ireland, *A Report of the National Protestant Congress* (Edinburgh: R.W. Hunter, 1895), p. 325.

21  These three examples are not meant to suggest that opinions about women religious were consistent and unchanged during the nineteenth century. Unfortunately, little academic research has been done on the shifts in popular attitudes towards Catholic women religious in the nineteenth century.

22  Rev. Bernard O'Reilly LD, *The Mirror of True Womanhood: A Book of Instruction for Women in the World* (Dublin: M.H. Gill & Son, 1883), pp. 250–1.

23  Bishop Ullathorne, *Three Lectures on the Conventual Life* (London: Burns, Oates & Co., 1868), p. 23.

24  C.S. Devas, *Studies of Family Life: A Contribution to Social Science* (London: Burns and Oates, 1886), pp. 144–5.

Alfonso Maria de Liguori's *Instructions on the Religious State* instructed his readers that 'souls who are most dear to God, who have attained the greatest perfection and who edify the Church by the odour of their sanctity, are, for the most part, to be found in religion'.[25] These passages reflected the Roman Catholic Church's teachings on the holiness of religious life.

These two discourses, the Protestant one that argued that women entered religious life under duress and the Catholic discourse of a 'higher calling', had one thing in common: both dismissed the agency of women entering religious life. This chapter questions these discourses and examines women's agency in 'choosing' religious life.[26] Religious life was not a natural option in a Protestant country where Catholicism was still contested. In addition, not all Catholic parents welcomed the departure, which could be permanent, of their daughters from their family circle. Women who encountered obstacles to their entry into religious life constructed an identity that legitimated their choice.

Gail Malmgreen, in her examination of the Methodist revival, comments that Methodist women zealously took advantage of the expanding number of religious opportunities for public activity.[27] Like Methodist women, Catholic women saw religious life as a opportunity for their spirituality to fuse with philanthropic 'works of mercy'. This chapter will examine the factors that influenced women who entered religious life. Many women became acquainted with religious life through childhood and family relationships, through philanthropic activities in their adult years or through the guidance of a spiritual advisor. Towards the end of the century, more and more women became exposed to religious life in schools managed by women religious. Family members, Catholic and Protestant, were not always supportive of women's entry

25 *Liguori's Instructions on the Religious State*, ed. Giovanni Battista Pagani (Derby: Richardson and Son, 1848), pp. 121–2. While no direct evidence has been found that this text was read by nineteenth-century sisters, a copy of Pagani's book was found in the archives of the mother house of the Sisters of Charity of St Paul the Apostle in Selly Park, England.

26 The use of this concept of 'choice' is troublesome as there is no consensus on its historical meaning. Some historians and sociologists theorise 'choice' as though individuals make choices without outside influences. This chapter conceptualises 'choice' in a particular manner: 'choice' was determined by the social conditions that influenced the quality and quantity of the options available for women at a particular place and point in time. The social conditions in which this choice was embedded are essential in understanding the identity of women religious.

27 Malmgreen, 1987, p. 67.

into religious life. When their desire to become women religious was opposed, women turned to religious ideology for justification. In this way, many were successful in achieving their aim of becoming women religious.

## Spirituality

The feminisation of the church and the extension of women's work into the public sphere through religiously motivated philanthropy are familiar themes for those investigating nineteenth-century women and religion.[28] Sue Morgan asserts that religious belief and feminism were the two most 'formative ideological influences' for nineteenth-century women.[29] Although these ideologies appear disparate, historians have placed great importance on their significance. Leonore Davidoff and Catherine Hall emphasised the importance of religion in middle-class women's lives: religion offered women the 'key' to a world where they were 'valued for their spiritual worth' and where a 'religious career' was a legitimate option.[30] It was religious belief, according to Patricia Crawford, that informed women's social actions and encouraged some to take on social responsibilities. This 'conventional' form of religion socialised women[31] and encouraged many to fight for moral causes in the public sphere. This socialisation proceeded in a unique way for Catholic women, through the expansion of religious congregations.

Women entered these congregations for a variety of reasons. Necrologies and many biographies of women religious, with their distinct focus on piety, emphasised the other-worldly 'call' of a vocation.[32] In the more sceptical, secular world, this spiritual dimension has been hastily dismissed and replaced by more practical reasons, such as the lack of marriage partners or the desire for a professional career. The influence of spirituality needs to be addressed, despite the difficulties. The evidence found in convent archives indicated that this 'call', as heard by aspirants to the active religious life, reflected more than the desire for a prayerful,

---

28 Rendall, 1985, pp. 73–107; Gill, 1994, p. 84; Malmgreen, 1987, p. 56; Morgan, 2002, p. 163.
29 Susan Morgan, 'Faith, Sex and Purity: The Religio-Feminist Theory of Ellice Hopkins', *Women's History Review*, 9 (2000), 13–34 (p. 13).
30 Davidoff and Hall, 1987, pp. 147–8.
31 Patricia Crawford, 'Women, Religion and Social Action in England, 1500–1800', *Australian Feminist Studies*, 13 (1998), 269–80 (p. 270).
32 Many congregations called their obituaries of women religious 'necrologies'. For more on the use of necrologies, see Chapter 6.

contemplative life. This desire for a relationship with God was revealed in three ways: first, through a yearning for communion with God, second, through the desire to remedy spiritual or physical poverty, and third, through a wish to lead an industrious life not restricted by cloister walls. The relationship with God was often interwoven into a relationship with the poor. This trio of objectives merged into a vocation for active religious life.

The spiritual dimension of the attraction to religious life cannot be ignored: convent annals, letters, necrologies and aspirant registers credited the desire for a personal relationship with God as a primary factor in attracting women to religious life. This was the first of the trio of objectives that led to the vocation for active religious life. Anne Croft, who became the second Mother Superior of the Society of the Holy Child Jesus, vividly recalled the sound of the bells of the convent of the Carmelites and recorded in her memoir: 'I could hear the nuns entoning [sic] their solemn chant, and the thought came to me, how beautiful it was to sing the praises of God; and then a longing desire seized me and I wished that I could join them!'[33] For Croft, these bells symbolised a way of life that venerated God and drove her 'longing desire' for a spiritual way of life. Necrologies offered similar sentiments. Margaret Bacon was drawn by a 'wish to live for God'.[34] Alice Finegan wished to 'leave the world for God'.[35] These narratives reflected a distinct separation between religious life and the secular world; women religious were not interested in fulfilling their Catholic spirituality as lay women.

These accounts also expressed the need to attend to spiritual or physical poverty outside the convent, the second objective in the trio. Edith Teresa Wray wished to serve the poor 'for our lord's sake'.[36] Amelia Connor, who had wished to be a nun from childhood, was 'drawn to the love of the works'.[37] Margaret Forrest was attracted to 'living and working with the poor'.[38] These women saw their vocation in conjunction with 'works of mercy'. Caroline Norton, after completing her formal education, instructed orphans and organised the Confraternity of the Rosary in her parish. She was not content with fulfilling her philanthropic duties as a lay person. Norton felt called to a religious life,

---

33 SHCJ: 'Memoir of Mother Angelica Croft, Second Superior General of the Society of the Holy Child Jesus', 1913, pp. 3–7, 10.
34 DC: Box 1, no. 10: 'Seminary Particulars', 1889–1917.
35 Ibid.
36 Ibid.
37 Ibid.
38 Ibid.

but did not wish to be 'praying the whole day'. She entered the Daughters of Charity of St Vincent de Paul in 1864 and as Soeur Teresa had a varied career teaching first at the Liscard orphanage and then seven years later at the Deaf and Dumb Institute in Woodhouse.[39] Her desires did not deny the importance of prayer; rather she emphasised her need for a prayerful, productive life outside cloister walls.

This vocation was seen by women religious as a personal invitation from God to live a holy and spiritual life. Their vocation was about salvation: both their own and that of others. Constitutions of active women's congregations reinforced this mixed life by conflating personal virtue with the salvation of others.[40] The Society of the Holy Child Jesus specified in its constitutions that:

> it is more especially the duty of all Religious to follow Him more closely, and to imitate Him more perfectly. And they should not only endeavour to render themselves perfect in every virtue, but with the assistance of Divine Grace, they should strive to do all in their power to help others in the way of Salvation.[41]

This type of active religious life was not about 'praying all day'. This third aspect of their vocation, the emphasis on the active element, 'to help others in the way of Salvation' or to provide for 'the instruction of the ignorant and the relief of the afflicted', was of great significance to this variant of religious life.[42] It was an essential part of the spirituality of active, simple-vowed congregations. Many constitutions allowed philanthropic work to supersede spiritual activity when 'the urgent necessities of the Poor require it'. Daughters of Charity could change the hours of their spiritual exercises or omit some of them when their work with the poor was of a more urgent nature:

> They shall always endeavour to acquit themselves faithfully of their spiritual exercises, having particular need of them to preserve themselves in a

39  DC: *Notes on Deceased Sisters* (1916), p. 1. The necrologies of 'notable' Daughters of Charity were included in a publication entitled *Notes on Deceased Sisters* and annually distributed to each convent. 'Sister Servant' was the name used by Daughters of Charity to refer to the local superior who managed the activities of a convent.

40  The rule and constitutions of a religious institute defined the aims and parameters of their way of life. For more on the importance of the constitutions, see Chapter 8.

41  SHCJ: Box 54 R 24 'Constitutions of the Society of the Holy Child Jesus', 1887, part I, section I, no. 1.

42  SCSP: *Rules and Constitutions of the Sisters of Charity of St Paul in England*, [1864], chapter 1.

state of grace, and in the fervor necessary to persevere constantly in the labors of their vocation; and although they should make no scruple of sometimes changing the hour of these exercises, or even of omitting some, *when the urgent necessities of the Poor require it*, still they shall take care never to neglect them through negligence, in devotion or too great an inclination for exterior things, which is sometimes cloaked under a false pretext of charity.[43]

This excerpt from the rule of the Daughters of Charity emphasised the significance of their work with the poor. Other congregations conflated prayer and work. The Poor Servants of the Mother of God in the first years after their foundation had to make 'meditation at our work because we were so few and we had no one but the Sisters to do anything, and we often worked until 11 or 12 at night'.[44] This need to pray and work simultaneously did not devalue the significance of their spiritual exercises. As their work was a form of prayer, combining the two, when necessary, was acceptable, although not ideal. Women religious were warned not to abuse this practice. The balance between their 'works of mercy' and interior life was tenuous. The previous excerpt from the Daughters of Charity rule noted that spiritual exercises allowed the Daughters of Charity to 'preserve themselves in a state of grace' and were a source of the fervour that was necessary in order to 'persevere constantly'. Their spiritual life was integral to the effectiveness of the philanthropic life.

Many women religious declared that their interest in religious life began during childhood. Twenty-five per cent of the aspirants who entered the Daughters of Charity of St Vincent de Paul indicated that they had 'wished from childhood to become a sister'.[45] Mary Forrest always 'thought of being a nun'.[46] Catherine Nolan 'wished to be a nun from the time of first communion'.[47] Mary Gunning heard the 'divine call' in her early teens after observing two Daughters of Charity of St Vincent de Paul on the streets of Paris.[48] Necrologies in other congregations also

---

43 DC: 'J.M.J. Rules of the Daughters of Charity Servants of the Poor Sick, Common Rules of the Daughters of Charity', 1920, chapter 8, section I. Emphasis is my own.

44 SMG: I/D 'Sister Alacoque's Annals', p. 10.

45 DC: Box 1, no. 10: 'Seminary Particulars', 1889–1917, Elizabeth Ann Bradley. Thirty-one of 124 women whose interviews were documented during 1889–1900 indicated that they had wished to enter religious life as a young child.

46 Ibid, Mary Forrest.

47 Ibid, Catherine Nolan.

48 DC: *Notes on Deceased Sisters* (1919), pp. 1–2.

noted an early desire to enter religious life. Ann Marie Bond's necrology chronicled that she 'desired from her earliest years to become a Religious'.[49] This desire, whether coming at a young age or later in life, was seen, in the language of these nineteenth-century women, as a 'call' from God.

## Catholic clergy

Catholic clergy were often called on to interpret this 'call' from God. Clerical recommendations were important for the entry of women into religious life, especially when an aspirant was not known to the congregation. Women discerning a vocation to religious life often approached their parish priest to discuss their religious vocation. He would question an aspirant's vocation and then advise her as to her readiness for religious life. Caroline Clements, a convert of Reverend Thomas Clarke SJ of Tunbridge Wells, sought his advice about her vocation. Clarke directed Clements to Cornelia Connelly, founder of the Society of the Holy Child Jesus and a woman 'for whom he had a great regard';[50] Clements subsequently entered the Society. Catherine Mary Pilley, a teacher in private schools and later a teacher at the school for the Deaf and Dumb in Boston Spa, was told by a Vincentian father that she had a religious vocation. He advised her 'after serious consideration' to enter the Daughters of Charity of St Vincent de Paul.[51] She did. Mary Lewis felt herself 'called by God' and at the age of twenty-three, on the advice of her Jesuit confessor, joined the Daughters of Charity of St Vincent de Paul.[52] Mary Anne Costello entered the Daughters of Charity of St Vincent de Paul on the advice of a 'pious Irish missionary'.[53]

The role of the clergy was particularly important in the early years of a congregation's existence, before educational institutions and kinship relationships began to play such an important role in introducing women to religious life. Peter Gallwey, a Jesuit based in London, was known for his 'zealous hunger of souls' and was a prodigious promoter of religious life. He recommended at least eight women to the Daughters of the Heart of Mary between 1859 and 1886. In 1859, their annals noted that 'Miss Caroline Langdale came to Kensington to learn

49 RSM Bermondsey: 'Some Lives of the Sisters of Mercy Bermondsey', 1840–74, pp. 168–9.
50 SHCJ: 'Necrologies', p. 188.
51 DC: *Notes on Deceased Sisters* (1938), pp. 126–7.
52 DC: *Notes on Deceased Sisters* (1906), pp. 91–2.
53 DC: *Notes on Deceased Sisters* (1919), p. 61.

something about the Society, for which Fr Gallwey thinks she has a vocation'.[54] Constance Beauchamp was converted by Fr Gallwey and received at the Jesuit church on Farm Street in 1882; she also entered the Daughters of the Heart of Mary.[55] Elizabeth Postle, another of Gallwey's penitents, was proposed by him in 1859.[56] Gallwey introduced Mary Mostyn,[57] Mary Halpert Bousfield[58] and Hester Blishen[59] to the Daughters of the Heart of Mary. Ada Vertue wished to enter an enclosed order but Gallwey persuaded her to join the Daughters of the Heart of Mary.[60] Gallwey's name also appeared frequently in the records of the Daughters of Charity of St Vincent de Paul. Evelyn Marshall, after her conversion, placed herself under the spiritual direction of Gallwey and she eventually entered the Daughters of Charity of St Vincent de Paul.[61] Gallwey was not the only priest to advocate women's religious life so vigorously. The Notre Dame de Namur annals indicate that no fewer than fifty women owed their vocation to the Redemptorist Louis de Buggenoms.[62] Fr Cullen SJ sent 'a good many Postulants' to the Poor Servants of the Mother of God.[63]

Convent records accorded clergy a prominent role in an aspirant's entry into religious life. Clerical advice was often requested and respected, but not always heeded. The Oratorian Frederick Faber directed Etheldreda Fitzalan Howard towards the contemplative Carmelites but her 'love and compassion' for the poor, according to her necrology, caused him to abandon this idea. One wonders if Faber's reassessment of Howard's vocation was caused by Howard's own preference for a more active congregation. Fr Philip (William Thomas) Gordon, who became Howard's confessor after Faber's death in 1863, had a 'different view' of Etheldreda's vocation and she became a Daughter of Charity.[64] The

54 DHM: C3 '1st Diary, Kensington', October 1859.
55 DHM: C4 'Death Notices English/Irish Provinces – Before 1900', Constance Beauchamp.
56 DHM: C3 'Provincial Council Meetings', 2 April 1859.
57 DHM: C4 'Death Notices English/Irish Provinces – Before 1900', Mary Mostyn.
58 Ibid, Mary Halpert Bousfield.
59 DHM: C3 'Provincial Council Meetings', 21 March 1859.
60 DHM: C4 'Death Notices English/Irish Provinces – Before 1900', Ada Vertue.
61 DC: *Notes on Deceased Sisters* (1935), pp. 107–8.
62 SND: 'Clapham Annals II: Notre Dame in England', 1851–1860.
63 SMG: I/D 'Beaumont', 1875, p. 24.
64 Cecil Kerr, *Memoir of a Sister of Charity: Lady Etheldreda Fitzalan Howard* (London, Burns Oates & Washbourne, 1928), p. 20.

Bishop of Southwark, Thomas Grant, arranged Mary Potter's entrance into the Mercy congregation in Brighton. Potter found that she did not quite 'fit' with the Mercy style of spirituality. Her novice mistress believed she was better suited to a contemplative life. Mary Potter left the Sisters of Mercy in Brighton and eventually became founder of the Little Company of Mary. [65] Theresa Butti felt herself called to a vocation as a young girl and was advised by her confessor to enter the Irish Sisters of Charity, but instead she became a Daughter of Charity of St Vincent de Paul. Butti's necrology explains that she was determined to follow the example of Anna Maria Blundell, who had entered the year before in 1856.[66] Not all Fr Gallwey's penitents followed his advice. Eleanor Maxwell, whose mother wished all nine of her daughters to consecrate their lives to God, was directed by Gallwey towards the Order of the Good Shepherd. However, Eleanor's attraction to the poor led her to the Daughters of Charity of St Vincent de Paul.[67] Although convent narratives frequently suggested that women were obediently following the advice of clergy, some women did make decisions based on their own assessment of whether a religious congregation met their vocational needs.

Convent necrologies and biographies described spiritual longing as the primary *raison d'être* for a vocation, and clergy were important in giving women direction. However, this discourse masked other factors that were relevant in making the decision to enter religious life. Socialisation and conditioning were factors that must be acknowledged. Florence Bagshawe dated her 'first seeds of vocation' to her first communion at age eleven. A more detailed examination of her life history suggests additional factors that could have contributed to her vocation. Florence Bagshawe's uncle was Edward Gilpin Bagshawe, the Bishop of Nottingham, and two of her aunts, Mrs Latter and Lady Macfarlane, invited and financially assisted the La Retraite congregation during their first years in England.[68] In addition, she attended La Retraite convent boarding school, and this would have introduced her to the lifestyle of women religious. These factors were all elements of the 'first seeds of her vocation' and will be assessed in more detail in the remainder of this chapter.

65  Elizabeth A. West, *One Woman's Journey: Mary Potter: Founder – Little Company of Mary* (Richmond, Victoria, Australia: Spectrum Publications, 2000), pp. 21, 27–8.
66  DC: *Notes on Deceased Sisters* (1918), p. 95.
67  DC: *Notes on Deceased Sisters* (1924–25), p. 1.
68  RLR: Mother Imelda, 'Sevenoaks', dated 20 November 1951 or 1957.

## Kinship relationships

Historians of women religious have acknowledged the importance of kinship relationships to the growth of congregations.[69] Women's understanding of religious life could be obtained from family members who were religious. In many families, there was a distinct trend of support for and entry into religious communities. Miriam Boyle, who entered the Daughters of Charity of St Vincent de Paul, had a sister in the Holy Cross and Passion congregation and one cousin in the Armagh convent of the Sisters of Loreto. In addition, two of her brothers and four cousins were priests.[70] The future Holy Child Jesus sister Christina Snow had three brothers who were clergy and four sisters who were religious.[71] Louisa Blundel's sister Frances became a Benedictine nun at Princethorpe. Her youngest sister, Tottie, became a Franciscan at Taunton, and her younger brother entered the Benedictines at Fort Augustus. In September 1887, she joined one paternal aunt, two maternal aunts and several cousins who were Daughters of Charity of St Vincent de Paul.[72] Monica Weld's family included two aunts who were nuns, one Jesuit uncle and two cardinals. She became a Daughter of Charity of St Vincent de Paul in 1882.[73] Five of the ten McCann sisters entered religious life; two entered the Congregation of St Joseph of Peace.[74] In families where a pattern of entering religious life existed, women would have a practical knowledge of conventual life: its benefits and its drawbacks. They were aware that religious life was a viable alternative to marriage or a single life.

Kinship relationships between religious sisters in the same congregation were common in nineteenth-century England. The Glaswegian sisters Helen and Jane Donnelley, aged thirty-three and twenty-six, entered the

---

69 Caitriona Clear, *Nuns in Nineteenth-Century Ireland* (Dublin: Gill, 1987), p. 144; Marta Danylewycz, *Taking the Veil: An Alternative to Marriage, Motherhood, and Spinsterhood in Quebec, 1840–1920* (Toronto, Canada.: McClelland and Stewart, 1987), pp. 112–13; M.R. MacGinley PBVM, *A Dynamic of Hope: Institutes of Women Religious in Australia* (Darlinghurst, New South Wales: Crossing Press, 2002); Mary Peckham Magray, *The Transforming Power of the Nuns: Women, Religion, and Cultural Change in Ireland, 1750–1900* (Oxford: Oxford University Press, 1998), pp. 14–15; Barbara Walsh, *Roman Catholic Nuns in England and Wales, 1800–1937: A Social History* (Dublin: Irish Academic Press, 2002), pp. 135–7.
70 DC: *Notes on Deceased Sisters* (1929), p. 2.
71 SHCJ: 'Necrologies', pp. 87–9.
72 DC: *Notes on Deceased Sisters* (1930), pp. 149–53.
73 Ibid (1922), pp. 3–4.
74 CSJP: 'Lest We Forget', Agnes McCann.

convent of the Daughters of Charity in Manchester together in 1885. The Fielding twins, Eliza and Emma, aged twenty, entered the Sisters of Mercy in Birmingham and were professed together.[75] Lucy Hall, aged thirty-five, entered the Daughters of the Heart of Mary and was followed two years later by her widowed mother, Mrs George Hall, aged seventy-five, and her elder sister, Ellen, aged forty-one.[76] The four Lomax sisters, Augusta, Chrysola, Elizabeth and Pauline, took their vows with the Sisters of Notre Dame de Namur in the years between 1862 and 1886.[77] Celebratory comments in annals noted the welcome of biological family members. The annals of the Faithful Companions of Jesus in Chester reported that 'after a long sojourn in the world, one of our former pupils, entered the community and on the Feast of the Immaculate Conception, she was followed by her sister'.[78] This was Mary Power, aged twenty-eight, who entered on 8 September 1873 and was followed three months later by her twenty-one-year-old sister, Ellen. The Isleworth convent annals of the Faithful Companions of Jesus recorded in February 1899: 'we had the joy of welcoming a dear postulant, the niece of the Superior'.[79]

Convert families also played an important role in the expansion of religious congregations.[80] Converting to Catholicism was not a decision made without serious deliberation. Such a step often meant not only ostracism from friends and family but also financial hardship.[81] The number of converts entering religious life is difficult to quantify as

75  RSM Handsworth: 1/200/9/1 Handsworth Annals, 1897, p. 208.
76  DHM: C3 'Provincial Council Meetings', 7 November [1898].
77  SND: Registers of Professed Sisters for the British Province (1845–1900).
78  FCJ: A654 'Chester Annals', 1873, p. 136.
79  FCJ: A1856 'Isleworth Annals', 1899, p. 2.
80  Robert J. Klaus, *The Pope, the Protestants, and the Irish: Papal Aggression and Anti-Catholicism in Mid-Nineteenth Century England* (London: Garland Publishing, 1987), pp. 17–18, 25. The prominence of some converts such as Frederick Faber, Henry Manning and Augustus Welby Pugin has led to an overemphasis on the number of converts who entered the Roman Catholic Church in the nineteenth century. W. Gordon-Gorman lists over 3,500 of the more prominent nineteenth-century converts in his *Converts to Rome: Since the Tractarian Movement to May 1899* (London: Swan Sonnenschein & Co., 1899) but this listing is incomplete. Unfortunately nineteenth-century record-keeping practices in Catholic parishes and dioceses make it difficult to quantify the number of conversions.
81  Pauline A. Adams, 'Converts to the Roman Catholic Church in England, circa. 1830–1870' (doctoral thesis, Somerville College, Oxford, 1977), pp. 120–2.

convert status was typically not recorded in most profession registers.[82] However, analysis of profession registers from the Daughters of Charity of St Vincent de Paul and the Society of the Holy Child Jesus allow some statistical inferences. Nine per cent of women who entered the Daughters of Charity were converts.[83] The Holy Child Jesus sisters noted convert status of only half of the professed Holy Child sisters. The proportion of converts in this sample, most certainly understated, was fifteen per cent. Cornelia Connelly, founder of the Society of the Holy Child Jesus, was a convert herself, and the large percentage of converts in her congregation may reflect her personal encouragement.[84] In addition, a good percentage of these convert religious sisters had siblings in the same congregation or in other religious institutes. Over nine per cent of the Daughters of Charity of St Vincent de Paul converts and over eleven per cent of the Society of the Holy Child Jesus converts were siblings. Three convert Daughters of Charity had siblings in other congregations. These statistics are too isolated to be considered representative for all religious congregations; however, they do suggest that the process of conversion may have promoted a degree of piety and religious commitment that encouraged entry into religious life. Pauline Adams's study of Catholic converts found a marked attraction of converts to religious life and pointed out that for some lay men and women, the power of their conversion 'had the affect almost equivalent to a religious vocation'. Her study also revealed that second-generation converts were as prolific in their entries into religious life as their forebears.[85]

Anecdotal evidence of the significance of convert families and kinship relationships is readily found in convent records. Sir Reginald and Lady Margaret Egerton were received into the Catholic Church a few months before their daughter Winefride's birth. She became a Daughter of Charity, and her two sisters also entered religious life.[86] Mary Burns's parents were influenced by the Oxford Movement and began studying to

82 Gordon-Gorman, 1899, p. xi. Gordon-Gorman notes that 130 converts in the nineteenth century became nuns, but as these women appear to have been from relatively prominent families, it is unlikely that this is a complete list of all converts who became women religious.
83 The date of baptism is recorded in the profession register of the Daughters of Charity of St Vincent de Paul. This was used to calculate the number of women who became converts. Approximately half of the Daughters of Charity who converted were over fifteen years of age.
84 These statistics were derived from the sisters database. See the Appendix.
85 Adams 1977, pp. 139, 148, 171.
86 DC: *Notes on Deceased Sisters* (1954), p. 42.

become Catholics in 1847. They were received into the Catholic Church with their five daughters, aged one month to ten years. All five daughters entered religious life: Mary became a Daughter of Charity of St Vincent de Paul and her four sisters became Ursulines. Her only brother became a Catholic priest.[87] The Ryder family converted in 1846. Three of the Ryder sons became priests and one daughter became a nun.[88] The Bellasis family produced three women religious (two of whom entered the Society of the Holy Child Jesus) and two priests. Convert Henrietta Kerr entered the Sacred Heart noviciate; four years later her two brothers retired early from the army and the navy to enter the Jesuit noviciate.[89]

Biological relationships bear further scrutiny in the context of England as they were significant factors in the growth of congregations in the nineteenth century. In the congregations analysed in Table 2.1,[90] over fourteen per cent of members were siblings and another one per cent were biologically related as aunts, nieces and sometimes mothers. Table 2.2 shows that almost two per cent of women religious had siblings or other relations who were in other religious communities or were clergy. Barbara Walsh noted that twenty per cent of the Irish-born component of the Daughters of Charity from 1847 to 1926 had siblings in religious life.[91] At the Sisters of the Sacred Hearts of Jesus and Mary from 1870 to 1926, eleven per cent were biologically related.[92] This trend was consistent with that of

87  Ibid, 1914, pp. 86–7.
88  Adams, 1977, pp. 2–3. Cited from Harrowby MSS, Ryder MSS, unpublished memoir by Cyril Ryder, 'A Son's Reminiscences'.
89  Ibid, p. 171.
90  Profession registers from each congregation were reviewed. Biological relationships were ascertained from names of parents as well as anecdotal evidence in annals, correspondence, necrologies, etc. It is likely that the extent of kinship relationships has been understated, especially those that were not sibling relationships.
91  The British Province of the Daughters of Charity of St Vincent de Paul was formed in 1885, and included women who entered the Daughters of Charity in England, Ireland, Scotland and Wales and who worked primarily in these regions. The Irish province was created in 1970. Barbara Walsh's calculations are based on the list of Irish-born Daughters of Charity that she obtained from the Daughters of Charity archives in Blackrock, Co. Dublin. Her figure of twenty per cent does not include the 230 English-born Daughters of Charity who worked in the British Province in the nineteenth century. English-born sisters amounted to thirty-two per cent of the professed sisters who worked in the British Province. My analysis includes all the women who worked in the British Province in the nineteenth century.
92  Walsh, 2002, p. 136.

Table 2.1 Sibling and kinship relationships within ten congregations, 1801–1900

| Congregation | Foundation on date in England | Total of professed sisters | Number of professed sisters with one or more siblings | Siblings as a % of total professed sisters | Number of other kin | Other kin as a % of total professed sisters |
|---|---|---|---|---|---|---|
| Religious Sisters of Mercy | 1839 | 1340 | 105 | 7.8 | 4 | 0.3 |
| Sisters of Charity of St Paul the Apostle | 1847 | 690 | 119 | 17.2 | 1 | 0.1 |
| Daughters of Charity of St Vincent de Paul | 1857 | 715 | 146 | 20.4 | 31 | 4.3 |
| Notre Dame de Namur | 1845 | 854 | 175 | 20.5 | 6 | 0.7 |
| Faithful Companions of Jesus | 1830 | 897 | 107 | 11.9 | 1 | 0.1 |
| Poor Servants of the Mother of God | 1869 | 276 | 20 | 7.2 | 7 | 2.5 |
| Society of the Holy Child Jesus | 1846 | 348 | 67 | 19.3 | 3 | 0.9 |
| Daughters of the Heart of Mary | 1846 | 138 | 8 | 5.8 | – | – |
| St Joseph of Peace | 1884 | 39 | 11 | 28.2 | 5 | 12.8 |
| St Joseph of Annecy | 1864 | 68 | 4 | 5.9 | – | – |
| Total | | 5,365 | 762 | 14.2 | 58 | 1.1 |

Source: Appendix.

Table 2.2 **Kinship relationships within and outside religious life within ten congregations, 1801–1900**

| Congregation | Total professed sisters | Number of kinship relationships within congregations | Number of kinship relationships as a % of total professed sisters | Number of kinship relationships outside congregations | Number of kinship relationships outside congregations as a % of total professed sisters |
|---|---|---|---|---|---|
| Religious Sisters of Mercy | 1,340 | 109 | 8.1 | 5 | 0.4 |
| Sisters of Charity of St Paul the Apostle | 690 | 120 | 17.4 | 5 | 0.7 |
| Daughters of Charity of St Vincent de Paul | 715 | 177 | 24.8 | 45 | 6.3 |
| Notre Dame de Namur | 854 | 181 | 21.2 | 5 | 0.6 |
| Faithful Companions of Jesus | 897 | 108 | 12.0 | 3 | 0.3 |
| Poor Servants of the Mother of God | 276 | 27 | 9.8 | 10 | 3.6 |
| Society of the Holy Child Jesus | 348 | 70 | 20.1 | 2 | 0.6 |
| Daughters of the Heart of Mary | 138 | 8 | 5.8 | 3 | 2.2 |
| St Joseph of Peace | 39 | 16 | 41.0 | 4 | 10.3 |
| St Joseph of Annecy | 68 | 4 | 5.9 | 1 | 1.5 |
| Total | 5,365 | 820 | 15.3 | 83 | 1.5 |

Source: Appendix

nineteenth-century women religious in other national contexts. Caitriona Clear noted that fifteen per cent of the women who entered the Limerick Sisters of Mercy from 1838 to 1900 were siblings; and in the Good Shepherd convent in Limerick twenty-two per cent of those who entered between 1861 and 1900 were siblings.[93] Barbara Misner, in her study of nineteenth-century women religious in the United States, concluded that over seventeen per cent of religious sisters had at least one family member in religious life.[94] Marta Danylewicz's figures on kinship relationships in Quebec indicate that the Sisters of Misericorde benefited from the influence of family members: twenty-one per cent had biological sisters in the same congregation; an additional nine per cent had siblings who were diocesan clergy or in other religious institutes.[95] Over thirteen per cent of the women who entered the sisters of the Congregation of Notre Dame in Quebec from 1840 to 1920 had at least one sister in the community; another nine per cent had at least one sibling in another community and thirteen per cent mentioned relatives in religious life.[96]

Barbara Walsh credits Irish family networking as the basis of kinship relationships and concludes that it was 'rare to find the same level of close kith and kin among English, Scots and Welsh born entrants'. Walsh interprets this as 'evidence of the absence of extended family unit networking' among the English, Scots and Welsh.[97] However, if one compares the incidence of sibling relationships as seen in Table 2.3, the sibling relationship percentages are fairly consistent with those in the population of the English-born sisters in each congregation. Approximately forty-six per cent of the members of the ten congregations sampled were English-born and forty-eight per cent of the kinship relationships were with English-born sisters.[98] Forty-one per cent of the members of the ten congregations were Irish-born and approximately forty-seven per cent of the kinship relationships were with Irish-born sisters. While the relationship between

---

93  Clear, 1987, p. 144.
94  Barbara Misner SCSC, *'Highly Respectable and Accomplished Ladies':* *Catholic Women Religious in America 1890–1850* (London: Garland Publishing, 1988), p. 133. Misner's sample of eight congregations includes 1,441 women religious, of whom 250 had at least one biological family member in religious life.
95  Danylewycz, 1987, p. 113. This analysis included those sisters who entered Misericorde from 1848 to 1920.
96  Ibid, p. 112.
97  Walsh, 2002, p. 136.
98  It is likely that many English-born sisters had Irish ancestry, but it is not possible to attribute 'Irishness' based on surname.

Table 2.3  Sibling relationships and countries of birth within ten
congregations, 1801–1900

| Country of birth | Number of siblings | Sibling relationships as a % of total number of siblings | Number of professed sisters | Number of professed sisters as a % of total number of professed sisters |
|---|---|---|---|---|
| England | 364 | 47.8 | 2,460 | 45.9 |
| Ireland | 357 | 46.9 | 2,216 | 41.3 |
| Other | 32 | 4.2 | 446 | 8.3 |
| Unknown | 9 | 1.2 | 243 | 4.5 |
| Total | 762 | 100.0 | 5,365 | 100.0 |

*Source*: Appendix.

Irish birth and kinship was stronger, extended family networking was strong in English-born women who became religious.[99]

Leonore Davidoff convincingly argues that siblings were 'key links' in patterns of migration, waged work and obtaining housing and other types of support.[100] This was equally true for women's religious congregations, where siblings were important to the growth of religious life. This pattern of kinship relationships suggests that women religious communicated their satisfaction with religious life to their siblings and other family members. Although constitutions and custom books proscribed 'excessive' family communications,[101] plentiful evidence exists documenting that family relationships continued after profession. Frances Taylor, founder of the Poor Servants of the Mother of God, referred to this family networking in a letter to the local superior at St Helens:

> It would save time and trouble if when girls write to their sisters or cousins –
> 'speak to Rev. Mother for me,' – to write back at once and say, 'Write to
> Rev. Mother yourself and make your application.' Can't this be fixed so that
> I need not be asked every time?[102]

99  Family and convent networks will be discussed in Chapter 6.
100  Leonore Davidoff, 'Where the Stranger Begins: The Question of Siblings in Historical Analysis', in Leonore Davidoff, ed., *Worlds Between: Historical Perspectives on Gender and Class* (Cambridge: Polity Press, 1995), pp. 206–21 (p. 206). Davidoff also argues that sibling relationships are virtually ignored in historical scholarship.
101  This will be discussed in more detail in Chapter 7.
102  SMG: I/A2a, p. 64: letter dated 11 July 1884 from Frances Taylor to Mother Aloysius Austin (Margaret Busher).

Women religious communicated with family members and encouraged their female relations to enter religious life. The historian Sylvia Pinches comes to a similar conclusion after reviewing the convent records of the Dominicans of St Catherine of Siena:

> What also comes out of a study of these records, in conjunction with other sources, is the network of connections which ran through the Catholic community in the midlands, and beyond, to London, and to Belgium. The nodes were, in many cases, the nuns themselves. Far from having cut themselves off from their families on entering religion, many nuns maintained a wide correspondence with family and friends, keeping their correspondents in touch with each other, and abreast of the activities, and needs, of the convent.[103]

Family networks were significant to the expansion of religious life and can explain, in part, the prevalence of biological relationships within congregations and within religious life in general.

### Family opposition

Not all women entering religious life were assured of family support. Evidence of family resistance exists not only in the convent narratives but also in some of the religious texts found in nineteenth-century convents. Alfonso Maria di Liguori's *Instructions on the Religious State* acknowledged the adverse effects that parents could have on a vocation:

> when a person resolves to abandon the world, he finds his worst adversaries in his parents, who either from interest or affection, generally allow themselves to become the enemies of God, and endeavour to turn their children away from their vocation, instead of giving their consent.[104]

Liguori's treatise, in regard to parental influence, was as applicable in the nineteenth century as when it was written in the eighteenth century.[105] Mary Theresa White's entry into the Society of the Holy Child Jesus was a 'severe blow' to her Catholic father. After 'bitterly opposing her

---

103 Sylvia Pinches, 'Roman Catholic Charities and Voluntary Societies in the Diocese of Birmingham, 1834–1945' (master's thesis, University of Leicester, 1997), p. 26.
104 *Liguori's Instructions on the Religious State*, pp. 38–9. Despite Liguori's use of the masculine pronoun, his text was meant for both men and women considering religious life.
105 Parental consent was important; only rarely did religious congregations accept women without at least one parent's approval. This will be discussed in more detail in Chapter 4.

entrance and overwhelming her with reproaches', he accepted her decision but his attitude remained that of 'silent disapproval'.[106] Sister Mary
Alphonse de Liguori (Iphigenie de Paiva) conspired with her sister
Isabelle to gain Isabelle's entry into Notre Dame de Namur. In her letter
of 29 October 1850, she thanked Mère Constantine for accepting
Isabelle as a postulant, adding, 'I am going to send her to you without
my brother knowing and I think I shall be able to keep it hidden from
him as long as necessary. She [Isabelle] is happy about it.'[107] The Irish-
born Eugenie Ryan had attended the boarding school of the Society of
the Holy Child Jesus for two years. When she approached her parents
regarding her interest in becoming a Holy Child Jesus sister, they insisted
she return to Ireland and join in the social life appropriate to a young
woman of her age. Over the next two years, Eugenie Ryan complied with
her parents' wishes. Her participation at parties and social events produced three offers of marriage: she refused them all. Finally convinced by
her resolve, Eugenie's parents granted her request and she left Ireland to
become a postulant at the Holy Child Jesus convent. Ryan's biographer
observed that 'It was a bitter blow to both father and mother, but their
strong Irish faith realised the honour God was doing their darling
Eugenie in calling her to be His own spouse, and they accepted the sacrifice with characteristic generosity.'[108] Similarly, William and Susan
Cuddon removed their twenty-three-year-old daughter Susanna from the
Benedictine convent where she had been educated despite (and perhaps
because of) her attraction to Benedictine life. Susanna's necrology
acknowledged her acquiescence to have them 'settle her advantageously
in life'. Her biographer judged that her obedience to her parents was 'the
Will of God' but eventually Susanna:

> could no longer resist His divine Call, and in anguish of mind she entreated
> her affectionate Parents not to hinder her from devoting herself entirely to
> the Divine Service. Their religious principles were too deeply founded to
> suffer them to hesitate one moment in consenting to the sacrifice demanded
> of them, they gave their consent to her entering a Convent.[109]

106  SHCJ: S. Mary Mechtilde, *Mother Mary Walburga SHCJ whose Years of
     Labor in the Society were its Seed Time in America* (Rosemont,
     Pennsylvania, USA, 1949), pp. 8–9.
107  SND: BX BB/2 in BH1 F1 'Blackburn Community Matters', 29 October
     1850.
108  M.M. Xavier Gwynn SHCJ, *From Hunting Field to Cloister* (Dublin:
     Clonmore and Reynolds, 1946), pp. 15–18.
109  RSM Bermondsey: 'Some Lives of the Sisters of Mercy Bermondsey',
     1840–74, p. 6.

Similar stories of family opposition are not uncommon in convent documents. These stories provided evidence of the significance of the 'call' to religious life. Parents, even Catholic ones, were not unanimously enthusiastic about their daughters entering religious life. Whether active or contemplative, religious life removed a daughter from frequent contact with her family. Although parents were allowed to visit their daughters, these visits were infrequent and they were not encouraged. Parents also lost the productive capacity of the daughter, as child-bearer, as wage-earner and as family care-giver. Eugenie Ryan's biographer remarked that there was 'no question of Eugenie's entering until sister Julie was old enough to take her place at home'.[110] Eugenie was the eldest of seven children, six of whom were female. She could not be released from her family duties until Julie, two years younger, could take her place in the family structure.

The language used in these biographies and necrologies revealed a tension between the family ideology and the religious ideology. The centrality of family life was disturbed by a daughter's entry into religious life and her permanent removal from the family circle. This tension was addressed in the narratives in several ways. First, parents were acknowledged for the great sacrifice they were making. The recognition of Eugenie's parents' 'bitter blow' conceded that their rights as parents had been supplanted. In exchange for the loss of their daughter, they were publicly acknowledged and honoured for their 'generous sacrifice'. The narrative recognised the personal sorrow and loss of the parents, but extolled their strong religious principles, which provided them with strength to make this sacrifice. Second, the narratives emphasised the 'will of God' in causing the breach in family life. It was by this higher authority that such a step could be taken, even against the will of parents. The 'will of God' legitimised the family break-up and a woman's separation from the biological family unit. The religious ideology that supported the 'will of God' as the supreme arbiter superseded the family ideology that defined the gendered responsibilities of a daughter. Lastly, the implication was always that the 'will of God' must be obeyed. When Susanna Cuddon finally confronted her parents it was because she 'could no longer resist his Divine call'. She had no choice but to comply with the 'will of God' despite the resulting opposition to her parents' wishes.

Throughout these narratives, the will of the parents, the will of the church and the will of God were readily acknowledged. The will of the woman entering religious life, however, was de-emphasised. It was each woman's submissive behaviour and her acquiescence to parental authority that was initially highlighted. The narratives almost divest

110   Gwynn, 1946, pp. 15–16.

these women of any responsibility in selecting religious life. What was underscored was the dominance of the 'will of God', because it was God who selected them for religious life. As quoted at the beginning of the chapter, Frances Taylor, founder of the Poor Servants of the Mother of God, reminded the novice Sister M. Campion (Louise Troughton) that religious life was about 'doing God's will' and that women became nuns because "The Master has come and called us'.[111] Frances Taylor placed the 'will of God' at the forefront of a woman's entry into religious life and negated any possibility of personal choice. The declaration of her vocation was not portrayed as an example of unfeminine wilfulness, but seen as an embrace of God's will. Women used this religious ideology to mask their active efforts of asserting their desire to enter religious life.

Whereas some convert families embraced religious life, others rejected it for their children. Agnes Moser converted with her parents at the time of the Oxford Movement.[112] She admired the work of the religious sisters she met while travelling in Boulogne and expressed an interest in religious life. Her father, attempting to dissuade her, advised her that she would have to 'work hard, scrub floors, rise at an unearthly hour &c.'. Despite his vehement disapproval, in 1874 she became a postulant at Carlisle Place, London, and she later became a Daughter of Charity of St Vincent de Paul. Her father held firm to his censure; he died that year and refused to see her on his deathbed.[113] Coventry Patmore and his family converted to Catholicism in 1864 after his second marriage to Marianne Byles, a convert he met in Rome. The author of the oft-debated and disputatious *Angel in the House*[114] sent his daughter Emily to the Holy Child Jesus boarding school in Mayfield.[115] When nineteen-year-old Emily expressed her desire to become a sister in the Society of the Holy Child Jesus, he was convinced this was a temporary attraction and requested she wait until she was twenty-one. Emily Patmore obediently spent the next few years travelling with her family, during which time she

---

111  Devas, 1927, p. 305.
112  The Oxford Movement, begun by Anglican clergymen at Oxford in 1833, attempted to renew the Church of England by reviving in it certain Catholic doctrines and rituals. Owen Chadwick, *The Spirit of the Oxford Movement* (Cambridge: Cambridge University Press, 1990).
113  DC: *Notes on Deceased Sisters* (1933), pp. 30–1.
114  Langland, 1995, p. 62. This poem promoted the image of woman as the middle-class 'angel' or moral salvator. The *Angel in the House* will be discussed in more detail in Chapter 6.
115  [Louise Wheaton], *A Daughter of Coventry Patmore, Sister Mary Christina, SHCJ* (London: Longmans, Green and Co., 1924), p. 68.

rejected one suitor. When she turned twenty-one, she again proposed entering the Society of the Holy Child Jesus and Coventry Patmore gave his grudging approval. There is some irony in that Emily Patmore did not become the domestic angel in the house but, instead, became Sister Mary Christina of the Society of the Holy Child Jesus.

Women who converted to Catholicism without their families' support were often ostracised by their families and left to fend for themselves financially. Convent records reported sympathetically on their plight and admired their pious resignation. Convert women could become boarders in a convent while they were seeking wage-earning positions with respectable Catholic families. Some converts turned to religious life as a haven from their difficulties, but congregations were wary of this type of vocation. Provincial meeting minutes of the Daughters of the Heart of Mary report that Miss Sculy's admission was being debated because 'her vocation seemed to be rather the result of necessity than of choice'. The mother general reasoned that 'with a more intimate knowledge of the Society acquired during her noviciate' both Miss Sculy and the congregation could more easily decide the depth of her vocation.[116] Miss Sculy does not appear on the profession registers of the Daughters of the Heart of Mary, which suggests that she had no vocation for this particular congregation. Other converts were more successful in their efforts to become women religious. Evelyn Marshall's mother considered her daughter's conversion a 'great disloyalty to the faith of her fathers, and she refused to receive her back into the home' and disapproved of her entry into the Daughters of Charity of St Vincent de Paul.[117] Frances Bridges, the daughter of an Anglican clergyman, was cut off from her family when she entered the Society of the Holy Child Jesus.[118] Joan Perkin calls the rejection of marriage 'the ultimate rebellion', but to some families, entering religious life must have appeared even more defiant.[119]

The biological family formed the basis of social order,[120] and the gendered discourse surrounding family life was centred on a vision of

---

116  DHM: C3 'Provincial Council Meetings', 9 April 1873.
117  DC: *Notes on Deceased Sisters* (1935), pp. 107–8. Marshall was given permission to return home and nurse her younger sister who was ill with scarlet fever. During this time, her mother accepted her religious vocation and eventually converted to Catholicism.
118  Gwynn, 1946, pp. 25–6.
119  Perkin, 1988, pp. 226–32.
120  Leonore Davidoff, 'The Family in Britain', in F.M.L. Thompson, ed., *The Cambridge Social History of Britain 1750–1950* (Cambridge: Cambridge University Press, 1990), pp. 71–131 (p. 106).

domesticity that placed the unmarried adult daughter firmly in the family circle as help-meet to fathers or mothers, unmarried brothers or overly burdened sisters.[121] Daughters and sisters were emotional, cultural and economic assets integral to the family unit.[122] Convent narratives document the acceptability of a woman's entry into religious life despite her removal from the family circle by maintaining that it was the 'will of God'. The narratives recognised the parents' loss and applauded their faith upon their acceptance of the 'will of God'. But not all families accepted this 'will of God' with grace. Continued family disapproval was acknowledged in the narratives and proved to be another 'cross' to bear for women who entered religious life contrary to their parents' wishes. The agency of these women entering religious life was concealed by a religious ideology that promoted obedience to 'God's will'.

## Education

Catholic education also played a role in the growth of religious life in the nineteenth century. Young girls were educated to fulfil the role of the traditional middle-class Victorian wife and mother.[123] Their education was meant to inculcate them with feminine virtues, religious morality and domestic knowledge. It was this 'cultivation of characteristics particularly feminine – self-denial, forbearance, fidelity', according to Joan Burstyn, that women would use to 'teach the whole world how to live in virtue'.[124] One contributor to *The Month*, a Catholic literary journal, opined that the main endeavour of Catholic education was to form 'good Catholic women, strong in faith, faithful in virtue'.[125] This focus on Catholic faith and virtue, when taught by women religious, encouraged another model of womanhood, that of religious life. By the latter half of the nineteenth century, the most important recruiting tool for the growth

121  Davidoff and Hall, 1987, pp. 321–56.
122  Davidoff, 1995, p. 214.
123  Joan N. Burstyn, *Victorian Education and the Ideal of Womanhood* (London: Croom Helm, 1980), p. 20; Felicity Hunt, 'Divided Aims: The Educational Implications of Opposing Ideologies in Girls' Secondary Schooling, 1850–1940', in Felicity Hunt, ed., *Lessons for Life: The Schooling of Girls and Women, 1850–1950* (Oxford: Basil Blackwell, 1987), pp. 3–21 (p. 4); Frances Widdowson, *Going up into the Next Class: Women and Elementary Teacher Training, 1840–1914* (London: Women's Research and Resources Centre, 1980), pp. 31–3.
124  Burstyn, 1980, p. 32.
125  *The Month* (1894), 520.

of vocations was formal education in Catholic schools. Prayer and piety were as much a part of the school curriculum as were reading and writing. Education was the central focus of seventy per cent of simple-vowed women's congregations in nineteenth-century England and Wales.[126] Women religious taught children and adults, in day schools, boarding schools, night schools and industrial schools. Vocations came from all types of educational institutions, but some sources of vocations were more common than others.

The link between boarding school education and vocations was particularly strong as boarding school students were considered prime candidates for religious life. In her reminisces of La Retraite boarding school, Florence Bagshawe explained:

> what a benefit it was to have been at school at Sevenoaks. The fervour of the little community impressed me very much & I can remember that while we were lying snugly in bed we heard the 3 nuns chanting their office in the cold chapel![127]

Her boarding school experiences influenced her decision to enter religious life. Congregations were aware of this important source of vocations. Upon establishing the first Faithful Companions of Jesus convent in Somers Town, London, the founder, Marie Madeleine Victoire de Bengy d'Houët, was anxious for the establishment of a boarding school for girls of the 'upper ranks' as the means for recruiting 'subjects capable of doing the good which her zeal foresaw could be affected in this country'. In a letter dated 8 March 1840, D'Houët explained, 'If we had a house for young ladies, as we had intended, we should obtain subjects for our society'.[128] Cardinal Nicholas Wiseman, in a letter to Cornelia Connelly, founder of the Society of the Holy Child Jesus, declared that:

> The middle classes, till now almost neglected in England, form the mass and staple of our society, are the 'higher class' of our great congregations out of the capital, have to provide us with our priesthood, our confraternities, and our working religious.[129]

Middle- and upper-class young women who attended boarding schools were considered suitable candidates for religious life.[130]

126  Walsh, 2002, p. 172.
127  RLR: Mother Imelda, 'Sevenoaks'.
128  *The Life of Madame de Bonnault d'Houët: Foundress of the Society of the Faithful Companions of Jesus* (Dublin: M.H. Gill & Son, 1885), p. 219.
129  John P. Marmion, 'Cornelia Connelly's Work in Education, 1848–1879', doctoral thesis, University of Manchester, 1984, p. 389.
130  The issue of class is addressed in more detail in Chapter 7.

Annals of congregations on occasion made reference to former students entering religious life. The 1859 Gumley House annual letter reported that the boarding school at Gumley House, Isleworth, had five new postulants:

> Five have entered from Gumley House alone; three, immediately from the school-room; the others, after having spent a few years in the world, and felt its emptiness, returned gladly to pass their lives in the hallowed home that had sheltered their youth.[131]

The Faithful Companions of Jesus in Upton celebrated a boarding school vocation in 1897 and noted in their annals:

> On Ascension Day, one of our former pupils came from her home in Dublin to join the Noviceship; she had for the past 4 years earnestly wished to enter, but only now obtained her parents' consent. This is the 2nd Upton pupil in the Noviciate, and we have hopes of some others joining later. This awakening of vocations among our children is a great consolation to us, as for many years, the Upton school-room seemed forgotten by the Heavenly Bridegroom of souls![132]

This deficiency in boarding school vocations was a disappointment to the annalist writing this entry, but she was hopeful that additional candidates from the 'Upton school-room' would enter religious life. This narrative also illustrates the dichotomy between the sisters of the congregation and others living 'in the world'. Convent documents often portrayed religious life as stable, safe and replete with religious sanctity whereas 'the world' was portrayed as empty, turbulent and contentious. Convent life, as will be discussed in more detail in Chapter 5, was much more complex than this simplistic metaphor suggests.

Some young women were attracted to convent life by the personal charisma of some women religious. Emily Barker entered St Leonards boarding school at the age of sixteen and like many others was attracted to the life of the Holy Child Jesus sisters by the 'strong personal influence' of her Prefect Mother Aloysius (Mary Ann Frankish).[133] Eugenie Ryan requested the religious name Aloysius as she felt she owed a great deal to the guidance of the same Mother M. Aloysius.[134] Mother M. Gertrude (Anne Catherine Day) was also noted in the Holy Child annals and in necrologies as fostering many religious vocations, including that of Margaret Mary Ellis, educated at the convent school in

131   FCJ: A923, 'Gumley House Annual Letter', 1859.
132   FCJ: A1842 'Upton Annals', 1897, p. 6.
133   SHCJ: 'Necrologies', p. 79.
134   Gwynn, 1946, p. 26.

Blackpool,[135] and Elizabeth Kenworthy, whose vocation was 'lovingly guarded' by Mother Gertrude.[136] Sister M. Catherine (Clarissa Reeves) saw many of her pupils become Daughters of Charity of St Vincent de Paul, and other pupils, her necrology noted, 'are to-day fervent members of other Religious Orders'.[137] Amelie Teúliere was directress of the Kensington orphanage, where 'several became religious'.[138] The charges of Sister M. Magdalen (Honora Finucane) entered the Children of Mary confraternity, and later, her necrology noted, 'many became religious'.[139]

The attraction to religious life can be measured in a less anecdotal way. The data in Table 2.4 is derived from the school registers of the St Leonards and Mayfield boarding schools.[140] The Holy Child Jesus records list each student's name, the date of entry into the school and in many cases whether the student subsequently married, entered religious life or died. Unfortunately, approximately one-third of the students are not categorised at all. Despite this missing information, the results show a distinct pattern that corroborates the link between boarding school students and vocations. In the case of St Leonards boarding school, seventeen per cent of the attendees entered religious life. The much smaller sample at Mayfield indicates that twenty-two per cent of boarding school attendees entered religious life. Further, there was a definite predisposition for a student to enter the congregation managed by the boarding school she attended; approximately six per cent entered the Society of the Holy Child Jesus from St Leonards boarding school and eight per cent Mayfield respectively. However, other congregations also gained religious vocations. There is no indication as to why these women did not enter the Society of the Holy Child Jesus. However, several explanations can be suggested. The Society of the Holy Child Jesus was a teaching congregation, and those not interested in education would not have wished to enter it. Twenty of the St Leonards students entered congregations that were not teaching congregations. Twenty-nine women entered contemplative orders; they were seeking a life fully devoted to prayer and not active, philanthropic works. Also, the charism of a congregation, that spirit of

135  SHCJ: 'Necrologies', p. 57.
136  Ibid, p. 29.
137  DC: *Notes on Deceased Sisters* (1923), p. 70.
138  DHM: C4 'Death Notices English/Irish Provinces – Before 1900', Henriette Amelie Teúliere, p. 3.
139  DC: *Notes on Deceased Sisters* (1914), p. 93.
140  St Leonards boarding school opened in 1850. Mayfield opened as a junior boarding school in 1871.

Table 2.4  Boarding school vocations, Society of the Holy Child Jesus

|  | Number of St Leonards students 1850–79 | % of St Leonards students | Number of Mayfield students 1872–79 | % of Mayfield students |
|---|---|---|---|---|
| Entered Society of the Holy Child Jesus | 29 | 6.3 | 5 | 8.5 |
| Entered other religious institute | 49 | 10.7 | 8 | 13.6 |
| Married | 169 | 36.7 | 13 | 22.0 |
| Died | 51 | 11.1 | 4 | 6.8 |
| Unknown | 162 | 35.2 | 29 | 49.1 |
| Total | 460 | 100.0 | 59 | 100.0 |

Source: SHCJ: Vol. 42, pp. 207–23

the congregation that was a mix of its history, theology, spirituality and philanthropic activities, would have played a role in women's choice of congregations. Another factor, which will be investigated in a more comprehensive manner in Chapter 7, has to do with the status of the congregation.

Women from educational institutions other than boarding schools were also attracted to religious life. Elizabeth Broadbent, taught by the Holy Child sisters at St Ignatius parish night school in Preston, met Cornelia Connelly dressed in her 'best', her 'blue merino crinoline and Leghorn bonnet trimmed with lily of the valley', to discuss her vocation to religious life. She became Sister M. Claver, a lay sister who held a variety of domestic functions during her lifetime, working alternatively as the convent's portress, infirmarian and baker.[141] The Gumley convent annals of 1859 noted that 'In this year the Poor School has presented its first flowers to our Divine Lord; three of the children have entered, two of whom have already received the Habit'.[142] These two women were received as lay sisters into the Faithful Companions of Jesus. Former students who attended poor schools, parish schools, industrial schools and night schools did enter religious life. However, the evidence is infrequent and anecdotal. While these three examples denote women becoming lay

141  Sr Ursula Blake and Sr Annette Dawson, *Positio: Information for the Canonization Process of the Servant of God Cornelia Connelly (née Peacock) 1809–1879*, 3 vols (Rome: Sacred Congregation for the Causes of Saints, 1983), II, p. 924.
142  FCJ: A923 'Gumley House Annual Letter', 1859.

sisters, it cannot be assumed that those entering religious life from boarding schools entered as choir sisters and those entering from all other institutions entered as lay sisters. As will be discussed in more detail in Chapter 7, a sister's status was dependent on a variety of factors. It was possible for a woman who would have been accepted as a lay sister in one congregation to be accepted as a choir sister in another.[143]

Teacher training colleges also proved successful in attracting young women to religious life. Our Lady's, the Notre Dame de Namur teacher training college in Liverpool, opened its doors in 1856 and trained many Catholic schoolteachers.[144] The training college attracted many students because of its Catholic pedagogy and the practical training available at the nearby Notre Dame de Namur schools.[145] Our Lady's collegiate atmosphere produced a unique sense of camaraderie and school spirit. The school magazine, *A Voice*, first published in April 1863, updated alumni with news of the teaching staff, graduates and current students. The 'News of Former Students' column reported that:

> After the Christmas Examination of 1862, 38 students left to commence their career as Teachers, 10 under the safe & happy shelter of holy religion, 28 in the midst of the trials of the world. Two are already wearing the habit of Notre Dame and several others expect to be clothed on Low Sunday.
>
> Those who were acquainted with Margaret Whiteside and Mary Ryan will be interested to know that their names in religion are Mary Gabriella and Alphonse of St Joseph.[146]

*A Voice* boasted about its successful graduates: thirty-eight were employed and ten had entered religious life. The four remaining extant issues of *A Voice* published in 1864, 1866, 1867 and 1869, continued to proclaim the successes of graduates, making special note of those who

143  Some congregations maintained class divisions through the classification of religious sisters as lay sisters and choir sisters. Choir sisters were professed sisters who typically functioned as teachers, nurses and parish visitors. They could vote and take on administrative roles within the congregation. Lay sisters were professed sisters who typically functioned as domestic help within the congregation. Lay and choir sisters will be discussed in much greater detail in Chapter 7.

144  In 1856, the Society of the Holy Child Jesus opened its teacher training college in St Leonards. The Society of the Sacred Heart opened its teacher training college in Wandsworth in 1873.

145  Mary Linscott, *Quiet Revolution: The Educational Experience of Blessed Julie Billiart and the Sisters of Notre Dame de Namur* (Glasgow: Burns, 1966), p. 112.

146  SND: Box 13 MPTC *A Voice* (April 1863).

Table 2.5 Out Lady's training college vocations, Notre Dame de Namur, 1856–69

|  | Number of students | % of student |
|---|---|---|
| *Entered Notre Dame de Namur* | 43 | 14.3 |
| *Entered other religious institute* | 49 | 16.3 |
| *Entered teaching or other profession* | 121 | 40.3 |
| *Married* | 57 | 19.0 |
| *Died* | 30 | 10.0 |
| *Total* | 300 | 100.0 |

*Source*: SND: *A Voice*, 5 (1869).

entered religious life. This excerpt from *A Voice* encouraged a view of religious life that stressed its security compared with the insecurity of the 'trials of the world'. Kim Lowden, in her thesis examining Anglican and Catholic contributions to teacher training in nineteenth-century England, credits religious training at Our Lady's for encouraging women to embrace their 'primary duty' to God and the church, and to resist the 'earthly and material ties such as family, kinship, money, possessions'. She goes on to say that this 'encouraged students to see single life as a teacher as most desirable'.[147]

Some evidence of this desirability is shown in Table 2.5, which records vocations from Our Lady's.[148] Over thirty per cent of graduates of Our Lady's entered religious life. Almost half of these women became religious at Notre Dame de Namur. Of the forty-nine students who entered other congregations, a significant portion, twenty-five of them, entered the Sisters of Mercy. The Sisters of Mercy were the largest congregation at this time and, by 1869, had forty-eight convents spread over England and Wales. While their activities were varied, they taught in and managed many educational institutions in the nineteenth century. The remaining twenty-four students entered twelve congregations. Kim Lowden demonstrates in her comparison of Anglican and Catholic teacher training colleges that women attending the Anglican

147 Kim Lowden, 'Spirited Sisters: Anglican and Catholic Contribution to Women's Teacher Training in the 19th century', doctoral thesis, Liverpool Hope University, 2000, pp. 96–7.
148 It is difficult to know how many women entering Our Lady's had previously announced their interest in religious life and had been encouraged by religious congregations, especially those heavily involved in education, to complete their teacher training before becoming postulants.

colleges were more likely to marry than were their Catholic counter-parts. Fifty per cent of Anglican teacher training college graduates married, while only nineteen per cent of Our Lady graduates married. Lowden suggests that it was Our Lady's strong matriarchal culture which influenced women to reject conventional women's roles in favour of service to God. This service could be as a religious sister or as a secular Catholic teacher.[149]

Boarding schools and teacher training colleges provided an environment very similar to that found in women's religious congregations. Women's congregations fashioned these matriarchal institutions to reflect their spiritual and philanthropic ethos and then placed them in a structure that was distinctly conventual. Students were conditioned by this conventual lifestyle, which mixed a distinct theology and spiritual ethos with a teaching apostolate in a women-only environment. It is not implausible that those who thrived under this regimen would consider a vocation in a religious community. For those who succeeded in this environment, it was a logical progression from boarding school or teacher training college to postulant and novice and finally professed sister. In addition, the influence of women religious as mentors cannot be overlooked. Women religious were role models, and would develop students who they believed had a vocation. Serving God and ameliorating the spiritual, educational and physical poverty of the poor in a secure environment that supplied for their physical needs could be more attractive than the uncertainties of marriage or single life in the 'outside world'. Status and security were possible within this environment. Despite these advantages, this life was not suitable for those without a certain sense of piety and spirituality and without a liking for a communal, rigorous, disciplined and ordered lifestyle.

## Conclusion

Women who entered religious congregations carefully assessed their options. They were in a position to do this because there were practical means of becoming acquainted with religious life. Kinship relationships, convent education and clerical recommendations all provided a means to assess conventual living. Being a 'spouse of Christ' offered numerous advantages: it guaranteed a focus on spiritual life, a valuable profession, opportunities for leadership and advancement and a safe haven from the 'outside world'. It offered a spiritual idealism that had an element of social action. The philanthropic work varied by congregation and appealed to many women.

149  Lowden, 2000, p. 101.

In the nineteenth century, women's identity revolved around their roles within the family unit. They were expected to be wives, mothers and daughters. Convent documents such as necrologies and biographies reinforced the standard tenets of nineteenth-century femininity by highlighting the obedience and piety of women even when faced with family opposition to their entering religious life. These narratives supported the religious ideology that emphasised the supremacy of the 'will of God' over the family ideology that stressed the family responsibilities of an unmarried daughter. There existed in Catholic culture an alternate ideal of femininity. Religious discourse legitimated a woman's removal from the biological family unit. Religious life involved a redefinition of self from one's identity as daughter, sister or widow. Nancy F. Cott in *The Bonds of Womanhood* (1977) discusses how religiosity contributed to self-definition and shaped social identity for lay women.[150] This reshaping was more prominent in religious life as each woman was defined not only as an individual nun but as a member of a religious congregation. What this chapter has begun to establish is the nascent formation of this identity of women religious. For some, this identity emerged in childhood; others were influenced by siblings or their experiences in convent schools. Whatever the vehicle for their interest, the first step in the process of the creation of the identity of the religious sister had taken place. The next chapter will examine the formation of the identity of a nun throughout her postulancy and noviciate period, the most critical juncture in the formation of the identity of women religious.

150  Nancy F. Cott, *The Bonds of Womanhood: 'Woman's Sphere' in New England, 1780–1835* (London: Yale University Press, 1977), p. 20.

# 3

# Forming a novice[1]

Train well. Teach much, lay good strong foundations, and let a determined will and God's grace do the rest.[2]

As young girls and women, daughters were taught according to a curriculum that included the practical details of running a home, their spiritual and moral responsibilities and suitable social and charitable obligations.[3] The importance of this 'moral motherhood'[4] in the nineteenth century led to a wide array of women's conduct manuals that instructed mothers on the appropriate training of daughters. Sean Gill has suggested that the emphasis on women and morality did much to encourage a 'cult of pious domesticity' that strengthened patriarchy in the family and in society.[5] Mothers taught their daughters the ideals of service and self-sacrifice;[6] Sarah Stickney Ellis claimed exultantly that

1 An earlier version of this chapter was published as 'Laying "good strong foundations": The Power of the Symbolic in the Formation of a Religious Sister', *Women's History Review*, 16 (2007), 403–15.
2 SMG: 'Mother Foundress' Letters to the Institute (1877–1900)', 1957, p. 52, circular letter dated 15 February 1897 from Frances Taylor to the Tertian sisters.
3 Leonore Davidoff, *The Best Circles: Society Etiquette and the Season* (London: The Cresset Library, 1986), p. 54; Carol Dyhouse, 'Mothers and Daughters in the Middle-Class Home, c. 1870–1914', in Jane Lewis, ed., *Labour & Love: Women's Experience of Home and Family 1850–1940* (Oxford: Basil Blackwell, 1986), pp. 27–48 (p. 39).
4 John Tosh, 'Authority and Nurture in Middle-Class Fatherhood: The Case of Early and Mid-Victorian England', *Gender & History*, 8 (1996), 48–64 (p. 53).
5 Sean Gill, *Women and the Church of England from the Eighteenth Century to the Present* (London: Society for Promoting Christian Knowledge, 1994), p. 66.
6 Carol Dyhouse, *Girls Growing Up in Late Victorian and Edwardian England* (London: Routledge & Kegan Paul, 1981), p. 26; Deborah

female satisfaction was achieved through selflessness.[7] These principles were also inculcated in the training of women religious in the nineteenth century; they were integral to the development of 'good strong foundations'. The identity of women religious was carefully crafted from their first entry into the convent as postulants through to their years in the novitiate. They were trained in the spiritual, vocational and communal aspects of religious life. This training process was in many ways literal but also developed women religious through the power of the symbolic.[8] The symbols of religious life – the habit, the new name and the ceremonies that marked their entrance into religious life – were as important as the texts that were read. The formation that occurred in a postulant and a novice created the basis of the identity of women religious. It was a paradoxical identity, and in this chapter its meaning will be explored in various contexts.

## Postulants

Fervent religious devotion, zeal for philanthropic activity and attraction to religious life were important precursors to successful active vocations. However, the existence of these attributes did not assure a woman entry into a congregation. The Roman Catholic Church listed various criteria for those entering religious life, the foremost being that they must lead 'irreprehensible lives', free from 'vicious defects and habits' that could lead to scandal. Impediments to religious life included incurable or hereditary diseases which would make women unfit for their religious duties, 'defects of liberty' such as marriage, 'defects of justice' such as debts needing to be paid, and serious family responsibilities (such as a parent being financially dependent on the aspirant).[9] Certificates of baptism and confirmation were reviewed and formal recommendations from clergy were important, especially if the candidate was not known to the

---

Gorham, *The Victorian Girl and the Feminine Ideal* (London: Croom Helm, 1982), p. 79.

7 Sarah Stickney Ellis, *The Daughters of England: Their Position in Society, Character and Responsibilities* (London: Fisher, Son & Co., 1845), p. 29.

8 There can be many forms of 'power' in religious life. The 'power of the symbolic' refers to the power obtained by the novice through the process of her formation as a religious sister.

9 Rev. Arthur Devine, *Convent Life; Or, The Duties of Sisters Dedicated in Religion To the Service of God, Intended chiefly for Superiors and Confessors* (London: The Passionists, 1889), pp. 20, 40–2. Constitutions often had a section regarding 'Postulants and Admission' that included some

congregation.[10] The final step, an interview with the local superior or novice mistress, was critical; she determined whether the candidate might have the requisite attributes for religious life and allowed her to enter the congregation as a postulant or dismissed her as having 'no vocation'.

Once the candidate was past these hurdles, the real testing began. The postulancy period typically lasted three to six months:[11] this was a decisive period when postulants evaluated if they were suited for the religious life that a congregation offered. Of equal significance, the congregation evaluated the postulant to determine if she was suited for the rigours and privations of a spiritual, vocational and communal life. Spirituality and piety were seldom the difficulty for postulants. Their attraction to religious life and the clerical recommendation presumed an adequate level of both. It was often the more practical aspects of religious life that arrested their progress. Religious life could be physically and mentally taxing, in addition to being spiritually demanding. The conditions of poverty, chastity and obedience could be arduous. In addition, living a communal life posed its own unique difficulties.

A woman often began her postulancy period with a religious retreat, followed sometimes with a formal hooding ceremony.[12] Eugenie Ryan's hooding as a Holy Child Jesus postulant was very simple: the founder, Cornelia Connelly, placed a short white veil, or hood, on her head and bestowed on her a blessing; in the background a choir of nuns chanted the verse 'Monstra te esse matrem' in the 'Ave Maris Stella'. After the hooding, the religious community sang the *Magnificat* in 'thanksgiving for the graces bestowed on the new postulant'.[13] Formal rituals and ceremonies, even this small one, were an important component of religious life. Ceremonies marked important milestones. The hooding ceremony signalled to the individual and the congregation the changing status of a woman: from lay woman to postulant.

Each postulant was assigned to a convent where she would undertake three to six months of prayer, study, manual labour and philanthropic work. During this time, the postulant lived with the religious community

of these impediments. Typically, the impediments were scrupulously used to screen postulants, but exceptions were made in certain circumstances.

10 The influence of the clergy is discussed in more detail in Chapter 2.

11 The postulancy period could last a few months longer than the prescribed period if the novice mistress needed more time to determine if the postulant was suited to religious life.

12 Sometimes called 'receiving the cap' or 'capping'.

13 M.M. Xavier Gwynn SHCJ, *From Hunting Field to Cloister* (Dublin: Clonmore and Reynolds, 1946), pp. 24–5.

but was not involved in all facets of community life. The Little Sisters of the Assumption postulant commenced her postulancy period with an eight-day retreat. Her days would begin with the chanting of the Little Office of our Lady, meditation and Mass.[14] Her study included lectures on the constitutions, study of doctrine and church history, lessons in plainchant and spiritual reading.[15] Holy Child Jesus postulants were instructed in the principles of religious life and the 'special spirit' of the congregation. Lizzie Carr recalled meeting the founder Cornelia Connelly to discuss the 'call to religious life', 'the immense love of Our Lord in the Blessed Sacrament' and 'the grace of perseverance'.[16] This period of prayer and study was important to understanding the spirit and objectives of the congregation. Perseverance was a particularly relevant issue. In one sample of postulants from the Daughters of Charity of St Vincent de Paul, half of the postulants left during this initial testing period.[17] This high percentage was indicative of the difficulties that this form of communal life held for many women.

Manual labour was another important facet of postulants' education. The Little Sisters of the Assumption postulant would be employed in a 'hidden way' in household duties.[18] Two Holy Child Jesus postulants, Lizzie Carr and Emily Patmore, 'had to wash up the dishes and plates in the children's refectory'. Afterwards, they laboured in the laundry. Emily Patmore 'hated it when she first began, but now she loved it; there were so many acts of mortification to be made'.[19] Some postulants were unused to this type of physical labour, but it was a significant part of their training. Not only did it teach practical domestic skills, but it taught, especially for those women of a higher class, humility and obedience. It weeded out postulants who were not suited for religious life. Dutiful performance of manual labour showed the resilience of the postulant. Necrologies lauded women who achieved this level of self-abnegation. Theresa Hadfield's necrology indicates that 'nothing appalled her, not even manual labor of

14  The Little Office of Our Lady is a liturgical devotion to the Blessed Virgin. It is a shorter version of, and sometimes said in addition to, the Divine Office.
15  Elizabeth W. Whitehead, *A Form of Catholic Action (The Little Sisters of the Assumption)* (London: Sands & Co., 1947), pp. 50–1.
16  [Louise Wheaton], *A Daughter of Coventry Patmore, Sister Mary Christina, SHCJ* (London: Longmans, Green and Co., 1924), pp. 104–8.
17  DC: Box 1, no. 2: 'Seminary Remarks'. This note book contains a list of women who became postulants between 1885–1893. 205 of the 411 postulants are not recorded in the profession register and therefore apparently did not proceed to the profession of vows.
18  Whitehead, 1947, p. 50.
19  [Wheaton], 1924, p. 24.

which she knew very little; she laughed at her blunders'.[20] This necrology was particularly instructive as Hadfield, the daughter of the well-known architect Mathew Ellison Hadfield, was unaccustomed to this type of physical labour. Her necrology taught about privations and difficulties that must be withstood to become a good religious.

Postulants also performed the 'works of mercy' that were fundamental to the philanthropic efforts of the congregation. The postulant Mary Potter visited the 'sick, poor and housebound' with a professed sister. She learned 'basic skills of attendance at the bedside of those suffering or dying' and she taught in the parish school.[21] Mary Langdale went with a professed sister to 'visit the Poor and helped in the little day school'.[22] Emily Patmore and Lizzie Carr taught at the Holy Child Jesus schools.[23] These brief introductions to 'works of mercy' tested the postulant's aptitude and willingness for such work. The working environment could vary dramatically from an elite convent boarding school, with its modern facilities, to a more crowded, ill-equipped poor school. A congregation's work with the poor and marginalised attracted many idealistic young women. These were the same types of young women who joined the settlement movement in the latter part of the nineteenth century. They were willing, according to Martha Vicinus, to 'sacrifice their security and ease for work among the poor'. However, idealism did not always lead to permanent settlement workers; reliable volunteers were difficult to find.[24]

Idealism could turn to disillusionment. Middle-class young women were not always ready to face the physical realities of working in close proximity to children brought up in the slum conditions of urban locales. These children could be dirty, smelly and sickly and they did not always respond with gratitude to the efforts of the settlement workers or women religious. One postulant remained at the Sisters of Mercy in Bermondsey only a few days before being overcome, according to the annalist, 'by her disgust for the miseries and want of cleanliness which must be sometimes found in the

20  DC: *Notes on Deceased Sisters* (1907), p. 64.
21  Elizabeth A. West, *One Woman's Journey: Mary Potter: Founder – Little Company of Mary* (Richmond, Victoria, Australia: Spectrum Publications, 2000), p. 23.
22  DC: 'Remarks on the Life of Sister Mary Langdale', p. 3.
23  [Wheaton], 1924, p. 108.
24  Martha Vicinus, *Independent Women: Work and Community for Single Women, 1850–1920* (London: Virago Press, 1985), pp. 219–25. For more on the settlement movement see Katharine Bentley Beauman, *Women and the Settlement Movement* (London: The Radcliffe Press, 1996).

poor places we visit'.[25] Log books from board schools of the 1870s noted with repetition problems faced by schoolteachers: ill, hungry and lice-ridden children, children who lacked the proper clothing or disregarded middle-class hygienic practices, children whose attendance at school was irregular owing to familial responsibilities, and 'cultural and economic norms of behaviour' that differed greatly from middle-class expectations.[26] Comments in annals inferred similar difficulties in some poor school class-rooms. 'The children are numerous', the Daughters of the Heart of Mary meeting notes indicated, 'but difficult'.[27] John Marmion in his analysis of Holy Child Jesus student examination papers found notations written by sisters which indicated that pupils were 'rude & bold, idiotic, nonchalant, idle, giddy, weak & bragging, uncharitable, reserved and sly, insolent, boorish, talkative, given to calling names, insubordinate, a greedy bear'.[28] Reverend Frederick Edwards criticised the behaviour of the students at his Woodford Green parish school, noting that 'their manners and rudeness was shocking', they were disrespectful of their parents, they fought fre-quently and 'as for obedience, they did not know what it meant'.[29] The romance of the 'works of mercy', when replaced by this lived experience, could dissuade some idealistic postulants from this life.

During the postulancy period, a postulant's 'dispositions' and her 'progress in virtue' were monitored carefully.[30] This period concluded with an assessment of the postulant's suitability for the next stage: the novitiate. The founder of the Sisters of Charity of St Paul the Apostle, Geneviève Dupuis, directed Sister Marie Geneviève (Louisa Bowen), who managed the House of Studies, to:

> tell me how many of your postulants will be ready to receive the holy habit on our return. I mean who have really profited by the training and the instructions they have received. If you cannot answer for their spirit of obedience, their docility and charity with their companions, do not present

25  RSM Bermondsey: 'Bermondsey Annals', 1856, p. 316.
26  Dina M. Copelman, *London's Women Teachers: Gender, Class and Feminism 1870–1930* (London: Routledge, 1996), pp. 83–93. Meg Gomersall noted that 'girls did not necessarily adopt the approved models of behaviour simply because this is what was taught to them in the schools'. Meg Gomersall, *Working-Class Girls in Nineteenth-Century England* (London: Macmillan Press, 1997), p. 118.
27  DHM: C3 'Acts of Superior Authority 1858–1920', 24 September 1881.
28  John P. Marmion, 'Cornelia Connelly's Work in Education, 1848–1879', doctoral thesis, University of Manchester, 1984, p. 299.
29  SMG: I/D/17 'Foundation in Woodford Green 1894', 2 August 1895.
30  [Wheaton], 1924, pp. 104–5.

them for the clothing. These are the virtues they ought to try to practise else they are not to become Novices.[31]

What is noteworthy was that Dupuis did not mention piety or prayer-fulness but instead cited the more practical attributes of living a religious life: obedience, docility and charity. These attributes, especially charity, were important for living together in a religious community, as will be discussed in more detail in Chapter 6.

Many postulants left convents when they realised they were not suited for religious life. Others who stayed the course, but were deemed unsuit-able, sometimes for health reasons and sometimes for general inaptitude, were told they had 'no vocation'.[32] Cornelia Connelly, referring to the clothing of a postulant, wrote: 'She is the only one that has been chosen out of the three postulants – one of whom has been quite declined & the other on further trial deferred'.[33] Cautious acceptance of women into the novitiate underscores the importance of the postulancy period.

At the end of the postulancy period, the progress of a postulant would be reviewed and the designated members of the community would vote on whether to accept her into the novitiate.[34] In small congregations such as the Daughters of the Heart of Mary, it was the council that voted to accept or reject a postulant.[35] Their report of Jane Mitchell was quite positive:

> during six weeks which she had spent in the house, [she] has shown great intelligence, amiability, excellent dispositions for the religious state and an ardent desire to be received into the Society. She is 25 years of age. The question was put to the vote with the following result. As postulant . . . Miss Jane Mitchell; accepted unanimously.[36]

31 SCSP: Box 1:46, letter dated 13 February 1864 from Geneviève Dupuis to Sister Marie Geneviève (Louisa Bowen).
32 Barbara Walsh has addressed the topic of 'no vocation' but much more work needs to be done. Barbara Walsh, *Roman Catholic Nuns in England and Wales, 1800–1937: A Social History* (Dublin: Irish Academic Press, 2002), pp. 130–4.
33 SHCJ: Vol. XVII, p. 31, Letter dated 3 February 1876 from Cornelia Connelly to Bishop James Danell.
34 A chapter was an administrative body typically made up of professed sisters that elected congregation leaders, approved the reception of novices and the profession of vows and legislated in non-routine matters. Chapter 8 will discuss the government structures of a congregation in greater detail.
35 The Daughters of the Heart of Mary were organised into 'reunions' rather than individual convents. A reunion included the superior, the novice mis-tress, the first and second assistant and usually one or two councillors.
36 DHM: C3 'Provincial Council Meetings', 23 December 1858.

In the Sisters of Mercy, it was the chapter of professed sisters that voted on each postulant. If the postulant was 'truly humble and conformable to the spirit of the Institute' she would be allowed to 'solicit in Chapter the Religious Habit', and if she received the majority of votes, she would commence her novitiate.[37] Once accepted as novices, women were able to participate more fully in community life. Their formal acceptance as novices was celebrated in the ceremony of reception, commonly called the clothing ceremony.[38]

### The clothing ceremony

Ceremonies, processions and devotions had an important function in the Roman Catholic faith. Devotions provided a 'common language' and an aesthetic outlet for Catholics of all classes and ethnic backgrounds. Mary Heimann's comprehensive analysis of Catholic devotions in nineteenth-century England suggested that increasingly 'more Catholics heard mass, received communion and made confessions, and did so more often; confraternities and other religious societies multiplied in number and grew in membership'.[39] Religious congregations often used ceremonies, processions and devotions as educational vehicles in their 'works of mercy', but these were also useful as a means of deepening the relationship between women religious and their congregation. In religious congregations, two ceremonies marked the most significant events in the life of women religious: the ceremony of reception and the profession ceremony.

The ceremony of reception symbolised the transformation of a postulant into a novice; it marked her entry into the novitiate. Here, the power of the symbolic was most striking. This ceremony, which typically occurred at the beginning of the novitiate, reflected centuries of Catholic tradition. The symbolism and sacredness attached to every facet of the rituals performed within the ceremony were emblematic of the visible transition from one state of life to another.

The first clothing ceremony held at the church of the Most Holy Trinity for the postulants of the newly founded Sisters of Mercy Bermondsey

37  RSM Bermondsey: 200/3/3, 'Rule and Constitutions of the Religious Sisters of Mercy of Our Blessed Lady of Mercy', [1835?], part 1, chapter 8, section 2.
38  Not all institutes marked the beginning of the novitiate period with the clothing ceremony. The Daughters of Charity of St Vincent de Paul were typically clothed seven to ten months after they entered the novitiate.
39  Mary Heimann, *Catholic Devotion in Victorian England* (Oxford: Clarendon Press, 1995), pp. 65–6.

convent in 1839 was striking and all the more noteworthy because it was the first public ceremony of an active, simple-vowed congregation in England. The Vicar Apostolic of the London District, Bishop Thomas Griffiths, insisted that the clothing ceremony of the first six Mercy postulants, one of whom was a member of the Catholic aristocracy, should be a public event. Griffiths saw this as important moment for Catholics in England; the public nature of the clothing ceremony marked the legitimacy and steadfastness of a Catholic Church that had survived the suppression of the Catholic faith in England for almost 300 years. The public nature of the clothing ceremony offered an important opportunity to promote the Sisters of Mercy and religious life to a well-to-do crowd of Catholics and Protestants and to encourage future postulants and benefactors. Catherine McAuley recounted the ceremony in great detail to the Irish Mercy sisters:

> On the morning of the ceremony, the Church, which accomodates [sic] four thousand was crowded to excess. Tickets had been circulated by the Bishop's direction – and none, that we could call poor, was amongst them. The seats next the sanctuary were filled with nobility . . . sermon preached by Doctor McGuire – explaining the nature of the order and the spiritual and corporal works of Mercy.[40]

Just ten years after the Catholic Emancipation Act, this clothing ceremony garnered a good deal of positive publicity for the Roman Catholic Church and the Sisters of Mercy. The entrance of Lady Barbara Eyre, sister of the Earl of Newburgh, was clearly a coup. Her high status and wealth would contribute greatly to the expansion of their 'works of mercy' and the status of the Sisters of Mercy.[41] The pomp and circumstance of the entire event, from the hymns to the procession of priests, nuns and postulants, were intended to elevate the status of Roman Catholicism. This clothing ceremony even received a mention in *The Times*, which reported that the novices 'renounced the world, and dedicated themselves to works of charity' but added, perhaps with a tinge of cynicism, that the collection towards the funds of the convent was 'apparently a very good one'.[42]

Not all clothing ceremonies were as public and high-profile, but they were all significant events celebrated by the congregation and the new

---

40 Mary C. Sullivan, ed., *The Correspondence of Catherine McAuley, 1818–1841* (The Catholic University of America: Four Courts Press, 2004), pp. 223–4. Letter dated 17 December 1839 from Catherine McAuley to Sister M. Elizabeth Moore.
41 RSM Bermondsey: 'Bermondsey Annals', 1840, p. 25.
42 *The Times* (14 December 1839), p. 7.

novices. They were well-orchestrated rituals, with hymns, prayers and dialogue carefully chosen to reflect the solemnity of the undertaking. Eugenie Ryan's private reception ceremony was held at the St Leonards convent chapel and included her biological sisters, who were attending the Mayfield Holy Child Jesus boarding school. On 11 December 1872, dressed in white, Bertha and Rosie Ryan followed behind their biological sister Eugenie and the procession of professed sisters and novices holding lighted candles and singing the *Magnificat*:

> After the Bishop had blessed the habit and veil to be worn by the future novice, it was the children's privilege to carry the garments from the sanctuary to the cloister, where Eugenie was to exchange her bridal splendour for the simplicity of the religious habit.[43]

This was certainly the most dramatic and symbolic segment of the clothing ceremony: the Catholic laywoman dressed in bridal attire was transformed into a religious sister.[44] She crossed the threshold from lay to religious life.

As indicated by the above passage, this transformation involved a physical change. Unlike a postulant, a novice wore a religious habit, and this was a significant symbol of her identity. Although the habit differed from that of a fully vowed professed sister, it still marked her as a religious sister and was a contentious and powerful symbol in mid-century England. This outward symbol of catholicity was not visible when the Sisters of Notre Dame de Namur, leaving from Bruges to found their first convent in England, boarded *The Earl of Liverpool* in 1845. Fearful of a negative response from an anti-Catholic populace, they preferred to arrive in England as inconspicuously as possible. They remained cautious of appearing in public as Catholic religious sisters. Later that year, Sister Clarie (Clarisse Noel) explained to Mère Constantine: 'We can go to Falmouth in our religious habit because we are in a carriage, but if we had to go out into the town, prudence would not permit it. Although people like us, not everyone does, far from it; the Protestant ministers, especially the Methodists, look unfavourably upon the prospect of our

43  Gwynn, 1946, p. 26.
44  Not all congregations sanctioned elaborate bridal attire at the clothing ceremonies. Of those that did, at least two changed their policies in the nineteenth century. By 1859, the Sisters of Mercy in the Diocese of Southwark no longer wore elaborate bridal attire. Novices of the Daughters of the Heart of Mary stopped wearing white bridal attire in their clothing ceremonies in 1869. RSM Bermondsey: 'Bermondsey Annals', 1859, p. 28; DHM: C3 'Provincial Council Meetings', 26 January 1869.

classes opening.'[45] The Notre Dame sisters did wear their habit to Sunday Mass, and Sister Clarie observed that 'We were edified on leaving church to see these good people observe us and weep with emotion'.[46] By 1849, the Notre Dame sisters had stopped wearing secular dress while travelling, remarking that 'we seem to be more respected'.[47] That same year, Sister Clarie observed: 'I think that Letitia, the little postulant, will be quite capable of taking the class, but as she is only in secular dress I am not to sure how well she will be respected'.[48] The habit was now a symbol of respectability, and this in Cornwall, a markedly Methodist region of England.

The Sisters of Mercy recounted similar experiences with regard to religious dress. In 1841, to avoid anti-Catholic antagonism, they did not wear their habits while travelling from Dublin to Birmingham.[49] Thirteen years later, the Bermondsey Sisters of Mercy left London for the Crimea in their religious habit. The 'Bermondsey Annals' indicated that:

> They travelled in the religious habit, without bonnet and cloak, usually worn on the visitation, which they afterwards felt to be a particular inspiration of Divine Providence, their appearance as Nuns, proving of great importance not only in the course of their journey, but also among those for whose service they were sent.[50]

They felt safe travelling in their habit, and this likely reflected the public acceptance of women religious and, more significantly, the work they performed in the public sphere. The habit proclaimed their catholicity, clearly problematic in Protestant England, but the sisters' philanthropic efforts, particularly their work with the soldiers in the Crimea, made the wearing of the habit less contentious.

As these two examples demonstrate, the sisters witnessed a shift in the public's response to their religious dress. The pattern that emerged, within these and other examples from convent archives, suggests that few

45 SND: PN.h/1 'English Translation of Letters to Namur', letter dated 18 December 1845 from Sister Clarie (Clarisse Noel) to Mère Constantine.
46 Ibid, letter dated 1 November 1845 from Sister Clarie (Clarisse Noel) to Mère Constantine.
47 SND: BX PRV/2 in BPND, box marked 'Province History 2: Notre Dame in England 1845–1850', pp. 134–5.
48 SND: BH2 Clapham CL.h/1 'Transcribed Letters from Clapham to Namur 1848–1850', letter dated 28 January 1849 from Sister Clarie (Clarisse Noel) to Mère Constantine.
49 Sullivan, 2004, p. 440. Letter dated 25 September 1841 from Catherine McAuley to Sister M. Frances Warde.
50 RSM Bermondsey: 'Bermondsey Annals', 1854, p. 216.

convents were welcomed by Protestants when they first arrived in a particular locale. This antagonism towards women's congregations, sometimes more vociferous than at other times, slowly dissipated once their
'works of mercy' were shown to be useful to the community. The annalist of the Daughters of the Heart of Mary indicated that after five years
in Clapham 'the prejudices of the Protestants around us subside even the
Archdeacon our former enemy now acknowledges that we are very quiet
and do much good'.[51] Admittedly, this examination of the shift towards
the acceptance of women religious is an anecdotal one and this particular question deserves a more thorough analysis.

Dress, as the sociologist Anthony Giddens has observed, signals the
divide in gender, class and occupational status. Modes of dress are often
employed to promote standardisation rather than difference.[52] Such standardisation in dress was important to nineteenth-century women's congregations. Most congregations had very detailed specifications with
regard to the habits of novices and professed sisters. According to their
*Guide*, a text used by some of the early Mercy convents, the habit of the
Sisters of Mercy was black, with no badge or ornament, and 'neatly
plaited from throat to waist'. The choir sister's habit had a train that measured three and a half fingers in length. The breadth of the habit was four
to five yards, according to the size of the wearer. The cincture was of
black leather and about two inches wide.[53] A further two pages of
instructions completed the specifications of the habit and elaborated on
the subtle distinctions between the habits of lay and choir sisters. The

51  DHM: C3 'London Diary: Clapham', April 1852.
52  Anthony Giddens, *Modernity and Self-Identity: Self and Society in the Late
    Modern Age* (Cambridge: Polity Press, 1991), p. 99.
53  RSM Handsworth: [M. Francis Bridgeman RSM], *Guide for the Religious
    Called Sisters of Mercy. Amplified by Quotations, Instructions, &c. Part I.
    & II.* (London: Robson and Son, 1866), pp. 112–13. In 1864, Mother Mary
    Francis Bridgeman invited English and Irish Sisters of Mercy to Limerick to
    attend a meeting that resulted in the publication of the *Guide* and the
    *Abridgement of a Guide for the Religious called Sisters of Mercy* (1866). The
    meeting and the resulting texts were intended as tools for 'preserving uni-
    formity' in the autonomous convents of the Sisters of Mercy. The texts held
    no juridic force, but were probably used in England by some, but certainly
    not all, of the Mercy convents. They were likely used by the convents in
    Nottingham and Derby, as they sent representatives to the Limerick meeting,
    and their branch houses (Oldham, Mansfield, Ashton, Rochdale, Belper,
    Calton, Atherstone and Mount Carmel). I found one copy of the
    *Abridgement* which included an inscription indicating the approval of the
    Bishop of Clifton in 1886. Therefore it is likely that the Bristol convent, and

habit could be used to differentiate status and class between novices and professed sisters, and lay and choir sisters.[54] It was a very practical and visible way to partition the past life of a lay Catholic woman from her present life as a religious sister.

On the day of her clothing, a novice also received a new name. Bertha Ryan of the Society of the Holy Child Jesus received the name Mary Magdalen; the name 'expressed her intense personal love of Our Lord and her desire to lead a life of reparation'.[55] Sister Clarie gave the name Joachim to Maria Alphonsa Lane, explaining that 'she is very fond of St. Joachim, that's why she asked for that name'.[56] Soeur Marie (Henriette Chatelain) of the Daughters of Charity of St Vincent de Paul gave Etheldreda Howard the religious name Mary, 'wishing to give her young companion pleasure'.[57] Sometimes novices could request a particular religious name, but they were often assigned a name by the mother superior or novice mistress. This religious name became intrinsic to the new identity of the religious sister. She honoured and prayed to the saint after whom she was named, and in many congregations, the saint's feast day was celebrated in her honour. The Everton annalist noted that 'The Sisters asked for recreation at breakfast in honour of the patron saints of the Cook and Infirmarian Srs. Clare and Jeanne Berchmans'.[58]

## Novices

The rituals in the clothing ceremony, most particularly the acquisition of the habit and the new name, were symbolic of the relinquishing of the old identity as a lay person and the formation of this new identity as a

its branch houses, Bridgwater and Westbury-on-Trym, may have also used this text. Also, there is correspondence dating from the turn of the century that indicates that other convents were using the *Guide* and *Abridgement*. RSM: *Bermondsey Annals*, 1864, pp. 57–8. Mary Peckham Magray, *The Transforming Power of the Nuns: Women, Religion, and Cultural Change in Ireland, 1750–1900* (Oxford: Oxford University Press, 1998), pp. 121–5; Catherine C. Darcy RSM, *The Institute of the Sisters of Mercy of the Americas: The Canonical Development of the Proposed Governance Model* (Lanham: University Press of America, 1993), p. 127.

54  Lay and choir sisters will be discussed more thoroughly in Chapter 6.

55  Gwynn, 1946, p. 84.

56  SND: PN.h/1 'English Translation of Letters to Namur', letter dated 7 January 1847 from Sister Clarie (Clarisse Noel) to Mère Constantine.

57  DC: 'Sr. Etheldreda Fitzalan Howard', p. 31.

58  SND: BX EV/1 in BH2, 'Everton Annals', 13 August 1880. St Clare of Assisi's feast day is 11 August and the anniversary of St John Berchman's death is 13 August (his feast day is 26 November).

religious sister. During the next two years, the novice would continue her formation; her guide and instructor during this period was the novice mistress.[59] She would become an intimate part of a novice's daily life; she was a teacher of things practical, vocational and spiritual. As a spiritual director, she was responsible for transmitting the congregation's unique spirituality to future generations of sisters.[60] The novice mistress carefully studied the character and qualities of each novice. She was to:

> encourage them from the first to great openness of spirit, and frankness of manner. The most marked defects which they have brought from the world, those defects especially which present an obstacle to the foundation of a religious character are first to be corrected & she is to proceed gradually & patiently in the work of laying a solid foundation of the virtues.

She was required to be 'a living rule and a model of every religious virtue' so that she could lead the novices to the attainment of this 'solid foundation of virtues'.[61] At the end of the novitiate, the novice mistress was in the position to assess the novices' readiness for the final step, the taking of simple vows.

The novitiate curriculum included manual work as well as vocational training. Sister Mary Christina (Emily Patmore) taught at the village school during the day. In the evening, she turned the mangle in the laundry.[62] Holy Child Jesus novice training included 'useful' tasks such as 'house-work, washing, gardening, needlework; after dinner, novices went to wash up pots and pans and clean the kitchen';[63] there was 'scrubbing to be done, and laundry work and hay-making and vegetable gardening, as well as teaching'.[64] Sister Mary of St Francis (Laura Petre) 'was seen to sweep the rooms and the corridors, to prepare the vegetables for the cook, to wash up the dishes after meals'.[65] Novices were trained to be 'indifferent' to the

---

59 Most congregations had a two-year novitiate which could be increased or decreased under specific circumstances.
60 Patricia Ranft, *A Woman's Way: The Forgotten History of Women Spiritual Directors* (New York: Palgrave, 2000), p. 173.
61 RSM Handsworth: 1/200/4/4, 'Instruction for Novice Mistress', no date but copied between 1848 and 1884.
62 [Wheaton], 1924, pp. 117–18.
63 SHCJ: 'Memoir of the Rev. Mother Angela Croft', Second Superior General of the Society of the Holy Child Jesus, 1913, p. 26.
64 [Wheaton], 1924, pp. 117–18.
65 A.M. Clarke, *The Life of the Hon. Mrs. Edward Petre (Laura Stafford-Jerningham) in Religion Sister Mary of St. Francis, of the Congregation of the Sisters of Notre-Dame de Namur* (London: Art and Book Company, 1899), p. 213.

employment given to them and to 'prefer the work which obedience puts into their hands'.[66] Dina M. Copelman noted that domestic work was also included in the curriculum at teacher training colleges; it cut down on college expenses and trained young women in 'humble femininity'.[67] Manual labour served as an outward sign of humility, which was deemed an important quality inculcated in novices and secular teachers.

Vocational education was also included in novitiate training. Much of it was very practical as it was taught while performing the congregation's 'works of mercy'. Novices could be found in the classroom, the infirmary or the homes of the parish poor. However, as will be discussed more thoroughly in Chapter 5, vocational training for those entering the professions, particularly education and nursing, became more formalised during the latter part of the nineteenth century. Congregations actively sought and obtained formal training and certification and even encouraged women to obtain teachers' certificates prior to entering religious life.

An important component of novitiate education was an understanding of the spirituality and the history of the congregation as well as a thorough grounding in Catholic doctrine, church history and basic theology. Mary Potter, Cornelia Connelly, Frances Taylor and other founders emphasised a theology of religious life that was inculcated in the novices in their congregations.[68] Mary Potter, founder of the Little Company of Mary, believed strongly in the necessity for women to study and understand theology despite the contemporary view that study of the 'sacred sciences' was gendered masculine, not feminine.[69] According to Bishop William Ullathorne, women religious 'pass through a complete course of ascetic and spiritual instruction, are made acquainted with the Rule and constitutions, and are informed in all the laws and customs of the Order'.[70] The founder of the Sisters of Charity of St Paul the Apostle, Geneviève Dupuis, visited the novitiate weekly to explain to novices a passage from *Spiritual Combat* or the Sunday's Epistle and Gospel.[71] The

66  RSM Handsworth: 1/200/4/4 'Instruction for Novice Mistress'.
67  Copelman, 1996, pp. 137–8.
68  Caritas McCarthy SHCJ, *The Spirituality of Cornelia Connelly: In God, for God, with God* (Lewiston, New York, USA: Edwin Mellen Press, 1986); Eithne Leonard, 'The Making of a Foundress: Frances Margaret Taylor 1832–1869' (unpublished dissertation, St Louis University, 1982), p. 71; West, 2000, p. 37.
69  West, 2000, p. 12.
70  Bishop Ullathorne, *Three Lectures on the Conventual Life* (London: Burns, Oates & Co., 1868), p. 25.
71  George V. Hudson, *Mother Geneviève Dupuis, Foundress of the English Congregation of the Sisters of Charity of St Paul the Apostle 1813–1903*

novice mistress of the Daughters of the Heart of Mary presented weekly
conferences which began with prayer and a reading, along with a short
summary of 'useful and edifying remarks'. These conferences were meant
to unite the Daughters of the Heart of Mary with 'holy eagerness, a spirit
of recollection, simplicity, and charity'.[72] As novice mistress, Potter
taught methods of prayer and introduced the spirituality of Simon de
Montfort to the novices.[73] The Mother Superior of Holy Child Jesus,
M. Angelica (Anne Croft), met the novices regularly and, according to
one Holy Child Jesus novice, 'read Father Faber's Hymns to us; at other
times she talked with us about the Saints, of our Society and its works'.
Croft trained the sisters using the constitutions and 'was most strict
about the virtues of humility, obedience, charity and the spirit of prayer;
these, she said, were the four wheels upon which religious life runs, and
she reproved severely any fault against them'.[74]

Not all women succeeded in this rigorous environment. It is difficult
to calculate definitively the percentage of novices that did not complete
their novitiate. In one sample, approximately ten per cent of novices left
the Daughters of Charity during their novitiate period. A third left for
health reasons; the remaining explanations were more varied and
included such reasons as 'no vocation', 'little capacity', 'scrupulousness'
and 'did not have much intelligence'.[75] Margaret Anna Cusack, while a
Poor Clare nun in Kenmare, Ireland, wrote that 'nuns were equally
careful not to encourage persons to enter convents unless they believed
they were really fit for such a life. To this rule, however, I must admit I
have known some exceptions'.[76] And these exceptions, women who were

---

(London: Sheed & Ward, 1929), p. 107. Undated notes found in the archives
of the Sisters of Charity of St Paul the Apostle indicate that *Spiritual Combat*
was an 'admirable manual' that 'should be taught as a class-book, small portions being learnt at a time, and given an account of by the Postulant to her
Mistress, who ought not only to examine her Postulant in its sense but also
in its practice'. SCSP: Box 80 'Instructions Rules etc', p. 3.

72  DHM: *Rule of Conduct for the Daughters of the Heart of Mary*
    (Roehampton: James Stanley, 1896), p. 28.
73  Ibid, pp. 12, 111. See West's critical examination of Mary Potter's theology
    in Section 3.
74  SHCJ: 'Memoir of the Rev. Mother Angela Croft', 1913, pp. 26–8.
75  DC: Box 1, no. 2: 'Seminary Remarks'. This book contained notes on women
    who entered as postulants from 1885–1893. Forty of the 411 women were
    recorded in the profession register as having left during the novitiate.
76  [Margaret Anna Cusack], *Five Years in a Protestant Sisterhood and Ten
    Years in a Catholic Convent, an Autobiography* (London: Longmans, Green,
    1869), p. 211.

professed but later found to have 'no vocation', often caused great difficulties in a convent environment. This demonstrated the necessity for the
scrupulous testing of novices.

As well as providing spiritual and vocational instruction, the novitiate regimen tested a novice's aptitude for religious life and developed
the novice's sense of identification with the community.[77] The novitiate
experience was meant to instil uniformity in spirit by moulding and
training women in a consistent fashion. Its objective was also to foster
an *esprit de corps* and encourage teamwork and loyalty. This code of
behaviour provided novices with an understanding of their congregation's mission and strengthened their ties to each other and to the congregation. The training of a novice was intended to develop a deeper
level of dedication to religious life and to the congregation. This sense
of community and corporate identity will be discussed in more detail in
Chapter 6.

## Profession ceremony

At the end of the novitiate training, the designated members of the community would vote to determine whether the novices were ready to enter
religious life. Those who received the majority of the affirmative votes
would begin preparation for their profession and the taking of the simple
vows. Profession ceremonies varied by congregation, but like the ceremonies of reception, they were carefully orchestrated, meticulous and
full of symbolism and ritual. Specially selected prayers, psalms and songs
linked the portions of the ceremony. Typically, the entire congregation
took part, entering the church two by two: first postulants, then novices,
then professed. Finally the mother assistant, the mother superior and the
novices being professed entered together. The bishop, or a priest dele-
gated by the bishop, and an assembly of priests awaited their entry by the
altar.

The symbolism of the profession ceremony reflected the importance of
the change in identity from novice sister to professed sister. In the ceremony of the Sisters of Mercy, the bishop, as he placed the black veil on
a novice's head, intoned 'Receive the holy veil, the emblem of chastity
and modesty, which mayest thou carry before the judgment seat of our
Lord Jesus Christ, that thou mayest have eternal life, and mayest live for
ever and ever.' After the mother superior fastened her veil, the newly professed sister rose and declared, 'He has placed His seal on my forehead.

77 A more thorough discussion of the corporate identity of women religious can
 be found in Chapter 6.

That I should admit no other lover but Him.'[78] During the profession ceremony of Sister M. Christina (Emily Patmore), the bishop placed a ring
on her finger and proclaimed:

> I espouse thee to Jesus Christ, the Son of the Most High Father, and may
> He protect thee.
> 　　Receive therefore this ring, the pledge of the fidelity of the Holy Spirit,
> that thou mayest be called the spouse of God, and if thou serve Him faith-
> fully, thou shalt be crowned eternally.[79]

The novice responded to questions regarding the verity of her vocation
before she read aloud and signed her act of profession. The act of pro-
fession was unique to each congregation. It was a simple vow, made to
God but received by the bishop on behalf of the Roman Catholic Church.
Sister Mary Walburga (Mary White) pronounced her vows as a Holy
Child sister on 27 July 1861 with the words:

> Almighty and Everlasting God, I, Mary Theresa White, in religion, Sister
> Mary Walburga, being in all respects most unworthy of Thy Divine regard,
> but confiding nevertheless in Thy infinite pity and mercy, and moved by the
> desire of serving Thee, in the presence of the most Blessed Virgin Mary, and
> all the Heavenly Court, vow to Thy Divine Majesty, perpetual Poverty,
> Chastity and Obedience, in the Society of the Holy Child Jesus.[80]

The formula of the Sisters of Mercy promised to God 'Poverty, Chastity,
and Obedience, and the service of the Poor, Sick, and Ignorant'.[81] The
three vows of poverty, chastity and obedience were typically part of the
act of profession of all simple-vowed congregations, but the Sisters of
Mercy added a fourth vow of service.[82] The newly professed made herself
prostrate and was prayed over by the bishop, priests and sisters. Upon
arising, she genuflected before the mother superior and was raised up to

---

78　Archdiocesan Archives of Liverpool (henceforward AAL): *Ceremonial for
　　the Reception and Profession of the Religious Sisters of Mercy* (Dublin:
　　Browne & Noland, 1894), pp. 34–5.
79　[Wheaton], 1924, p. 129.
80　Mary Mechtilde SHCJ, *Mother Mary Walburga SHCJ whose Years of Labor
　　in the Society were its Seed Time in America* (Rosemont, Pennsylvania:
　　1949), p. 10.
81　AAL: *Ceremonial for the Reception and Profession of the Religious Sisters
　　of Mercy*, 1894, pp. 30–1.
82　Many religious institutes had a fourth vow. For example, the Order of the
　　Presentation of the Blessed Virgin Mary and the Religious of the Sacred
　　Heart had a fourth vow, which was to devote themselves to education of
　　young girls. The Soeurs de la Misericorde (de Seez) had a fourth vow to
　　devote themselves to the care of the sick.

receive the embrace of the mother superior and all her religious sisters. The ceremony ended; the sisters holding lighted candles exited the church in the order in which they entered.[83]

The three important personages in this ceremony were the novice, the bishop and the mother superior. The novice was the primary actor in the ceremony: by pronouncing her simple vows to God, she became a 'spouse of Christ' and a member of a religious community. In her act of profession, Sister Mary Walburga vowed to 'Thy Divine Majesty, perpetual Poverty, Chastity and Obedience, in the Society of the Holy Child Jesus'. These vows were not made to the bishop or to the church, but to God, to be enacted in the Society of the Holy Child Jesus.[84] In addition, the vow of obedience was interpreted to reflect obedience to the constitutions of the congregation and to the head of the congregation, in most cases the mother superior. Bishop William Bernard Ullathorne explained that this vow of obedience was 'not an unlimited one' but one that was 'clearly defined' according to each congregation's constitutions.[85] The bishop played a dominant role in the ceremony itself and represented the Roman Catholic Church. He exercised considerable authority in his diocese, and his function in the ceremony reflected his high status and power in the church. As the celebrant of the ceremony, he blessed the novice's veil and her ring with holy water and then incense. He delivered the sermon. When the novice requested to be received to 'Holy Profession', the bishop asked if she was 'sufficiently instructed'. As she made her act of profession, he elevated the Sacrament. His was the dominant voice in the ceremony. The mother superior represented the congregation. She presented the novice to the bishop and subsequently received her into the congregation. She directed the novice to the altar and to the bishop, who questioned her. The superior also had a voice in this ceremony. She directed the novice to 'Offer to God the sacrifice of praise.' She charged the novice to rise after she was sprinkled with holy water, then embraced her. As mother superior, she received the act of profession from the novice.[86] The roles played out by the three major

83  AAL: *Ceremonial for the Reception and Profession of the Religious Sisters of Mercy*, 1894, pp. 25–42.
84  P. Chas. Augustine OSB, DD, *A Commentary of the New Code of Canon Law*, 8 vols (London: B. Herder Book Co., 1918), III, p. 55.
85  Bishop Ullathorne, *A Plea for the Rights and Liberties of Religious Women, with reference to the Bill proposed by Mr. Lacy* (London: Thomas Richardson and Son, 1851), p. 6.
86  AAL: *Ceremonial for the Reception and Profession of the Religious Sisters of Mercy*, 1894, pp. 25–45.

participants were characteristic of the power structure within the nineteenth century. The bishop represented the power and authority of the
church. The mother superior represented the authority of the congregation. The novice offered herself to the church when she made her act of
profession. All three actors were active, not passive, participants. They
all exerted a degree of control over the events of the ceremony.

The profession ceremony was the culmination of the formal training
process of a novice and marked the end of a rite of passage that began
when she entered the congregation as a postulant. The novitiate served
an important function in the training of women religious and the formation of their identity. It was a shared experience that created a bond
between novices. The novices were involved in most aspects of religious
life, and their spiritual, vocational and communal training was intended
to form not only a good sister, but a loyal member of the congregation.

## Conclusion

It was during their postulancy and novitiate training that women
obtained an understanding of the spiritual, vocational and communal
nature of religious life. This training was meant to instil in them the
meaning of the vows of poverty, chastity and obedience and their future
role as spouses of Christ, using both the literal and the symbolic. The
focus on manual labour was a great equaliser and tested the ideals of
many of these women. Importantly, women religious were meant to obedient. Yet this obedience was not simply about being docile. Obedience
was meant to build 'good strong foundations' by building character and
commitment. Obedience was symbolic of constancy, steadfastness and
loyalty. The clothing and profession ceremonies reflected their significance and power as spouses of Christ; they emphasised the sacredness of
the life of women religious. They were symbolic markers of their progress
and their distinctive commitment. The congregation was at the centre of
such commitment. 'Good strong foundations' were encouraged so that
women religious could face external forces, whether they be intransigent
bishops, obstinate clergymen, demanding benefactors or disapproving
Protestants. Their training in church history, doctrine and spirituality as
well as their formal vocational training indicated they were meant to be
educated and effective evangelisers. They were critical to their working
identities, as evangelisers and professional women, as will be examined
in Part II.

# Part II

# Working identities

# 4

# Evangelising

The Sisters shall on the first day of every year make a renewal of their vows to excite in their hearts an increase of fervour in the service of their Heavenly Spouse by so solemn a recollection of the obligations they have contracted.[1]

This passage from the constitutions of the Religious Sisters of Mercy reminded the Mercy sisters of the significance of the work they performed in the 'service of their Heavenly Spouse'. This was their solemn obligation, and the renewal of their vows each year was meant to revitalise their efforts towards their 'works of mercy'. Their work and the work of other active simple-vowed women religious was a striking, visible and dynamic factor in the growth of philanthropy in nineteenth-century England. Despite this, the philanthropic and evangelical activity of women religious is virtually invisible in historical texts.[2] The persistent image of women religious projected in these texts was of women with 'eyes cast down', subservient and obedient to a church hierarchy that denied or limited their public voice. In addressing the needs of their church, nineteenth-century women religious are judged by historians as passive, not active. Rather than shaping the course of their activities, they are seen in these historical texts as mutely following the directives of the

1 RSM Bermondsey: 'Rule and Constitutions of the Religious Sisters of our Blessed Lady of Mercy' [1835?], inscription dated 1844, part 1, chapter 10, article ii.

2 For the purposes of this discussion, religious activism is defined as charitable and reforming efforts that were directed by religious belief. These efforts did not have as their end goal the creation of state legislation, but were focused, as this chapter will argue, on evanglisation. This does not imply that the work of women religious was without contemplative content. Many nineteenth-century women religious found the 'sustenance' to perform their 'works of mercy' firmly rooted in their spirituality.

Catholic hierarchy.[3] At times, credit for their achievements has been assumed to belong to male colleagues or ecclesiastical officials. However, as will be seen in the next two chapters, the contribution of Catholic women religious to nineteenth-century religious activism is much greater than the current historiography would suggest.

'Activism' is a term laden with multiple meanings. It evokes a sense of vigorous action and confrontation, it is directed towards an objective and it supports a particular cause. Nineteenth-century women's activism is usually seen within the narrow confines of the women's movement, suffragette rallies or reformist movements such as the Ladies' Association Against the Contagious Diseases Act. Religious activism has often been an ignored subset of women's activism, partly because of its emphasis on salvation[4] and the preservation of the faith and partly also, perhaps, because of its inattention to legislative reforms. In addition, religious activism carried with it discomfiting representations of a subordinated ideal of womanhood as found in the ideologies of many religious denominations in the nineteenth century.[5] This ideal represented women as 'help-meets' who were characteristically imbued with humility and piety. Their activism was connected with their religious affiliation and based on their role as assistants or helpers to male ministers or priests.[6]

3  Anthony Fahey, 'Female Asceticism in the Catholic Church: A Case-Study of Nuns in Ireland in the Nineteenth Century', doctoral thesis, University of Illinois at Urbana-Champaign, 1982, p. 154.

4  Salvation was a prominent theme in many religious denominations during the nineteenth century; Salvationists, evangelicals and nonconformists all saw their efforts towards salvation as an important component of their spirituality. Robert J. Klaus, *The Pope, the Protestants, and the Irish: Papal Aggression and Anti-Catholicism in Mid-Nineteenth Century England* (London: Garland Publishing, 1987), p. 121; Lynne Marks, 'The "Hallelujah Lasses": Working-Class Women in the Salvation Army in English Canada, 1882–92', in Franca Iacovetta and Mariana Valverde, eds, *Gender Conflicts: New Essays in Women's History* (Toronto: University of Toronto Press, 1992), p. 89; Linda Wilson, *Constrained by Zeal: Female Spirituality amongst Nonconformists, 1825–1875* (Carlisle, England: Paternoster Publishing, 2000), pp. 64–5.

5  Susan Morgan, 'Faith, Sex and Purity: The Religio-Feminist Theory of Ellice Hopkins', *Women's History Review*, 9 (2000), 13–34 (p. 13). Sue Morgan considers that this lack of interest in religion as a category of analysis stems from the secular language of history and the 'central role played by evangelical Protestantism in the formulation of highly oppressive construction of domesticated womanhood'.

6  Judith Rowbotham, 'Ministering Angels, not Ministers: Foreign Missionary Movement, c. 1860–1910', in Sue Morgan, ed., *Women, Religion and*

Some historians have seen beyond these preconceptions. Sue Morgan's research, for instance, suggests that Ellice Hopkins and her colleagues were more than reactionary Christian women attempting to rehabilitate sexual morality; they were creators of a 'surprising radical, unorthodox construction of gender and sexual morality'.[7] Deborah M. Valenze's work on female preachers portrays these women as mobilisers of working-class leadership who spread popular evangelicalism in the first half of the nineteenth century.[8] Sean Gill links women's 'moral and spiritual qualities' to their involvement in public campaigns for social reform.[9] Susan Mumm suggests that Anglican women religious felt they were on a mission 'to Christianize and feminise the godless and masculine outside world'.[10] Martha Vicinus claims that Anglican sisterhoods and evangelical organisations offered important examples of women's leadership and management as well as evidence for women's power.[11] Katharine Gleadle finds evidence of the feminist tradition in the radical Unitarian Church of the 1830s.[12] The gendered nature of missionary work has just begun to be addressed by religious and social historians. In 1992, Delia Davin bemoaned the lack of research in this area.[13] Since then, edited collections and journal articles have begun to address this need.[14] Rhonda Semple's study of the role that gender played in the

*Feminism in Britain, 1750–1900* (Houndmills: Palgrave Macmillan, 2002), pp. 179–96 (p. 183).

7   Morgan, 2000, p. 13.

8   Deborah Valenze, *Prophetic Sons and Daughters: Female Preaching and Popular Religion in Industrial England* (Princeton, New Jersey: Princeton University Press, 1985), pp. 73, 138.

9   Sean Gill, *Women and the Church of England from the Eighteenth Century to the Present* (London: Society for Promoting Christian Knowledge, 1994), p. 4.

10  Susan Mumm, *Stolen Daughters, Virgin Mothers: Anglican Sisterhoods in Victorian Britain* (London: Leicester University Press, 1998), p. 94.

11  Martha Vicinus, *Independent Women: Work and Community for Single Women, 1850–1920* (London: Virago Press, 1985), pp. 83–4.

12  Katherine Gleadle, *The Early Feminists: Radical Unitarians and the Emergence of the Women's Rights Movement, 1831–1851* (London: Routledge, 1995), p. 1.

13  Delia Davin, 'British Women Missionaries in Nineteenth-Century China', *Women's History Review*, 1 (1992), 257–71 (p. 257).

14  Eleanor Francis-Dehquani, *Religious Feminism in an Age of Empire: CMS Women Missionaries in Iran, 1869–1934* (Bristol: University of Bristol, 2000); Gulnar Eleanor Francis-Dehquani, 'Medical Missions and the History of Feminism: Emmeline Stuart of the CMS Persia Mission', in Morgan, ed., 2002, pp. 197–212; Sean Gill, 'Heroines of Missionary Adventure: The Portrayal of Victorian Women Missionaries in Popular Fiction and Biography' in Anne

development of British Protestant missions in the nineteenth century provides a comparative assessment of the gendered notions of women's roles
in religion and society.[15] These examples of religious activism serve to
balance the feminine stereotype of a passive, modest, subordinate womanhood with a portrayal of strong, dedicated, reforming women.

Other notable historians have established that religious activity was
intricately linked to the hierarchical church. Women's prescribed role
was centred in the domestic sphere and their moral authority was a
source of influence and strength in the home. As Davidoff and Hall
have noted, this moral authority extended women's activities to include
philanthropic endeavours outside the home.[16] A middle-class woman's
domestic skills and moral authority made her the obvious person to
advise less fortunate women on domestic and spiritual matters. The
*Report on the Visitation of Females at their Own Homes in the City of
Westminster* noted that those less fortunate women who 'from various
circumstances, and often through personal and family afflictions, are

---

Hogan and Andrew Bradstock, eds, *Women of Faith in Victorian Culture:
Reassessing the Angel in the House* (Dublin: Macmillan Press Ltd, 1998),
pp. 172–85; Deborah Kirkwood, 'Protestant Missionary Women: Wives and
Spinsters', in Fiona Bowie, Deborah Kirkwood and Shirley Ardener, eds,
*Women and Missions: Past and Present, Anthropological and Historical
Perceptions* (Oxford: Berg, 1993), pp. 23–42; Laura Lauer, 'Opportunities for
Baptist Women and the Problem of the Baptist Zenana Mission, 1867–1913',
in Morgan, ed., 2002, pp. 213–30; Rowbotham, 2002, pp. 179–96; Judith
Rowbotham, '"Soldiers of Christ"? Images of Female Missionaries', *Gender &
History*, 12 (2001), 82–106; Susan Thorne, 'Missionary-Imperial Feminism',
in Mary Taylor Huber and Nancy C. Lutkehaus, eds, *Gendered Missions:
Women and Men in Missionary Discourse and Practice* (Ann Arbor, Michigan:
University of Michigan Press, 1999).

15  Rhonda A. Semple, *Missionary Women: Gender, Professionalism and the
Victorian Idea of Christian Mission* (Suffolk: Boydell & Brewer, 2003),
p. 2. This text, like so many others in its genre, is based on Protestant missionary efforts. Historiography on nineteenth-century English Catholic
women involved in overseas missionary work is sparse. The references to
overseas missionary work by women religious tend to be integrated in
biographies of notable nuns or congregation histories and not to be examined specifically as overseas missionary work. Edmund M. Hogan, *The
Irish Missionary Movement: A Historical Survey 1830–1980* (Dublin: Gill
and Macmillan, 1990) provides an excellent survey of broad-based Irish
missionary activities.

16  Leonore Davidoff and Catherine Hall, *Family Fortunes: Men and Women of
the English Middle Class, 1780–1850* (London: Hutchinson, 1987), p. 116.

brought into poverty and sin' needed 'counsel and help from the Christian female'.[17] As models of middle-class domesticity, Christian virtue and morality, middle-class women were thought to be a good influence on the lower classes.[18]

By the end of the nineteenth century, women's work as philanthropists expanded from home visitations and the organisation of fund-raising bazaars to running and managing large philanthropic organisations, albeit often under the aegis of the male clergy or management committees.[19] Frank Prochaska's study suggests that as benefactors and philanthropists, women were particularly keen to invest in those philanthropic endeavours that related to their experience and to their own sex. Their organisations centred on 'charities which dealt with pregnancies, children, servants, problems of ageing and distressed females'.[20] Women's Catholic congregations often concentrated their efforts on women and children. The medium used most often by women's congregations to evangelise the Catholic family was education, although their efforts in health care and social welfare also aimed to place the Catholic faith at the heart of the family unit. Maria Luddy has pointed to two strands of nineteenth-century philanthropy. One strand involved 'benevolent' philanthropists who addressed the spiritual and temporal needs of the working classes while the other involved 'reformist' philanthropists who demanded that legislation address the causes of poverty.[21] Women religious, and indeed many philanthropists in nineteenth-century England, can be primarily found among the first strand. Their conception of 'reform' was of a moral and spiritual nature, but it often encompassed attending to the temporal needs of the working class.

This chapter examines women religious as religious activists and links the services they performed to their religious identity. Their religious beliefs and practices were at the core of their existence and integral to their working lives. As missionaries, they were builders of the Roman Catholic Church and were a key factor in the extension of religious

17 *Report on the Visitation of Females at their Own Homes in the City of Westminster* (1854), p. 3.
18 Catherine Hall, 'The Early Formation of Victorian Domestic Ideology', in Sandra Burman, ed., *Fit Work for Women* (London: Croom Helm, 1979), pp. 15–32 (pp. 25–8.)
19 F.K. Prochaska, *Women and Philanthropy in Nineteenth-Century England* (Oxford: Clarendon Press, 1980), pp. 142–4, 222; Vicinus, 1985, p. 72.
20 Prochaska, 1980, p. 30.
21 Maria Luddy, *Women in Ireland, 1800–1918: A Documentary History* (Cork: Cork University Press, 1995), p. 201.

devotion and the consolidation of Catholic culture in nineteenth-century England. These developments were fuelled not only by the substantial numbers of women entering religious life but also by the increasing number of requests from bishops, clergy and lay Catholics for experienced women religious to develop and manage educational, health care and social welfare institutions. These institutions were marked with the congregation's special brand of evangelisation and were essential for the growth of Catholic missions in England. The missionary identity of women religious was a facet of their religious identity: they were active in both domestic and international missionary work.[22] This chapter, however, will examine their missionary identity as missionaries in England, the home mission field. The labour of women religious in the fields of education and health care and in the provision of social services was linked to their missionary activities. Their objectives were clearly articulated in congregation constitutions, many of which focused on salvation by decreeing that women religious laboured 'to procure the salvation and sanctification of the persons of either sex'[23] and 'for the Salvation and perfection of our neighbour'.[24] Their own salvation, and that of others, was at the core of their way of life as vowed women. As active women religious, they were called to evangelise in a very public manner.

## Missionary identity

In 1839, Nicholas Wiseman, then rector of the English College in Rome, appealed to the readers of the *Dublin Review* about the need for missionary clergymen,

> devoted to the task of going from town to town, relieving the overworked local clergy of part of their labours, by giving well-prepared and systematic courses of instruction and arousing the slumbering energies of congregations in which stronger excitement is required than the voice of ordinary admonition.[25]

22  Susan O'Brien, 'French Nuns in Nineteenth-Century England', *Past and Present*, 154 (1997), 142–80 (p. 145). Susan O'Brien notes that 'internationalism' and foreign expansion were among the new characteristics of nineteenth-century French congregations.

23  RLR: 'Constitutions of the Society of the Sacred Heart of Jesus', 1884, part 1, section 1, no. 1.

24  SHCJ: Box 54 R24 'Constitutions of the Society of the Holy Child Jesus', 1887, part I, section I, no. 1.

25  Nicholas Wiseman, 'Froud's Remains', *Dublin Review*, 6 (May 1839), 416–5. Wiseman is referring to parish congregations.

Wiseman, even before the large influx of Irish Catholics to England, acknowledged the urgency of revitalising the Catholic faith in England. Concern over 'leakage', which was to become such a focus of the church's evangelising efforts for the remainder of the century, was apparent even at this early date. In an article entitled 'How we Lose Our Poor', one contributor to *The Tablet* wrote that 'we must look for that terrible leakage which is carrying away every year so many souls from the Catholic pale'.[26] Wiseman promoted his solution, religious congregations, despite the displeasure of some of the vicars apostolic and later bishops, who would rather have encouraged secular clergy, whose loyalties would be to the diocere.[27]

'Arousing the slumbering energies' of lapsed Catholics was a fundamental focus of the efforts of Catholic clergy throughout the nineteenth century; missions and retreats were the standard approaches used to revive Catholic parishes throughout England. They were oftentimes dramatic and emotive events led by peripatetic missionaries preaching redemption and hellfire, offering confession and the Eucharist in the hope of creating 'converts' and re-evangelised Catholics.[28] Missions encouraged a variety of pious activities including receiving communion, frequent confession, reciting the rosary, following the stations of the cross and attending pilgrimages and processions. Prayer and devotion were encouraged through novenas, benedictions, expositions of the Blessed Sacrament, the *Quarant'Ore* and special devotions to the Holy Family or the Sacred Heart. Devotional aids such as scapulars, medals and rosaries were also advocated.[29] Missions lasted for days or weeks, and their achievements were heralded by the Catholic faithful. In 1897, Monsignor William Charles McKenna VG reminisced about the missions

---

26  'How We Lose Our Poor', *The Tablet* (10 February 1883), 201–2.
27  John Bossy, *The English Catholic Community, 1570–1850* (London: Darton, Longman & Todd, 1975), p. 360; see also the discussion in chapter 2 of regular and secular clergy.
28  These methods of evangelisation were favoured by Primitive Methodists and some temperance campaigners. R. W. Ambler, *Ranters, Revivalists and Reformers: Primitive Methodism and Rural Society, South Lincolnshire, 1817–1875* (Hull: Hull University Press, 1989); L. Billington, 'Popular Religion and Social Reform: A Study of Revivalism and Teetotalism, 1830–50', *Journal of Religious History*, 10 (1979), 266–93; G. M. Ditchfield, *The evangelical revival* (London: University College London Press, 1998).
29  Mary Heimann, 'Devotional Stereotypes in English Catholicism, 1850–1914', in Frank Tallett and Nicholas Atkin, eds, *Catholicism in Britain and France since 1789* (London: The Hambledon Press, 1995), pp. 13–25 (p. 22).

of the Rosminians Luigi Gentili and Moses Furlong, commenting that they produced 'a marvellous effect on Catholics at the time, and gave new life, as it were, to religion in every congregation' in Manchester.[30]

The Faithful Companions of Jesus annalist rejoiced over the first mission preached by Redemptorists in Middlesbrough in 1874. A team of five priests spent over six weeks in Middlesbrough, and over 800 children and 700 adults received the sacrament of confirmation.[31] The annalist noted that:

> A great number of persons who had given up their Religion for years, made their peace with God. An old woman who had not approached the Sacraments during forty years and who had not practiced her Religion since childhood, came to our Mothers to ask them to make her examination of conscience, as she did not know how or where to begin.[32]

These sisters laboured with the Redemptorist fathers in their missionary endeavours, by preparing those who had 'given up their Religion'[33] for the reception of the sacraments and teaching and encouraging Catholic devotions. The 'West Hartlepool Annals' of 1895 provided an example of the Faithful Companions of Jesus teaming up with the Redemptorists at yet another mission:

> At the close of the instructions, the good Father who was charged with the children inaugurated a confraternity of the Holy Angels. 87 girls who had given their names were present – principally girls who had left school and who are too young to be admitted to our Lady's Congregation. During the Mission, our Mothers gave special instructions every evening for Adults. Of 72 girls who attended regularly, all, with one exception continue to attend Holy Mass on Sundays and to confess & communicate. May they persevere in their good dispositions.[34]

The Faithful Companions of Jesus were an active part of this missionary activity, preparing young and old for the reception of the sacraments. Older girls, who had left school to work at home or in factories, were inaugurated into confraternities managed by the Faithful Companions of Jesus. Confraternities, as will be discussed below, were instrumental in the development of the Catholic Church in England. The West

30  'Recollections of Catholicity in Manchester', *The Harvest* (1897), 219.
31  FCJ: A656 'Middlesbrough Annals', 1874, p. 6.
32  Ibid, p. 6.
33  K. Blott, *A Hundred Years: A History of the F.C.J.'s in Middlesbrough 1872–1972 with Particular Reference to the Growth of St Mary's Convent School* (Middlesbrough: H. & F. Stokeld Printers, 1972), p. 19.
34  FCJ: A1205 'West Hartlepool Annals', 1895, pp. 44–5.

Hartlepool annalist noted the importance of children as evangelisers. She remarked that the children:

> formed a little crusade to force their parents to attend the mission, [sic] they kept asking, praying aloud at home, & even some of them cried till they got their parents to attend & go to Church & Mass. They told them they would be killed or drowned or something dreadful would be sure to happen to all of them if they would not go, and after that they would be burned for ever in hell.[35]

Children were considered to possess an 'instinctive religious sense' which made them the focus of evangelisation. The evangelisation of children was common in many religious denominations in the nineteenth century, but it has been argued that Roman Catholics were the 'pioneers of large-scale revivalist work among children'.[36] Women religious, given the breadth of their educational and social welfare institutions, were in a perfect position to lead these revivalist efforts. The Preston Faithful Companions of Jesus annalist observed:

> During Lent the children down to the very youngest in the Infant School are encouraged to be Apostles of the Sacred Heart 1st by praying for the 'Black Sheep' of the parish especially those of their own family & 2nd by trying to persuade their parents & relations to approach the holy Sacraments. The priests have come across many instances in which men & women out of the Church for many years have made their peace with God, owing to the entreaties & persuasion of their children.[37]

The educational and social welfare institutions managed by women religious provided the ideal context for teaching Catholic morality and religious devotions to Catholic children; their outreach, through the evangelical efforts of these children, extended even further, to the families of these children.

35 Ibid, p. 48.
36 John Sharp, 'Juvenile Holiness: Catholic Revivalism among Children in Victorian Britain', *Journal of Ecclesiastical History*, 35 (1984), 220–38 (pp. 220–1). Other texts on religion, education and children illustrate the use of children as instruments of adult conversion. See for example C. Colton, *History and Character of American Revivals of Religion* (London: Frederick Westley & A.H. Davis, 1832); John Kent, *Holding the Fort: Studies in Victorian Revivalism* (London: Epworth Press, 1978); Thomas Walter Laqueur, *Religion and Respectability: Sunday Schools and Working Class Culture 1780–1850* (London: Yale University Press, 1976), pp. 7–8.
37 FCJ: A1854 'Preston Annals', 1899, p. 45.

Male missionary congregations, especially the Rosminians, Passionists and Redemptorists, were renowned for their preaching abilities on missions and retreats. They contributed significantly to the building of Catholic communities, the renewal of Catholic devotion and the creation of a distinct Catholic identity in England.[38] But the preaching of the mission and the resulting revival of enthusiasm for Catholicism was only a first step. Lapsed Catholics needed to be properly prepared for the sacraments and trained in their religious duties to ensure that their fervour and religious spirit would not be fleeting. The writer of the Salford annals noted proudly that the Faithful Companions of Jesus participated in the 'great work' of the four Dominican Fathers who had given a mission at St John's by instructing eight Protestants and preparing thirty others for the sacraments.[39] Women religious were lauded for their missionary efforts. In 1892, Father William J. Connolly of the Battersea mission wrote to 'Reverend Mère' in Namur that the convent of Notre Dame was the 'backbone of the Battersea Mission'. Connolly noted that the sisters' 'piety, hard work, and intelligent zeal in carrying on the Schools and preparing the children for the Sacraments, and in so many other ways quietly and unobtrusively assisting the clergy in the spread of religion' were fundamental to the mission.[40] A Jesuit priest, F. Swift, giving their annual retreat in 1897, advised the Faithful Companions of Jesus:

> You are as truly Apostles of Christ as those He called long ago in Galilee, and you have a work to do as such in the Church of God. You have more power in some ways even than priests, more intimate intercourse with Souls! How grand a vocation! You train souls, to lay their fundamental principles, not according to the new-fashioned ways, but as true Christians.[41]

His choice of words is telling. These women religious were 'Apostles', not help-meets or assistants. He acknowledged their 'power' and the importance of their work of salvation.

38 D. Aidon Bellenger, 'Religious Life for Men', in V. Alan McClelland and Michael Hodgetts, eds, *From without the Flaminian Gate: 150 Years of Roman Catholicism in England and Wales 1850–2000* (London: Dartman Longman + Todd, 1999), pp. 142–66 (pp. 158–9); John Sharp, *Reapers of the Harvest: The Redenptorists in Great Britain and Ireland 1843–1898* (Dublin: Veritas, 1989), p. 125.
39 FCJ: A740 'Salford Annals', 1884, p. 23.
40 SND: BX BS/4 in BH1 F1 letter dated 19 August 1892 from Fr William J. Connolly to Reverend Mother General.
41 FCJ: A1842 'Isleworth Annals', 1897, pp. 9–10.

This work of salvation was pivotal to the identity of women religious. They frequently referred to themselves as missioners. This term, used in describing laity, clergy and women religious, referred to their efforts at converting 'souls to God'.[42] A Poor Servant of the Mother of God, Sister Mary Colette (Frances McCarthy), commented in a letter to the sisters at Brentford that 'The Sisters at Roehampton are becoming great missioners – one goes up every week to London & spends a week in Green Court'. Their refuge work, saving the souls of the 'penitent' women at Green Court, 'poor girls who have been leading very bad lives but who wish to repent',[43] was one aspect of their efforts as missionaries. The Faithful Companions of Jesus annalist recorded that 'Notwithstanding our occupations as missioners, we have spent the year 1883 calm & peaceably'.[44]

The missionary focus of the Faithful Companions of Jesus expanded beyond national boundaries. Marie Madeleine Victoire de Bengy d'Houët, founder of the Faithful Companions of Jesus, sent sisters from France to England, Ireland, Switzerland, Italy and North America in the course of the nineteenth century. Their international remit was inscribed in their constitutions:

> It is a thing conformable to our vocation to travel into different countries, and to live in whatever part of the world it may be, where we hope to renew greater service to Almighty God, and to be more useful for the spiritual good of our neighbour.[45]

They were not unique in their international remit. The Sisters of Mercy, founded in Ireland in 1831, began their expansion outside Ireland in 1839 with the Bermondsey foundation in England. They extended their franchise internationally to Newfoundland in 1842, Pittsburgh in 1843, Jamaica in 1890, Perth, Australia, in 1846 and New Zealand in 1849. The Sisters of Notre Dame de Namur, founded in 1804, also spread internationally in accord with their founder Julie Billiart's directive to instruct the children of the poor 'in the most abandoned places'.[46]

---

42 Paul Bull, *The Missioner's Handbook: A Guide for Missioners, Evangelists, and Parish Priests* (London: Grant Richards, 1904), pp. 1–5.

43 SMG: letter dated 23 March 1885 from Sr Mary Colette (Frances McCarthy) to sisters. Green Court was located in Soho, London.

44 FCJ: A731 'Middlesbrough Annals', 1883.

45 FCJ: *Summary of the Constitutions* (Dublin: M.H. Gill & Son, 1882), no. 2.

46 SND: *Règles et Constitutions des Soeurs de Notre-dame* (Namur: [1859]), article 2: 'L'esprit des membres de l'Association, est un esprit de simplicité, d'obéissance, de charité; e leur désir est de consacrer leurs soins aux pauvres des lieux les plus abandonnes.'

Notre Dame sisters left Belgium for England in 1845.[47] They also founded convents in the Congo, South Africa, the United States, Canada and Guatemala in the nineteenth century. Founders of women's congregations saw no physical boundaries to the scope of their missionary work, and the Roman church encouraged their efforts. While Rector of St Bede's College in Manchester, L.C. Casartelli expounded on the missionary activity of women religious and praised them unreservedly:

> And it would be obviously impossible to give an account of the enormous number of nuns and sisters of nearly all our female congregations whose work, in every part of the globe, from frozen Alaska to tropical Africa, forms so large and so important an element of the missionary success of the Catholic church.[48]

The term 'missionary' is sometimes associated only with far-off non-Christian lands, but women religious were considered 'missioners' and 'missionaries' in both this international and the domestic context.[49]

Congregations celebrated visits from sisters who were missionaries in far-off lands. These visits brought home the importance of international expansion to the congregation's objectives. It reinforced their identity as missionaries at home and in more exotic locales. Women religious communicated the excitement of the foreign missions to their students. The Manchester Faithful Companions of Jesus annalist observed:

> The news of our Foreign Missions is always received by our children with great pleasure. Canada above all has a special charm for them. When we relate instances of the life and work of our dear Mothers we often hear this exclamation 'Oh! If I were a nun how I would like to go to Canada!' But not content with desires they have sent some useful objects amongst others a white vestment to the poor Missions of Canada.[50]

Congregations received many requests to supply foreign missions. In 1890, a foundation team of seven Bermondsey Sisters of Mercy left for Kingston, Jamaica, to teach at an industrial school for girls and an orphanage for boys.[51] The Poor Servants of the Mother of God

---

47  Jean Bunn SND, 'The Archives of Notre Dame de Namur in Britain', *Catholic Archives Journal*, 13 (1993), 3–12 (p. 3).
48  L.C. Casartelli, *Catholic Missions* (London: Catholic Truth Society, 1891), p. 9.
49  Davin, 1992, p. 260.
50  FCJ: A740 'Brook Street, Manchester Annals', 1884, p. 4.
51  RSM Bermondsey: 'Bermondsey Annals', 1890, pp. 288–9.

dispatched five sisters to Georgetown and three to Barbados in 1898.[52] Some women were specifically attracted to foreign missions. At the age of fourteen, Edith Mary Fielding heard a sermon on Chinese martyrs and decided that her vocation was to be a foreign missionary.[53] Her first fourteen years as a Daughter of Charity of St Vincent de Paul were spent managing various convents and their institutions. Then, at the age of forty-two, she was sent to China. Her necrologist noted, 'Her vocation for China was not the result of any enthusiastic desire . . . but she felt Our Lord asked this sacrifice of her.'[54] Despite this necrologist's emphasis on her obedience, Fielding's early attraction to the foreign missions, noted in a published biography, suggests a more active role in this placement. In 1899, the Hartlepool annals reported that 'our little community was privileged to add two of its members to the band of missionaries destined to carry out the great work of our Society in America. As true Faithful Companions of Jesus, they answered the call of Notre Mère & made the sacrifice demanded of them with great generosity.'[55] This missionary discourse was couched in a language that was steeped in the ideals of self-sacrifice and holy mission.

Whether at home or abroad, missionary work demanded time and used scarce resources. Frances Taylor, founder of the Poor Servants of the Mother of God, complaining of a shortage of sisters, observed, 'It is really like a battlefield – every outpost needs more soldiers.'[56] Mother M. Evangelista (Honora Gaffney), second Mother General of the Sisters of St Joseph of Peace, declared to her sisters, 'Let us try to be valiant women and do great things for God.'[57] Women religious used language that was vigorous and powerful in order to inspire their sisters to remain steady at their work of salvation. The metaphor of the soldier was common in some congregations; women religious were soldiers battling for the salvation of souls. Their weapons were their moral authority, their personal example and their identity as women religious. Peter Gallwey, Jesuit and strident apologist of nineteenth-century

52 SMG: I/A3b, p. 76, letter dated 4 January 1898 from Frances Taylor to Mother Aloysius Austin (Margaret Busher).
53 Lady Cecil Kerr, *Edith Fielding Sister of Charity* (London: Sands & Company, 1933), pp. 13–17.
54 DC: *Notes on Deceased Sisters* (1920–21), p. 118.
55 FCJ: A1854 'West Hartlepool Annals', 1899, p. 27.
56 SMG: I/A3b, p. 36, letter dated 10 March 1892 from Frances Taylor to Mother M. Lucy (Maria Forrestal).
57 CSJP: *Reflections and Counsels of Mother M. Evangelista to her Spiritual Children* (1963), p. 11.

women religious, described women's congregations as 'an exceptional body like the army and the navy, eminently useful to the State and the country, and necessarily governed by exceptional laws'.[58] For him, women religious were an integral part of the good of the nation, even a Protestant nation.

### Education, social welfare and health care

Education was considered the English Catholic hierarchy's most pressing problem. A letter from the bishops in 1852 declared that the education of the poor was 'one of the most important duties confided to the Church' and that 'No congregation should be allowed to remain without its schools, one for each sex.' The bishops concluded that 'It is the good school that secures the virtuous and edifying congregation.'[59] But educating the vast numbers of working-class Catholics was problematic for a financially impoverished Catholic Church. Religious congregations, particularly women's congregations, played an important role in achieving the aims of the English Catholic hierarchy. The educational institutions that women's congregations built and managed ranged from orphanages to teachers' colleges, from poor schools to boarding schools, from industrial schools to night schools. The subjects taught were wide-ranging: from reading and writing to more vocational skills such as needlework and laundry or ladies' accomplishments such as music, drawing and art. All were eligible for educational development: men and women, girls and boys, Protestants and Catholics, employed and destitute, rich and poor. Contemporary sources noted the slow but steady rise throughout the nineteenth century of children educated in Catholic schools: 30,207 in 1843; 71,666 in 1870; and 108,300 in 1875. But the numbers of Catholic children outside the Catholic school system remained problematic for Catholics. In 1843, over two-thirds of Catholic children, a total of 65,307, were not being educated in Catholic schools. Thirty years later, forty-five per cent, approximately 57,000 children,

---

58  Father Gallwey SJ, *Convent Life and England in the 19th Century: Two Sermons Preached in the Church of the Immaculate Conception, Farm Street, Mid-Lent, March 7th 1869, On Occasion of an Appeal on Behalf of the Little Sisters of the Poor* (London: Burns, Oates & Co, 1869), p. 51.
59  *The Synods in English: Being the Text of the Four Synods of Westminster*, ed. Rev. Robert E. Guy OSB (Stratford-on-Avon: St Gregory's Press, 1886), pp. 266–8. This excerpt is from the synodal letter dated 17 July 1852. Guy is using the term 'congregation' to mean a parish community.

were educated elsewhere.[60] To encourage widespread participation, education occurred both during the day and in the evening hours. While the scope of educational endeavours was wide-ranging, the focus of education was on women and children, with an overriding emphasis on the working class. For many congregations, educating the higher classes was looked upon as a source of income to fund the education of the poor.

By 1897, seventy per cent of women's congregations in England and Wales[61] were actively involved in education; through their educational institutions they worked towards the 'salvation of souls' that was so integral to their objectives. The Faithful Companions of Jesus constitutions noted that 'The end of the Society is, not only to work with divine grace, for our own salvation and perfection but also to employ ourselves with all our strength, with the help of the same grace to promote the salvation and perfection of our neighbour.'[62] The constitutions of the Society of the Holy Child Jesus established that the sisters' aims were not only to work towards their own salvation but also to labour for the 'salvation and perfection of our neighbour'.[63] Their method of evangelisation occurred primarily within the classroom: Catholic faith and morality permeated the academic curriculum. Education was the means of teaching religious rites and instilling piety. Catholic education provided for the secular education of Catholics, but, more importantly, served to promulgate the Catholic faith, devotionally as well as doctrinally.[64]

As discussed earlier, perhaps the most striking evidence of women's work as missionaries was their efforts in preparing children and adults for the sacraments. The first convents founded in towns and villages were often overwhelmed by great numbers of children and adults needing instruction. In a letter dated 8 July 1850, Soeur Clarie (Clarisse

60 Mary J. Hickman, *Religion, Class and Identity: The State, the Catholic Church and the Education of the Irish in Britain* (Aldershot, England: Avebury, 1995), p. 187; John P. Marmion, 'The Beginnings of the Catholic Poor Schools in England', *Recusant History*, 17 (1984–85), 67–83 (p. 69).
61 Barbara Walsh, *Roman Catholic Nuns in England and Wales, 1800–1937: A Social History* (Dublin: Irish Academic Press, 2002), p. 172.
62 FCJ: *Summary of the Constitutions*, p. 1.
63 SCHJ: Box 54 R24 'Constitutions of the Society of the Holy Child Jesus', 1887, part 1, section 1, no. 2.
64 Edna Hamer, *Elizabeth Prout, 1820–1864: A Religious Life for Industrial England* (Bath, England: Downside Abbey, 1994), p. 101. For more on the importance of 'visual piety' see David Morgan, *Visual Piety: A History and Theory of Popular Religious Images* (Berkeley: University of California Press, 1999); Susan O'Brien, 'Making Catholic Spaces: Women, Décor, and Devotion in the English Catholic Church, 1840–1900', in Diana Woods, ed.,

Noel) described to Mère Constantine the challenges they faced upon arriving at Blackburn:

> What a vast field lies open to us! Hundreds of children stagnate here, without instruction, or what is worse, go to Protestant schools to drink in knowledge which leads them to destruction. What a grace to be chosen to snatch so many souls from the power of the devil![65]

Six weeks later, Soeur Clarie reported, 'The poor Blackburn Sisters have written to tell me that before Sunday they have to examine nearly 400 girls who are going to be confirmed. Sr. M. Alphonse has lost her voice, which is a great nuisance just now.'[66] This 'vast field' was noted by other congregations. In the first year of the foundation of the Mercy community at Bermondsey, the sisters prepared between 200 and 300 children and adults for confirmation.[67] The diary of the Daughters of the Heart of Mary reported that on 31 May 1864, 'Forty children – boys and girls – of this parish made their First Communion.' The annalist described this event in Kensington:

> It was the first time that this pious custom was carried out with such solemnity. The parents as well as the children were moved by it and we hope for some fruits of grace from this touching occasion. It is a striking witness to the progress of Catholicism in England. Only a few years ago these public acts could not have been allowed; such as these children appearing in the street dressed in white with veils and wreaths of white roses – processions of the Bl. Sacrament in the garden in view of the people – the Cardinal in his vestments carrying the relic of St. Simon Stock in solemn procession, etc.[68]

This exultant, triumphal language describing the solemnity and the pomp of the public ceremony reflected the annalist's elation at the 'progress' of Catholicism in England and the acceptance, at least in some locales, of public Catholic processions. For women religious, preparing children and

---

   *The Church and the Arts* (Oxford: Blackwell Publishers, 1992), pp. 449–64. Susan O'Brien presents convincing evidence of how women religious played an important role in promoting the devotion to female saints through donations of statues, pictures and stained glass.

65  SND: BX PRV/1, p. 21, letter dated 8 July 1850 from Soeur Clarie (Clarisse Noel) to Mère Constantine. The *Catholic Directory* of 1850 and 1851 does not list educational institutions in Blackburn during these years.
66  SND: BH2 Clapham CL.h/1, letter dated 23 August 1850 from Soeur Clarie (Clarisse Noel) to Mère Constantine.
67  RSM Bermondsey: 'Bermondsey Annals', 1839, p. 14.
68  DHM: C3 'London Diary: Clapham', 31 May 1864.

adults to receive the Catholic sacraments was an important aspect of instilling religious piety and was connected with their missionary activities. This work was pivotal in the convent narratives and an important part of their *raison d'être* in the nineteenth century. It was an important way of combating 'leakage'. Missionary success was measured through the numbers of people converted but also through the numbers of infant baptisms, communions taken, confessions heard and other sacraments administered to Catholics.[69] Unfortunately, national statistics regarding conversions and reception of sacraments do not exist; however, Mary Heimann's work has shown that the number of Catholic churches, chapels and stations tripled in fifty years, from 472 to 1,490. Thirty-five of these parishes organised confraternities and sodalities in 1850, and by 1880 this figure had jumped to 556.[70] More importantly, Catholic churches offered a growing variety of devotional activities including catechising, confession, benediction and exposition of the Blessed Sacrament, public rosary, *Quarant'Ore* and the stations of the cross.[71] These figures point to an increase in devotional activities and church attendance, although the extent of devotional fervour is difficult to ascertain.

Missionary success was also measured by good behaviour. The *Catholic Directory* in 1838 observed that the Presentation nuns in Manchester transformed the 'neglected children of the poor', who were taught 'their duties to God, their neighbour, and themselves'. More importantly, through their efforts:

> The youthful mind is brought into contact with everything that is pure and attractive in religion, and is stamped with those heavenly impressions which no length of time can efface. Here, in fine, the obedient child, the modest virgin, the discreet matron, and the virtuous wife are formed in the nursery of piety, and become useful members, nay, ornaments of society; whilst but for [the] existence of this institution, they might become prey to the deplorable consequences of ignorance and vice.[72]

69 Casartelli, 1891, p. 10. Casartelli discusses this in terms of foreign missions but the success of the missions in England would also be measured in this manner.

70 Mary Heimann, *Catholic Devotion in Victorian England* (Oxford: Clarendon Press, 1995), pp. 174–81. Calculated from Appendix I, Devotional Statistics of the Churches, Chapels, and Stations in England and Wales. Heimann's work could be further developed by investigating the link between the growth of confraternities and sodalities and the efforts of women religious.

71 The *Quarant'Ore* consists of a solemn exposition of the Blessed Sacrament for forty hours.

72 *Catholic Directory* (1838), 85.

Working-class children were portrayed as a blank slate who, under the influence of the Presentation nuns, would become attentive and pious Catholics.[73] This rhetoric was highly romanticised and optimistic. The York annals of the Institute of the Blessed Virgin Mary presented a very different illustration of the difficulties that teachers in poor schools faced in their first few days of teaching at a new school:

> The scene that met them [the sisters] on their arrival will long be remembered – a disorderly crowd of wild-looking creatures, for the most part barefooted . . . Squalid and dirty, shouting and screaming, mounting every available projection upon which they could perch themselves.[74]

The York annals illustrate the challenges faced by some women religious when embarking on their evangelical efforts. Many sources commented positively on the results of convent school discipline on the children of the working class. Good behaviour and religious practice were important objectives of nineteenth-century schooling; Catholic sources frequently indicated that convent-run schools were effective on both counts.[75] Reverend Francis Hopkins, the parish priest at St Mary's, Birmingham, requested that the Sisters of Mercy take over management of the boys' school. He felt that the boys in his mission were falling behind the girls, who were being educated by the Mercy sisters. The Handsworth annalist noted that since Sister M. Aloysius (Elizabeth Carless) and the recently professed Sister Joseph (Mary Emily Whitehead) took charge of the school, 'the change in the aspect of the School, and in the Conduct of the Boys has often been commented upon by the School Inspectors. Their attendance at Sunday Mass and their regularity in approaching the Sacraments show how much has been effected for them by the devotedness with which the Sisters have given themselves to this great work.'[76]

Women religious also educated those who could not attend school in the daytime. The January 1862 entry in the annals of the Daughters of the Heart of Mary reported that:

73 Educational and religious institutions often acted as agents of cultural socialisation instilling societal ideals of morality. Anne Digby and Peter Searby, *Children, School and Society in Nineteenth-Century England* (London: The Macmillan Press, 1981), p. 23. Laqueur argues that the working classes in their Sunday schools stressed moral and ethical values such as honesty, orderliness, punctuality and hard work. Laqueur, 1976, pp. 7–9.
74 Sr M. Gregory Kirkus IBVM, *The Institute of the Blessed Virgin Mary: An Historical Sketch of the Institute in England* (1993), pp. 12–13.
75 Admittedly, some Catholic sources may be biased.
76 RSM Handsworth: 1/200/9/1 'Handsworth Annals', 1886, p. 122.

schools are to be opened in the evening for poor girls working in the day, to give them the instruction that they cannot otherwise get and to save them from the dangers to which they would be exposed in the bad company they would keep in the evening.[77]

The annalist's comment regarding 'bad company' exposed another important *raison d'être* of the evening courses. The courses were often intended to regulate the behaviour of girls and women and entice them away from situations and activities that were deemed immoral. In 1898, *The Harvest* praised the Cross and Passion sisters, who had for twenty-seven years guided the young women of Ancoats by 'counsel and example' to 'form their mind and character' and 'keep them from evil influences and train them in Christian virtues'.[78] The Sisters of Mercy *Guide* remarked that female industrial school students required 'more careful religious training' than other female students as they were less likely to be under parental control; they also had the 'means of procuring dress and other indulgences'.[79] The regulation of working-class morality was the key to the reforms that women religious were attempting.[80] How far this invitation to 'respectability' was actually internalised and how much it was acceded to in exchange for vocational training is difficult to ascertain.

The needs of the middle and upper classes were addressed in convent boarding schools. Training for married life and motherhood was explicit in boarding school advertisements. 'Great attention is paid to the cultivation of those qualities essential to the happiness of home-life and society', stated the advertisement for the Faithful Companions of Jesus of Gumley House. The Catholic High School of Our Lady of Sion in Chepstow Villas combined 'Catholic and moral training with a secular education conducted upon the latest modern principles'.[81] The Convent of Jesus and Mary in Willesdon operated a high school for boarders and

---

77 DHM: C3 'London Diary: Clapham', 10 January 1862.
78 *The Harvest* (October 1898), 253.
79 RSM Handsworth: [M. Francis Bridgeman RSM], *Guide for the Religious Called Sisters of Mercy. Amplified by Quotations, Instructions, &c. Part I. & II.* (London: Robson and Son, 1866), p. 14.
80 Frank Mort, *Dangerous Sexualities: Medico-Moral Politics in England since 1830* (London: Routledge & Kegan Paul, 1987), p. 37. Frank Mort posits that the regulation of working-class morality proved a key component of reform programmes through the century. See also Lucy Bland, *Banishing the Beast: English Feminism and Sexual Morality, 1885–1914* (London: Penguin, 1995).
81 *Catholic Directory* (1900), 454.

day scholars in which the sisters promoted as their 'first aim' the 'religious training of their pupils'.[82] These advertisements also pinpoint how central religious training was to the education of a young lady.

Another aspect of the missionary work involved promoting confraternities and sodalities; these associations of laity possessed a distinct spiritual life and were often devoted to a specific spiritual or charitable purpose. They were invested with a certain cachet; the prominence and recognition associated with membership to a confraternity or sodality was strongly emphasised in convent annals. The investiture ceremony and the awarding of medals of the sodality or confraternity were solemn events in the academic calendar. These groups were selective: membership was based on appropriate behaviour and religious piety rather than social status. The Daughters of the Heart of Mary formed a sewing class in connection with the Confraternity of St Joseph; these children had the privilege of making their own clothes. Only 'well-behaved' girls could become members of the confraternity. The white pinafore, 'presented with some ceremony before the altar of the Blessed Virgin', was the 'badge of membership', and proud wearers led their school on all 'occasions of state'.[83] These 'badges', whether medals or a particular type of clothing or the honour of leading the school on religious feast days, were significant as they allied children to the Catholic Church.

Confraternity and sodality members were often involved in a highly ritualised prayer life that was communally oriented. They were vital supporters of the Catholic Church, both financially and spiritually, and encouraged regular participation in the sacraments and other Catholic devotions. They were sometimes co-opted by congregations to extend the missionary and charitable work of the congregation. The Sisters of Mercy at Bermondsey organised the Confraternity of St Aloysius, where the 'little Associates by their subscriptions and work had Masses offered for the Holy Souls, clothed many children and relieved poor families, besides making offerings to the church of flowers and linens for the altars'.[84] The Confraternity of the Blessed Sacrament required monthly communion in common, and the young boys and men wore a sash and medal on special occasions.[85] At St John's in Salford, the Children of Mary would 'consecrate a great part of their time to visit different houses whose inhabitants they strive to gain to the service of God'. One Child

---

82  Ibid, p. 455.
83  DHM: Patricia Vaulk, 'The Society of the Daughters of the Heart of Mary in England', p. 11.
84  RSM Bermondsey: 'Bermondsey Annals', 1865, p. 64.
85  Ibid, 1885, p. 274.

of Mary received the special attention of the Faithful Companions of Jesus annalist when she:

> undertook to oblige some persons to go to Mass on Sunday; so that they might be ready in time, she used to help them to prepare breakfast, then she accompanied them to Mass & continued the same line of conduct until they had quite taken the habit of assisting regularly at the Holy Sacrifice. She also conducted three adults to the school to be instructed, they now lead an edifying life & one of them is about to enter a religious community.[86]

This young woman had absorbed the evangelistic ethos and became an active agent in promoting church attendance and the reception of the sacraments. Later in 1897, the annals indicated that each Child of Mary had been assigned a portion of Salford, and 'as the object of their zeal' the Children of Mary endeavoured to 'make all the Catholics in their district attend Sunday Mass'.[87] Members of confraternities and sodalities took on the role of missionaries for their own class. Children of Mary were represented in many of the Catholic processions held in parishes to celebrate various religious feast days. The Sisters of Mercy described the 1884 Corpus Christi procession in Walthamstow as 'one of the most beautiful ceremonies they ever witnessed'. The annalist noted in great detail:

> Besides the Sisters of Charity with their little boys, there were the Brothers of Mercy with their boys and boy-band, the Sisters of Mercy with the Girls from Walthamstow, many Priests, and Bishop Patterson, bearing the Blessed Sacrament.[88]

Candlelit ceremonies, incense-filled churches and orderly processions complete with 'boy-bands' involved many young Catholics in the devotional life of the church and provided diversity to their daily lives.

Women's congregations were crucial to the evangelisation of Catholics and the devotional revival that ensued in the nineteenth century. Mary Heimann has suggested that this devotional revival was accessible to Catholics of all classes and that Catholic devotions provided a shared experience between the ultramontane, Irish and 'Old' Catholics.[89] This mutual accessibility was due in part to the work of women's congregations as they involved themselves with every class of society and consistently promoted the Catholic faith by encouraging participation in the sacraments and

---

86 FCJ: A656 'Salford Annals', 1874, p. 142.
87 FCJ: A1843 'Salford Annals', 1897, p. 30.
88 RSM Handsworth: 1/200/9/1 'Handsworth Annals', 1884, p. 115.
89 Heimann, 1995, p. 276. See Chapter 1 for more on ultramontane, Irish and 'Old' Catholics.

attendance at Catholic devotions. The insufficient numbers of clergy and male missionaries as well as the vast numbers of Catholics helped shape the nature of the work of salvation. Evangelisation was also women's work. The efforts of women religious in encouraging religious practice and devotions were essential in the battle against 'leakage', and women's congregations had an important role in the work of salvation of nineteenth-century England and Wales.

The missionary efforts of women religious also extended to their work in health care. Sisters nursed the wealthy and the working class of all denominations and ages. Specially built institutions such as Nazareth House, managed by the Poor Sisters of Nazareth, offered permanent accommodation and health care for 'crippled, deformed and incurably afflicted' girls. St Margaret's Hospital, run by the Dominican sisters at Stoke-on-Trent, also catered to 'female patients afflicted with incurable diseases'. Providence Hospital, managed by the Poor Servants of the Mother of God, received 'Surgical and medical cases'.[90] Other congregations like the Sisters of Bon Secours and the Soeurs de la Misericorde de Sees focused on home health care.

Women's congregations provided health care services in order to offer spiritual and temporal care for the sick and dying. Father Peter Gallwey SJ wrote on behalf of the Little Sisters of the Poor:

> So long as the pestilence and the conflagration and the storm and the wickedness of man fill up the beds in our hospitals, O! Let the Nun find her way to the bedside, to console, to nurse, to prepare for eternity.[91]

The constitutions of the Daughters of Charity highlight the dual objectives of their work with the sick:

> The end for which the Daughters of Charity are sent to a Hotel-Dieu or hospital, is to honor our Lord Jesus Christ, the Father of the Poor sick, both corporally and spiritually; corporally, by serving them and giving them food and medicine, and spiritually, by instructing the sick in what is necessary for their salvation and causing them to make a good general confession of their whole past life; that by this means, those who die may depart hence in the state of grace and they who recover may take the resolution never more to offend God, with the help of his grace.[92]

The instruction of the sick was also part of the remit of nursing sisters. Barbra Mann Wall has skilfully argued that American women religious

90  *Catholic Directory* (1891), 456.
91  Gallwey, 1869, p. 11.
92  DC: 'J.M.J. Rules of the Daughters of Charity Servants of the Poor Sick: Particular Rules for the Sisters in Hotels-Dieu and Hospitals'.

found that nursing the sick and dying allowed women religious to become 'mediators to God' and 'served as an independent means for women to acquire sacramental authority'.[93] Convent documents illustrate that this was a factor in the work of women religious in England. Gallwey explained that 'work done at the death-bed' could have 'eternal' benefit.[94] The act of bringing the dying into the church was important to women religious. This may explain their frequent efforts, at least in England, to build institutions for the terminally ill and dying, rather than for those who needed surgical or medical treatment.[95]

## Conclusion

Women religious were an integral part of the Catholic mission. Their religious identity was focused on their efforts towards their own salvation and that of others. Academic and vocational education under the sisters' tutelage was imbued with a specifically Catholic morality that emphasised the importance of the Catholic sacraments and devotional forms of worship. Women religious became an integral part of the parish infrastructure as they prepared young and old for the sacraments of the Catholic Church. They organised and supported confraternities, sodalities and mothers' clubs, and their emphasis on religious devotion shaped a Catholic culture that, in the nineteenth century, became more integrated into the life of the church.

Catholic texts laud bishops and priests for their efforts in revitalising Catholicism. Integral to their efforts were those of women religious. Religious sisters provided a stable and consistent form of evangelisation that was, in some cases, a daily influence in Catholic lives. The practical nature of their philanthropic and evangelical work was the necessary link between the revivalist efforts of male preachers and the lives of Catholics practising their faith. Women religious were significant contributors to the growth of the nineteenth-century Catholic Church through their religious activism. Through their 'service' to their 'heavenly spouse', they

93 Barbra Mann Wall, *Unlikely Entrepreneurs: Catholic Sisters and the Hospital Marketplace, 1865–1925* (Columbus, Ohio, USA: Ohio State University Press, 2004), p. 137.
94 Gallwey, 1869, p. 11.
95 Of the fifteen English hospitals managed by women's congregations in 1900, only three accepted medical and surgical cases. The remainder were for individuals needing convalescence (6) or individuals suffering from incurable diseases (2), mental illness (1), deafness and blindness (2) and inebriety (1). *Catholic Directory* (1900), 414.

sought to create a devout religious morality in those they came in contact with. While evangelisation was intrinsic to their religious identity, they also worked towards ameliorating temporal needs for education, health care, food, shelter and employment. This aspect of the work and the development of their professional identity will be examined in the next chapter.

# 5

# Professionalising[1]

It is not praising a nun to say that she is a good teacher or a good cook
(though these qualities are valuable acquisitions to their Community), but
the praise of a nun is to say 'She is a good religious'.[2]

The labour of women religious in the fields of education and health care
and in the provision of social services was intricately linked to their missionary and professional identity. As discussed in the previous chapter,
salvation – their own and that of others – was at the core of their way of
life as simple-vowed women religious. Their objectives were clearly articulated in congregation constitutions which decreed that women religious
laboured 'for the salvation of souls'. As women religious, they were
called to evangelise. Connecting these activities to their missionary identity is straightforward, but adding to their cache of identities a 'professional identity' can be, problematic and discomfiting. This difficulty is
not associated solely with Catholic women religious. As Kathryn Gleadle
observed in her work on nineteenth-century British women radicals and
Unitarians, 'Evangelical notions of women's religious and moral vocation were reconciled uneasily with the notion of the female professional.'
Religious activism, even if parochial, extended the boundaries of their
identity and propelled many women religious into roles as administrators, educators and health care professionals.[3] These professional roles

---

1  An earlier version of this chapter was published as Carmen M. Mangion,
   ' "Good Teacher" or "Good Religious"?: The Professional Identity of
   Catholic Women Religious in Nineteenth-Century England and Wales',
   *Women's History Review*, 14 (2005), 223–42.
2  SMG: 'Mother as We Knew Her', 1957, p. 106.
3  Lynn Abrams, *The Making of Modern Woman: Europe 1789–1918* (London:
   Pearson Education, 2002); Patricia Crawford, 'Women, Religion and Social
   Action in England, 1500–1800', *Australian Feminist Studies*, 13 (1998), 269–
   80; Mary Hilton and Pam Hirsch, eds, *Practical Visionaries: Women,
   Education and Social Progress, 1790–1930* (London: Longman, 2000);

became an important facet of their identity. As congregations grew and the number of convents increased, a sister's work became more specialised. This occupational focus and the emergence of teaching and nursing as professions were factors in women religious acquiring a professional identity. This in turn conveyed an authority and status that was important to their self-identity and to the ways in which they were perceived by the public.

There were two major obstacles to acknowledging the professional identity of women religious. First, there was the contradiction between the 'caring' work that women religious performed and the professional dimension of their roles as teachers, nurses or social service providers. This was problematic not only for women religious, but for all women who entered the 'caring' professions in the nineteenth century. Second, there was a fear that the religious dimension of their role might distract from its technical functions. Judith Moore in her study of the professionalisation of nursing noted that scholars often discount religious commitment as an important stimulus for advancing women in the professions.[4] Yet, despite these obstacles, women, many inspired by religious commitment, worked diligently to raise the level of academic and practical qualifications needed to attain professional status for educators and nurses. Another factor that hindered women from achieving professional status was the gendering of professions. Anne Witz has commented that this created a tier structure where 'semi-professions', such as the 'caring' professions, were deemed inferior.[5] These issues speak to the contested nature of professions, especially where women were concerned.

These obstacles to achieving professional status were not easily overcome by women religious. Yet several historians have drawn attention to the professional nature of the work and contributions of women religious. According to scholar Sarah Curtis, French women religious 'virtually invented the modern teaching profession in nineteenth-century France'.[6] The teaching practices of the United States-based Congregation of St Joseph have been characterised as 'modern' by the historians Carol K.

---

Sue Morgan, ed., *Women, Religion and Feminism in Britain, 1750–1900* (Basingstoke: Palgrave Macmillan, 2002).

4 Judith Moore, *A Zeal for Responsibility: The Struggle for Professional Nursing in Victorian England, 1868–1883* (Athens: University of Georgia Press, 1988), p. xv.

5 Anne Witz, *Professions and Patriarchy* (London: Routledge, 1992), p. 60.

6 Sarah A. Curtis, *Educating the Faithful: Religion, Schooling, and Society in Nineteenth-Century France* (Dekalb, Illinois: Northern Illinois Press, 2000), p. 64.

Coburn and Martha Smith. Their analysis of congregation teaching manuals suggests that their teaching model encouraged flexibility and the absorption of new ideas.[7] Colin Jones has argued that seventeenth-century French nursing sisters were not passively following the instructions of medical doctors, nor were they merely 'carers' who performed non-skilled tasks. Nursing sisters utilised the diet of the sick poor as a therapeutic tool, ran the institution's pharmacy, operated charitable dispensaries and performed minor surgical procedures such as blood letting, dressing wounds and lancing boils.[8] The nursing historian Sioban Nelson has suggested that nineteenth-century women religious in Australia and North America operated state-of-the-art hospitals that were furnished with the latest medical technology.[9] Rosemary Radford Ruether has asserted not only that women religious were self-supporting and educated, but that their ownership and management of large properties made them the most independent women professionals in nineteenth-century America.[10] These revisionist works emphasise the technical competence and skill of women religious rather than the 'caring' nature of their work.

Can this technical competence and skill be understood as professional competence? This depends on how a profession is defined. Scholars of professions have acknowledged that any definition is problematic as professions are historically and culturally contingent.[11] In medieval and early modern times, a profession was 'a calling, a sacred duty, a commitment not only to the service of others but to the larger social good'.[12] This definition was expanded in the eighteenth century, owing, as some

7 Carol K. Coburn and Martha Smith, *Spirited Lives: How Nuns Shaped Catholic Culture and American Life, 1836–1920* (Chapel Hill and London: The University of North Carolina Press, 1999), p. 138.

8 Colin Jones, 'Sisters of Charity and the Ailing Poor', *Social History of Medicine*, 2 (1989), 339–48 (p. 340).

9 Sioban Nelson, *Say Little, Do Much: Nurses, Nuns, and Hospitals in the Nineteenth Century* (Philadelphia: University of Pennsylvania Press, 2001), pp. 159–60.

10 Rosemary Radford Reuther, 'Catholic Women', in Rosemary Radford Ruether and Rosemary Skinner Keller, eds, *In Our Own Voices: Four Centuries of American Women's Religious Writing* (San Francisco: Harper San Francisco, 1995), pp. 17–60 (p. 21).

11 Elizabeth Smyth, Sandra Acker, Sandra Bourne and Alison Prentice, eds, *Challenging Professions: Historical and Contemporary Perspectives on Women's Professional Work* (Toronto: University of Toronto Press, 1999), p. 4.

12 R.D. Gidney and W.P.J. Millar, *Professional Gentlemen: The Professions in Nineteenth-Century Ontario* (London: University of Toronto Press, 1994), p. 10.

historians argue, to the changes of industrialisation.[13] Penelope J. Corfield has noted that the distinction between 'profession' and 'occupation' became more specific in modern times. Corfield has argued that the turning point of professionalisation began in the eighteenth century with the regulation of the professions and the creation of professional organisations.[14] Historians in their definition of a profession generally include four basic attributes. First, professions require a formalised training process and tests of proficiency that denote a 'special competence' which, secondly, sets professions apart from occupations and offers social prestige to professionals. Thirdly, professional services to others are regulated by professional associations and/or governmental bodies which, fourthly, limit entry into the professions.[15]

Commentators in the nineteenth century defined a profession in somewhat fluid and markedly gendered terms. Margaret Bateson in *Professional Women upon their Professions* (1895) advised her readers of the 'happy labour women may expect to find in certain of the professions and avocations that are now open to them'.[16] She advocated the entry into a profession for the woman for whom 'June comes not'. Her definition was broad and included 'any form of work which a woman is paid by the public, or entrusted by the public to do, and which she performs under that full sense of responsibility which we term the professional, in contradistinction to the amateurish spirit'.[17] Her distinction of the term 'profession' relied on the skilled and remunerative nature of the work performed. H. Byerley Thomson in his *The Choice of a Profession: A Concise Account and Comparative Review of the English Professions* (1857) very hesitantly defined a profession as an occupation where 'a man for a reward places at the public service his intellectual labour, and the fruits of intellectual knowledge, and experience'. Later in his introductory chapter, Thomson acknowledged that 'turning to the profession of education, we find the fair sex appearing as an important element'. His

13  Rosemary O'Day, *The Professions in Early Modern England, 1450–1800: Servants of the Commonweal* (London: Longman, 2000), p. 7.
14  Penelope J. Corfield, *Power and the Professions 1700–1850* (London: Routledge, 1995), pp. 19–26.
15  Ibid, pp. 19–26; Lee Holcombe, *Victorian Ladies at Work* (London: Archon Books, 1973), p. 19; Geoffrey Holmes, *Augustan England: Profession, State and Society, 1680–1730* (London: George Allen & Unwin, 1982), p. 3; Smyth, Acker, Bourne and Prentice, 1999, p. 5.
16  Margaret Bateson, *Professional Women upon their Professions* (London: Horace Cox, 1895), p. 3.
17  Ibid, pp. v–viii.

definition of a profession relied on the attributes of public service and intellectual labour, and he significantly included women teachers as professionals. Both texts reflect the ambiguity of nineteenth-century definitions of professions as well as an exclusivity about professions. The expansion of the provision of higher education and the emphasis on technical training for many occupations resulted in an expansion of nineteenth-century occupations that could be termed 'professional'.[18] Teaching and nursing were two of those occupations upgraded to professional status as training became more methodological and institutionalised and occupations became more regulated.[19]

## Women religious as educators

After mid-century, the education of Catholics, particularly the children of the working class, became an imperative objective of the newly organised Catholic hierarchy.[20] The First Provincial Synod in 1852 declared, 'wherever there may seem to be an opening for a new mission, we should prefer the erection of a school, so arranged as to serve temporarily for a chapel'.[21] Teaching congregations from the continent and Ireland were entreated by Catholic bishops and clergy to initiate foundations in England. Approximately seventy per cent of the women's religious institutes located in England and Wales had education as a primary focus in the nineteenth century.[22] Although religious education was certainly an important aspect of Catholic education, the English bishops convened at that First Provincial Synod were adamant that secular education should be 'modern' and competitive with that in non-Catholic schools.[23]

The English Catholic Church lacked the funds to develop the requisite number of Catholic educational institutions, which meant that the

18  H. Byerley Thomson, *The Choice of a Profession: A Concise Account and Comparative Review of the English Professions* (London: Chapman and Hall, 1857), pp. 1–2.
19  Holcombe, 1973, p. 19.
20  On 29 September 1850, Pope Pius IX re-established the English Catholic hierarchy, the canonical form of church government which included a hierarchy of bishops and archbishops who had episcopal authority over clergy and laity. See Chapter 1.
21  *The Synods in English: Being the Text of the Four Synods of Westminster*, ed. Rev. Robert E. Guy OSB (Stratford-on-Avon: St Gregory's Press, 1886), p. 86.
22  Barbara Walsh, *Roman Catholic Nuns in England and Wales, 1800–1937: A Social History* (Dublin: Irish Academic Press, 2002), p. 172.
23  *The Synods in English*, 1886, pp. 26–9.

Catholic hierarchy actively pursued government aid. In 1839, the Catholic Institute was organised as a fund-raising body for both Catholic schools and chapels. Educational fund-raising efforts were transferred to the newly organised Catholic Poor School Committee in 1847. Its remit was to increase the number of Catholic schools and assure the availability of adequate teacher training. From 1847, when the Committee of the Privy Council of Education distributed grants to twelve Catholic parish schools, these Catholic organisations managed the grant-requesting process and sought to maximise government grants.[24] The government had agreed that grants could be given to Catholic schools so long as government inspectors could monitor their facilities and secular teaching practices. Thereafter, grant-aided schools were the norm and grant amounts distributed by the government to Catholic schools continued to increase. The education historian John Marmion argues that Catholic Sunday schools and poor schools existed because of the acceptance of government grants, and that teaching bodies moved away from the 'ministerial style of instruction' in order to obtain and maintain grant-aided status.[25] Grant-aided schools also required certificated school teachers, and women's congregations throughout the nineteenth century adjusted their teacher training programmes in order to comply with government certification requirements.

Until the development of the first Catholic teacher training college, most of the teacher training obtained by women religious occurred within the confines of the convent and encompassed both theoretical and practical on-the-job training. The 'trainers' were often women religious who were experienced educators and were considered technically skilled in teaching. In 1849, Sister of Mercy Mother M. Aloysia (Mary Elizabeth Jackson), superior of St Anne's Convent in Birmingham, was 'very conspicuous in her zeal for education, and trained numbers of the teachers under the New System'.[26] In 1852, the Catholic Poor School Committee began subsidising the teacher training school run there.[27] The Sisters of Charity of St Paul the Apostle designated their Selly Park novitiate as the

24  J.L. Altholtz, 'The Political Behaviour of English Catholics, 1850–67', *Journal of British Studies*, 4 (1964), 89–103 (p. 92). The Committee of the Privy Council became the Department of Education in 1856.
25  John P. Marmion, 'The Beginnings of the Catholic Poor Schools in England', *Recusant History*, 17 (1984–85), 67–83 (p. 80).
26  RSM Handsworth: 4/300/2/3 'Documents Pertaining to St Anne's and St John's Convents'.
27  John P. Marmion, 'Cornelia Connelly's Work in Education, 1848–1879', doctoral thesis, University of Manchester, 1984, p. 311.

house of studies. Teacher training was included in the novitiate curriculum for those sisters who would teach in their mission schools.[28] From 1853, there was a separate teacher training school for the Sisters of Charity of St Paul the Apostle at St Chad's Catholic Church in Birmingham.[29] These training efforts were financially supported by the Catholic Poor School Committee, which awarded a grant of £30 to subsidise each participant in teacher training.[30]

The efforts of religious congregations prior to 1856 had focused on developing internal teacher training programmes. Lay Catholic women interested in teaching had no option but to obtain training at non-Catholic teacher training colleges.[31] At the instigation of the Catholic Poor School Committee, the Sisters of Notre Dame agreed to open Our Lady's, a teacher training college for Catholic women in Liverpool. This institution was to become the largest of the Catholic teacher training colleges in the nineteenth century. Within the first ten years, half of the 1,648 certificated Catholic schoolmistresses had received their training at Our Lady's.[32] The first Notre Dame sisters destined to teach and manage Our Lady's obtained their diplomas in December and began teaching classes on 2 February 1856.[33] Our Lady's geared its curriculum towards producing Catholic certificated teachers who would mix academic principles with Catholic values. The Catholic education offered by women religious presented a far broader curriculum and philosophy than was required for

---

28 George V. Hudson, *Mother Geneviève Dupuis, Foundress of the English Congregation of the Sisters of Charity of St Paul the Apostle 1813–1903* (London: Sheed & Ward, 1929), p. 138.

29 J.J. Scarisbrick, *Selly Park and Beyond: The Story of Geneviève Dupuis and the Congregation of the Sisters of Charity of St. Paul the Apostle* (Selly Park, England: Sisters of Charity of St Paul the Apostle, 1997), p. 35.

30 Hudson, 1929, p. 139.

31 Queen's College for Women, founded in 1848, and Bedford College, founded in 1849, were the first teacher training colleges in England that granted graduates certificates of proficiency.

32 Parliamentary Papers (1866), *First Report of the Royal Commission Appointed to Inquire into the Working of the Elementary Education Acts, England and Wales*, c.4863, p. 45.

33 *The Foundations of the Sisters of Notre Dame in England and Scotland from 1845 to 1895* (Liverpool: Philip, Son & Nephew, 1895), p. 51; W.J. Battersby, 'The Educational Work of the Religious Orders of Women: 1850–1950' in George Andrew Beck, ed., *The English Catholics, 1850–1950* (London: Burns Oates, 1950), pp. 337–64 (p. 348); Mary Linscott, *Quiet Revolution: The Educational Experience of Blessed Julie Billiart and the Sisters of Notre Dame de Namur* (Glasgow: Burns, 1966), p. 110.

national certification.[34] Two additional women's Catholic teacher training colleges were founded in England. In 1856, the Society of the Holy
Child Jesus opened its teacher training college at St Leonards, and the
Society of the Sacred Heart opened its teacher training college at
Wandsworth in 1873. These institutions provided Catholic women
with the technical training to become teachers with a specific Catholic
orientation.

Many congregations now sent women religious to one of the three
Catholic teacher training colleges rather than provide in-house training.
The Hull Sister of Mercy Mother M. Stanislaus (Teresa Dawson)
attended St Leonards training college in 1865, a year after she had taken
her first vows.[35] Sister M. St Ethelbert (Mary Burns) of La Retraite
attended teacher training college after her profession in 1894.[36] These
Catholic teacher training colleges became instrumental in training
Catholic women religious. One annalist of the Society of the Holy Child
Jesus noted that 'many of our most valuable Religious had come from
among the Students, and the methods of teaching in our Schools had been
systematised and much improved'.[37] Perhaps even more telling than this
anecdotal information were the results of the analysis of the records of
Our Lady's. They indicate that over thirty per cent of those who attended
Our Lady's from 1856 to 1867 entered religious life.[38]

For most of the nineteenth century, the focus of women's congregations was on primary education. By the end of the century, however,
women's congregations began to address the need for secondary education. In 1894, the Holy Child Sisters launched a Catholic teacher training college, specifically for secondary school education in London. The
future principal Sister St Raphael (Mary Paley) and Sister Mary of Assisi
(Angela Mary Bethell) attended Bedford College and earned their
Cambridge teaching diplomas at the end of 1895. In 1896, the society

34  Susan O'Brien, 'Religious Life for Women' in V. Alan McClelland and
    Michael Hodgetts, eds, *From without the Flaminian Gate: 150 Years of
    Roman Catholicism in England and Wales 1850–2000* (London: Darton
    Longman + Todd, 1999), pp. 108–41 (p. 121).
35  Maria G. McClelland, *The Sisters of Mercy, Popular Politics and the Growth
    of the Roman Catholic Community in Hull, 1855–1930* (Lewiston, NY: The
    Edwin Mellen Press, 2000), p. 147.
36  RLR: Catherine Applegate, 'La Retraite: Origins and Growth', 1979, p. 75.
37  Marmion, 1984, p. 359.
38  SND: Box 13 MPTC, *A Voice*, 5 (1869). Calculated from copies of the school
    magazine, *A Voice*, first published in April 1863, which updated alumni with
    news of the teaching staff, alumni and current students. See Chapter 2.

opened its training college in Cavendish Square, London.[39] This offered further opportunities for teacher training for Catholic women. Such efforts to improve the teaching qualifications of lay Catholic women and women religious were encouraged by the Catholic hierarchy. Bernard O'Reilly, Bishop of Liverpool, commended the Faithful Companions of Jesus in 1899 for sending some of their sisters to secondary education training.[40] Bishop Thomas Grant of the Diocese of Southwark encouraged women religious to obtain government teaching certificates 'to keep with the times and procure for our children the same advantages of apparatus, accommodation, etc as were enjoyed by the children of state-aided schools, a thing impossible without such aid'.[41]

Congregation annals frequently recorded news of women religious sitting for teaching exams or obtaining further education in order to obtain teaching certificates. The annalist of the Sisters of Mercy in Handsworth noted with pride that Mother M. Elizabeth (Elizabeth Stocker) and Sisters M. Bernard (Maria Kelly) and M. Gertrude (Mary Ledwith), along with Mary McHale (who later became Sister M. Juliana), passed their teaching examinations in 1849. She proudly announced that 'these were the first Catholic certificated Mistresses in England'.[42] In 1855, the annals of the Birmingham Sisters of Mercy noted that 'Rev Mother Sr. M. Catherine and Sr. M. Camillus went to Nottingham for the purpose of obtaining government certificates for teaching'.[43] Annals of the Derby Sisters of Mercy noted that three sisters were sent to Our Lady's Teacher Training College in December 1870 to be 'examined for certificate' in order to obtain permanent grants for their schools.[44] Two Poor Servants of the Mother of God, Sisters M. Lucy (Maria Forrestal) and M. Claver (Sarah Synnot), took cooking lessons at the National School of Cookery in South Kensington in 1879.[45] Another Poor Servant of the Mother of God, Sister M. Gabriella (Helen Corbett) attended college in the late 1890s.[46] In addition, some congregations assiduously kept abreast of the changes in their profession. The

39  SHCJ: 'Memoir of Mother Angelica Croft, Second Superior General of the Society of the Holy Child Jesus', 1913, pp. 191–3.
40  FCJ: A1854, 'Upton Annals', 1899, p. 44.
41  RSM Bermondsey: 'Bermondsey Annals', 1875, pp. 238–9.
42  RSM Handsworth: 1/200/9/1 'Handsworth Annals', 1849, pp. 31–2.
43  RSM Handsworth: 2/200/9/1 'Birmingham Annals', 1855, Jun 15.
44  RSM Handsworth: *Sisters of Mercy Derby 1849–1999: A Sesquicentennial Celebration* (1999), p. 12.
45  SMG: I/B 'Annals', 1879, p. 43.
46  SMG: 'Mother As We Knew Her', 1957, p. 154.

Blackburn Notre Dame superior travelled to Liverpool in 1863 to learn about the New Education Code.[47] In 1873, the superior of the Everton Valley Notre Dame convent took 'nearly all the Sisters teaching in the Government Schools to Mt Pleasant, to hear a Conference from Monseigneur Capel on education'.[48]

Many congregations were assiduous in directing sisters to obtain the qualifications needed to teach in grant-aided schools. They began by training women religious internally, but later developed Catholic teacher training colleges which were grant-funded and provided Catholic women, both lay and religious, with the opportunity to train to become elementary and secondary teachers in a Catholic setting. They subsequently passed government teaching examinations in order to obtain their teaching certificates. Susan O'Brien's work has noted that the Catholic teacher training colleges provided a superior education and the academic results of students were excellent.[49] This evidence points to women religious embracing the formalised training process and the tests of proficiency that denoted a 'special competence' in education.

Public acknowledgement of the merits of women religious teachers was plentiful in Catholic sources. Catholic magazines such as *The Harvest* praised women religious unreservedly. The October 1898 issue stated:

> The Sisters are not only Certified Government Teachers, but as they furnish a constant supply of competent and approved teachers, they form a permanent staff devoted to the profession of teaching.[50]

Commendations also appeared in government sources. One of Her Majesty's Inspectors of Schools, Thomas William Marshall, reported after a visit to one convent school in 1850:

> They have also institutes especially devoted to education, the most inappreciable advantage of being familiar not only with scientific systems but with those living traditions which grow out of the experience of a long service of years and are easily perpetuated amongst successive generations of teachers, all animated by the same spirit and acting, not as individuals who cannot bequeath to others their own influence and example, but as communities which are always the same, though their members change or disappear.[51]

47  SND: BX BB/1 in BH1, 'Blackburn Annals', 11 February 1863.
48  SND: BX BB/1 in BH1, 'Blackburn Annals', 3 August 1873.
49  O'Brien, 1999, p. 121.
50  'Grand Bazaar on Oct 27, 28, 29 31', *The Harvest* (October 1898), 253.
51  Michael Murphy, 'The Associated Catholic Charities of the Metropolis for the Educating, Cloathing [sic] and Apprenticing the Children of Poor

This reference praised not only their devotion to education and the constancy of their teaching efforts but also their familiarity with 'scientific systems' of education. This acknowledgement of the technical skills and academic qualifications of these religious sisters strengthens the claim that Catholic schools managed by women religious were providing an academic as well as a moral education.

While numerous examples of approbation exist, not everyone was satisfied with the quality of the 'intellectual' education obtained in Catholic schools. In May 1894, the Catholic journal *The Month* published 'On the Secondary Education of Catholic Women', whose author cautioned that 'convent schools have accentuated the spiritual side of education somewhat at the expense of the intellectual side'.[52] He observed that convent schools were 'following the times but they followed "afar off"', and, the author remarked, no one realized better than the nuns themselves that they were not '"up to date"'.[53] This public discussion on the merits of convent education suggests that women religious teaching in boarding schools may have placed more emphasis on religious education and less on academic subjects. Many Catholic boarding schools were not grant-aided, so government-mandated curriculum guidelines were not applicable. However, there is evidence of the importance of academic subjects in boarding schools. By 1900, some boarding schools were touting their Oxford or Cambridge examination pass rates in advertisements found in the *Catholic Directory*. The Faithful Companions of Jesus at Gumley House announced that 'Total passes in University Examination for the past 11 years [were] over 86 per cent, in July 1899, 100 per cent'.[54] Anecdotal evidence both praised and condemned the quality of education in Catholic schools; more research is needed in order to accurately assess the merits of nineteenth-century Catholic education.

Despite the focus on training and certification, women religious viewed their religious vocation as a sacred calling from God. Teaching was simply a means to an end, and, as discussed in the last chapter, that end was centred on evangelisation. It is unlikely that nineteenth-century women religious would have acknowledged their own professional identity. Such self-recognition would have been problematic for them as, in

Catholics and Providing an Asylum for Destitute Orphans, 1811–1861', p. 139. Cited from the National Archives: CCE AR 1850/1, pp. 818–19.
52  A.J.S., 'On the Secondary Education of Catholic Women', *The Month* (May 1894), 26–33 (p. 33).
53  Ibid, pp. 27–8.
54  *Catholic Directory* (1900), p. 45. It is not known how many young women actually took the University Exams.

their view, it would have secularised their efforts. Frances Taylor, founder of the Poor Servants of the Mother of God, explained:

> We must understand that our temporal duties are only secondary means, and are not to be regarded as the chief substance of the religious life. How many clever people there are in the world outside, and how little their talent is worth, if it is not directed to a supernatural end! It is not praising a nun to say that she is a good teacher or a good cook (though these qualities are valuable acquisitions to their Community), but the praise of a nun is to say 'She is a good religious'.[55]

Sister Mary Linscott, historian of the Sisters of Notre Dame de Namur, concurred with Frances Taylor; she opined that the early mothers general thought of teaching not as a profession, but as a 'sublime work in which it was a privilege to be engaged'.[56] While teaching qualifications and skills were important, and religious congregations encouraged and in many cases mandated technical training for women religious, their focus was on their identity as religious, not as professionals.

## Conclusion

Teaching had become a profession by the end of the nineteenth century: many teachers were trained professionals, educated in teacher training colleges, qualified by government certification and employed by the local authority. When religious congregations began managing grant-aided schools, the academic curriculum of these Catholic schools fulfilled the requirements laid down by governmental bodies. While the quality of this Catholic education still needs to be more thoroughly analysed, evidence exists that most schools run by women religious offered an education that at least compared with, and sometimes exceeded, non-Catholic education. Many congregations actively sought and obtained formal training and certification for the sisters who taught in their schools; they created Catholic teaching colleges to ensure that training could be obtained in a Catholic setting. These trained religious sisters obtained a 'special competence'. Their efforts were visibly in the service of others and, in some circles, they earned a certain 'social prestige'. They were professionals by the standards of the times.

Women religious saw their mission in terms of service. They were at the forefront of philanthropic and educational activity for Catholics in England. The work they performed did not address the core causes of the

---

55  SMG: 'Mother as We Knew Her', 1957, p. 106.
56  Linscott, 1966, pp. 125–6.

social problems of the day, but concentrated on basic education and occupational training supplemented by large doses of Catholic religious doctrine. They moved within what they perceived as their sphere of influence. The reform they advocated revolved around Catholic evangelisation. Their efforts, while adhering to orthodox values, do not warrant denigration; they were religious reformers.[57] They were crucial to the regeneration of the Catholic Church in England. They engaged in activities that would instil religious piety and, perhaps more importantly in their eyes, prevent recidivism in immoral or irreligious behaviour.

It was this religious identity in combination with the professional identity that contributed to acceptance of women religious in the public sphere and in the Protestant consciousness. Identity is not static or rigid or one-dimensional. Women religious developed multiple identities that formed the cohesive whole. Acknowledging this wide-ranging but cohesive identity recognises their active roles in public life. As educators, their objective was to transform those they taught into pious, loyal Catholics in order to build and strengthen the foundation of the Roman Catholic Church. They were ultimately faithful to this religious identity, in their eyes a holy vocation.

57 Susan Morgan, *A Passion for Purity: Ellice Hopkins and the Politics of Gender in the Late-Victorian Church* (Bristol: University of Bristol, 1999), p. 89. Sue Morgan posits that churchwomen's agenda for social change was their expression of religious feminism and should not be denigrated for its adherence to orthodox values.

*Figure 1* Society of the Holy Child Jesus novices gathering greenery in Mayfield.
Reproduced by permission of the Society of the Holy Child Jesus.

*Figure 2* Sisters of Mercy, Liverpool novitiate.
Reproduced by permission of the Institute of Our Lady of Mercy.

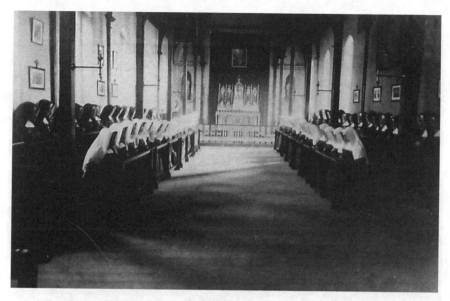

*Figure 3* Poor Servants of the Mother of God, professed sisters and novices, in novitiate chapel in Roehampton. Reproduced by permission of the Generalate of the Poor Servants of the Mother of God.

*Figure 4* Sisters of Mercy on the convent roof of the Crispin Street convent, London. Reproduced by permission of the Union of the Sisters of Mercy.

150

*Figure 5* Six Daughters of Charity of St Vincent de Paul in the priory garden, Mill Hill. Reproduced by permission of the Daughters of Charity, British Province.

# Part III

# Corporate identities

# 6

# Building corporate identity

The evangelical revival of the late eighteenth century made religion the central focus of middle-class culture and located the family unit at the centre of religious faith and morality.[1] The family discourse that evolved from this revival in the next century incorporated many related themes: the centrality of the home, the primacy of a domestic ideology and the gendered nature of the public and private spheres.[2] These themes were the focus of a domestic literature which set out to propagate the civilising effects of family life. This family discourse became memorialised in tracts, conduct manuals and the press.[3] The family was positioned as the foundation of the 'economic, religious, social and emotional life of the middle class'[4] and became significant to an understanding of nineteenth-century social and political culture.

Subsequently, many social commentators encouraged a domestic ideology and a related idealisation of motherhood which identified the wife and mother as the guardian of the home and family. She was regaled as a caring, supportive and selfless help-meet who created a peaceful oasis for her husband. In her role as mother, she provided moral and spiritual

1 Leonore Davidoff and Catherine Hall, *Family Fortunes: Men and Women of the English Middle Class, 1780–1850* (London: Hutchinson, 1987), p. 78; Catherine Hall, 'The Early Formation of Victorian Domestic Ideology', in Sandra Burman, ed., *Fit Work for Women* (London: Croom Helm, 1979), pp. 15–32 (p. 23).
2 Eleanor Gordon and Gweneth Nair, 'The Myth of the Victorian Patriarchal Family', *The History of the Family*, 7 (2002), 125–38 (pp. 125–6).
3 Leonore Davidoff, Megan Doolittle, Janet Fink and Katherine Holden, *The Family Story: Blood, Contract and Intimacy, 1830–1960* (London: Longman, 1999), p. 101.
4 Leonore Davidoff, 'The Family in Britain', in F.M. L. Thompson, ed., *The Cambridge Social History of Britain 1759–1950*, 3 vols (Cambridge, 1990), II, pp. 77–131 (p. 80).

guidance to her children.[5] Sarah Stickney Ellis, one of the foremost promoters of this domestic ideology, claimed that women's authority derived from this domestic role. She reasoned that:

> The women of England, possessing the grand privilege of being better instructed than those of any other country, in the minutiæ of domestic comfort, have obtained a degree of importance in society far beyond what their unobtrusive virtues would appear to claim. The long-established customs of their country have placed in their hands the high and holy duty of cherishing and protecting the minor morals of life, from whence springs all that is elevated in purpose, and glorious in action. The sphere of their direct personal influence is central, and consequently small; but its extreme operations are as widely extended as the range of human feeling.[6]

Ellis elides women's domesticity, high moral standards and sphere of direct influence into a proud, patriotic call for all women to use their influence as 'women of England' for the glory of Britannia. Yet by referring to the 'minutiæ' of domestic comfort, their 'unobtrusive virtues' and their 'small' sphere of personal influence, she placed limits on women's influence. Coventry Patmore's sentimental *The Angel in the House* (1854) became symbolic of this idealised, but limited, version of womanhood. His protagonist Felix was inspired by his beloved Honoria and determined that:

> Where she succeeds with cloudless brow,
> In common and in holy course,
> He fails, in spite of prayer and vow,
> And agonies of faith and force:
> Her spirit, compact of gentleness,
> If Heaven postpones or grants her pray'r,
> Conceives no pride in its success,
> And in its failure no despair;[7]

5 For more on family in nineteenth-century England, see Joan N. Burstyn, *Victorian Education and the Ideal of Womanhood* (London: Croom Helm, 1980); Davidoff, Doolittle, Fink and Holden, 1999; Sara Delamont and Lorna Duffin, *The Nineteenth-Century Woman: Her Cultural and Physical World* (London: Croom Helm, 1978); Deborah Gorham, *The Victorian Girl and the Feminine Ideal* (London: Croom Helm, 1982); Carol Christ, 'Victorian Masculinity and the *Angel in the House*', in Martha Vicinus, ed., *A Widening Sphere: Changing Roles of Victorian Women* (Bloomington and London: Indiana University Press, 1977), pp. 146–62.

6 Sarah Stickney Ellis, *The Women of England, their Social Duties, and Domestic Habits* (London: Fisher, Son & Co., 1839), p. 54.

7 [Coventry Patmore], *Angel in the House: The Betrothal* (London: John W. Parker and Son, 1854), p. 69.

I praised her, but no praise could fill
The depths of her desire to please,[8]

Honoria, the object of Felix's affection, was portrayed as a woman whose effortless morality was inherent in her womanly nature. She was gentle, unassuming, even passive in success or failure, and her 'desire to please' revealed her selflessness.

These mythological representations of womanhood dominated the discourse of domesticity in Victorian society.[9] The quintessential English woman was Ellis's obsequiously self-effacing woman and Coventry Patmore's gentle, moral and passive woman; she became the epitome of middle-class English womanhood. This model, acceptable to both Catholics and Protestants, took her place at the centre of the family unit, where beliefs about self and identity developed. The family was thus the most critical site of inclusion and exclusion where identities and loyalties were shaped through habits and rituals.[10] For women entering religious life, the religious community replaced the biological family and new habits and rituals shaped the evolving identity of a religious sister. This developing identity did not eliminate other identities, such as daughter, sister or even wife and mother, but these former identities receded as the identity of 'nun' advanced. The family discourse, so integral to nineteenth-century ideals and conduct, did not disappear; instead, it was utilised by women's congregations to develop the corporate identity of women religious. This chapter will examine how the family metaphor was utilised by women's congregations and adjusted to mould the behaviour and attitudes of women religious. The family metaphor was useful and perhaps even lived in some convents, but as congregations grew, the more useful tool used to assimilate a disparate group of women was a corporate identity. This corporate identity, interweaved with the family discourse, was often idealised but women religious acknowledged the tensions inherent in communal living. While this corporate identity legitimated and empowered women religious, it also restricted their actions and created artificial boundaries through the institutionalisation of religious life. Consequently, the congregation

8  Ibid, p. 101.
9  Claudia Nelson and Ann Sumner Holmes, 'Introduction', in Claudia Nelson and Ann Sumner Holmes, eds, *Maternal Instincts: Visions of Motherhood and Sexuality in Britain, 1875–1925* (London: Macmillan Press, 1997), pp. 1–12 (p. 1). This mythological woman dominates the discourse on domesticity but she remains a contentious figure as this discourse did not always reflect lived experience.
10  Davidoff, Doolittle, Fink and Holden, 1999, pp. 13, 91.

became a powerful source of individual and corporate identity for women religious.

## The congregation as family

Familial imagery and nomenclature were inherent in many medieval and early modern institutions such as guilds and fraternities,[11] and women's monastic orders also employed the familial model in communities.[12] This practice was also followed by nineteenth-century women religious, who used the family metaphor in structuring their communities and their identities. Women religious were not simply unrelated members of one household sharing domestic space and economic and domestic arrangements. They were connected by more than contract and service.[13] The Society of the Holy Child Jesus, founded in Derby in 1846, noted prominently in its constitutions that it was 'forming one religious family'.[14] This rhetoric of the 'religious family' prevailed through this and other congregational documents. Why was the family metaphor so dominant? The family discourse was an important facet of nineteenth-century social and political culture. It was a familiar model which all could identify with. The familial model was incorporated in various nineteenth-century establishments including the British army, women's teacher and nursing training colleges, settlement houses, freemason groups, millenarian sects and trade unions.[15] It represented a commitment to structure, order, obedience and loyalty; these were familiar themes of the family discourse. Congregations used the family metaphor, so prevalent in Victorian culture, to develop a corporate identity and mould behaviour and attitudes.

Despite the frequent use of the family metaphor, the congregation was a corporate entity, replete with various elements of government: an elected superior, an advising body of administrators and published constitutions. The congregation was the overarching structure within religious life. It was the site of learning, spirituality, administration and authority. Organisationally, simple-vowed women's religious

---

11  Ibid, p. 8.
12  Claire Walker, *Gender and Politics in Seventeenth-Century English Convents: English Convents in France and the Low Countries* (Basingstoke: Palgrave Macmillan, 2003), pp. 57–8.
13  Davidoff, Doolittle, Fink and Holden, 1999, p. 33.
14  SHCJ: Box 54 R24, 'Constitutions of the Society of the Holy Child Jesus', 1887, section 3.
15  Davidoff, 1990, pp. 109–12.

congregations fell under two main groupings: those with a centralised structure and those that were organised as autonomous convents.[16] As a centralised congregation expanded geographically and founded convents in other locations, one convent was chosen as the mother house. Notre Dame de Namur had its mother house in Namur, Belgium. The mother house of the Faithful Companions of Jesus was located in Paris, France. The mother house was an administrative centre, home to the general superior and her council. International centralised congregations were often further subdivided into geographic administrative units called provinces, and a provincial house would become the administrative centre in a particular geographic location. For example, Upton, in Cheshire, became the provincial house of the Faithful Companions of Jesus in 1886. The Daughters of Charity of St Vincent de Paul located their provincial house in Mill Hill, London, in 1885. The mother house or provincial house provided a space that allowed for the development of common lifestyles and collective identities as well as opportunities for the cultivation of social networks.[17]

As a physical place, the congregation was often represented by the mother house or provincial house. This geographic space was symbolic of both the beginning and the end of religious life. It was oftentimes the location of the novitiate and the infirmary. The novitiate, as discussed in Chapter 3, would have had special resonance for women religious. It was their *alma mater*, the site of the initial years of their formation. Women religious would commonly end their lives in the infirmary alongside aging friends and colleagues and in the midst of familiar memories of their religious life: the novitiate where they were trained, the chapel where they were professed and rooms that had been used for recreations and retreats. The mother house or provincial house was also a place of rejuvenation. Women religious returned here annually for retreats and recuperation. In 1895, the Faithful Companion of Jesus chronicler recorded:

> On July 20th the prizes were distributed by our chaplain, and on the following day our children left us. We then enjoyed a few holidays 'en famille' before setting out on our yearly migration to Upton.[18]

16  Chapter 8 will explore the administrative structures and governance of congregations.
17  Michael Savage, 'Space, Networks and Class Formation,' in Neville Kirk, ed., *Social Class and Marxism: Defences and Challenges* (Aldershot, England: Scolar Press, 1996), pp. 58–86 (p. 69).
18  FCJ: A1205 'Liverpool Annals', 1895, p. 64.

After a busy school year managing night schools and Sunday schools, one boarding school and six poor schools, the Liverpool community prepared themselves for their journey to the provincial house in Upton. They would reunite with others from their congregation: novice mistresses, fellow classmates from the novitiate and former work colleagues. This was the time and place to revitalise their physical and spiritual energy and renew old friendships.

The convent was another important geographic space; it was the smaller unit of congregation life and, for the majority of women religious, the location of their daily lives. The convent was where they lived, worked, prayed and recuperated from their labours alongside other women with similar beliefs and aspirations. These daily relationships embraced both familial warmth and familial tensions.

Life within religious congregations centred on the figure of the mother. The most obvious evidence of the centrality of motherhood within a religious community its the naming conventions. Those in leadership roles, such as the superior general, mother superior, local superior, assistant superior, bursar and mistress of novices, were referred to as 'Mother'.[19] These positions were administrative but their specific roles and responsibilities, as defined in the constitutions, had a familial edge to them. For example, the mother superior expected obedience, love and respect. The Mercy constitutions advised that sisters were to:

> obey the Mother Superior as having authority from God, rather through love than servile fear. They shall love and respect her as their Mother, and in order that she may be enabled to direct them in the way of God's service.[20]

The mother superior had responsibilities that reinforced her familial function as head of the family, which included maintaining 'regular discipline', admonishing 'with charity those who may transgress', inflicting 'penances as may be judged expedient' and comforting and supporting the 'dejected'.[21] The Faithful Companions of Jesus constitutions advocated that the superior have specific qualities:

> Il faut encore qu'elle sache unir en temps et lieu la sévérité et la douceur, qu'elle soit pleine de sollicitude pour celles qui lui sont confiées; qu'elle ne

19  This is the usual naming convention in congregations, however naming conventions do vary. For example, there are congregations and orders where all professed choir sisters are referred to as mothers or dames.

20  RSM Bermondsey: 200/3/3 'Rule and Constitutions of the Religious Sisters of Mercy of Our Blessed Lady of Mercy' [1835?], part 1, chapter 7, section 1.

21  Ibid, part 2, chapter 2, sections 2 and 3.

craigne pas le travail, qu'elle possède une instruction suffisante, en un mot que ses supérieures puissent avoir confiance en elle et lui communiquer leur autorité sans inquiétude. En effet, les maisons pourront être d'autant mieux gouvernées, pour la plus grande gloire de Dieu, que l'autorité confiée aux supérieures particulières sera plus étendue.[22]

According to this piece of prescriptive text, the leaders of women's congregations were women of strength and resolve who governed wisely and with a firm hand but also bestowed kindness and compassion upon their charges. Mother superiors were instructed to attract daughterly love and encourage daughterly obedience. These mothers were not simply meant to be authoritarian mothers who maintained discipline and inflicted penances for transgressions, but they were also to be understanding mothers who comforted dejected sisters and showed compassion for sisters who were disciplined. This view of motherhood was laden with images of authority, discipline and caring: it was a powerful model for femininity. This model, according to Susan O'Brien, described a mother superior's 'status and power and indicated the manner in which authority was wielded'.[23]

Convent documents placed significant emphasis upon the authority of the ecclesiastical superior as 'father' of the congregation. Just as biological families placed the eldest male as the recognised head of household and the dominant authority in the family,[24] women religious used the ecclesiastical superior, oftentimes a bishop, as their father figure. This was important at a time when dependence on men was seen as the 'natural and proper state of womanhood' and a 'badge of respectability'.[25] Yet the relationship between the congregation and its father figure was seldom one of absolute submission to his authority. The authority of the earthly father figure was circumscribed by the constitutions and the

22 FCJ: *Constitutions de la société des soeurs fidèles compagnes de jésus* (Vannes: Imprimerie Galles, 1879), part 6, chapter 4, no. 2: 'She should also know how to combine at one and the same time severity and gentleness, to be full of solicitude for those entrusted to her; she should not fear hard work and should have sufficient education; in a word she should be such that her superiors may have confidence in her and delegate to her, without anxiety, their authority. Indeed the houses will be so much the better governed, for the greater glory of God, the more the authority entrusted to individual superiors is extended.'
23 Susan O'Brien, ' "Terra Incognita": The Nun in Nineteenth-Century England', *Past and Present*, 121 (1988), 110–40 (p. 136).
24 Davidoff and Hall, 1987, p. 329.
25 Gordon and Nair, 2002, p. 126.

government of the congregation.[26] Women religious held tightly to their authority as 'mothers'. These female-headed households were typically not economically or socially dependent on their ecclesiastical 'father'. In addition, the 'law of the father' on earth was undermined by the ultimate authority of the father in heaven.

The vast majority of women religious functioned in this familial model as daughters. Their prescriptive literature instructed them as to the appropriate daughterly behaviour, which integrated piety, obedience and perhaps, most importantly, loyalty. The constitutions of the Poor Servants of the Mother of God noted that:

> the confidence given by a subject to a superior is that of daughter to mother, & of friend to friend; its end is to promote union of spirit & to afford to all sympathy & consolation in the trial & difficulties of life.[27]

Disobedient daughters, according to the constitutions of the Sisters of Charity of St Paul the Apostle, must:

> submit without a murmur to the penances she imposes on them. Even the severity with which she may think it necessary at times to treat them must not make them the less regard her as their Mother, nor hinder them from placing the most implicit confidence in her guidance, nor from having recourse to her in all their difficulties, whether corporal or spiritual.[28]

Sisters were instructed that their relationship with their superior was more than simply one of submission to one's superior but was equivalent to that of daughter and mother. The 'union of spirit' engendered by such a relationship was paramount to the success of a congregation, and sisters were to have confidence in their superior's decisions. The focus of daughterly duties concentrated on loyalty to the superior. This loyalty had a dual function; it represented not only fidelity to an individual, but also allegiance to the corporate entity. This prescriptive literature was meant to teach and to regulate behaviour between sisters and mother superiors in order to maintain religious discipline and encourage loyalty to the congregation.

It is difficult to ascertain how successful leaders of congregations were in merging authority with compassion. Excerpts from correspondence, typically from local and general superiors, acknowledged, sometimes

---

26  See Chapter 8 for more about the relationship between bishops and women religious.

27  SMG: I/C/1/4 'Constitutions SMG Vol 1st' and 'Constitutions SMG Vol 2nd', section 35, 'Of Intercourse with Superiors'.

28  SCSP: *Rules and Constitutions of the Sisters of Charity of St Paul in England* [1864], chapter 9, no. 15.

with kindness, sometimes with impatience, that some women religious had difficulties in adjusting to religious life or changes in their particular circumstances. The early years of religious life could be particularly difficult; women were often, for the first time, physically separated from their biological family. La Retraite constitutions encouraged their members to:

> quit father, mother, brothers, sisters and all they possessed in the world . . . to change it into a spiritual affection which loving them more, with this love, which well regulated charity requires, as one must do, who being dead to the world and self, but living for J.C. our Lord who, she has chosen in place of father, mother, brothers, sisters and all things.[29]

These directives were aimed at minimising biological family identity and maximising corporate identity. For many women religious, they would have been difficult directives to follow. In some cases, their severity was mitigated by compassionate women religious like Sister M. Rock (Hannah O'Dea), who was recognised for her 'kindness, especially to postulants, who, she used to say "miss their mothers during the first months". She was a real mother to them.'[30] Sister M. Bernard (Moran), who had been the primary financial support for her biological family, found comfort in Mother M. Evangelista's (Honora Gaffney) counsels and wrote:

> Mother [Evangelista] seemed to understand everything and consoled me with the advice that 'God will not be outdone in generosity,' and would make it up to my family, the events proved that she was correct and everything went well and God blessed them in every way . . . She was always interested in my home affairs. I used to take my letters to her and she would ask about them all.[31]

The founder of the Sisters of Charity of St Paul the Apostle, Geneviève Dupuis, informed Sister M. Felix Stanislaus (Anne Sandwell):

> I have written to Mother Rose to ask her to go and see your good father and if he is in any immediate danger to telegraph Mother Mary to send you to see him, but of course you would have to go to Mother Rose's Convent to sleep – and as soon as God would have taken your father to Himself – you would have to return to Leeds. Have great courage and fortitude.[32]

29  RLR: 'Constitutions of the Society of the Sacred Heart of Jesus', 1884, chapter 2, section 4.
30  SMG: 'Necrology Book I: 1872–1945', 1956, pp. 34–5.
31  CSJP: Sr Catherine Ferguson, 'Sisters of St Joseph of Peace: History of the Sacred Heart Province, 1884–1984', 1983, p. 81.
32  SCSP: Box 1:47 letter dated 7 May 1885 from Geneviève Dupuis to Felix Stanislaus.

These examples demonstrate the sympathetic response of congregation leaders to the difficulties some women religious faced in managing their relationships with their biological families during times of personal crisis. Annals from various congregations included similar references to sisters visiting family members in times of death and illness despite the severe strictures of constitutions and customaries. Yet in convents managed by less sympathetic superiors or superiors who followed the constitutions scrupulously, requests for family visits or sympathy for difficult adjustments could be treated with less compassion.

Relationships within conventual establishments could be as contentious as those in biological families. The rule of the Daughters of Charity of St Vincent de Paul provided an entire chapter entitled 'Of the Charity and Union which should exist among them' which advised Daughters of Charity to:

> cherish and respect one another as Sisters that our Lord has united together for his service by the special profession of works of Charity, and they shall do their utmost to maintain perfect union among themselves. For this purpose, they shall quickly banish from their hearts every feeling of aversion and envy, and be on their guard not to make use of any unkind expression in speaking to each other; but behave together with Christian meekness and respectful cordiality, which should always appear on their countenance, and in their words.[33]

The rule also directed that they 'shall willingly bear with their companions in their imperfections as they would wish to be borne with by them'.[34] These injunctions acknowledged the tensions that existed in communal living arrangements and prescribed the ideal behaviour of a religious sister. 'Perfect union' was the objective and so aversion, envy and unkind expression were to be replaced by Christian meekness and respectful cordiality. Similar models of feminine behaviour were found in secular conduct manuals. Sarah Lewis in *Woman's Mission* described the mission of single women, who were to establish 'peace, and love, and unselfishness' and promote 'the most minute particular of elegance, of happiness, or moral good'.[35] These prescribed notions of femininity were useful in identifying the expected normative behaviour of single and religious women. Yet despite these admonitions, fractious relationships existed.

Disagreements and personality clashes also featured in the narratives concerning community life. In 1848, Sister Clarie (Clarisse Noel)

33  DC: 'J.M.J. Rules of the Daughters of Charity Servants of the Poor Sick, Common Rules of the Daughters of Charity', 1920, chapter 5, section 1.
34  Ibid.
35  [Sarah Lewis], *Woman's Mission* (London: John W. Parker, 1839), p. 130.

updated Mère Constantine on the conduct of the sisters in the Penryn convent:

> Little M. Borromee is going on reasonably well although Sr. M. Aloyse complains about her from time to time. I don't say she is completely to blame, but in her turn Sr. M. Borromee complains about her. Human weakness which however does not prevent them from getting on well together. It is necessary for each of us to have her share of suffering since we are not angels.[36]

Sister Clarie acknowledged tensions that existed between sisters in convent communities and the 'human weakness' that was inherent in all relationships. Human weakness is also evident in a letter from the founder of the Poor Servants of the Mother of God Frances Taylor, where she admonishes Sister M. Campion (Louise Troughton),

> I don't feel quite sure of your perfect charity to Margt. M. I don't want you to be blind to her faults, but to see them with the eyes of a loving, tender sister. Is your manner right? Do you say things in a gentle sweet way, or in a short, tart tone?[37]

Geneviève Dupuis, the founder of the Sisters of Charity of St Paul the Apostle, alluded to familial tensions in her annual letter to her growing congregation in 1877:

> I have had many joys upon my Feast from your devotedness, but of them all my greatest was to see you all so united in your affections. For it made me feel that we are all, what I long and pray that we may ever be, one family . . . But, dear children, more, much more, do I value the gold of your charity. When I know that it is in your hearts I am a happy mother, and I may say with all truth that the greatest grief I ever feel, comes from any, I will not say breach, but even the slightest diminution of that charity which we ought to have for each other. The joy of my Feast Day is based upon this, more than on anything else – that in uniting in your expression of love towards me you are united the more one with another.[38]

Although their charity had made her a 'happy mother', Dupuis acknowledged and mildly chastised the sisters for their occasional lack of charity

36 SND: PN.h/1 'English Translation of Letters to Namur', letter dated 5 January 1848 from Sister Clarie (Clarisse Noel) to Mère Constantine.
37 SMG: A6, p. 98, letter dated 18 May from Frances Taylor to Sister Mary Campion (Louise Troughton).
38 George V. Hudson, *Mother Geneviève Dupuis, Foundress of the English Congregation of the Sisters of Charity of St Paul the Apostle 1813–1903* (London: Sheed & Ward, 1929), pp. 261–2. This annual letter from Geneviève Dupuis was dated 15 January 1877.

towards each other. She referred to both their united affections and her earnest desire that they would be 'one family'. This would have been difficult given the large number of 'family' members. By 1877, thirty years after its foundation in England, the Sisters of St Paul the Apostle would have been a congregation of approximately 248 professed sisters, novices and postulants in forty-two convents and the mother house in Selly Park.[39] The family metaphor remained an integral component of the congregation narrative even when the size of the congregation would seem to suggest that it had lost its utility.

Another difficulty in using the family metaphor developed from the peripatetic nature of religious life. The convent community could be static or transient. Some women religious remained in a convent for their entire working lives; others were moved from convent to convent every few years. In diocesan-based congregations such as the Sisters of Mercy, convents were typically independent of each other and often a sister remained in the convent that she entered as a postulant.[40] Centralised congregations such as Notre Dame de Namur or the Daughters of Charity of St Vincent de Paul were more likely to relocate individual sisters to where their skills were needed. Sister M. Ebba (Constance Malone) was sent to Devon after taking her first vows as a sister of Notre Dame de Namur. Five years later, she was transferred to Brixton in London, and then, three years later, to Clapham, London. By 1888, she was based in Sheffield, where she remained for twelve years. Then in 1896, she was removed to Blackburn in Lancashire for only one year until she was relocated to her final convent, in Everton Valley, Liverpool.[41] An analysis of the records of the Daughters of Charity of St Vincent de Paul shows a similar pattern; on average, a Daughter of Charity relocated five times during her lifetime.[42] In a retreat given by founder Frances Taylor, she advised the sisters of the Poor Servants of the Mother of God that:

> You must be prepared to go from house to house dear Children, and from charge to charge. One week you will have a Superior whom you like very much: you will be able to tell her all your little troubles and she will understand you, and you feel so happy in your intercourse with her. Next week

39  SCSP: 'Box 26 Registers of Postulants and Novices', 1847–1900. Calculated from this register.
40  Some convents, for example the convent in Hull, did become the mother house for branch convents of the Sisters of Mercy within the diocese.
41  SND: Mission Database.
42  DC: Register of Sisters of the British Province: the average number of placements per sister was calculated from this register.

you may have a Superior to whom you cannot speak, or you imagine you cannot, and feel some sort of difficulty.[43]

Taylor counselled the sisters that the location and the nature of their labours was not predetermined, was not constant and was not in their control. She also acknowledged the multiplicity of relationships between sisters and mother superiors.

The nature of the philanthropic work of congregations, especially at this time of great growth, required a workforce that was mobile and adaptable. Nineteenth-century women religious became this flexible workforce. The pattern of spiritual activities, as defined by the constitutions, was consistent from one convent to another in a congregation. However, there was a redefining of their working and personal relationships either when sisters were relocated to a new convent or when new sisters were transferred into a convent. These moves would disturb the web of relationships that had been previously built up between the sisters. One annalist noted after being informed that her mother superior was leaving the convent, 'Our dear Sister Superior left for Namur[;] every one was sad as she had told the Sisters she was not returning. Recreation at dinner but not the usual cheerfulness as can well be imagined.'[44] Although good-byes were sometimes difficult, it would not be unusual for the replacement sister to be known by other sisters in the convent. One Notre Dame annalist noted that the convent had received a 'letter from Namur' announcing that 'our dear Sister Superior was destined for Clapham and that dear Sister Gilbert du St Sacrament whom several sisters knew would replace the late Superior'.[45] The Blackburn annals noted the arrival of Sister Agnes of the Seven Dolours (Jane Rigby) and novice Sister M. Silva to 'replace two of our Sisters who are going to study in Liverpool'.[46] This physical movement offered women religious an opportunity for new friendships and new relationships. No doubt, also, it meant disappointments and frustrations for some sisters. Frequent changes meant getting used to new ways and personalities, and this could create tension as well as enjoyment. Some transfers could be necessitated by difficult relationships; oral tradition maintains that some women were moved from one convent to another because they were a troublesome influence in the convent. The development of relationships

43  SMG: 'An Eight Days' Retreat for the Poor Servants of the Mother of God given by Mother Foundress (M. Mary Magdalen of the Sacred Heart, S.M.G.)', p. 87.
44  SND: NH h/2 in BH3, 'Northampton Annals', 28 August 1899.
45  Ibid, 2 September 1899.
46  SND: BX BB/1 in BH1, 'Blackburn Annals', 26 September 1873.

was both enhanced and inhibited by the relocation of sisters from one convent to another.

## Particular friendships

Another reason for frequent moves could be the wish to discourage 'particular friendships', either those that existed or those that had a potential to exist. Women religious were encouraged to form sisterly relationships with each other. Yet those relationships had prescribed limitations. 'Particular friendships', also called 'private friendships' or 'intimate friendships', were prohibited. The constitutions of the Sisters of Charity of St Paul the Apostle included an entire section entitled 'Of Charity and Meekness and Private Friendships'. To avoid 'private friendships', sisters 'must make it a point to be at all times altogether, except when the duties of their respective offices, or other unavoidable circumstances' would make it impracticable, and 'it is in a particular manner forbidden that two Sisters should be alone together; that is – either alone with no others in the same room, or apart from the rest of the Community, when it is assembled together for work or any other purpose'.[47] The Daughters of Charity of St Vincent de Paul had similar injunctions:

> Although they should entertain much love for one another, they should carefully avoid particular friendships, which are the more dangerous that they appear less so; because they are ordinarily concealed under the mantle of charity, though they are, in reality, nothing but disorderly affections of flesh and blood they shall, therefore, avoid them with as much, or even more care than aversions: these two vicious extremes being capable of ruining, in a short item, a whole Company.[48]

Proscriptions against 'particular friendships' were also included in necrologies. Miriam Boyle's necrology noted that when she entered the seminary in Paris, she rushed to embrace a friend from Drogheda. She was immediately admonished and told that seminary sisters were 'not allowed to embrace each other'.[49] Exclusive relationships were thought to hinder a deep, intimate relationship with God. Proscriptions against these relationships were typically contained in the section of the constitutions pertaining to charity. The excerpt from the Daughters of

47  SCSP: *Rules and Constitutions of the Sisters of Charity of St Paul in England* [1864], chapter 5.
48  DC: 'J.M.J. Rules of the Daughters of Charity Servants of the Poor Sick', chapter 6, nos I and II.
49  DC, *Notes on Deceased Sisters* (1929), 5.

Charity just discussed comes from a section entitled 'Of some means of preserving Charity and Union among themselves'. These friendships could cause dissatisfaction within the community by creating factions and rivalries between women religious.[50] Particular friendships were discouraged because congregation leaders believed they could presage the denouement of religious life on an individual and, more detrimentally, a corporate level. Sadly, some fulfilling nineteenth-century friendships may have been terminated if they were deemed inappropriate.

Although prescriptive literature vigorously denounced particular friendships, 'devoted' and 'holy' friendships were sanctioned. Catherine M. Pilley's necrology included a quote from another religious sister, who explained: 'We were great friends, and though our characters were quite different we were devoted to each other without allowing our friendship to degenerate into too great familiarity.'[51] The obituary of Mother Imelda Poole, published in *The Month* in 1895, noted that:

> Mother Imelda Poole, whose name has already been mentioned, was knit to Mother Drane in the bonds of a holy friendship, the depth and intensity of which the pages of the Memoir before us attest in numberless ways.[52]

The relationship between Poole and Drane functioned as an exemplar for an acceptable, even laudable, 'holy friendship'. These narratives suggest that boundaries defining particular friendships were not fixed; there appeared to be a fine line dividing disruptive particular friendships from deep and devoted 'holy friendships'. This line appeared more easily negotiated when women held positions of authority in the congregations. However, there may have been other 'holy friendships' between women who held less visible positions in the community that were not commented on in convent narratives. The difficulties of 'particular friendships' seemed to stem from the impact of these friendships on the community. Scholars of American and Irish women religious have found that some 'particular friendships' may have challenged the authority of the mother superior and disrupted the 'spiritual peace' of the community,

---

50  Mary Peckham Magray, *The Transforming Power of the Nuns: Women, Religion, and Cultural Change in Ireland, 1750–1900* (Oxford: Oxford University Press, 1998), p. 51, 72; Janice Raymond, *A Passion for Friends: Toward a Philosophy of Female Affection* (London: The Women's Press, 1991), p. 92.

51  DC: *Notes on Deceased Sisters* (1938), 128–30.

52  Herbert Thurston, 'Two Modern Dominicanesses', *The Month* (October 1895), 183–204 (p. 197).

leading to divisions within the community.[53] Susan Mumm, writing on Anglican sisterhoods, has found some instances where 'particular friendships' were encouraged, but for the most part intimate emotional relationships were thought to 'impair bonding to the group as a whole'. This again points to the possible detriment of the 'particular friendship' to the community's cohesiveness.

Close, single-sex relationships were not unusual in the nineteenth century. Lillian Faderman's work on 'romantic friendships' indicates that intimate, emotional friendships of this style were not taboo until the 1920s, when women's changed status and medical knowledge led to the proscription of such relationships. The change in attitudes towards these relationships began in the late nineteenth century, when middle-class women became more financially secure and the idea that women were sexual beings who needed to express their sexuality became more commonplace. This encouraged more ambivalent attitudes towards close female friendships.[54] Elizabeth Edwards, who has explored relationships among female leaders of women's colleges in the nineteenth century, saw homoerotic friendships as primarily a source of emotional support. Yet these relationships were problematic because those who held positions of power within institutions found it difficult to balance their emotional and sexual needs with this power.[55] These tensions could be even more visible in convents. Schoolgirl crushes could diminish once a girl left school, but women entering religious life could not always avoid contact with each other. This was, perhaps, another reason why congregation literature was so vigorous in proscribing particular friendships.

## Camaraderie

Although particular friendships were taboo, camaraderie and merriment did have their place in the convent. Recreation was a specific time established in a convent's horarium when women religious could replenish

53 Carol K. Coburn and Martha Smith, *Spirited Lives: How Nuns Shaped Catholic Culture and American Life, 1836–1920* (Chapel Hill and London: The University of North Carolina Press, 1999), p. 79; Magray, 1998, pp. 56, 66.

54 Lilian Faderman, *Surpassing the Love of Men: Romantic Friendship and Love between Women from the Renaissance to the Present* (London: The Women's Press, 1981), pp. 16–20.

55 Elizabeth Edwards, 'Educational Institutions or Extended Families? The Reconstruction of Gender in Women's Colleges in the Late Nineteenth and Early Twentieth Centuries', *Gender and Education*, 2 (1990), 17–35 (pp. 26–9).

their physical and spiritual energy. It was a valued way of spending time together as a community. Extra recreations were given to celebrate important events, to reward the sisters or to cheer the sisters during times of sorrow. The sisters of Notre Dame de Namur were given extra recreation to celebrate the Royal Wedding of 1893,[56] and in Battersea a recreation was granted 'on account of the depressing influence of a very dense fog'.[57] The Battersea annals noted 'Boarder attacked by Diphtheria – went to hospital. Rec. to cheer sisters'.[58] Recreation was used to celebrate important and sometimes even mundane events. But how was recreation spent?

While the constitutions of many congregations prescribed that recreation was a time to refrain from 'childish levity, excessive laughter, unbecoming gestures and conversations, all forbidden plays, or any that might lead to want of delicacy',[59] evidence suggests that some of these prescriptions would, on occasion, be moderated. Holy Child Jesus recreations spent with Mother Angelica (Anne Croft), the second superior of the congregation, could be full of 'merriment or piety'. They included pious activities such as reading Father Frederick Faber's hymns or discussing various saints, but 'sometimes we had bits of fun, and then she [Mother Angelica] would laugh heartily and enjoy it as much as we did. Very often we spent a good part of the recreation in singing in which she joined.'[60] Frances Taylor admonished her sisters in a 'Letter on Recreation':

> Recreation is not a time in which to indulge in our passions, or in any way to throw off the yoke of religion. It is a religious exercise, just as taking our meals is a religious exercise. We have to eat and drink in a religious manner, so have we to take recreation in a religious manner.[61]

'Recreation in a religious manner', however, was not so strictly defined. On a snowy winter's day, novices, postulants and professed sisters, including Taylor, had a 'snowball match'. One participant noted:

> None escaped except Mother herself and one or two old Sisters. Out of respect we did not throw snowballs at them. Mother made up for it by

56  SND: BX BB/1 in BH1, 'Blackburn Annals', 28 August 1899.
57  SND: BX BS/1 in BH1, 'Battersea Annals', 30 November 1899.
58  Ibid, 8 October 1898.
59  DC: 'J.M.J. Rules of the Daughters of Charity Servants of the Poor Sick', chapter 3, section 2.
60  SHCJ: 'Memoir of Mother Angelica Croft, Second Superior General of the Society of the Holy Child Jesus', 1913, pp. 26–8.
61  F.C. Devas SJ, *Mother Mary Magdalen of the Sacred Heart (Fanny Margaret Taylor): Foundress of the Poor Servants of the Mother of God 1832–1900* (London: Burns, Oates & Washbourne, 1927), p. 161.

asking one of these [sic] to pick up something from under a little tree. The Sister said she could not see anything there. Mother said: 'Where is your faith? Feel for it!' The Sister did so, and meanwhile Mother shook the tree and she got covered all over with snow.[62]

The writer of this passage also noted, 'it was the only recreation of the kind we ever had'.[63] This example, like the ones before it, point to the intersection of a 'recreation in a religious manner' with joyfulness and 'bits of fun'.

Necrologies revealed the liveliness of certain sisters at recreation. Sister M. Cecelia (Emily McCann) was 'loved by all for her joyous nature. The gravity of the classroom was thrown off when the hour arrived for the Community recreation; she was then as a sunbeam radiating cheerfulness around her.'[64] Mother Mary Vincent (Gertrude Bishop) was a 'personality' whose 'originality and her ready wit, combined with a certain Puck-like whimsicality, made her a most amusing member of the community recreation'.[65] Sister M. Bernard (Margaret Furlong) 'would make up little rhymes, which of course made much fun'.[66] Sister M. Aquin (Anne Farrell) was 'gifted with a real sense of humour, Sister had a store of amusing anecdotes for recreation. She also had the art of bringing out the spiritual side in conversation, reflecting her deep interior life.'[67] These extracts celebrated these women religious for their joyfulness at recreation. They balanced levity with piety. Sister Joseph Mary was 'charitable' and her spirit was 'supernatural'. Sister M. Aquin told amusing anecdotes and her conversations reflected her deep interior life. This balance is critical to the understanding of how joyfulness and humour were laudable elements of religious life.

Camaraderie and friendship were extended to women religious outside the convent. Annalists frequently recorded visits of sisters and superiors belonging to another convent within the congregation. In 1852, Mother Mary Clare (Georgiana Moore) sent Mother M. Angela (Elizabeth Graham) with five other sisters to found the Mercy convent in Brighton;

---

62 SMG: 'Mother as We Knew Her', 1957, p. 70. The editor of the collection of reminiscences indicated that some of the newer sisters were under the impression that Taylor was 'hard'. She wished to develop a more comprehensive picture of Taylor that would 'remain when they were all dead and gone'. It appears that these reminiscences were collected beginning in 1901.
63 Ibid, pp. 70–1.
64 CSJP: 'Lest We Forget', Emily McCann.
65 SHCJ: 'Necrologies', p. 243.
66 SMG: 'Necrology Book I: 1872–1945', 1956, pp. 90–1.
67 Ibid, pp. 37–8.

three of these sisters returned to Bermondsey after the house was operational.[68] When the Mercy sisters in Abingdon were seriously ill, the Sisters of Mercy at Bermondsey sent the assistant superior, Sister M. Walburga (Helen Law), and a lay sister, Sister M. Joseph (Catherine O'Hara), to nurse them back to health.[69] A Notre Dame sister at Everton travelled to the Mount Pleasant convent to hear a conference from Monseigneur Capel on education.[70] These brief visits offered women the opportunity to expand their expertise and to assist other convents but also served as an opportunity to share experiences and to develop further relationships with other women religious in the same congregation.

These convent networks extended internationally as well. In 1861, the Notre Dame de Namur Liverpool annalist remarked that Mdlle Victorinie Boukier, Superior of Cleveland in the United States of America, attended the General Council meeting in Liverpool and was able to 'pay us a visit, which filled us with great joy'.[71] In 1872, Mother Mary Vincent (Ellen Whitty), former superior of the mother house in Dublin and current superior of the convent in Brisbane, Australia, stopped at Bermondsey. Her visit 'was a source of mutual pleasure, for she gave an interesting and most edifying account of the labours of our Dear Sisters in that New Continent'.[72] The annals of the Faithful Companions of Jesus noted:

> On September 12th & 13th, we passed some delightful recreation with dear Mother Philomena Higgins, who with our Beloved Revd Mother General's permission had come to visit us. The accounts of the hardships & work of our dear Mothers & Sisters in the far West renewed in us fervent desires of doing more for our Lord & for our dear Society, which can form such heroic souls & imbue them with a spirit of such joyful sacrifice.[73]

These visits recognised and endorsed the international efforts of the congregations.

For women religious, the congregation was an imagined community. Like Benedict Anderson's 'nation', the congregation was sometimes a sizeable entity, in effect, a diaspora of women religious. Women religious were unable to know everyone in the congregation yet they imagined

---

68  RSM Bermondsey: 'Bermondsey Annals', 1852, p. 191. When new convents were opened, experienced Sisters of Mercy would often be loaned temporarily to them.
69  Ibid, 1867, p. 117.
70  SND: BX EV/1 in BH2, 'Everton Annals', 3 August 1873.
71  SND: C3 'London Diary: Clapham', 1847–80, 8 August 1861.
72  RSM Bermondsey: 'Bermondsey Annals', 1872, p. 194.
73  FCJ: A1856 'Isleworth Annals', 1899.

their unity and connectedness.[74] As missionary entities, women's congregations expanded from their origins on the continent and in England and Ireland, to North America, South America, Australia, New Zealand, Asia and Africa. Visits like that of Mother Philomena Higgins which recounted the 'hardships & work' and the transformation of this 'spirit of . . . joyful sacrifice' conjured an image of the women religious that populated these far-flung convents. Women religious imagined the 'deep, horizontal comradeship' with each member of the congregation; this reinforced their corporate identity.[75] They considered themselves part of international institutions that had a profound impact on Catholics and non-Catholics in other nations. They empathised with the hardship, sacrifice and the 'heroic' nature of the work that their sisters performed all over the world. It was unlikely that homogeneity existed, but exposure to members of their international congregation reinforced the sense of mission that each congregation promoted.

This sense of mission also connected women from different religious institutes. Interaction between women religious of various congregations and orders was often noted in convent annals and occurred with some frequency. Congregations offered temporary shelter to sisters of other communities when they were founding a new convent. The Daughters of the Heart of Mary lodged the Carmelites in 1866 and Little Sisters of the Assumption in 1880.[76] Convents welcomed nuns and sisters who needed temporary lodging. In 1880, five German Dominican nuns and postulants on the way to South Africa lodged at the Mercy convent in Bermondsey for a few days until their ship was ready to sail.[77] The Poor Servants of the Mother of God hosted two Passionist nuns from Bolton for three months in 1877 while they were fund-raising for their new convent.[78] The Dominican nuns of Carisbrooke convent lodged at the Sisters of Mercy in Bermondsey while giving evidence on some legal proceedings. The Bermondsey annals of 1871 noted that their visit was

> only a short stay but it was the beginnings of an affectionate intercourse; and the kind Dominican Nuns testified their grateful sense of the hospitality with which they were received by sending some handsome bunches of artificial flowers for the Altar of their own making.[79]

74  Benedict Anderson, *Imagined Communities: Reflections on the Origin and Spread of Nationalism* (London: Verso, 1991), p. 6.
75  For more on the missionary identity of women religious, see Chapter 4.
76  DHM: C3 'London Diary: Clapham', 29 June 1880 and 12 February 1866.
77  RSM Bermondsey: 'Bermondsey Annals', 1880, p. 256.
78  SMG: I/D 'Memories of the Early Days', p. 15.
79  RSM Bermondsey: 'Bermondsey Annals', 1871, p. 191.

Congregations shared their knowledge and experience with each other. When the Sisters of St Joseph of Peace arrived from Knock, Ireland, at their new home in Nottingham in December 1883, the Sisters of Nazareth welcomed them with a party in their honour. They were a source of encouragement to the Irish sisters and were helpful in such practical details as the making of their habits.[80] Two Sisters of Mercy, M. Elizabeth (Ellen Rigby) and M. Xavier (Rosanna Spence), visited the schools of the Sisters of Notre Dame, who gave them 'all the help they could and who on many other occasions had shown the greatest kindness to our Sisters who sought information with regard to school management'.[81] In 1873, Ursulines from Glasgow consulted with the Notre Dame sisters and visited their 'Town Schools' and then 'came to the Convent and took tea'.[82] In 1875, the Faithful Companions of Jesus sought advice from the Battersea Sisters of Notre Dame about educational practices. The Battersea annalist noted that the three sisters 'wished to see the working of some of our schools. Sister Superior went out with them both in the morning & in the afternoon'.[83] Convent networks were important sources of professional expertise, practical information and fellowship.

Relationships between institutes may have originated through personal relationships between women religious; many women religious would have met while attending boarding schools or teacher training colleges. As shown in Table 3.4, ten to thirteen per cent of women who attended Holy Child Jesus boarding schools entered religious life in other religious communities. Just over sixteen per cent of women leaving Our Lady Teacher Training College between 1856 and 1869 entered religious life in an institute other than Notre Dame de Namur. Another logical reason for these inter-institute interactions was the preponderance of kinship relationships. At least one per cent of women had kin who were in other religious communities.[84] Annals occasionally noted the visits of biologically related sisters who were women religious. The Notre Dame annals noted that 'Two Sisters of Mercy from Mt Vernon came to see Sister M. Etheldreda, the sister of one, they took tea.'[85] In 1868, Sister M. Ursula Joseph (Mary Greene), then residing at the Bermondsey

---

80 CSJP: Sr Catherine Ferguson, 'The Founding and Growth of the Sisters of St Joseph of Peace' (Leicester, 1984), p. 3.
81 RSM Bermondsey: 'Bermondsey Annals', 1859, p. 28.
82 SND: BX EV/1 in BH2, 'Everton Annals', 27 August 1873.
83 Ibid, 11 November 1875.
84 This figure is understated as kinship was not recorded consistently in convent documents. See Chapter 2 for more information on kinship relationships.
85 SND: BX EV/1 in BH2, 'Everton Annals', 6 January 1876.

convent, was sent permanently to the Mercy convent in Abingdon. She was given permission to visit her biological sister, M. Josephine (Cecilia Green), a sister of Notre Dame de Namur, at that time residing into St. George's convent in Southwark.[86]

Despite the abundance of evidence for a cooperative network of relationships between congregations and orders in the nineteenth century, there is evidence that competition for candidates and congregational rivalry did exist. Mère Julie (Julie Marguerite Guillemet) was concerned in 1848 that the Somers Town convent was 'in [a] most painful and precarious' position because 'several religious communities were being introduced into England, and had settled in the neighborhood of our houses'. The founder of the Faithful Companions of Jesus, Marie Madeleine Victoire de Bengy d'Houët, quieted her concerns: 'Let us thank our dear Lord for sending these new religious communities to England that they may serve to increase His glory. If they take away our children, it is because God so wills it. Thus, as long as we accomplish His holy Will, and go to Him for all eternity, we should be very hard to please if this did not suffice us.'[87] However, it seems unlikely that this rivalry was a significant factor in congregational tensions in the nineteenth century. The pattern of convent expansion suggests there was limited competition with regard to convent locations as the needs of Catholics in England were so great.[88] Moreover, bishops wished convents in their dioceses to be financially viable, so they were unlikely to accept a convent in a location where it would compete directly with another convent. The congregation of La Retraite was refused entry into England twice as Bishop Danell indicated that it 'would be detrimental to the Society of the Sacred Heart and to other communities in his diocese'.[89] In general, cooperation and competition coexisted between various congregations in the nineteenth century. It seems likely that competition would have encouraged convent foundations to locate in areas where there were fewer convents.

86 RSM Bermondsey: 'Bermondsey Annals', 1868, pp. 118–19.
87 *The Life of Madame de Bonnault d'Houët: Foundress of the Society of the Faithful Companions of Jesus* (Dublin: M.H. Gill & Son, 1885), p. 237.
88 Walsh, 2002, pp. 63–88.
89 RLR: Catherine Applegate, 'La Retraite: Origins and Growth', 1979. Cited from a letter dated 30 May 1880 from Mère St Françoise de Sales to Reverend Mother General Mère Felt. La Retraite did finally get permission to found a house in England in 1880 but it was based on the Sisters' need for refuge (due to persecution in France) and was not considered a foundation. This caused some difficulties for them later when they attempted to found additional convents in England.

## Corporate identity

Another result of convent expansion was that the family metaphor, so often used in convent literature, became less representative of the lived experience. As congregations grew, in both number and size of convents, the lived experience varied from, at one end of the spectrum, a community atmosphere to, at the other end, an institutional environment. Susan O'Brien has astutely noted that despite the emphasis on the familial characteristics of convent communities, they could not 'reproduce the dynamics of the patriarchal family' and points to the importance of the founder of the congregation, whose personal touch and leadership were fundamental to the family metaphor.[90] After the founder's death, congregations attempted to preserve the spirit of the founder. They developed a body of literature that elaborated on the ideals of the founder and the charism of the congregation. After the death of Catherine McAuley in 1841, many of the women who joined her in the early days of the history of the Sisters of Mercy drafted their recollections of her life. In 1844 and 1845, Mother M. Clare (Georgiana Moore) wrote five letters documenting Catherine McAuley's life, these later were used in her composition of the life of Catherine McAuley which she wrote into the 'Bermondsey Annals'. Seven other memoirs were written by the sisters whom McAuley trained in the early years of the congregation's foundation. The Limerick Manuscript formed the genesis of the first published biography of Catherine McAuley written by Sister M. Vincent Harnett in 1864, twenty-one years after McAuley's death.[91] This was the first of four biographies of Catherine McAuley published in the nineteenth century.[92] The four-volume *Leaves from the Annals of the Sisters of Mercy* by Sister Mary Austin (Margaret

90  O'Brien, 1988, p. 136.
91  Mary C. Sullivan RSM, *Catherine McAuley and the Tradition of Mercy* (Dublin, Ireland: Four Courts Press, 1995), pp. 27–9. These narratives are today named the Dublin Manuscript, the Derry Large Manuscript, the Derry Small Manuscript, the Limerick Manuscript, the Dundalk Manuscript, the Liverpool Manuscript and a second Cork Manuscript. They are not all unique documents. Sullivan's research indicates evidence of copying and sharing of manuscripts.
92  [Mary Vincent Harnett], *The Life of Reverend Mother Catherine McAuley, Foundress of the Order of Mercy* (Dublin: John Fowler, 1864); [Mary Austin Carroll], *Life of Catherine McAuley, Foundress and First Superior of the Institute of Religious Sisters of Mercy* (New York: D. & J. Sadlier & Co., 1866); [Mary Magdalen de Pazzi Bentley], *Popular Life of Catharine McAuley* (New York: P. J. Kenedy and Sons, 1887); K.M. Barry, *Catherine McAuley and the Sisters of Mercy* (Dublin: Fallon and Son, 1894).

Carroll), published between 1881 and 1895, developed the history of the
Religious Sisters of Mercy from the days of its foundation on Baggot
Street to its expansion to England, Scotland, Australia, New Zealand,
Newfoundland, the United States, South America and Central America.
Additionally, Catherine McAuley's counsels were collected in *A Little
Book of Practical Sayings, Advices and Prayers of Our Reverend
Foundress, Mother Mary Catharine [sic] McAuley Who Commenced the
Institute of Our Blessed Lady of Mercy December 12, 1831, and died
November 11, 1841*, compiled by Mary Clare (Georgiana Moore) in
1868. *The Maxims and Counsels of Our Beloved Foundress, Mother
Mary Catherine McAuley, Gathered From Her Life, Letters, Sayings, and
the Annals of the Order, Arranged for Every Day in the Year* was pub-
lished in Ireland in 1900. The Sisters of Mercy, whose convents were
autonomous and diocesan-based, felt an urgent need to preserve
Catherine McAuley's imprint on the Religious Sisters of Mercy and they
drafted and published a body of literature to achieve this objective.

Other congregations followed a similar pattern of drafting and publishing material about their founder. The Faithful Companions of Jesus
published three biographies based on congregation histories as well as
the memoirs by their founder Marie Madeleine Victoire de Bengy
d'Houët.[93] Many undated but bound texts were found in the archives of
the Poor Servants of the Mother of God.[94] Edited collections of correspondence and written memoirs by the early sisters promoted Frances
Taylor's memory and memorialised the spirituality of the congregation
she founded. But they also were tools to instruct and mould the behaviour of future sisters. Sister Mary Alacoque (Mary Murphy) recounted in

93 F. Abbé Martin, *Vie de Madame de Bonnault D'Houët Fondatrice de la
Société des Fidèles Compagnes de Jésus* (Paris: Librairie Saint-Joseph, 1863);
*The Life of Madame de Bonnault d'Houët: Foundress of the Society of the
Faithful Companions of Jesus* (Dublin: M.H. Gill & Son, 1885); R.P.
Stanislaus, *Notice sur la vie, les vertues et les oeuvres de la Servante de Dieu
Marie Madeleine Victoire de Bengy, Viscountesse de Bonnault d'Houët*
(Paris, France: J. Mersch, 1895).

94 SMG: 'An Eight Days' Retreat for the Poor Servants of the Mother of God
given by Mother Foundress (M. Mary Magdalen of the Sacred Heart,
S.M.G.)'; 'Mother Foundress' Letter on Recreation' (Lourdes); 'Meditation
from "Retreat for Novices in Preparation for Taking Vows"'; 'Notes of
Conferences given to Local Superiors by Mother Foundress, Mother Mary
Magdalen of the Sacred Heart Poor Servant of the Mother of God';
'Instructions of Mother Foundress on Our Holy Rule on Confession, etc.
Taken from her Letters, and from Sisters' Notes'; 'Manual of the Institute of
the Poor Servants of the Mother of God and the Poor', 1897.

her *Memories of the Early Days* that 'Mother had taught such good custody of eyes people thought that the Sisters were blind'.[95] In nineteenth-century religious congregations, 'custody of the eyes' represented self-effacement and humility, and was a behaviour to be lauded. This growing body of literature functioned at many levels. It was meant to communicate the founder's ideals, teach appropriate behaviour patterns and preserve unity.

Memoirs, biographies, guides, histories and edited works were part of the corpus of a congregational history that was recorded and communicated. These documents united women religious and reinforced their connection to their congregation and their identity as members of that congregation. Just as families were united by common ancestry, women religious revered the founder of their congregation. They prayed at their founders' tombs, celebrated their anniversaries and read and reread their writings. The Daughters of Charity, who considered both Vincent de Paul and Louise de Marillac as their founders, read Vincent's conferences during meal times and prayer times. The reading list of the Daughters of the Heart of Mary included Adelaide Marie Champion de Cice's *Practice of Virtues*. These texts were both family histories and conduct manuals. They were accessible to all sisters. Even those sisters who could not read would have been able to absorb their content during meal times and recreations when these texts were read aloud. The manuscripts enabled women to identify themselves as members of a specific group with a unique purpose. Women religious developed an awareness of belonging to a unique congregation.

Congregational identity was reinforced by remembering and reminding. In his work on identity, Robert Pope declares that identity is 'forged through historical events, recorded, passed on and partly reconstructed in the form of myths around which people can unite'. 'Collective remembering' is one important method of uniting a group.[96] As has been discussed in Chapter 3, the novitiate training included a thorough teaching of the founder's ideals as well as the congregation's history.[97] These ideals and this history were alluded to again and again during annual retreats, anniversaries and occasions of celebration. Sister Mary (Etheldreda Fitzalan Howard), 'Poet Laureate' of the Daughters of Charity of St Vincent de Paul, wrote vow songs and special 'welcomes' to superiors,

95 SMG: I/D 'Sister Alacoque's Annals', p. 11.
96 Robert Pope, 'Introduction', in *Religion and National Identity: Wales and Scotland c.1700–2000*, ed. by Robert Pope (Cardiff: University of Wales Press, 2001), pp. 1–13 (p. 7).
97 See Chapter 3 for more on the novitiate and the formation of identity.

bishops and cardinals for celebrations of feasts and Golden Jubilees.[98] Congregations also encouraged the writing of biographies of significant women religious other than founders. Howard also penned the *Life of Sister Marie Chatelain* (1900), which was edited by Lady Amabel Kerr.[99] The Sisters of Notre Dame published *The Foundations of the Sisters of Notre Dame in England and Scotland from 1845 to 1895* (1895) to tell the story of their foundation in England. These are but a sample of texts internally published by religious congregations to remember their significant sisters and the history of their congregation. There are many more unpublished manuscripts in convent archives that document other lives and events. Despite the strong rhetoric of humility and self-effacement, leaders of congregations were heralded as important role models for younger and older sisters, and they were an integral part of the congregation's history and identity. Elizabeth Smyth, in her work on the historical writings of nineteenth- and twentieth-century Canadian women religious, argues that this literature had both a practical and a spiritual value. Temporal events were framed as part of the spiritual journey of the congregation and the individuals being celebrated.[100]

This remembering embraced not only the 'great and the good' but also the ordinary sister. In some congregations, every sister was memorialised on her death with a necrology that was sent from convent to convent to be read aloud. In these congregations, every sister, whether she was a convent superior or a convent cook, was remembered. Necrologies memorialised piety. They were teaching tools, oftentimes simply a list of pious attributes and personal characteristics, but they were also reminders of the history of the congregation. The Congregation of St Joseph of Peace entitled its book of necrologies 'Lest We Forget', an apt title for such remembrances. This effort of creating a communal history emphasised the founders and early congregation history but also memorialised individual women religious and reinforced their identity as members of a congregation.

Corporate identity was both tangible and intangible. The tangible factors were reflected visibly in the iconography of the congregation found first and foremost in the name of the congregation, but also in the

98   DC: *Sister Etheldreda Fitzalan Howard*, p. 33.
99   Ibid, p. 142; Amabel Kerr, *Sister Chatelain or Forty Years' Work in Westminster* (London: Catholic Truth Society, 1900).
100  Elizabeth Smyth, '"Writing Teaching Us Our Mysteries": Women Religious Recording and Writing History', in Beverly Boutilier and Alison Prentice, eds, *Creating Historical Memory: English-Canadian women and the Work of History* (Vancouver: UBC Press, 1997), pp. 101–28. In this essay, Smyth examines the 'power of institutional memory' by exploring the historical writing of nineteenth- and twentieth-century Canadian women religious.

habit that women religious wore and the convents and institutional space that women religious inhabited.[101] The Faithful Companions of Jesus were named after the women who travelled with Jesus during his active ministry and remained with him at the time of his death; they were his 'faithful companions'.[102] The Sisters of the Most Cross and Passion wore on their black habit the symbol of their spirituality: inside a white heart was inscribed 'Jesu Xpi Passio', which translated into the 'Passion of Jesus Christ' in Hebrew, Greek and Latin. Below this inscription were three nails which represented the suffering and death of Jesus.[103] Their spirituality revolved around the remembrance of the sufferings of Jesus.

The convent space and institutional space also reflected the iconography of a congregation. The Incarnation was a special focus of the Poor Servants of the Mother of God. Their convents included paintings of the Incarnation, and the Feast of the Incarnation was celebrated with great joy.[104] These images and symbols reflected the spirituality of the founders. They were also corporate markers which bound women to a congregation and its spirituality. Other corporate markers were reflected in the philanthropic work of the congregations, the special prayers and meditations and the traditions that were a part of congregational life.

Nineteenth-century women religious referred often to the spirit of their founder and their congregation. This spirit was unique for each congregation. It was a mix of spirituality and theology as envisioned by the founders of the congregation. Frances Taylor chose the Incarnation as the spiritual focus for the Poor Servants of the Mother of God. As Susan O'Brien explains, Taylor 'saw herself and the sisters as people who, hidden and unknown themselves, were bringing the Word to the world, just as Mary had been the servant of God and the bringer of his life'.[105] The spirit of the Poor Servants of the Mother of God, as divined by Frances Taylor, was based on Ignatius's theology.[106] Caritas McCarthy's in-depth study of

---

101  O'Brien, 1988, p. 137.
102  Mary Campion McCarren FCJ, *Faithful Companion of Jesus: Venerable Marie Madeleine Victoire de Bengy, Viscountess de Bonnault d'Houët 1781–1858, Foundress of the Society of Sisters Faithful Companions of Jesus* (London: Catholic Truth Society, 1981), p. 21.
103  Edna Hamer, *Elizabeth Prout, 1820–1864: A Religious Life for Industrial England* (Bath, England: Downside Abbey, 1994), p. 14. 'Jesu' is Hebrew, 'XPI' is Greek and an abbreviation for 'Christ' and 'Passio' is Latin. I am very appreciative of Dr Edna Hamer for taking the time to explain this to me.
104  O'Brien, 1988, p. 137.
105  Ibid.
106  Eithne Leonard SMG, 'The Making of a Foundress: Frances Margaret Taylor 1832–1869' (postgraduate thesis, St Louis University, 1982), p. 74.

Cornelia Connelly's spirituality indicates that Connelly encouraged the Holy Child Jesus sisters to adopt the 'full contemplative involvement in the mystery of the Incarnation'.[107] Susan O'Brien notes that their emblem of the holy child 'showed the infant Jesus with arms outstretched in a gesture which was childlike in trust and confidence yet foreshadowed the crucifixion'.[108] The founder of the Sisters of Notre Dame de Namur, Julie Billiart, chose as the objects of the Sisters' devotions the Holy Child Jesus in the crib and the Sacred Heart of Jesus.[109] The spirituality of the congregation was a significant part of this corporate identity.

The formation process described in Chapter 3 prepared women for their integration into the corporate structure of the congregation. A woman redefined herself first as a postulant and then as novice and, finally, as a professed sister and a member of a particular congregation. This process involved imbibing the history, traditions and spirituality of the congregation. Women from sometimes disparate backgrounds were moulded by the same corporate imprint in order to build unity and an *esprit de corps*. These women bound themselves to the tangible philanthropic goals and spiritual ethos of the religious congregation.

This corporate identity provided a source of strength, self-definition and accomplishment for women religious, as did the dominant discourse of selflessness and its barrage of messages on humility and piety. The individual identity receded as the corporate identity evolved. The visual image of this is striking: the homogeneity of a mass of women dressed in the habit of their congregation. It is difficult to see each individual woman. Instead, what dominates is the mass itself. The message was clear: this unity in spirit and philanthropy led to corporate power. Corporate identity provided for a 'sheltered space', as described by Coburn and Smith in their work on American women religious, where women created a 'sacred space' outside motherhood and marriage.[110]

## Conclusion

The family discourse was dominant in Victorian culture and provided a useful metaphor for congregations. The model of the good mother was

107   Caritas McCarthy SHCJ, *The Spirituality of Cornelia Connelly: In God, For God, With God* (Lewiston, New York, USA: Edwin Mellen Press, 1986), p. 124.
108   O'Brien, 1988, p. 137.
109   Myra Poole, *Prayer, Protest, Power: The Spirituality of Julie Billiart Today* (Norwich: Canterbury Press, 2001), p. 75.
110   Coburn and Smith, 1999, p. 10.

used by congregation leaders to balance the dual qualities of compassion and discipline. Acting as a good daughter or sister was about loyalty, to both the mother superiors and the congregation. Prescriptive literature was important in defining the roles and responsibilities of mothers and daughters and hinted at the tensions in these relationships. Correspondence and annals demonstrated the complexity of the relationships between mothers and sisters and sisters and sisters. Sometimes the absolute tone of prescriptive literature could be moderated; lived experience could vary from the directives of the prescriptive literature.

Women religious created a communal structure which provided women with group affiliation and networks of friendships. These communities were not socially isolated. Women achieved self-fulfilment along with companionship. This structure provided a distinct identity that bound women together and separated them from the outside world. The shared corporate identity was consistently being remembered, commemorated and memorialised. It was the values of community life as well as a distinct spirituality that appealed to women who entered religious congregations. Religious life provided support, solidarity and safety but also required a degree of humility and self-effacement that was difficult for some. Despite the badge of corporate identity, differences existed, and differences of class and ethnicity were difficult to camouflage, as will be discussed in the next chapter.

# 7

# Class and ethnicity

The theme of perfection resonates throughout the nineteenth-century writings of and about women religious. Catherine McAuley reminded the Sisters of Mercy that 'Religion refines and elevates the character. A perfect Religious is a perfect lady.'[1] Thomas Marshall, one of Her Majesty's Inspectors of Schools, saw women religious as:

> belonging to a higher grade of society – this is almost universally the case in female communities – yet in the previous cultivation of their minds, the possession of more ample attainments, and a far more careful and complete preparation for the task to which they are consecrated.[2]

In Catholic circles, women religious were hailed as models of gentility who epitomised the hegemonic ideal of feminine behaviour. There was an air of superiority surrounding them, in part because of the religious nature of their role, but also because of representations of their gentility and breeding. Perfection was not an exclusively Catholic or a religious expectation. Patricia Branca noted that Victorian society expected women to be:

> perfect ladies, perfect wives, and perfect mothers. The Victorian woman was to have an observing eye, a calculating head, a skilful hand, concise speech, a gentle step, external tidiness and internal purity.[3]

1 [Georgiana Moore], ed., *A Little Book of Practical Sayings, Advices and Prayers of Our Reverend Foundress, Mother Mary Catharine [sic] McAuley Who Commenced the Institute of Our Blessed Lady of Mercy December 12, 1831, and died November 11, 1841* (London: Burns, Oates & Co., 1868), p. 13.

2 Michael Murphy, 'The Associated Catholic Charities of the Metropolis for the Educating, Cloathing [sic] and Apprenticing the Children of Poor Catholics and Providing an Asylum for Destitute Orphans, 1811–1861' (1995), p. 139. Cited from National Archives, CCE AR 1850/1, p. 818.

3 Patricia Branca, *Silent Sisterhood: Middle-Class Women in the Victorian Home* (London: Croom-Helm, 1975), p. 152.

Conduct manuals published in the nineteenth century instructed Victorian women on how to achieve this perfection.[4] Women religious had their own specialised version of these secular conduct manuals. Constitutions, customs books, religious biographies and necrologies were some of the texts used to instruct women religious on the means of achieving perfection. Perfection was not only represented in a religious sense but also linked to ideas of gentility, decorum and, by default, class.

Class is central to studying religion in nineteenth-century England,[5] and it follows that class is relevant to our understanding of identity and women religious. Another important dimension to this analysis of identity is ethnicity, especially as forty-one per cent of the women who entered religious congregations in England and Wales were Irish-born.[6] The relationship between English and Irish-born sisters added another complex layer to an understanding of convent life but one that is more difficult to tease out of the convent documents. This chapter will consider the relationship among class, ethnicity and identity in nineteenth-century religious congregations by first examining the social status and the national origins of religious institutes. There was a social hierarchy among religious institutes, based on class, ethnicity and social status, that in many ways reflected the class structure within nineteenth-century England. The introduction of active, simple-vowed religious congregations altered this hierarchy and widened the parameters of religious life by removing some of the class barriers that restricted some women's entry into religious congregations. Next, the social composition of select congregations and congregation leadership will be examined analytically to discern further nuances to the relationship between class, ethnicity and leadership. The complicated lay–choir dichotomy is another important feature of this discussion.[7] The division between lay and choir sisters was clearly defined within a congregation, yet qualifications for entry into a congregation as a lay or a choir sister varied between religious institutes.

4  Ibid, pp. 12–24.
5  K.S. Inglis, *Churches and the Working Classes in Victorian England* (London: University of Toronto Press, 1963).
6  See Table 7.2.
7  Susan O'Brien, 'Lay-Sisters and Good Mothers: Working-Class Women in English Convents, 1840–1910', in W.J. Sheils and D. Wood, eds, *Women in the Church: Papers Read at the 1989 Summer Meeting and the 1990 Winter Meeting of the Ecclesiastical History Society*, Studies in Church History, (Oxford: Ecclesiastical History Society, 1990), pp. 453–65 (p. 457). Susan O'Brien has noted that in 1870, about half of the 200 unenclosed and partially enclosed convents in England included lay sisters.

Nineteenth-century boundaries of religious life diverged from the narrowly constructed parameters of religious life in early modern England. Catholic daughters of the aristocracy and gentry entered solemn-vowed, enclosed orders in England, and, after the Reformation, on the continent.[8] As choir sisters, they were typically educated enough to recite the Divine Office in Latin and brought in a substantial dowry. They were eligible to vote in chapter and to hold office and were involved in the contemplative life of the order. Very little is known of the background of women who entered as lay sisters, but their responsibilities often lay in managing the convent household and performing domestic tasks in the convent. The lay sister brought either no dowry or a much smaller one. She had no voting rights, could not hold office and had a less rigorous prayer life; her domestic tasks took precedence and she was more likely to pray litanies and rosaries in the vernacular rather than the Divine Office.[9] This lay–choir dichotomy was endemic in this period.

This pattern was not uniquely English; it was consistent with the customs of many continental religious orders. Aristocratic French nuns in the seventeenth and eighteenth centuries were unlikely to interact with the poor in the manner of the simple-vowed sisters such as the Filles de la Charité or Filles de Sainte-Geneviève; it was the less socially connected women who entered the *filles séculières*. According to Elizabeth Rapley, the French aristocratic elite 'accepted the principle of active religious life for women, on the understanding that their own daughters would not be affected'. These daughters entered the older, higher-status contemplative orders. Their status as nuns was higher than that of the active, simple-vowed sisters; they were not a part of the movement of the *filles séculières*.[10] This type of class

---

8  Claire Walker, *Gender and Politics in Seventeenth-Century English Convents: English Convents in France and the Low Countries* (Basingstoke: Palgrave Macmillan, 2003), p. 29. Claire Walker's prosopographical analysis of 530 nuns indicates that ninety-two per cent of women religious entering English congregations as choir nuns on the continent between 1591 and 1710 were daughters of gentlemen, esquires, baronets, knights and peers. This sample, admittedly, is quite small. Caroline Bowden's research indicates that at least 1,950 nuns lived in exile in 1675, and this figure does not include the Mary Ward sisters. Caroline Bowden, 'Community Space and Cultural Transmission: Formation and Schooling in English Enclosed Convents in the Seventeenth Century', *History of Education*, 34 (2005), 365–86 (p. 366).

9  In some congregations, women who functioned as lay sisters were referred to as coadjutrix sisters.

10  Elizabeth Rapley, *The Dévotes: Women and the Church in Seventeenth-Century France* (London: McGill-Queen's University Press, 1990), p. 116. Rapley discusses these two congregations in great detail on pp. 79–100.

congruence continued into the nineteenth century. Ralph Gibson has noted that the elite institutes such as the Carmelites, Visitandines, Clarisses, Ursulines and the religious of the Sacred Heart were more likely to recruit from the daughters of the wealthy aristocracy than from the working classes in the nineteenth century.[11] Women who entered active, simple-vowed congregations in France came from the social classes that they served.[12]

Religious life in England followed a different trajectory owing to the penal laws and the suppression of Catholicism. Unlike in France, there was no explosion of congregations similar to the *filles séculières*. The Institute of Mary, founded by Mary Ward, was the sole English contribution to this movement until the nineteenth century. Its 'works of mercy', performed surreptitiously in York and Hammersmith from the late seventeenth century, did not attract a great deal of attention or many postulants. However, there were changes to this established pattern in the late eighteenth century. The French Revolution, as discussed in Chapter 1, resulted in twenty-three communities of contemplative nuns fleeing the continent and making their homes in England. The amelioration of the penal laws in the form of the Catholic Relief Acts in 1778 and 1791 and then the enactment of the 1829 Catholic Emancipation Act made conventual life, and in particular the growth of female active, simple-vowed congregations, a viable possibility in England.[13] English women no longer had to travel to the continent to become nuns, and religious life was no longer the exclusive purview of the English Catholic elite. The development and dramatic growth of women's simple-vowed, active congregations expanded the boundaries of religious life by expanding the base of Catholic women who could become women religious. And this cohort of Catholic women, as outlined in Chapters 1 and 2, eagerly seized this opportunity to enter religious life.

## Congregations and ethnicity

In the nineteenth century, contemplative, solemn-vowed orders retained a higher status than active, simple-vowed congregations and were often

11 Ralph Gibson, *A Social History of French Catholicism, 1789–1914* (London: Routledge, 1989), p. 116.
12 Sarah A. Curtis, *Educating the Faithful: Religion, Schooling, and Society in Nineteenth-Century France* (Dekalb, Illinois: Northern Illinois Press, 2000), p. 45.
13 J. Derek Holmes, *More Roman than Rome: English Catholicism in the Nineteenth Century* (London: Burns and Oates, 1978), pp. 19–52. See Chapter 2 above for more on nineteenth-century English Catholicism.

the prerogative of the English gentry and aristocracy. They upheld their high status by requesting a substantial dowry for entry and this served to monitor the social origins of the women who entered their orders. Women from the English gentry and aristocracy did enter active, simple-vowed congregations, but preferred French, Belgian or Irish congregations rather than native English congregations. Susan O'Brien suggests that this had to do with social compatibility and class as well as ethnicity.[14] An analysis in greater detail of the ethnicity of the ten congregations examined in this book sheds some light on additional factors that linked religious institutes and ethnicity.

The first foreign simple-vowed congregation to found a convent in England, the Faithful Companions of Jesus, was a relatively young congregation, established in France by Marie Madeleine Victoire de Bengy d'Houët in 1820. Her reasons for expanding to England were related as much to security and survival as they were to mission. Religious institutes were the target of anti-clerical activity during the French Revolution, and this anti-clericalism re-emerged periodically in nineteenth-century France. Political turmoil, as well as missionary objectives, encouraged many French religious congregations to expand their networks of branch convents outside France. Many relocated to nearby England as a precautionary measure, considering that if anti-clerical activity threatened their communities in France, they could quickly cross the Channel to the safe haven of established convents in England. The outbreak of the revolution of 1830 was a cause for great concern; the safety of D'Houët's fledgling congregation, then consisting of ten convents spread throughout France, was at risk. She considered founding new convents outside France, and a Jesuit advisor provided the link to exiled priest, John Joseph Henry Nérincks, who was ministering to the French émigré community at Somers Town, London, and was looking for a religious congregation to manage his girls' boarding school. On 19 October 1830, Marie Madeleine Victoire de Bengy d'Houët and Mère Julie (Marguerite Julie Guillemet) departed for England to survey London as a possible site for their first non-continental convent. Finding the situation in Somers Town amenable, they took possession of the boarding school on 16 November 1830.[15]

14 Susan O'Brien, '"Terra Incognita": The Nun in Nineteenth-Century England', *Past and Present*, 121 (1988), 110–40 (p. 135).
15 *The Early History of the Society of the Sisters Faithful Companions of Jesus as related in the Memoirs of the Venerable Marie Madeleine Victoire de Bengy Viscountess de Bonnault d'Houët*, translated by Patricia Grogan FCJ (Margate: FCJ Martell Press, 1981), pp. 46–50.

The Faithful Companions were not the only congregation to select England for reasons of safety and mission. As can be seen in Table 7.1, among the eighty religious congregations that founded convents in England in the nineteenth century, French-founded institutes dominated; they comprised fifty-four per cent of all congregations.[16] Decade after decade, with the exception of the 1830s, the majority of congregations founding their first convents in England came from France. This was not simply due to anti-religious sentiment in France. Despite the political vicissitudes, persecution of religious institutes in nineteenth-century France did not reach the extremes of the French Revolution. Active, simple-vowed congregations, unlike contemplative orders, were considered productive entities by French civil administrations, and despite the fervent Catholicism of their members, many congregations remained functional in France.[17] French foundations were numerous for other reasons also. Catholic connections to France were strong and French congregations were well known to clergy and bishops in England. Hundreds of French clergymen emigrated to England; approximately six per cent of the Catholic clergy who worked in England between 1801 and 1914 were French-born.[18] Susan O'Brien has noted that many priests and bishops 'looked to France for a ready-made supply of properly formed and trained religious sisters who came from a culture which . . .

16 Susan O'Brien, 'Religious Life for Women', in V. Alan McClelland and Michael Hodgetts, eds, *From without the Flaminian Gate: 150 Years of Roman Catholicism in England and Wales 1850–2000* (London: Darton Longman + Todd, 1999), pp. 108–41 (p. 114). O'Brien notes sixty-two foundations by 1887, of which thirty-two were French and five were Belgian.

17 Nicholas Atkin, 'The Politics of Legality: The Religious Orders in France, 1901–45' in Frank Tallett and Nicholas Atkin, eds, *Religion, Society and Politics in France Since 1789* (London: The Hambledon Press, 1991), pp. 149–66 (p. 150); Lynn Jarrell OSU, 'The Development of Legal Structures for Women Religious between 1500 and 1900: A Study of Selected Institutes of Religious Life for Women', doctoral thesis, Catholic University of America, 1984, p. 303.

18 Charles Fitzgerald-Lombard, *English and Welsh Priests 1801–1914: A Working List* (Bath, England: Downside Abbey, 1993). This book contains brief biographical sketches of all known priests (8,753) working in England and Wales in the nineteenth century. My analysis by their country of birth indicates that 496 priests working in England and Wales from 1801 to 1914 were French-born. Unfortunately, the country of birth for 39.3 per cent, or 3,436, of the priests listed is unknown so the number of French-born priests is likely to be understated.

Table 7.1 Countries of origin of congregations founded in England and Wales, 1801–1900

| Decade | France | England | Belgium | Italy | Germany | Ireland | Netherlands | India | Total | % French foundations each decade | % of foundations each decade |
|---|---|---|---|---|---|---|---|---|---|---|---|
| 1801–10 | 0 | 0 | 0 | 0 | 0 | 0 | 0 | 0 | 0 | – | – |
| 1811–20 | 0 | 0 | 0 | 0 | 0 | 0 | 0 | 0 | 0 | – | – |
| 1821–30 | 1 | 0 | 0 | 0 | 0 | 0 | 0 | 0 | 1 | 100.0 | 1.3 |
| 1831–40 | 0 | 0 | 0 | 0 | 0 | 2 | 0 | 0 | 2 | – | 2.5 |
| 1841–50 | 4 | 1 | 1 | 1 | 0 | 0 | 0 | 0 | 7 | 57.1 | 8.8 |
| 1851–60 | 6 | 5 | 0 | 1 | 0 | 0 | 0 | 0 | 13 | 53.8 | 16.3 |
| 1861–70 | 6 | 3 | 4 | 0 | 0 | 0 | 1 | 0 | 14 | 42.9 | 17.5 |
| 1871–80 | 10 | 1 | 1 | 0 | 2 | 0 | 0 | 0 | 14 | 71.4 | 17.5 |
| 1881–90 | 8 | 3 | 2 | 2 | 0 | 1 | 0 | 1 | 15 | 53.3 | 18.8 |
| 1891–1900 | 7 | 2 | 2 | 2 | 1 | 0 | 0 | 0 | 14 | 50.0 | 17.5 |
| Total | 43 | 15 | 10 | 4 | 3 | 3 | 1 | 1 | 80 | – | 100.0 |
| % total | 53.8 | 18.8 | 12.5 | 5.0 | 3.8 | 3.8 | 1.3 | 1.3 | | | |

Source: Appendix.

educated English people admired'.[19] Many religious congregations culti-
vated this continental preference; convent boarding schools advertised
their qualifications in the *Catholic Directory* and *The Tablet* and offered
a 'French education'. The Society of the Sacred Heart declared that its
Acton establishment was 'decidedly French' and 'the whole system pre-
cisely the same as that at Sacre Coeur, Paris'.[20] Sister Clarie (Clarisse
Noel), writing about one postulant to Mère Constantine, noted that the
postulant was educated in Paris and then remarked, 'People appreciate
us for French but not for English'.[21] Despite this propensity to found convents in England, few French sisters remained in or were transferred to
England after the initial foundation. Of a sample of 2,440 women from
four French-founded congregations, only four per cent, ninety-two
women, were French-born.[22]

The Irish pattern of convent foundations in England differed from that
of the French.[23] French congregations were often centralised, and each
founded one initial convent in England. Local women entered French
congregations and this led to further convent foundations. Irish religious
institutes tended to be decentralised and each might found more than one
convent in England. Only three Irish congregations opened convents in
nineteenth-century England, but these three congregations sent foundation teams from Ireland that established sixteen convents prior to 1900.[24]
The Sisters of Mercy founded their first convent in Bermondsey in 1839

19 Susan O'Brien, 'French Nuns in Nineteenth-Century England', *Past and Present*, 154 (1997), 142–80 (p. 149). This essay discusses in great detail the factors that 'pulled' French congregations to found convents in England.
20 *Catholic Directory* (1844), p. 115.
21 SND: PN.h/1 'English Translation of Letters to Namur', letter dated 2 November 1845 from Soeur Claire (Clarisse Noel) to Mère Constantine.
22 These four congregations were the Sisters of Charity of St Paul the Apostle, the Daughters of Charity of St Vincent de Paul, the Faithful Companions of Jesus (which contributed fifty-three sisters – almost sixty per cent of the French-born sisters) and the Daughters of the Heart of Mary. The Sisters of Notre Dame de Namur were actually founded in Namur, Belgium, and con-tributed only two French-born sisters and thirteen Belgian-born sisters to their congregation in nineteenth-century England.
23 This is only a cursory discussion of migration patterns of religious institutes. More research would allow for a better understanding of the international expansion of women's religious institutes.
24 In the nineteenth century, fourteen Sisters of Mercy convents were founded in England and Wales from various convents in Ireland; one Presentation convent was founded in Manchester in 1836; and the Irish Sisters of Charity founded one convent in 1890.

and quickly dominated the number of conventual establishments and the number of religious sisters in England. Fourteen convents were founded by the Sisters of Mercy directly from Ireland; another seventy-six convents were founded by the original fourteen and their progeny by 1900. This remarkable pattern of expansion may reflect the popularity among bishops of their decentralised government structure.[25]

Table 7.2 reveals another aspect of ethnicity: Irish-born women were a dominant presence in convents in England. In the sample of ten congregations, forty-one per cent were Irish-born compared with forty-six per cent who were English-born. The immediate question that arises, one unfortunately inadequately answered by extant sources, was whether these Irish-born women had specifically immigrated to join religious congregations in England or were members of Irish immigrant families who had settled in England for economic reasons. Congregations in England needed more women religious than could be found locally; Ireland was a natural recruiting ground owing to its proximity, its abundance of Catholic women and their willingness to emigrate.[26] Some congregations in England regularly quested for postulants in Ireland. Mother M. Evangelista (Honoria Gaffney) faced a shortage of postulants and travelled to her home town in Ireland in search of women interested in religious life in England.[27] The Irish-born Holy Child sisters M. Aloysius (Eugenie Ryan) and M. Walburga (Mary Theresa White) journeyed to Ireland in 1894 in search of potential postulants.[28] Probably the most vocal recruiter of Irish-born women was Frances Taylor, founder of the Poor Servants of the Mother of

25  More on this in Chapter 8.
26  Research on nineteenth-century patterns of Irish emigration demonstrates that unmarried Irish women frequently migrated, with and without their families, as a result of the economic conditions in Ireland, both before and after the Great Famine. Hasia Diner, *Erin's Daughters in America: Irish Immigrant Women in the Nineteenth Century* (Baltimore, Maryland, USA: The John Hopkins University Press, 1983); Charlotte MacDonald, *A Woman of Good Character: Single Women as Immigrant Settlers in Nineteenth-Century New Zealand* (Wellington, New Zealand: Bridget William Books, 1990); Janet A. Nolan, *Ourselves Alone: Women's Emigration from Ireland, 1885–1920* (Lexington, Kentucky: University Press of Kentucky, 1989).
27  CSJP: Catherine Ferguson CSJP, 'Sisters of St Joseph of Peace: History of the Sacred Heart Province, 1884–1984', 1983, p. 36. One-third of the professed sisters who entered in nineteenth-century England were from Roscommon County, Mother M. Evangelista's county of birth.
28  SHCJ: Anne Murphy, 'SHCJ and Ireland', in *History Society of the Holy Child Jesus: Beginnings* (1996), pp. 47–51 (p. 47).

Table 7.2 Countries of birth of entrants (subsequently professed) in ten congregations, 1801–1900

| Congregation | Total | England | % | Ireland | % | Other | Not known |
|---|---|---|---|---|---|---|---|
| Sisters of Mercy | 1,340 | 686 | 51.2 | 451 | 33.7 | 83 | 120 |
| Sisters of Charity of St Paul the Apostle | 690 | 291 | 42.2 | 349 | 50.6 | 32 | 18 |
| Daughters of Charity of St Vincent de Paul | 715 | 230 | 32.2 | 406 | 56.8 | 74 | 5 |
| Notre Dame de Namur | 854 | 549 | 64.3 | 222 | 26.0 | 73 | 10 |
| Faithful Companions of Jesus | 897 | 367 | 40.9 | 428 | 47.7 | 98 | 4 |
| Poor Servants of the Mother of God | 276 | 21 | 7.6 | 200 | 72.5 | 3 | 52 |
| Society of the Holy Child Jesus | 348 | 225 | 64.7 | 61 | 17.5 | 34 | 28 |
| Daughters of the Heart of Mary | 138 | 82 | 59.4 | 29 | 21.0 | 22 | 5 |
| St Joseph of Peace | 39 | 1 | 2.6 | 38 | 97.4 | 0 | 0 |
| St Joseph of Annecy | 68 | 8 | 11.8 | 32 | 47.1 | 27 | 1 |
| Total | 5,365 | 2,460 | 45.9 | 2,216 | 41.3 | 446 | 243 |

*Source*: Appendix.

God. Taylor made the 'great round of Convents – Presentation, Mercy, Loreto, Faithful Companions, Irish Sisters of Charity, French Dominicans' and remarked that she was 'molta contenta' as she met with 'kind charitable nuns' and returned to England with numerous qualified postulants.[29] In 1870, Taylor's three weeks in Ireland netted fifty applications from aspirants.[30] She referred to the newly accepted 'band of postulants' from Ireland as 'pure, innocent and pious even amidst the dangers of Dublin'.[31] These Irish-born women were an important part of the dynamic growth of religious congregations in England.

29  SMG: I/A3b, letter dated 19 July from Frances Taylor to the Roman community.
30  SMG: I/B 'Annals of the Congregation of the Poor Servants of the Mother of God Mary Immaculate in England', 1870, p. 7. Devas noted that she was able to accept only five of the applicants. F.C. Devas SJ, *Mother Mary Magdalen of the Sacred Heart (Fanny Margaret Taylor): Foundress of the Poor Servants of the Mother of God 1832–1900* (London: Burns, Oates & Washbourne, 1927), p. 143.
31  SMG: I/F3 (volume 3 of 5), p. 251a, letter dated 13 July 1891 from Frances Taylor to Alexander Fullerton.

If one looks at the entry of women into these ten congregations by decade, what becomes clear in Table 7.3 is that until the 1860s, the majority of women entering congregations were English-born. Irish-born women began to enter women's congregations in larger numbers in the 1860s, and by the 1870s, more Irish-born women entered English congregations than did English-born women. This pattern diverges from the general pattern of Irish migration, in which Irish-born inhabitants of England began to drop both in numbers and as a percentage of the total population after the 1861 census. This suggests that after the 1860s, Irish-born women were crossing the Irish Sea specifically to enter English convents or that more Irish-born women already living in England were finding religious life an attractive alternative. Educated Irish women may have found more opportunities for a vocation in England than in Ireland. Mary Peckham Magray and Suellen Hoy have noted that many Irish women emigrated to North America and Australia because large dowries were not required to be a choir sister.[32] Similarly, Irish women may have found congregations in England less restrictive with regard to dowry requirements. Or Irish-born women may have emigrated to England out of a sense of mission in order to minister to their own countrymen and countrywomen. An examination of some of the native English congregations may provide some further explanations for this phenomenon.

### Native English congregations

Some of the native English congregations offered a model of religious life that differed from that existing in French, Belgian or Irish congregations founded in England. They created opportunities for pious women who did not have sufficient financial resources to enter these religious congregations. This alone was not unusual: many congregations (as will be discussed later in this chapter) accepted dowerless women as lay sisters. But some English congregations, like the Little Company of Mary, did not have the two-tiered structure so prevalent in many congregations; they were not divided into lay and choir sisters. In addition, the Little Company of Mary demanded no dowry; the founder, Mary Potter, received women of ability regardless of their financial means.[33] And,

32  Mary Peckham Magray, *The Transforming Power of the Nuns: Women, Religion, and Cultural Change in Ireland, 1750–1900* (Oxford: Oxford University Press, 1998), p. 105; Suellen Hoy, 'The Journey Out: The Recruitment and Emigration of Irish Religious Women to the United States, 1812–1914', *Journal of Women's History*, 6/7 (1995), 64–98, (p. 64).
33  West, 2000, p. 88.

Table 7.3 Countries of birth of entrants (subsequently professed) in each decade in ten congregations, 1801–1900

|  | English-born | % | Irish-born | % | Other | Not known | Total | % |
|---|---|---|---|---|---|---|---|---|
| 1801–1810 | 0 | – | 0 | – | 0 | 0 | 0 | – |
| 1811–1820 | 0 | – | 0 | – | 0 | 0 | 0 | – |
| 1821–1830 | 1 | – | 1 | – | 0 | 0 | 2 | – |
| 1831–1840 | 11 | 0.0 | 10 | 27.8 | 14 | 1 | 36 | 0.7 |
| 1841–1850 | 160 | 0.1 | 58 | 23.1 | 27 | 6 | 251 | 4.7 |
| 1851–1860 | 401 | 0.2 | 247 | 35.6 | 19 | 26 | 693 | 12.9 |
| 1861–1870 | 413 | 0.2 | 309 | 38.0 | 64 | 28 | 814 | 15.2 |
| 1871–1880 | 432 | 0.2 | 509 | 50.3 | 25 | 46 | 1,012 | 18.9 |
| 1881–1890 | 552 | 0.2 | 547 | 44.3 | 73 | 64 | 1,236 | 23.0 |
| 1891–1900 | 468 | 0.2 | 535 | 41.9 | 205 | 68 | 1,276 | 23.8 |
| Unknown | 22 |  | 0 |  | 19 | 4 | 45 | 0.8 |
| Total | 2,460 |  | 2,216 |  | 446 | 243 | 5,365 | 100.0 |
| % Total | 45.9 |  | 41.3 |  | 8.3 | 4.5 |  |  |

*Source*: Appendix 1.

some congregations specifically recruited lower-middle-class and working-class women as women religious.

One of these congregations was Elizabeth Prout's Sisters of the Most Holy Cross and Passion, founded in Manchester in 1851. Clerics attempted to discourage the middle-class convert Mary Taylor from entering the congregation of the Most Holy Cross and Passion as they insisted that it 'was not a religious Order; it was only a lot of factory girls'. Many of the early professed sisters in this congregation worked in the factories and mills, and Manchester clerics opposed the congregation's development and expansion on the grounds that they feared that it was not respectable. Taylor entered despite clerical disapproval and later described how the congregation experienced 'the most determined opposition from all the priests in their neighbourhood, who treated them as persons devoid of reason for attempting the foundation of a new institute under what seemed to them such unfavourable circumstances'.[34] The Franciscan Missionaries of St Joseph, founded by Alice Ingham, herself a daughter of a cotton-carder and milliner, also accepted working-class women; at least one-third of the women who entered prior to 1900 were former mill-workers.[35] Margaret Hallahan, orphaned at the age of eleven,

34 Edna Hamer, *Elizabeth Prout, 1820–1864: A Religious Life for Industrial England* (Bath, England: Downside Abbey, 1994), pp. 74–80.
35 O'Brien, 1999, p. 117.

worked as a domestic servant in several households before she founded the Dominican Sisters of St Catherine of Siena in 1844 at the age of forty-two. Hallahan explained the reasoning behind her congregation's working-class membership: 'It seems to me that Our Lord will make use of our Order to break through the custom which has crept into England, that scarcely any were allowed to enter religion but the aristocracy, thus shutting the way of perfection and sanctity to the multitude'.[36]

The Irish-born Anne O'Brien had dreamed of becoming a nun, but at the age of twenty-two, she was living in a Protestant household, possibly supporting her widowed mother and younger siblings, and saw 'no way of getting into a convent'. She had no dowry to give and was short-sighted, which she understood as an impediment to entry into religious life. She read in the newspaper a small article written by Georgiana Fullerton about the newly founded Poor Servants of the Mother of God, which accepted pious women with a religious vocation but limited means. In 1871, she travelled to London to meet Frances Taylor, founder of the congregation.[37] Two years later, she was a professed sister and by 1875, as Sister Mary Gertrude, she was the assistant and novice mistress of this growing congregation. The Poor Servants of the Mother of God, founded in 1869, were another English congregation that regularly accepted women without dowries.[38] In the early years, they subsidised their philanthropic work through donations, laundry work, needlework and the operation of a printing press. Their 'works of mercy' ranged from visiting the poor (in their homes, in workhouses and in hospitals), organising mothers' meetings, preparing adults and children for the

36 Sylvia Pinches, 'Roman Catholic Charities and Voluntary Societies in the Diocese of Birmingham, 1834–1945' (master's thesis, University of Leicester, 1997), p. 25. Cited from Margaret Hallahan's *Positio*, document VII, located in the archives of the Dominican Convent in Stone, Staffordshire. Letter dated 1850 from Margaret Hallahan to Rev. Domini Aylward, O.P. Provincial.
37 SMG: I/D 'Sister Alacoque's Annals', p. 11.
38 Thirty-nine per cent of the sisters who entered the Poor Servants of the Mother of God entered without a dowry. Thirty-two per cent gave a dowry, and half of these dowries were less than £50. For the remaining twenty-nine per cent of the sisters listed in the profession register, no amount is entered in the dowry column, and it seems likely that they did not give a dowry. Unfortunately, there has been little work on calculating average dowry amounts in the nineteenth century. Barbara Walsh's work, which includes sisters who entered congregations up to 1937, indicates that dowry amounts for the Sisters of the Sacred Hearts of Jesus and Mary were usually around £120. Barbara Walsh, *Roman Catholic Nuns in England and Wales,*

sacraments, teaching at poor schools and managing refuges, hospitals and infirmaries. Frances Taylor continually stressed that 'Ours is the lowliest of all Congregations.'[39] This was not meant to denigrate the congregation; Taylor believed that such lowliness led to holy perfection. The congregation's social status proved attractive to some candidates. Dora Dean, niece of Frances Taylor, preferred the Poor Servants of the Mother of God to the 'lot of ladies at the Sacre Coeur'. Dean's comment alludes to the differences in social status between religious institutes in England; she purposely joined a congregation that she believed was 'despised and looked down on'.[40]

These English-founded congregations offered opportunities for dowerless middle- and working-class women to enter religious congregations where they were actively involved in their 'works of mercy' and internal government.

## Social composition of congregations

As the comment of Thomas Marshall, quoted above, indicates, women's religious congregations were often imagined as homogenous institutions whose membership included 'ladies' who belonged to a 'higher grade' of society. However, this was not always the case. Prescriptive literature gives the first hint of this varied social composition among and within congregations. In some congregations, sisters were urged to behave like ladies. Frances Taylor wrote to local superiors instructing them to 'Try hard to refine your Community: <u>good manners – a correct way of speaking – avoiding any roughness</u>, and <u>too loud laughing</u> – all so important. Try and get your Sisters to have an <u>ambition</u> to improve in this respect.'[41] Another sister remembered that 'Mother used to try and teach us good manners. She used to say we ought to try and be as polite as ladies, living in God's own house.'[42] Mary Potter, founder of the Little Company of

*1800–1937: A Social History* (Dublin: Irish Academic Press, 2002), p. 105. Mary Peckham Magray has noted that dowries in Ireland ranged from £500 to £600 but that after the Great Famine dowry amounts dropped to £200–£300. Magray, 1998, pp. 36–7.

39  SMG: 'Mother Foundress' Letters to the Institute (1877–1900)', 1957, p. 171.
40  SMG: I/A3a, p. 65, letter dated 9 February 1887 from Frances Taylor to unknown Sister.
41  SMG: 'Notes of Conferences given to Local Superiors by Mother Foundress, Mother Mary Magdalen of the Sacred Heart Poor Servant of the Mother of God', p. 16, letter dated 18 August 1897 from Frances Taylor to local Superiors.
42  SMG: 'Mother as We Knew Her', 1957, p. 68.

Mary, took 'great pains' to teach her sisters the 'the correct pronuncia-
tion of the Latin for our office, and gave us many a lesson on Religious
decorum . . .'[43] This prescriptive literature, focusing as it does on polite-
ness, pointed to expectations of gentility among religious sisters but also
hints that perhaps the women entering religious congregations were not
all well-versed in the Victorian ideal of lady-like behaviour.

Another way to examine the homogeneity of women's congregations
is to examine the social composition of individual religious communities.
The profession registers of the Sisters of Charity of St Paul the Apostle[44]
and the Daughters of Charity of St Vincent de Paul noted the father's
occupation for many of their professed sisters.[45] The Sisters of Charity of
St Paul the Apostle had education as their primary focus in the nineteenth
century and the sisters typically taught in small parish schools, managed
orphanages and involved themselves in parish visiting and religious
instruction. They made their first foundation in Banbury, England, in
1847, and by the end of the century, the mother house in Selly Park,
Birmingham oversaw fifty-four convents throughout England and Wales.
They were the second largest congregation in England and Wales.[46] The
Daughters of Charity of St Vincent de Paul were founded in Sheffield in
1857.[47] By the end of the nineteenth century, forty-one additional convents and numerous institutions were being managed by the Daughters
of Charity and they were the third largest congregation in England. They
managed a variety of institutions: crèches, orphanages, industrial, day
and night schools, reformatories, schools for the blind and homes for the
poor, working girls and the disabled. They were equally active in religious instruction and parish visiting. There were similarities between the
two congregations. Both were founded from France; neither had the division of lay and choir sisters. Both were flexible in terms of the 'works of
mercy' that they performed; they met the needs of the localities they

43  Little Company of Mary Archives, Nottingham: 14/4 'Recollections of
    Mother M. Cecilia Smith & Mother M. Catherine Crocker', 1878.
44  Barbara Walsh also examines the social composition of the Sisters of Charity
    of St Paul the Apostle, but her analysis covers 1847–1926 and focuses
    heavily on the Irish component. Walsh, 2002, pp. 141–9.
45  See the Appendix for methodology.
46  The relative size of each congregation is judged by the number of convents
    founded by the congregation.
47  The Daughters of Charity of St Vincent de Paul founded their first convent
    in Salford in 1847, but after one sister was physically accosted and the
    convent was set on fire, they returned to France in 1849. Their second foun-
    dation attempt in 1857 was more successful. DC: *Sisters of Charity of Saint
    Vincent de Paul in Great Britain and Ireland* (1955), p. 14.

Table 7.4 Classes of professed sisters in two congregations, 1847–1900

| Class | Occupational groupings | SCSP | % | DC | % | Total | % |
|-------|------------------------|------|-----|------|-------|-------|------|
| I | Professional occupations | 36 | 5.2 | 112 | 15.7 | 148 | 10.5 |
| I/II | Professional and intermediate occupations | 35 | 5.1 | 61 | 8.5 | 96 | 6.8 |
| II | Intermediate occupations | 269 | 39.0 | 357 | 49.9 | 626 | 44.6 |
| III/IV/V | Skilled/partly skilled/ unskilled | 158 | 22.9 | 136 | 19.0 | 294 | 20.9 |
| – | Unknown | 192 | 27.8 | 49 | 6.9 | 241 | 17.2 |
| Total | | 690 | 100.0 | 715 | 100.0 | 1,405 | 100.0 |
| % total | | | 49.1 | | 50.9 | | 100.0 |

*Source*: Appendix.

served. They had approximately the same number of sisters, although the Sisters of Charity of St Paul the Apostle had smaller convents and were less likely to manage large institutions.

The analysis of occupations uncovered other similarities and differences between the congregations.[48] Table 7.4 shows that approximately forty-nine per cent of the Sisters of Charity of St Paul the Apostle had fathers whose livelihoods were classified as professional and intermediate occupations (Classes I and II). Fathers of these professed sisters were property owners, architects, builders, contractors, accountants, insurance agents, clerks and solicitors. Seventy-four per cent of the women who entered the Daughters of Charity of St Vincent de Paul were also from Class I or II. Among the various occupations that were included in Class I, landowner's daughters made up one per cent of the Sisters of Charity of St Paul the Apostle and ten per cent of the Daughters of Charity of St Vincent de Paul. This ten per cent included some illustrious members of the Catholic aristocracy: there were Petres, Fieldings, Howards, Langdales, Arundels and Taafes who were professed Daughters of Charity.

The daughters of the English Catholic aristocracy and gentry were expected to enter the higher-status solemn-vowed, contemplative orders, but in the nineteenth century, some entered simple-vowed congregations.

48 This analysis has some limitations. Twenty-eight per cent of the fathers' occupations were not documented by the Sisters of Charity of St Paul the Apostle. In most of these cases, the profession register simply noted that the father was deceased and no occupation was noted. The registers of the Daughters of Charity of St Vincent de Paul are more complete; only seven per cent of the entries were missing the father's occupation.

Eleanor Maxwell, daughter of Lord William Maxwell and a relation of the Duke of Norfolk, head of one of the most prominent Catholic families in England, entered the Daughters of Charity of St Vincent de Paul in 1861. Her necrology, excerpted below, emphasised her humility by comparing her worldly status with the life she led as a religious sister:

> On one occasion some Priest was being shown over the house, seeing a Sister with sleeves tucked up, and a large minage apron on, he asked 'Is that a lay Sister?'; the Priest who was with him, and who knew Sister Mary, said, 'She is the aunt of the Duchess of Norfolk.'[49]

Etheldreda Fitzalan Howard, daughter of the Duke of Norfolk, caused astonishment seven years later when she entered the Daughters of Charity. Her spiritual director was criticised:

> How could he think of directing his penitent to the Sisters of St. Vincent de Paul? Carmel, where her sister had entered several years before – well and good! Members of the highest nobility in France, even Queens and Princesses, had entered amongst the daughters of St. Teresa; but to be a Sister of Charity, where there are no lay Sisters, and where St. Vincent desired only 'good village girls,' where the life is hard and the work rough and even menial! What could Father Gordon be thinking of?[50]

Howard was sent to Carlisle Place in London and as Sister Mary spent her first nine years as a Daughter of Charity teaching boys and girls in the day school. She found that London children were 'not like the children at Arundel, who were so respectful to "Miss Ethel", but a crowd of more or less disciplined little people'.[51] Her necrologist also highlights her humility in her attempts to conceal her aristocratic connections:

> our dear Sister regarded no title so noble as that of Daughter of Charity, and did all in her power to hide her identity; her companions would often laughingly remark that this desire on her part to remain unknown was no compliment to her parents.[52]

One wonders, though, if the remarks of her companions were meant to be gentle teasing or whether they reflect some tension between women of different class backgrounds.[53] What is significant about the Daughters of

---

49  DC: *Notes on Deceased Sisters* (1924–25), p. 2.
50  Ibid (1928–29), p. 75.
51  Ibid, p. 77.
52  Ibid, p. 86.
53  [Mary Austin Carroll], *Leaves from the Annals of the Sisters of Mercy*, 3 vols (New York: The Catholic Publication Society, 1881), I, p. 357. Carroll mentions tensions regarding Lady Barbara Eyre's entry into the Sisters of Mercy.

Charity was the frequency with which the Catholic aristocracy and gentry entered this congregation, which had no lay – choir divide and was lower in social status than contemplative orders. Founders Vincent de Paul and Louise de Marillac had intended that this institute be for 'rough village girls'. Yet, in England, as the analysis has shown, women of middle and upper classes entered the Daughters of Charity of St Vincent de Paul with great frequency.

The largest cohorts of women entering the two congregations from 1865 onwards belonged to Class II. The majority of the women in this class, in both congregations almost thirty-four per cent, were farmers' daughters, most of whom were Irish-born.[54] Perhaps it is not altogether surprising to find so many Irish farmers' daughters finding their place in English convents given the limited employment opportunities for Irish men and women during the agricultural depressions of the 1870s.[55] And this corresponds with the trend noted earlier in the chapter, that the greater number of Irish-born women entered the ten religious congregations sampled after 1870. The last occupational grouping to be examined is the skilled to unskilled grouping which made up Classes III, IV and V. Twenty-three per cent of the Sisters of Charity of St Paul the Apostle and nineteen per cent of the Daughters of Charity of St Vincent de Paul belonged in this grouping. These were typically daughters of tradesman, such as tailors, bootmakers, carpenters, etc. The majority of these women, fifty-seven per cent, were English-born, and thirty-four per cent were Irish-born.[56]

Despite the limitations of this study, particularly the missing data from the Sisters of Charity of St Paul the Apostle, it is possible to make some tentative comments about social class. It appears that women of the middle and working classes were more likely to enter the Sisters of Charity of St Paul the Apostle than the Daughters of Charity of St Vincent de Paul. This is corroborated by the trend documented in the analysis of the Class I occupational grouping, where the Daughters of Charity were found to be more attractive to upper-class women. This suggests that the elite women entering the Daughters of Charity may

54 Eighty per cent of the farmers' daughters in the Sisters of Charity of St Paul the Apostle and ninety-five per cent of the farmers' daughters in the Daughters of Charity of St Vincent de Paul were Irish-born.
55 Walsh, 2002, pp. 141–9. Walsh's book discusses this phenomenon in great detail. W.J. Smyth, 'The Making of Ireland: Agendas and Perspectives in Cultural Geography', in B.J. Graham and J. Proudfoot, eds, *A Historical Geography of Ireland* (London and New York: Academic Press, 1993).
56 The remainder were born elsewhere.

have raised its profile and status and encouraged more women of the higher classes to enter the congregation. There could be other structural reasons for this attraction. The Daughters of Charity managed many large institutions, whereas the Sisters of Charity of St Paul the Apostle were more likely to manage smaller institutions and work in parish schools. Perhaps the Daughters of Charity required more women with management skills than did the Sisters of Charity of St Paul the Apostle. Geography may also have been important. As was discussed in Chapter 1, the Sisters of Charity of St Paul the Apostle were relatively localised to the Midlands and the north, whereas the Daughters of Charity of St Vincent de Paul had a stronger presence in London and the south-east. Perhaps the cachet of London convents attracted women of the higher classes.

Also, these were not homogenous congregations; women religious came from many social classes. At least two out of ten sisters were from the professional classes (Class I and II) and two out of ten were from the skilled to unskilled labouring classes (Class III, IV and V). It was the 'middling sorts' that dominated the numbers of entrants. The daughters of merchants and civil servants filled the ranks of these two congregations and importantly, farming families from Ireland contributed many daughters to English congregations.

## Leadership and class

Did this heterogeneity of classes within congregations lead to more opportunities for women of the working class to become leaders in active, simple-vowed congregations?[57] The story is told of the 'pardonable motherly pride' of the Countess of Denbigh as she presented her daughter Edith Fielding to the Mother General of the Daughters of Charity of St Vincent de Paul in Paris in 1883. She declared that her daughter was 'capable of being made a Superioress at once'.[58] Fielding did indeed eventually take on many leadership roles in the Daughters of Charity, including that as the local superior of convents in Manchester, Dunfermline and Dover, before she left for mission work in China in 1903. However, women of the upper classes were not automatically given leadership roles within congregations. Lady Barbara Eyre, daughter of the Earl of Newburgh, joined the group of Catholic lay women organised by Father Peter Butler to care for the poor in Bermondsey

57 For this analysis, leadership is defined simply as holding the position of a mother superior.
58 DC: *Notes on Deceased Sisters* (1920–21), p. 117.

about a month or so after Elizabeth Agnew. When the decision was made to put the group on firmer footing and form a foundation of the Irish Sisters of Mercy, it was Agnew, daughter of General Agnew and cousin to the Member of Parliament Sir Andrew Agnew, who was selected along with Maria Taylor to enter the novitiate in Cork. Agnew was professed in Bermondsey in 1839, the year Lady Barbara Eyre began her postulancy and novitiate. As intended, it was Agnew who replaced Mother Mary Clare (Georgiana Moore), the mother superior at Cork who had been placed in Bermondsey as a temporary superior. When Agnew became superior in July 1841, Eyre, who had been professed a few months earlier, became the mother assistant. It appears likely that Agnew seemed more suited to lead the newly founded congregation than did Eyre. Six months later, Agnew's leadership was questioned and she was removed from office for not managing the Bermondsey congregation in accordance with the Sisters of Mercy constitutions. Mother Mary Clare Moore returned from Cork and was appointed superior and novice mistress of the Bermondsey convent.[59] No mother assistant was appointed. Eyre died eight years later, a respected member of the community and benefactress but one who did not hold any further leadership roles despite her aristocratic birth.

Margaret Furlong, later Sister M. Bernard, was born in Wexford in 1850 and entered the Poor Servants of the Mother of God in 1873. Little is known of her class background, but she did not contribute a dowry, and early convent correspondence indicates that she 'wants training' and had poor penmanship.[60] Like many other congregation sisters, she moved around from convent to convent, from London to Roehampton to Liverpool and Beaumont and even to convents in Rome and Paris.[61] Extant correspondence suggests that her transfers were due to her cleverness and ambition. In a letter to Mother M. Lucy (Maria Forrestal), Provincial of England and Ireland, the founder, Frances Taylor, wrote:

> You know Bernard will naturally <u>itch</u> to manage that laundry herself. Sisters never like obeying an inferior – it is most important that Bernard should not have the laundry on her back again, and that Spinola be allowed <u>fairly</u> and within limits her own way.[62]

59 RSM Bermondsey: 'Bermondsey Annals', 1838–39, pp. 12–27.
60 SMG: I/A3b letter dated 11 May [1891] from Frances Taylor to an unknown sister; letter dated 4 January 1898 from Frances Taylor to Mother Aloysius Austin (Margaret Busher).
61 Chapter 6 includes a discussion of convent transfers.
62 SMG: I/A2a, p. 74, letter dated 6 October 1885 from Frances Taylor to Sister M. Lucy (Maria Forrestal).

Taylor noted the tensions between these two sisters, and the reference to 'obeying an inferior' perhaps reflects a class difference between the two.[63] But Taylor also made note of Sister M. Bernard's ambitious nature. This 'good clever Sister' appeared to have the drive and the aptitude for management: she held responsibilities as a refectorian and housekeeper in the novitiate, later managed the laundry, and eventually became superior of the Liverpool, Roehampton and Paris convents.[64] It appears that her talent for leadership was recognized and utilised.

Table 7.5 allows us to analyse leadership in a less anecdotal manner. If we look at Classes I and I/II, we find that twenty-four per cent of the population of the Daughters of Charity of St Vincent de Paul were contributing one-third of the leaders. This high social class produced a greater than representative proportion of leaders. If we focus on those who did not become leaders in Class I, we find that seventy-two property owners' daughters did not take on leadership roles. It was possible that they did not have the skills, aptitude, personality or 'common sense' necessary for becoming a local superior.[65] Women belonging to Class II, most of whom were farmers' daughters, made up almost half of the population of the Daughters of Charity of St Vincent de Paul yet provided only forty-two per cent of the leadership.

The last grouping of Class III/IV/V, which includes daughters of carpenters, masons, painters and blacksmiths, made up nineteen per cent of the population and provided the Daughters of Charity of St Vincent de Paul with eighteen per cent of their leaders. These middle- and working-class women became leaders in proportion to their frequency in the population. Marta Danylewycz saw a similar pattern in her study of Quebecois congregations, and concluded that educated women of the lower classes could transcend their social origins to become leaders of a congregation.[66]

This analysis reflects only one congregation and, of course, cannot be taken as representative of all congregations. However, it points to a level of meritocracy in the Daughters of Charity of St Vincent de Paul. Although the majority of the leadership came from middle- and upper-

---

63  Sister M. Spinola entered with a dowry of £30; Sr M. Bernard did not contribute a dowry.
64  SMG: I/A3, letter dated 4 January 1898 from Frances Taylor to Mother Aloysius Austin (Margaret Busher).
65  These seventy-two women lived to an average age of sixty-four.
66  Marta Danylewycz, *Taking the Veil: An Alternative to Marriage, Motherhood, and Spinsterhood in Quebec, 1840–1920* (Toronto, Canada: McClelland and Stewart, 1987), p. 99.

Table 7.5 Occupational groupings and leadership of professed sisters in the Daughters of Charity of St Vincent de Paul, 1857–1900

| Class | Occupational groupings | Leaders | % | Non-leaders | % | Total | % |
|---|---|---|---|---|---|---|---|
| I | Professional occupations | 40 | 20.8 | 72 | 13.8 | 112 | 15.7 |
| I/II | Professional and intermediate occupations | 24 | 12.5 | 37 | 7.1 | 61 | 8.5 |
| II | Intermediate occupations | 80 | 41.7 | 277 | 53.0 | 357 | 49.9 |
| III/IV/V | Skilled/partly skilled/unskilled | 34 | 17.7 | 102 | 19.5 | 136 | 19.0 |
| – | Unknown | 14 | 7.3 | 35 | 6.7 | 49 | 6.9 |
| Total | | 192 | 100.0 | 523 | 100.0 | 715 | 100.0 |
| % total | | 26.9 | | 73.1 | | 100.0 | |

*Source*: Appendix.

class backgrounds, working-class women did become leaders in proportion to their frequency in the population. Ethnic origins are also important in this study of leadership, but in this congregation, being Irish-born or English-born made little difference with regard to leadership. Irish-born and English-born women were leaders in proportion to their frequency in the population.

## Lay sisters

The previous analysis of social composition looked specifically at two congregations that did not have the lay–choir social structure. However, this class dichotomy existed in many nineteenth-century congregations and is relevant to this chapter's examination of class, ethnicity and identity. It is difficult to write conclusively about lay and choir sisters and their relationships in the nineteenth century because the voice heard in most convent documents was typically the voice of the choir sister. In addition, much of the information regarding lay and choir sisters is found in prescriptive literature, such as constitutions, guides and manuals that may or may not represent the lived experience of the lay sister. Despite these limitations, these sources illustrate some important points about class and the lay–choir dichotomy in nineteenth-century congregations.

Dowry was an important factor in the distinction between a lay and a choir sister. In the initial years of a convent's foundation, it was likely that the specified dowry amounts would be strictly adhered to in order to assure the financial stability of a convent. But in some circumstances, in particular if a convent was financially stable or needed a particular skillset, insufficient dowry was not always a barrier to entry.

As mentioned in Chapter 2, the clergy played an important role in the dissemination of information about religious institutes, and they directed aspirants to the religious institute that they felt most suited their skills and class background. Mary Potter was drawn to the contemplative Carmelites but neither of her spiritual directors, the Redemptorist Peter Burke and Bishop Thomas Grant, thought it 'reasonable' for her to enter the Carmelites[67] as a lay sister. Burke advised her that there was 'No question of you being a lay sister' and pointed her to congregations that would accept her as a choir sister. The division between lay and choir sister was not fixed at a specific point in the social scale.[68] Mary Potter's middle-class education expanded her options for religious life as a choir sister in certain congregations. Burke offered Potter the following advice:

> I fancy you lean to some active Order. Then the question is: whether your attrait [sic] is merely for teaching children. In that case 'Notre Dame' would suit you and is easily entered. The order looks more to the subject than to her dowry. If you relish teaching and visiting the sick and poor, then, for my part, I would prefer the Sisters of Charity otherwise known as 'of St. Vincent de Paul'. Money, I imagine, is no great difficulty there either . . . I have given you a standard or gauge by which you can measure yourself.[69]

Burke and Grant pushed aside Potter's desire to enter a contemplative order. Possibly they felt she was unsuited for a cloistered life or the physical labours of a lay sister, or maybe the needs of a growing Catholic population led them to suggest religious life in active congregations. Burke suggested that the Sisters of Notre Dame de Namur or the Daughters of Charity of St Vincent de Paul, both active, simple-vowed congregations, could be more flexible with regard to dowry as they were both well established, financially stable congregations and the work they performed, teaching, was frequently waged. Future wages were an adequate substitute for a dowry. Education, especially in the latter part of the century, was an asset that could be used as a dowry. Cornelia Connelly, founder of the teaching congregation of the Society of the Holy Child Jesus, wrote to Bishop Thomas Grant regarding the postulant Marian McKay, a

67  West, 2000, p. 20.
68  O'Brien, 'Lay-Sisters', 1990, p. 455.
69  West, 2000, p. 20. Cited from Little Company of Mary Archives, Tooting Bec, London, Letters K: letter dated 14 November 1868 from Peter Burke to Mary Potter.

former student and current teacher in the Holy Child schools, 'She has no other dower than her education.'[70] In another letter written in 1871, Connelly referred to Helen Milanesi, a former pupil, who 'has no fortune, but her education takes its place & her pension at Mayfield will be paid on the Novices fund'.[71] There was great value in McKay's and Milanesi's education as it prepared them to become teachers in the Holy Child schools. The dowry requirements could be waived in some circumstances. Not all congregations were so flexible. Susan O'Brien has noted that the Institute of the Blessed Virgin Mary and the Society of the Sacred Heart were looking for 'qualities that could not be acquired in a teacher-training establishment'.[72] These congregations were much more likely to hold firm on their dowry requirements in order to encourage a higher class of postulant.

Convent literature indicates that from the spiritual perspective, it made little difference whether a sister was employed as a laundress or a local superior. Religious perfection was an achievable goal for both lay and choir sisters:

> The perfection of the Lay Sisters is as dear to God as that of the Choir Sisters; and their religious spirit and training is equally important to the Community of which they form part. Superiors, therefore are under the same obligations with regard to them as to the Choir Sisters, and it is their duty to have their religious and domestic training most carefully attended to.[73]

There was a nuanced reverence in convent literature for the lay sister and domestic work. Mercy choir sisters were told they should 'never forget that the Lay Sisters are, equality with themselves, the spouses of Christ, and are very dear to Him, because they represent, in a particular manner, His state of humiliation when He came not to be served but to serve'.[74] There was a certain prestige in being humble and subordinate. The Mercy *Guide* acknowledged that the 'perfection of the Lay Sisters is as dear to God as that of the Choir Sisters; and their religious spirit and training is equally important to the Community of which they form

---

70 SHCJ: Vol. XIII, p. 34, letter dated 1 July [1862] from Cornelia Connelly to Bishop Thomas Grant.
71 SHCJ: Vol. 49, p. 173, letter dated 24 February 1871 from Cornelia Connelly to Canon Danell.
72 O'Brien, 'Lay-Sisters', 1990, p. 455.
73 RSM Handsworth: [M. Francis Bridgeman RSM], *Guide for the Religious Called Sisters of Mercy. Amplified by Quotations, Instructions, &c. Part I. & II.* (London: Robson and Son, 1866), part III, 1866, p. 113. Referenced as *Guide* in later citations.
74 Ibid, p. 110.

part'.[75] Susan O'Brien has suggested that necrologies contain further evidence that lay sisters had special 'moral and spiritual privileges and insights' and were regarded as having close contacts with saints, the Virgin Mary and St Joseph.[76]

However, Victorian sensibilities did not recognise this sort of parity in the earthly sphere. There was a clear hierarchy of authority and power in religious congregations. Class background, formal education and practical skills influenced the positions that women religious held within the congregation. Elizabeth Langland has explored middle-class women's experiences and power and has noted that 'upper middle-class women cooperated and participated with men to achieve control managing the cultural capital that secured their own pre-eminence and authority in contrast to both the working class and the lower-middle classes'.[77] This aspect of power pertained to religious communities as well, and it was most clearly seen in congregations with a lay–choir dichotomy. Choir sisters used their status and their class to uphold their power in the congregation. Their dominance was reflected in the ways in which the lay–choir split segregated sisters: from the habits they wore to the titles by which they were addressed and the work they performed in the congregation. Even in those congregations where there was no lay–choir split, subtle differentiation underscored the significance of class background to one's position in a congregation.[78] Nineteenth-century commentators, for the most part, did not find this class dichotomy unusual.

The physical separation between lay and choir sisters often reinforced the difference in classes. This separation typically began at the reception and clothing ceremonies. Susan O'Brien has noted that the choir sisters of the Institute of the Blessed Virgin Mary were clothed at major events and festivals, typically by the bishop. Ceremonies for lay sisters were typically performed by a chaplain or his deputy before Mass.[79] There were specific differences in the habits they wore. The habits of the Faithful Companions of Jesus coadjutrix sisters were 'half a hand's breadth shorter' and their cloaks were shorter than their habits.[80] The food they ate was the same,[81] but in some congregations their recreations were held

75  Ibid, p. 113.
76  O'Brien, 'Lay-Sisters', 1990, p. 460.
77  Elizabeth Langland, *Nobody's Angels: Middle-Class Women and Domestic Ideology in Victorian Culture* (London: Cornell University Press, 1995), p. 37.
78  O'Brien, 'Lay-Sisters', 1990, p. 454.
79  Ibid, p. 458.
80  FCJ: *Rules for the Coadjutrix Sisters* (Dublin: M.H. Gill & Son, 1882), p. 25.
81  RSM Handsworth: 1/200/4/1, *Guide*, part III, 1866, p. 110.

separately.[82] Their prayer life was different also; while the Office was said by both lay and choir sisters, the lay sisters prayed the Office in English and in low tones.[83] The Mercy *Guide* indicated that in order for lay sisters to be instructed in their spiritual exercises, they must have a place 'set apart for themselves' and 'they go to Confession and Communion after the junior choir Sister in each grade, as they always rank junior to them'.[84] These elaborate methods of separation, whether in dress, space or activities, revealed how women religious upheld the class system of difference within their convent spaces.

According to convent documents, some prospective lay sisters held expectations that were incompatible with their function as lay sisters. They imagined 'they can but enter a convent, labour, care, contradiction, &c,. will be at an end, and they will be free to spend all the time they please in reading pious books and saying their prayers'. These assumptions, according to the Mercy *Guide*, should be realigned to the expectations of the choir sisters, and 'the future duties and the nature of the state of a Lay Sister should be fully explained to her' as they 'rarely realise to themselves that they embrace a life of labour and subjection by becoming Lay Sisters; this, therefore should be strongly represented to them'.[85] The Mercy *Guide* went on to explain:

> It would be dangerous to profess one who does not value and esteem the state of Lay Sister, or who desires one more elevated: this evil ambition would probably be still more strongly and fatally developed by years, and lead to discontent and other evils.[86]

82  For example, in both the Sisters of Mercy and the Society of the Holy Child Jesus. RSM Handsworth: [M. Francis Bridgeman RSM], *Abridgment of a Guide for the Religious Called Sisters of Mercy* (London: Robson and Son, 1866), p. 121. The *Abridgment* does note that the mother superior and the majority of the vocals (voting sisters) can, with the approval of the bishop, admit lay sisters to the choir sisters' recreation. However, the lay sister 'must be aware that this is a concession not a right'. Sister Ursula Blake and Sister Annette Dawson, *Positio: Information for the Canonization Process of the Servant of God Cornelia Connelly (née Peacock) 1809–1879*, 3 vols (Rome: Sacred Congregation for the Causes of Saints, 1986), II, p. 806.

83  RSM Handsworth: 1/200/4/1, *Guide*, part III, 1866, p. 112. The inference here is that the choir sisters said the Office in Latin. However, Susan O'Brien's research has indicated that in some congregations, the Office was not usually said in Latin. O'Brien, 'Lay-Sisters', 1990, p. 459.

84  Ibid, p. 113.

85  Ibid, p. 109.

86  Ibid, p. 113.

Lay sisters were expected to live a life of 'labour and subjection' and
Victorian choir sisters equated desiring a life 'more elevated' with 'evil
ambition'. Similar expectations were noted in the 1872 annals of the
Institute of the Blessed Virgin Mary, which indicated that a 'spirit of independence and equality' existed among the working classes, and lay sisters
were trained with a 'more than ordinary amount of prudence'.[87] Cornelia
Connelly also hinted at the tensions between lay and choir sisters in her
correspondence:

> I recommend you to tell Sr. Gonzaga to be very kind & full of charity
> towards the Lay Sisters – Nothing but real kindness & charity will bring
> them to the truth; – and to satisfaction & contentment with the great grace
> of their vocation.[88]

Some lay sisters, according to this prescriptive literature, expected religious life to elevate their personal status and perhaps move them beyond
the status of domestic servants. But the force of Victorian ideas of class
was much more powerful; lay sisters, although they were undoubtedly
'spouses of Christ', were typically expected to function as domestic servants, albeit very pious and devout domestic servants.

And what about the ethnicity of lay sisters? Seventeen per cent of the
sisters who entered the Society of the Holy Child Jesus in the nineteenth
century were Irish-born and approximately twenty-four per cent were
lay sisters. Among those women who were professed as Faithful
Companions of Jesus, there was also a slightly higher proportion of Irish-
born lay sisters than in the convent population. Fifty-five per cent of the
lay sisters were Irish-born but only forty-eight per cent of the population
was Irish. It is difficult to make any general conclusions on data from
only two congregations. In addition, both congregations staffed large
boarding schools, where a relatively high number of lay sisters were necessary to meet the needs of the boarding school students. There is no
extant information on the work experience of lay sisters prior to their
entry into religious life, although Susan O'Brien's research on the Society
of the Sacred Heart's lay sisters indicates that many had been domestic
servants prior to their entry into the Society.[89]

87  O'Brien, 'Lay-Sisters', 1990, p. 459. Cited from IBVM Archives, York, MS
    Annals V6/2.1872, p. 42.
88  SHCJ: Vol. VIII, p. 11, letter dated 4 May [1873] from Cornelia Connelly to
    Mother Catherine (Maria Tracey).
89  O'Brien, 'Lay-Sisters', 1990, p. 458. Of the fifty-five coadjutrix sisters
    who had a recorded previous occupation, three-quarters were domestic
    servants.

## Conclusion

The influx and dramatic growth of active congregations in England and Wales in the nineteenth century brought greater opportunities for women to enter religious life. Congregations varied in the philanthropic works they performed, in the people they served and in the women they attracted and accepted into religious life. Religious life was no longer the province of the wealthy elite. Increasingly, women of limited means had the opportunity to enter religious life as something other than lay sisters. Working-class congregations encouraged and accepted women without dowries. As the century progressed, teaching credentials proved necessary and as important as dowries, and women with one and not the other could find a place in some teaching congregations. Women entering active, simple-vowed congregations in nineteenth-century England and Wales were entering congregations that were inclusive of women from all walks of life. This meant that congregations in England and Wales were not all internally homogenous. The variety of congregations gave women more options of where and how they would spend their religious life. There were opportunities to exceed the limitations of one's social background. However, lay sisters still had their place within active, simple-vowed congregations. There were often elaborate methods of separation and differentiation that reinforced the class system that existed at the time despite the rhetoric of spiritual equality. Class and to a lesser extent ethnicity were important determiners of the place that women religious held in their congregations.

# 8

# Authority and governance

We must go out and conquer the world without being afraid of the difficulties or snares it sets in our way. There must be nothing petty about a Sister of Notre Dame. She must have the strong heart of a man, and a generous soul filled with the spirit of the good God.[1]

This directive found in the *Book of the Instructions of Blessed Mère Julie* (1909) was uncompromising. The founder Julie Billiart warned of impending struggles defeated only by the sister of Notre Dame's 'strong heart of a man' and her soul filled with the 'spirit of the good God'. Billiart knew first hand of the difficulties of following God's will. She established the sisters of Notre Dame in Amiens, France, in the aftermath of the French Revolution and encountered more than her fair share of trials provoked by both the church and state. Her conflict with Bishop Jean François Demandolx culminated in the sisters of Notre Dame departing Amiens for Namur, Belgium. Demandolx had wished to limit their work to his Diocese of Amiens, in part because there was a great need for Catholic teachers in Amiens, especially following the French Revolution, but also because in a diocesan congregation, his position as superior general would make his authority indisputable. In Namur, Bishop Charles Francis Joseph Pisani was more amenable to Billiart's plans for a more mobile sister of Notre Dame who would meet the needs of the poor 'of the most abandoned places'.[2] In addition, Billiart sought to organise the congregations as a pontifical, not a diocesan congregation, under the supervision of papally approved rule and constitutions and a mother general instead of a bishop, in order to send Notre Dame sisters wherever they were needed. In 1804, when the congregation was

1  SND: *Book of the Instructions of Blessed Mère Julie* (1909), p. 147.
2  SND: *Règles et Constitutions des Soeurs de Notre-Dame* (Namur: [1859]), article 3, 'L'esprit des membres de l'Association, est un esprit de simplicité, d'obéissance, de charité; et leur désir est de consacrer leurs soins aux pauvres des lieux les plus abandonnés'.

founded, the status of women's simple-vowed congregations was still questioned. Some episcopal and clerical authorities considered these 'modern female orders' unseemly because they performed their work outside the cloister and in public spaces.[3] Given the importance of a non-cloistered existence to her teaching sisters, Billiart wished to protect them from the caprice of episcopal authority.[4]

The conflict over authority and governance[5] that arose between Julie Billiart and Bishop Demandolx was not particularly unique; stories of similar conflicts are part of convent tradition in many religious institutes.[6] Active congregations of women operating in nineteenth-century England and Wales provided a different setting for such conflicts but similar tensions. This chapter analyses some of the issues surrounding the identity of women religious and their authority and governance. How did women religious understand the authority they exercised? How did they negotiate their authority in conjunction with their professional and religious identity? How effective were female leaders in achieving their congregation's objectives if these objectives ran contrary to episcopal objectives? This chapter argues that women religious used their religious identity to support their authority. They were not alone in this strategy. Nineteenth-century reformers like Josephine Butler and Ellice Hopkins were driven by religious motives to generate a very public outcry against social injustice. Josephine Butler believed she had received her mission

3 SHCJ: Vol. 51, p. 38: letter dated 6 March 1862 from Cornelia Connelly to Bishop Thomas Grant. Here, Connelly refers to the approbation of the constitutions of 'modern female orders'.

4 Mary Linscott, *Quiet Revolution: The Educational Experience of Blessed Julie Billiart and the Sisters of Notre Dame de Namur* (Glasgow: Burns, 1966), pp. 42–4.

5 These terms have specific meanings as used in this chapter. Authority refers to the power to demand obedience. Governance refers to the administrative structure and the rules in place that provide authority to govern.

6 Radegunde Flaxman, *A Woman Styled Bold: The Life of Cornelia Connelly, 1809–1879* (London: Darton Longman and Todd, 1991); Edna Hamer, *Elizabeth Prout, 1820–1864: A Religious Life for Industrial England* (Bath, England: Downside Abbey, 1994); Jo Ann Kay McNamara, *Sisters in Arms: Catholic Nuns through Two Millennia* (London: Harvard University Press, 1996); Elizabeth A. West, *One Woman's Journey: Mary Potter: Founder – Little Company of Mary* (Richmond, Victoria, Australia: Spectrum Publications, 2000). Almost any history of a congregation or founder published after 1980 will illustrate some difficulties that the congregation or founder faced when dealing with episcopal or clerical authority.

from God, and her public references to scripture served to reinforce her authority.[7] Ellice Hopkins used her religious beliefs to create a public ministry that attempted to elevate public morality.[8] These women, while supporting nineteenth-century notions of femininity, became archetypes of women's agency, authority and power.[9] Female voices such as theirs were not the norm, yet they successfully challenged other Christian men and women to join in their efforts. Women religious supported similar notions of femininity but their religious activism and evangelisation, as has already been discussed in previous chapters, was more subtle.[10] They were exemplars of women's authority despite the restrictions of a communitarian lifestyle lived under the aegis of a patriarchal church. Women religious, too, like the moral crusaders Butler and Hopkins, used their religious identity to buttress their authority.

Women religious exercised their authority in two contexts: within the convent and in the institutions they managed in the public sphere. This authority was not universally acknowledged. It was sometimes contested, oftentimes negotiated and always circumscribed. Gender was central to the tensions that surrounded the issues of governance and authority. But in nineteenth-century England, the religious identity of women religious and their approved rule and constitutions provided the

7 Alison Milbank, 'Josephine Butler: Christianity, Feminism and Social Action', in Jim Obelkevich, Lyndal Roper and Raphael Samuel, eds, *Disciplines of Faith: Studies in Religion, Politics and Patriarchy* (London: Routledge, 1987), pp. 154–64 (pp. 155–6).

8 Susan Mumm, '"I Love my Sex": Two Late Victorian Pulpit Women', in *Women, Scholarship and Criticism: Gender and Knowledge c. 1790–1900*, ed. by Joan Bellamy, Anne Laurence and Gill Perry (Manchester: Manchester University Press, 2000), pp. 204–21; Susan Morgan, 'Faith, Sex and Purity: The Religio-Feminist Theory of Ellice Hopkins', *Women's History Review*, 9 (2000), 13–34.

9 Susan Morgan, *A Passion for Purity: Ellice Hopkins and the Politics of Gender in the Late-Victorian Church* (Bristol: University of Bristol, 1999), p. 8; Patricia Crawford, *Women and Religion in England 1500–1720* (London: Routledge, 1993), p. 1.

10 Coburn and Smith argue that American women religious demonstrated their power and influence to shape Catholic culture and American life in their ability to act and create. This power and influence did not, however, lead to a 'public voice' on social issues involving women and children. Carol K. Coburn and Martha Smith, *Spirited Lives: How Nuns Shaped Catholic Culture and American Life, 1836–1920* (Chapel Hill and London: The University of North Carolina Press, 1999), p. 222. Religious activism is discussed in greater detail in Chapter 4.

legitimisation needed to exercise their authority within the convent and in the public sphere. Religious identity, derived from their membership in a congregation, was an important source of their authority. That this religious identity defined and limited the bounds of authority is indisputable, but the limits to the authority of active women religious were somewhat fluid during the nineteenth century, sometimes expanding, sometimes contracting. The interplay among the strong individual personalities of women religious, bishops and clergy served to expand or contract the scope available in their spheres of action. Importantly, it was an authority subject to the provisions of an international Roman Catholic Church. This international context could provide crucial support for those who stepped beyond the acceptable boundaries defined by the local bishop.

The issue of identity, both individual and corporate, is central to the question of authority and gender but it is problematic. Women who joined religious congregations had chosen to work within the structure of the Roman Catholic Church. They believed in its theological precepts, its road to salvation and the authority of a patriarchal hierarchy. The approbation of a congregation occurred through a complex process of approvals that was created and maintained by the male hegemony of bishops and Roman authorities. Catholic women could become religious only by entering a religious institute that had earned diocesan or papal approbation. The authority of women religious would always be circumscribed by this male hegemony. This makes it more difficult to determine the context and depth of their authority. They, like so many women of the nineteenth century, were subordinate to a patriarchal hierarchy which could disempower them. Yet they exerted the authority they associated with their identity as religious. Despite the dominant Victorian ideology that gloried in a model of femininity that was obedient, docile and domestic, and a Catholic ideology that clearly embraced these Victorian tenets of femininity, women religious behaved in a manner that sometimes ran counter to this ideology. The language they used often reflected obedience and humility, yet their actions did not preclude exerting their own authority or negotiating with the Catholic hierarchy to achieve ends that suited the congregation's objectives. The paradox was that obedience did not involve a lack of agency; women religious saw obedience as a means of deciding and collaborating to provide much-needed social services and evangelisation.

Women religious were part of the 'public life' of the church and, as theologian Lynn Jarrell argues, the way in which women religious lived their lives as consecrated women influenced the way in which the Roman

Catholic Church perceived their religious identity.[11] Women religious constructed an identity that acknowledged their authority, but at the same time promoted the concepts of obedience and humility. The authority of women religious was visible both within the convent structure and outside the convent walls. When they pushed against the boundaries of church practices, they were supported by the authority derived from belonging to a legitimated congregation. Using their religious identity as official church workers, women religious reinforced their own authority.

This chapter will examine the source and nature of the authority that congregations and women religious wielded in the public sphere. Governance becomes important to understanding authority within the convent and congregation. Understanding the different levels of authority and the interactions and relationships between women religious, bishops, confessors, clergy and the laity provides a key to the equation of women religious, governance and authority in the nineteenth century. Relationships between women religious and members of the clergy could abound with mutual respect, trust and friendship. However, when women religious appeared to overstep the boundaries that separated their authority from insubordination, the tension was very real. This chapter will argue that these nineteenth-century women used their identity as women religious to develop a model of womanhood that wielded significant authority while negotiating normative expectations.

## Forms of government

The authority of simple-vowed women religious was a function of their relationship to the Roman Catholic Church and was mediated through a legitimated congregation.[12] The legitimation of a new religious institute began with the approbation of the bishop. His support and

11 Lynn Jarrell, OSU, 'The Development of Legal Structures for Women Religious between 1500 and 1900: A Study of Selected Institutes of Religious Life for Women', doctoral thesis, Catholic University of America, 1984, p. 311.

12 Throughout the nineteenth century, there was no common church law which clearly defined the authority of bishops and female superior generals. According to the historian Rosa MacGinley, disputes that were adjudicated in Rome consistently reinforced the authority of the congregation over episcopal authority. In 1900, *Conditae a Christo* defined the juridical nature of pontifical and diocesan congregations. M.R. MacGinley PBVM, *A Dynamic of Hope: Institutes of Women Religious in Australia* (Darlinghurst, New South Wales: Crossing Press, 2002), p. 59.

encouragement were critical as his status in the church hierarchy gave him significant power in his diocese. He approved the establishment of a congregation and the work it performed, and was often influential in the creation of the congregation's rule and constitutions and method of governance. Congregations that remained diocesan typically opened branch convents within one diocese and were under the authority of the bishop as the superior general. Diocesan approbation, or diocesan rite, was always the first step in legitimating any institute, and for some institutes remained its final status.

Once congregations established their viability as diocesan congregations, they could, if they desired, take further steps to seek papal approbation, referred to as pontifical rite, which positioned them under the authority of the Pope in Rome. In the nineteenth century, newly founded congregations overwhelming chose this more time-consuming and rigorous path to papal approbation. Almost three-quarters of the simple-vowed congregations that made foundations in England in the nineteenth century were pontifical rite. Susan O'Brien hailed this papal form of government an 'important innovation' as it allowed a female superior general to receive her authority directly from Rome.[13] This was a 'great advantage', declared Frances Taylor, founder of the Poor Servants of the Mother of God in England, because 'it renders us independent of <u>all</u> bishops and governed by the Pope himself'.[14] Papal approbation opened new doors to expanded forms of legitimated authority for women religious in simple-vowed congregations.

Prior to 1854, the process for papal approbation could be lengthy and complicated and each congregation's story of the approval of the congregation and its rule and constitutions was distinctive. Under the guidance of Cardinal Archbishop Andreas Bizzarri, secretary of the Congregation of Bishops and Regulars, *Methodus quae a Sacra Congregatione Episcoporum et Regularium servatur in approbandis*

---

13 Susan O'Brien, 'Religious Life for Women', in V. Alan McClelland and Michael Hodgetts, eds, *From without the Flaminian Gate: 150 Years of Roman Catholicism in England and Wales 1850–2000* (London: Darton Longman + Todd, 1999), pp. 108–41 (p. 109). The forerunner to this form of government for women religious was the English Ladies, founded by the Mary Ward (1585–1645). For more on the incomparable Mary Ward and her ideas on government and authority see Laurence Lux-Sterritt's *Redefining Female Religious Life: French Ursulines and English Ladies in Seventeenth-Century Catholicism* (Aldershot: Ashgate, 2006).

14 SMG: I/A2b, p. 43, letter dated 22 January 1891 from Frances Taylor to Mother M. Austin (Margaret Busher).

*novis institutis votorum simplicium* was developed in 1854.[15]
*Methodus* established a new process for a congregation's approbation
that involved four distinct stages. The first stage was the general
approval of the objectives and purpose of the congregation. The second
stage gave the official decree of praise, the *decretum laudis*. For this,
congregations submitted a petition requesting approbation, letters of
recommendation from bishops and clergy, a draft of their rule and constitutions and a special report which included the objectives of the congregation, the history of its foundation, the numbers of convents,
postulants, novices and professed sisters and their status (lay or choir),
the means of financial support, the spirituality of the congregation and
its usefulness to the church.[16] The Pope would grant an official decree
of praise, the *decretum laudis*, if these documents demonstrated to the
Sacred Congregation of Bishop and Regulars that the congregation was
well-established, financially stable, spiritually robust and supported by
local bishops and clergy.[17] Once armed with the *decretum laudis*, the
congregation moved from the jurisdiction of the bishop to the jurisdiction of Rome.[18]

The third stage in the legitimation of a congregation was the review of
the rule and constitutions by canonical experts for their 'purity of

15  This following section is a summary of a process that was unique for each
    congregation, particularly before 1854 but even after that date.
16  Jarrell, 1984, p. 216.
17  Since its formation in 1622, the Sacred Congregation the Propagation of
    the Faith (*Propaganda Fide*) was responsible for the religious administra-
    tion of 'mission countries', i.e. countries that were non-Christian or were
    administered by non-Catholic governments. So, it was *Propaganda Fide*,
    not the Sacred Congregation of Bishop and Regulars, that handled English
    religious affairs until 29 June 1908 when Pius X's Constitution *Sapienti
    consilio* revised and limited *Propaganda Fide*'s remit, especially with
    regard to religious life. Matters regarding religious life in England and
    Wales then moved under the jurisdiction of the newly created Sacred
    Congregation of Religious. Jarrell, 1984, p. 284; MacGinley, 2002,
    p. 278.
18  Ibid, pp. 59–60. If the congregation did not merit a *decretum laudis*, it was
    issued with a *decretum commendatum*, which affirmed features of the con-
    gregation deserving commendation. The Congregation of Bishops and
    Regulars (or *Propaganda Fide* if a mission country) would suggest the alter-
    ations necessary for a *decretum laudis*. Many thanks to Dr Rosa MacGinley
    for our many long-distance discussions on this and other points regarding
    the evolution of juridical and legislative traditions throughout the long
    history of women's religious institutes.

Catholic thought' and practicality.[19] A congregation was defined by its rule and constitutions, which were constructed within certain parameters approved by Rome and modified by its founders to reflect the unique spirit of the congregation. Once the rule and constitutions were approved, the congregation entered the fourth stage, a testing period during which the approved rule and constitutions were 'lived'. The Bishop of Salford, Herbert Vaughan, referred to this last part of the process in his address to the Sisters of the Most Cross and Passion:

> The Holy See, our dear Sisters, is very slow in giving its approbation to a new constitution . . . Since that time it [the constitutions] has been thoroughly examined – it has been examined by consultors of the Holy See; a congregation of Cardinals has read through your rules, discussed them, and now the Holy See, the See of Peter, has put its seal to this constitution, and said, 'This is mine'; it claims special authority over it, so that now it cannot be destroyed, and cannot be annulled by any human hand but by that of Peter alone.[20]

The last ten years of this approbation process for the Sisters of the Most Cross and Passion would be spent 'living' their rule and constitutions. Further changes could be recommended by the congregation, and once these were approved, the congregation would receive juridic status. The rule and constitutions were an important source of authority for congregations and women religious. It was the rule and constitution that women religious first turned to in a dispute with a local bishop. The authority to act with or react against official representatives of the institutional church, be it a bishop or a member of the clergy, was found in the contents of rule and constitutions legitimated by Rome.

In diocesan-approved congregations, where the rule and constitutions were approved by the bishop, these legal documents could be altered, at any time, by or with the approval of the bishop. As will be seen in the example of Mary Potter and the Little Company of Mary, the bishop as superior general was the final decision-maker and arbiter of all disputes. Typically, he would not be occupied in the day-to-day matters of running a congregation, but the authority of the mother superior was dependent on his level of involvement. In most papally approved congregations, where disputes occurred with bishops, the

19 Hope Campbell Barton Stone, 'Constraints on the Mother Foundresses: Contrasts in Anglican and Roman Catholic Religious Headship in Victorian England', doctoral thesis, University of Leeds, 1993, p. 52.

20 *Records of the Foundation and Progress of the Congregation of the Sisters of the Most Holy Cross and Passion: 1851–1911* (Dublin, 1911), p. 42. I am indebted to Dr Edna Hamer for bringing this document to my attention.

superior general and her council were encouraged to settle issues themselves or submit to the final arbitration of the Sacred Congregation of
Bishops and Regulars in Rome. The difference in authority for a female
superior general appears, at first glance, almost negligible. After all, the
final arbiter of disputes, whether it be a bishop or the Pope, was always
male. Yet the difference between the two types of government in terms
of authority was quite significant.[21] Female superior generals and her
council had daily responsibility for the management of the congregation, which allowed a high degree of latitude in their activities. They
had the authority to innovate, to develop and to react to social conditions. Yet their authority was not without some limitations, as will be
discussed later. The interaction with the Roman authorities, in most
cases located thousands of miles away from the mother house, was
infrequent, and Rome was unlikely to interfere with a congregation's
routine operating decisions. When disputes did occur between congregations and bishops or where the bishop's interference was considered
contrary to the rule and constitutions, recourse was available to the
congregation.

Congregations under diocesan approbation could find their way of life
altered by episcopal interference in internal affairs. Mother M. Elizabeth
(Elizabeth Coyney), believing (incorrectly) that the mother house of the
Institute of the Blessed Virgin Mary in Munich had been closed down
during the secularisation of religious property in Germany, submitted the
York convent to the authority of the Bishop of Beverley, John Briggs, in
1857. The congregation's historian Sister Gregory Kirkus called this a
'tragic decision' and described the 'reign of terror' when the next bishop,
Robert Cornthwaite, subjected the sisters to his own interpretation of
women's religious life and interfered with their daily activities. He altered
the diet, devotions and clothing of the York convent. He encouraged
enclosure, quite contrary to the founder Mary Ward's original intent, and
cautioned sisters not to look out of street-facing windows or even to
think of events outside the convent walls.[22] Diocesan approbation did

21  The Sisters of Mercy constitutions gave the bishop 'broad powers' regarding
    their internal governance. Catherine C. Darcy RSM, *The Institute of the
    Sisters of Mercy of the Americas: The Canonical Development of the
    Proposed Governance Model* (Lanham: University Press of America, 1993),
    p. 23.
22  In 1609, Mary Ward founded the congregation that became known as the
    Institute of Mary in England (and the Institute of English Ladies on the con-
    tinent). In the nineteenth century, the Bar Convent in York began to call
    itself the Institute of the Blessed Virgin Mary, which was the name under
    which it received its final approbation by Rome in 1877. (In 2004, in

not often lead to this type of extreme episcopal interference in the affairs of a congregation; many bishops allowed mother superiors the latitude they needed to manage the day-to-day affairs of their congregation. However, the amount of authority allowed to mother superiors was determined at the discretion of the bishop.

Rome encouraged centralisation of papally approved congregations under a female superior general and a council made up of members of the congregation. Authority inside the convent rested on an intricately constructed hierarchy of women managing women. Most pontifical-rite congregations developed highly centralised hierarchical structures and systems of administration. The mother superior and her council, which usually consisted of at least one mother assistant, a bursar and a novice mistress, were responsible for managing the internal affairs of the congregation and the novitiate. They directed the purchasing, building and maintenance of physical structures including their convent and the institutions under their care. They supervised the staff of various institutions and philanthropic works such as schools, hospitals and reformatories as well as various mission activities including parish visiting and religious education. They managed the finances of the congregation, which included budgeting, planning, investing and fund-raising. They coordinated the congregation's business relationships, with tradesmen, government officials, clergy and episcopal officials. They trained future members of their congregation. In most cases, there was a high level of autonomy in their day-to-day activities. However, as with publicly registered bodies, this was not without strict accountability to various authorities. Individual convents reported their activities to their provincial house. Provincial houses reported to their mother house. Episcopal authorities had the right of annual visitation where they reviewed in detail the activities, financial and spiritual, of a convent and

respect to Mary Ward's founding vision, the Roman branch of the congregation was renamed the Congregation of Jesus.) Ward had intended that the institute be an active congregation of women religious centralised under the authority of a female superior general. In 1857, the congregation was centralised under the mother house in Munich, Germany. It was not until 1911, after many difficulties and concerted efforts on the part of subsequent mother superiors, that the York convent and subsequent branch houses were reunited with the mother house, now located in Nymphenburg, Germany. Sr Gregory Kirkus IBVM, *An I.B.V.M. Biographical Dictionary of the English Members and Major Benefactors* (London: Catholic Record Society, 2001), pp. 9–20. I am thankful to Sr Christina Kenworthy-Browne for the explanation of the various names of the congregation over its history.

congregation.[23] There was a consistent path of responsibility: novices were responsible to the novice mistress; the assistant superiors, bursars and novice mistress were responsible to the mother superior; the mother superior was responsible to the chapter and council; and the mother superior and her council were responsible to the bishop and Rome. This was an elaborately tiered structure with layers of authority and accountability. The centralisation allowed for uniformity in training under a central novitiate, expansion that was national or global rather than diocesan, and a flexible and portable pool of personnel that could be relocated where they were needed. As Chapter 6 has shown, it was successful in maintaining a certain *esprit de corps*. This form of governance validated the authority of women religious and legitimated their right to exercise their authority in relation to internal convent management and their evangelical and missionary vision.[24]

Some bishops saw pontifical approbation as a threat to their authority and a hindrance to their management of the diocese and preferred congregations to remain under their authority as diocesan-approved congregations. Congregation histories and annals document the persuasive techniques and intimidation used by some bishops to keep congregations diocesan. Cardinal Nicholas Wiseman and Bishop Thomas Grant pressured the founder Cornelia Connelly to place the Society of the Holy Child Jesus under diocesan authority.[25] They were unhappy that the constitutions she originally created, based on the Jesuit model, did not specifically address the authority of the bishop and even more radically included the election of a female superior general for life. This was consistent with the Jesuit form of government, which advocated that the

23　Barbara Walsh, *Roman Catholic Nuns in England and Wales, 1800–1937: A Social History* (Dublin: Irish Academic Press, 2002), pp. 89–124.

24　This was not a new idea. Male religious orders had begun the process of centralisation in the thirteenth century with the development of the Dominicans and Franciscan friars, who travelled across diocesan boundaries in their preaching ministries. The founder Mary Ward had attempted to integrate centralisation within the government of the Institute of Mary. In the seventeenth century, Ward's 'innovation' was not welcomed by English clergy or the Roman authorities. By the nineteenth century, women's simple-vowed congregations frequently used a centralised governmental structure. James R. Cain, 'Cloister and the Apostolate of Religious Women', *Review for Religious*, 27 (1968), 652–72 (p. 660).

25　Sister Ursula Blake and Sister Annette Dawson, *Positio: Information for the Canonization Process of the Servant of God Cornelia Connelly (née Peacock) 1809–1879*, 3 vols (Rome: Sacred Congregation for the Causes of Saints, 1983), II, p. 573.

superiors general were ratified by the Pope and 'received their authority from Christ and their commands were therefore to be received with faith and obedience'.[26] This level of authority was contentious and made for a sometimes difficult relationship between bishops and Jesuits. Such tensions became more complex when mixed in with issues of gender. Cornelia Connelly remained adamant that the Society of the Holy Child Jesus should become papally approved but it was not until 1887, thirty-three years after the constitutions of the Society of the Holy Child Jesus were submitted to Rome, that it received pontifical approbation.[27]

Similar difficulties were faced by Mary Potter, founder of the Little Company of Mary. She struggled under the increasing interference of the Bishop of Nottingham, Edward Gilpin Bagshawe. The relationship between Potter and Bagshawe began amicably enough and Bagshawe encouraged Potter's vision of a new congregation. But his 'guidance' of the community became intrusive and subverted Mary Potter's original vision. He expanded its activities from Potter's original intent, that of nursing the sick and dying in their homes, to teaching and parish visiting, which he saw as the greater need in his diocese. More critically, he ignored her vision of the inner spirit of the nascent community. Potter had intended to create a deep devotional life based on the 'Calvary spirit'. It was this devotional life, not philanthropic activities, that was supposed to focus the energies of the group and 'challenge and revitalise the surrounding culture'. Bagshawe, and indeed some of the first members of the community, did not share Potter's vision.[28] Bagshawe also intruded more and more in the daily life of the convent by approving all additions to and dismissals from the congregation and by managing all financial aspects of its work. He insisted on opening convents that Potter judged were financially and physically unfeasible.[29] Potter was made mother superior by Bagshawe in 1879, but dismissed within four months and replaced with someone more sympathetic to his way of thinking.

Mary Potter's frustration led her to seek permission from Bagshawe to go to Rome in 1882. Her intent, which she did not share with Bagshawe, was to seek papal approbation of the Little Company of Mary. This, she believed, was the only means to wrest control of her infant congregation from Bagshawe. In a short time, she made many

---

26  Ibid, II, pp. 761–2.
27  A discussion of the many difficulties that the Society of the Holy Child Jesus encountered can be found in Flaxman, 1991.
28  West, 2000, pp. 101–10. West provides a probing examination of the spiritual dimension of the charism of the Little Company of Mary.
29  Ibid, p. 80.

influential friends among the hierarchy in Rome, including Pope Leo XIII, who requested that she open a convent in Rome.[30] In 1883, she was successful in gaining approbation for her original constitutions. The Little Company of Mary was now a pontifical-rite congregation, and the Cardinal Prefect of Propaganda informed Bagshawe that he was no longer superior general of the congregation.[31] When Mary Potter returned to England in May 1886, she reorganised the congregation in line with the approved constitutions and, much to Bagshawe's dismay, closed down several convents.[32]

Bagshawe's interference with the Little Company of Mary had as much to do with his own understanding of episcopal authority as it had to do with the commonly held distrust of women in positions of authority. This was, of course, not solely a Catholic issue. The nineteenth-century physiologist Alexander Walker noted in 1839 that:

> It is evident that the man, possessing reasoning faculties, muscular power, and courage to employ it, is qualified for being a protector: the woman, being little capable of reasoning, feeble, and timid, requires protection. Under such circumstances, the man naturally governs: the woman as naturally obeys.[33]

Bishop William Ullathorne offered a similar opinion on women and authority:

> The troubles of the French Congregations of which you speak have all arisen from their adoption of the democratic method of election. Democratic government is bad enough form, but it is absurd for women. As a rule sentiment is their motive power; and sentiment in them is like India rubber, at once tough and elastic, yielding on pressure, but reasserting its old tenacity, until you can put light and principle in the place of sense and sentimentality. But it is hard to get these into some minds and some communities.[34]

These opinions on female authority were unequivocal: women lacked reasoning faculties and were ruled by 'sentiment', not 'light and principle'. Women religious were not of the same opinion. They believed in

30  Ibid, p. 139.
31  Patrick Dougherty, *Mother Mary Potter: Foundress of the Little Company of Mary (1847–1913)* (London: Sands & Co., Ltd., 1961), pp. 145–6.
32  West, 2000, p. 159.
33  Alexander Walker, *Woman Physiologically Considered, as to Mind, Morals, Marriage, Matrimonial Slavery, Infidelity and Divorce* (London: A.H. Bailey & Co., 1839), p. 131.
34  John P. Marmion, 'Cornelia Connelly's Work in Education, 1848–1879', doctoral thesis, University of Manchester, 1984, p. 398.

their abilities to manage and direct the activities, spiritual and temporal, of religious congregations.

## Collaboration

Many bishops supported the authority of women religious to manage their congregations. In some narratives, it is the collaboration of bishops and mother superiors that resounds through the texts. These relationships, when built on the bonds of friendship or mutual respect, boded well for the congregation. The letters to and from Mother Mary Clare (Georgiana Moore), founder of the Bermondsey Mercy convent, and Thomas Grant, Bishop of Southwark, were brimming with warmth, concern and mutual regard. The Sisters of Mercy researcher Mary Sullivan writes that for almost twenty years their working relationship and mutual respect contributed to the accomplishments of both. Bishop Grant wrote to Mother Mary Clare, 'Pray much for me between now and Friday as I am in great anxiety of mind about two matters in which I have to decide. They do not regard the Convents of course.'[35] His letter to her in 1868 regarding the acceptance of a novice who was ill with consumption was indicative of his trust in her judgement: 'Do whatever you believe is for the best'.[36] Edmund Knight, the former Bishop of Shrewsbury, was a favourite among the Upton Faithful Companions of Jesus. Their annals noted how he arrived one day, unannounced, and after visiting with the schoolchildren, he:

> returned to the parlour and surrounded by a few of our Mothers took tea and chatted as of old, making kind inquiries for all his friends and asking especially at what stage the cause of our Mother's canonization stood: that cause for which he had worked so devotedly in past years.[37]

At Middlesbrough too, the Faithful Companions of Jesus received the favourable attention of their bishop, Richard Lacy, whose:

> visits are frequent; his deeds of kindness are many, and on occasions he gives proofs of his paternal solicitude. As soon as he heard of Notre Mère's arrival, he came to welcome her, and has since expressed his pleasure at having made her acquaintance.[38]

35 Mary C. Sullivan RSM, *Catherine McAuley and the Tradition of Mercy* (Dublin, Ireland: Four Courts Press, 1995), p. 80.
36 RSM Bermondsey: 'Bermondsey Annals', 1868, pp. 120–1.
37 FCJ: A1210 'Upton Annals', 1896, p. 57.
38 FCJ: A1209 'Middlesbrough Annals', 1896, p. 79.

Bishops Knight's and Lacy's deference to the congregation's founder, Marie Madeleine Victoire de Bengy d'Houët, and Mère Zoe Girod, the newly elected superior general, is noteworthy.[39] These mothers general were important decision-makers in the Faithful Companions of Jesus and their approval was necessary for any new foundations, building programmes or other major congregation projects in England. Such relationships between congregations and bishops surpassed the usual platitudes of deference and respect evident in formal correspondence between bishops and women religious. They were congenial and productive, and full of mutual admiration and respect, 'paternal solicitude' and daughterly love.[40] Although it is difficult to quantify the frequency of such close relationships, collaborative relationships were frequently mentioned in convent documents.

The Faithful Companions of Jesus prayed fervently that the successor of Bishop John Carroll of Shrewsbury would be 'favourable to us'. When Samuel Webster Allen was appointed bishop they were pleased, as he 'has been a kind friend to Dee House'.[41] Margaret Anna Cusack, founder of the Congregation of St Joseph of Peace, wrote to Canon Douglas of Nottingham in 1885 about the importance of the support of clergy and bishops:

> God knows people talk of the Fathers of the Desert but I can only say they had a nice easy life in comparison with some of the 'mothers' of the 19th century. Ah! My Father pray for me, pray for me. If it were not for a few priests like yourself, and a very few bishops like Dr. Bagshawe I would long since have given up all my work in despair.[42]

The sympathetic nature of the episcopal support suggested by Margaret Anna Cusack and the Faithful Companions of Jesus was important to the efficient management of congregations and the achievement of their philanthropic aims. Cusack wrote favourably of Bishop Bagshawe, yet the same Bishop Bagshawe caused Mary Potter much anxiety. Convent documents make clear that circumstances could cause one bishop to clash with one mother superior but not another.

The relationship between clergy and religious communities was symbiotic. Bishops and clergy needed women religious to educate and

39  F.M. Capuchin Stanislaus, *Life of the Viscountess de Bonnault D'Houët: Foundress of the Society of the Faithful Companions of Jesus 1781–1858* (London: Longmans, Green and Co., 1913), p. 18. 'Notre Mère' in 1896 would have been Zoe Girod, who was superior general from 1896 to 1914.
40  For more on these 'familial' relationships see Chapter 6.
41  FCJ: A1842 'Upton Annals', 1897, pp. 90–1.
42  Susan Dewitt CSJP, *A Great Love of Peace* (Bellevue, Washington: CSJP, 2000), p. 20.

develop a pious, loyal and church-going laity. Women religious needed the approval of bishops to enter a diocese and perform their work. Their public acknowledgement and support were valuable, especially in competing for financial resources. Cardinal Henry Manning, Archbishop of Westminster, wrote a letter of support on behalf of St Joseph's Retreat, newly opened by the Daughters of the Heart of Mary, to encourage the 'faithful' to support their endeavours financially:

> I heartily commend this useful and pious institution to the generosity of the faithful, in order that the zealous Managers may be able to meet the outlay required for building and other expenses.[43]

These relationships benefited both the diocese and the religious congregations and represented the cooperation necessary to build a pious, united and church-going laity.

## Challenging clerical authority

Collaboration was certainly the ideal relationship. Women religious, however, faced with intransigent bishops or clergy, used the tools at their disposal to manage episcopal and clerical authority. Leaders of women's congregations were aware that bishops could inhibit the growth and spirit of their congregation, especially when a congregation was young and its leadership fairly new to religious life. The Poor Servants of the Mother of God, founded in 1869 by Frances Taylor, was one such congregation. Extant correspondence reveals Taylor's efforts to train her sisters in the art of management, which included not only managing the convent, the sisters and the philanthropic works, but also managing the clergy and bishops. She was concerned with issues of authority and educated her sisters as to their rights and obligations. Taylor specifically addressed the need to 'deal with Bishops and priests and Confessors'. She instructed her sisters:

> The Constitutions say we should show them due respect, be submissive to those placed over us, but yet keep them within the limits of their office . . . One thing we could resist a Bishop in is when he interferes in the spirit of the Institute, once it has been confirmed by Rome, and its Constitutions approved of. This is beyond his authority, and if he persisted in trying to change our spirit we should refer to the Sacred Congregation of Religious.

43 DHM: Special collection 'Old Letters and Documents', letter dated 8 March 1868 from Cardinal Henry Manning.

His power would cease if, for instance, he wanted us to do away with manual labour, and devote ourselves entirely to education.[44]

Frances Taylor's advice illustrates the tensions between obedience to a bishop and the authority inherent in the 'spirit of the Institute'. Taylor confirmed the importance of respect and submissiveness to the bishop. There was no question within religious congregations that the bishop was their ecclesiastical superior and he was owed their obedience. But, as Taylor noted, there were 'limits' to his power over their congregation and in certain circumstances resistance was acceptable. The 'spirit of the Institute' was enshrined in a congregation's constitutions and, once approved by Rome, it could not be altered by the congregation or the bishop. Taylor was concerned about a bishop's interfering with the 'spirit' of the Poor Servants of the Mother of God and her reference to education was perhaps indicative of pressures she may have faced to open or teach in parish schools.[45] Nineteenth-century bishops and mission priests were eager for educators. There were many examples, some well-known in contemporaneous convent circles, of their attempts to alter the philanthropic work of a congregation to include education. Taylor explained that recourse was available to the Poor Servants through pontifical bodies in Rome which had jurisdiction over religious institutes and adjudicated disputes.

At the heart of Taylor's instructions was the significance of the constitutions. Constitutions defined the aims and parameters of life within these communities. They were the guidelines that governed the scope of the temporal philanthropic work of the congregation, the spiritual duties of the sisters and some of the daily responsibilities of community life. Constitutions were designed to regulate the working relationships between a disparate group of women of a variety of ages, educational experiences, class positions and ethnic backgrounds. The constitutions

44  SMG: 'Instructions of Mother Foundress on Our Holy Rule on Confession, etc. Taken from her Letters, and from Sisters' Notes', p. 39. At the time when this letter was written, religious congregations in England would have turned to the *Propaganda Fide* if there were any interference by the bishop. The Sacred Congregation of Religious was not founded until 1908. It is likely that the editors of this bound typescript of letters replaced the name of the Sacred Congregation of *Propaganda Fide* with that of the Sacred Congregation of Religious to reflect the authority in place at the time of publication. The original of the letter has not been located.
45  As mentioned in Chapter 2, congregations with teaching as their main focus were enthusiastically welcomed to open convents in England. Many congregations that did not focus on teaching were encouraged to teach.

were central to the daily life of a sister from the beginning of her association with a community. Postulants attended weekly conferences on the constitutions. Novitiate instruction included daily study of the constitutions. Retreats attended by professed sisters included further reference to the constitutions. The constitutions were often read aloud at meal times.[46] They provided the model of religious life; the necrology of Sister Mary Ann Joseph (Angela Flemming) embodied the ultimate of praises: 'It could be said of her with truth that she was a living copy of the Rule'.[47]

Frances Taylor consistently referred to the constitutions as a source of authority. In writing about clergy and confessors she declared:

> About dealing with priests. I have said that we must keep them within limits – the limits of their office. The Confessor must not interfere with the arrangements of Superiors or government. His duty is with regard to the Sisters' conscience. If he told you not to report something which the Rule says you must report this would be beyond his power. Do not answer: 'I won't do it' – but 'I will think about it'. You are not bound to obey him in this – the Rule comes first.[48]

Here again Taylor emphasised keeping clergy to the 'limits of their office' and underscored the primacy of the constitutions. Constitutions empowered a congregation by providing an authoritative response to clerical challenges to the sisters' authority[49] and allowing them to legitimately resist unwarranted episcopal authority.

There are many examples in the correspondence of the Poor Servants of the Mother of God as well as other congregations that illustrate this tenuous balancing act as superiors submissively, but firmly, reminded bishops and clergy of the congregation's rights according to its constitutions. The vow of obedience was not made to the church or to a specific individual; it was made to God. It was interpreted to reflect obedience to the constitutions of the congregation, to the authority who had approved the constitutions (the Pope or the diocesan bishop) and to the head of the congregation, in most cases the mother superior. It was this obedience to their constitutions that allowed women religious to act contrary to the wishes of ecclesiastical officials. Women religious generally complied with the Victorian ideals of a respectful and obedient womanhood and they, in theory and usually in practice, deferred to the authority of the

46  RSM Bermondsey: 'Bermondsey Annals', 1843, pp. 105–6.
47  RSM Bermondsey: 'Obituaries from Ursula O'Connor to Clare Arrowsmith', pp. 180–5.
48  SMG: 'Instructions of Mother Foundress', p. 41.
49  Elizabeth Rapley, *The Dévotes: Women and the Church in Seventeenth-Century France* (London: McGill-Queen's University Press, 1990), pp. 178–9.

Roman Catholic Church, but in matters of conscience, they acted in the name of God. Strong leaders believed God created their congregation and they were duty-bound to protect it. In the *Instruction to the Holy Rule*, Frances Taylor stated:

> Then towards priests in whose Mission we work we must be submissive and civil – but never go with them against our Superiors' wishes or orders. This is the test of a loyal and true nun to her Institute and to her Superiors. Obedience to our Superior comes first; she holds God's plan to us: for His sake we obey her whether she is prudent or not. We are not to study her qualities, but see God in her orders, and obey them blindly for His sake.[50]

These three sentences underscore significant elements of the relationships between superiors and sisters. While women religious were expected to be submissive and civil to priests, this submissiveness was qualified; it did not encourage mechanical obedience to priests' requests. The 'true and loyal nun' was obedient, first and foremost, to her congregation and her superior. The first responsibility of women religious was to God, but what Taylor taught was that, according to the constitutions, God's plan must be seen in the instructions of the female mother superior. Sisters were expected to be obedient to their superiors and loyal to their congregation.

## Exerting authority

Throughout the nineteenth century, congregations were inundated with requests for new foundations and more sisters. The services women religious provided, particularly as educators, were desperately needed. As their missionary work increased, mother superiors and their councils cautiously balanced this expansion against their resources, of both money and personnel. Many requests to found new convents were rejected because of insufficient financial support or inadequate numbers of trained sisters. In April 1875, the Reverend Richard Power of Canterbury requested Sisters of Mercy for his parish but, with 'mature deliberation' Reverend Mother M. Camillus (Catherine Dempsey) refused his request. Not deterred, Power renewed his request again in August but, 'as Sisters could not be conveniently spared at this time', his request was again denied.[51] The founder Frances Taylor remarked in 1888, 'I think I have refused at least three foundations since I came back to England'.[52] Annals were replete with examples of women religious refusing the requests of bishops, clergy

50 SMG: 'Instructions of Mother Foundress', pp. 39–40.
51 RSM Bermondsey: 'Bermondsey Annals', 1875, pp. 233, 237.
52 SMG: I/F3 (volume 2 of 5), p. 115, letter dated 5 June 1888 from Frances Taylor to Alexander Fullerton.

and laity for convent foundations. Despite dramatic growth in the number of sisters, convents and congregations, the supply of sisters could not meet the demand. Women religious, especially through their educational institutions, had access to children and families, and their religious influence was unquestioned. They were in high demand for their pastoral and evangelical activities. While episcopal authority over congregations certainly existed, congregations had a level of independence in selecting convent locations. Mary Peckham Magray has observed, in the Irish context, that 'the idea that women religious had to be asked or invited to make foundations is convent myth to mask their agency and influence'.[53] Of course, in church law, religious congregations needed the bishop's approval before settling in his diocese. However, this legal reality disguised the agency of women religious as they discerned which requests for convent foundations to accept or reject.

A centralised government, with an elected superior general and her council, was problematic for some bishops. The authority typically given to a superior general to make financial decisions, to accept or reject missions, to appoint and transfer women religious and to accept or dismiss women as postulants and novices was not always accepted as congruent with a bishop's own authority and his need to manage the affairs of his diocese. The relationship between a mother house and the local convent could prove a hindrance for a bishop. Some episcopal requests were funnelled to the mother house by the local convent for approval. It was easier for bishops to administer their dioceses if convents reported directly to them. It was easier for priests if the schools were managed by the mission and not the convent. These were often highly contested areas of authority. Women religious were diligent in asserting their professional identity and ability as educators to manage their own schools. One of Her Majesty's Inspectors of Schools, E.M. Sneyd-Kynnersley, observed that women religious were 'by no means subservient to their priestly managers: at their back in case of dispute is reverend mother, and only the boldest priest would go to war with so excellent and so powerful a person'.[54]

One area where women religious leveraged their authority was in the withdrawal from a convent or diocese. An analysis of the closures of

53 Mary Peckham Magray, *The Transforming Power of the Nuns: Women, Religion, and Cultural Change in Ireland, 1750–1900* (Oxford: Oxford University Press, 1998), pp. 15–31. Magray's point was that congregations made calculated business decisions with regard to where and when they founded new convents.
54 E.M. Sneyd-Kynnersley, *H.M.I. Some Passages in the Life of One of H.M. Inspectors of Schools* (London: Macmillan and Co., 1908), pp. 237–8.

Table 8.1 Numbers of convents opening and closing in ten congregations, 1801–1900

| Congregation | Number of convents opened | Number of convents closed | % closed |
|---|---|---|---|
| Religious Sisters of Mercy | 119 | 18 | 15.1 |
| Sisters of Charity of St Paul the Apostle | 90 | 36 | 40.0 |
| Daughters of Charity of St Vincent de Paul | 39 | 5 | 12.8 |
| Notre Dame de Namur | 24 | 8 | 33.3 |
| Faithful Companions of Jesus | 18 | 3 | 16.7 |
| Poor Servants of the Mother of God | 23 | 13 | 56.5 |
| Society of the Holy Child Jesus | 13 | 4 | 30.8 |
| Daughters of the Heart of Mary | 16 | 4 | 25.0 |
| Congregations of St Joseph of Peace | 6 | 2 | 33.3 |
| Sisters of St Joseph of Annecy | 4 | 0 | – |
| Total | 352 | 93 | 26.4 |

Source: Appendix.

convents in ten congregations gives an understanding of how women religious exerted such authority when challenged by clerical or episcopal authority. Table 8.1 demonstrates the extent of these convent closures in the nineteenth century. The numbers of convents closed varied dramatically by congregation, from none to thirty-six. The percentage of convents closed in comparison with to the numbers of convents opened is a more telling statistic. On average, a quarter of convents opened by these ten congregations were closed down. Unfortunately, it is difficult to make absolute assertions about the reasons for convent closures because convent records are sometimes frustratingly vague in explaining them. The Bermondsey annals merely note in 1885 that the convent at Eltham was 'given up'.[55] Another convent was closed 'owing to a want of proper management'.[56] Annoyingly, we do not know whose management is 'wanting'. In many cases, there are no records explaining the reasons for the closure.

55  RSM Bermondsey: 'Bermondsey Annals', 1885, p. 273.
56  DC: Notes on Deceased Sisters (1915), p. 32.

One congregation that closed convents with particular frequency was the Sisters of Charity of St Paul the Apostle. Throughout the century, they opened ninety convents and closed thirty-six. Their strategy to 'choose the obscure and unknown corners of the world, its villages and hamlets – in preference even to its cities – for the exercise of their charity'[57] meant that some convents contained as few as two or three sisters.[58] Small convents could be quickly opened or closed, allowing for more flexibility to react to changed conditions. According to the congregation historian George Hudson, writing in 1929, many of the closures resulted from disagreements about the authority of the congregation in managing their convents and schools.[59] Geneviève Dupuis, founder of the Sisters of Charity of St Paul the Apostle in England, was, by many accounts, a dominant personality. Hudson observed:

> From the opening of the convent at Banbury Mother Dupuis had assumed a position of authority. She was willing to listen to Dr. Tandy for suggestions and advice, but she did not look upon him as a Director, with authority over the disposal of the Sisters, as the Director had at Chartres. But she looked to the Bishop as the authority in all matters, as the head of the Order.[60]

Despite episcopal authority 'in all matters', Dupuis disagreed with bishops when she felt duty-bound to do so. Dupuis remarked on her relationship with one particular bishop:

> I have never disobeyed the Bishop in any matter in which he had a right of comment, all assertions to the contrary notwithstanding. His advice, I am sorry to say, I have not always been able at all times to follow.[61]

In matters of conscience, her biographer explained, Dupuis was 'firm as a rock'.[62]

57  SCSP: *Rules and Constitutions of the Sisters of Charity of St Paul in England* [1864], chapter 1.
58  J.J. Scarisbrick, *Selly Park and Beyond: The Story of Geneviève Dupuis and the Congregation of the Sisters of Charity of St Paul the Apostle* (Selly Park, England: Sisters of Charity of St Paul the Apostle, 1997), p. 8.
59  George V. Hudson, *Mother Geneviève Dupuis, Foundress of the English Congregation of the Sisters of Charity of St Paul the Apostle 1813–1903* (London: Sheed & Ward, 1929), p. 133. 'Director' was the term often used in France for an ecclesiastical superior appointed by the bishop of the diocese. At this time, Dupuis recognised the director in Chartres as the ecclesiastical superior of the congregation; William Tandy's role as parish priest was much less authoritative.
60  Ibid, p. 132.
61  Scarisbrick, 1997, p. 24.
62  Hudson, 1929, p. 275.

There are many examples of her firmness with both bishops and priests. For instance, Dupuis closed the Burnley convent in 1859 when the parish priest demanded that 'the nuns should be independent of the mother house'.[63] The Bishop of Nottingham, Arthur Riddell, insisted on the removal of the local superior at the Great Marlow convent, Sister M. Juliana (Mary Mauson). Geneviève Dupuis replied, 'if I remove her I remove all the sisters, both at Marlow and at Danesfield'. In 1885, both convents were closed down.[64] In 1899, the Bishop of Nottingham, Edward Gilpin Bagshawe, wrote to Geneviève Dupuis indicating, 'I can only say that I deeply regret the interference of Mgr. Sabela, and of Lord Howard, with your undoubted rights. It appears to me to be altogether unjustifiable, and you could not possibly admit the principles.'[65] Sabela and Howard insisted on 'absolute control' of the teachers managing the schools in Wells. Dupuis would not agree to this and Sisters of Charity of St Paul the Apostle left this convent also.

Obedience to the bishop did not mean blindly submitting to the bishop's assumed authority. Correspondence between bishops and mother superiors is full of examples of women religious suggesting alternatives or explaining their ideas more fully in order to convince the bishop of the wisdom of their plans. Women religious made room to negotiate. The Sisters of Mercy *Guide for Religious* noted:

> Should the Bishop refuse a permission, &c. &c., we must never murmur: there is no imperfection in discussing such subject in council, and making respectfully such representation to the Bishop as the interests of the Community seem to demand; but such matters should not be made the subject of unnecessary conversation or comment in the Community or with externs.[66]

Women religious had the responsibility to advance the interests of their congregation and discuss sensitive issues with the bishop. In 1862, the founder Cornelia Connelly wrote to Bishop Thomas Grant, after he informed her that there were to be no further clothings or professions until a property dispute had been resolved:

> I took your letter recd by the 3 o'clock post and read it to Our Lady of Sorrows asking her in her own sweet meekness to listen to it – and the

---

63  Ibid, p. 133.
64  Diocesan Archives of Northampton: F IV.5 Convent Book, p. 66.
65  SCSP: Box 4:70, letter dated 19 December 1899 from Edward Gilpin Bagshawe to Geneviève Dupuis.
66  RSM Handsworth: [M. Francis Bridgeman RSM], *Guide for the Religious Called Sisters of Mercy. Amplified by Quotations, Instructions, &c. Part I. & II* (London: Robson and Son, 1866), p. 64.

interior answer I got was 'burn the letter and tell [the] Bp to forget what he wrote and to come and tell you what more you can do than you have done.' I have burnt it my Lord and now will you come and tell me what more I can do than I have done.[67]

Connelly relied on her 'interior answer', ironically inspired by the 'sweet meekness' of Our Lady of Sorrows, to negotiate with a bishop who did not appear to be open for negotiation. These negotiation tactics were deferential, yet represented an assertiveness that stemmed from the authority that women religious held as leaders of religious congregations.[68]

Women religious have often been portrayed as passive, following the direction of clerical and episcopal authority, relying on their guidance in internal and external affairs and acquiescing to the decisions made by those who were leaders of the Roman Catholic Church. Yet these examples show that women religious used their authority to respectfully negotiate with church authorities in matters that were in 'the interests of the Community'. When they faced conflicts with the male hegemony of the Roman Catholic Church, they used their constitutions to buttress their authority and leveraged the increasing demand for their services to remove themselves from situations that diminished their authority. Nineteenth-century women religious protected their constitutions, their congregation's spirit and their authority to make decisions.

## Conclusion

Theories of patriarchy consign women to the role of passive victims and deny their strength or authority. The Catholic Church has often limited women's function and authority because of their gender; however, women religious should not be seen as victims nor as free agents: both representations create an ahistorical view. Women religious exercised their authority and subsequently created another version of the gendered nature of womanhood. They were in a paradoxical space: although

---

67 Flaxman, 1991, p. 276. At this time, the congregation was still only diocesan-approved, so Bishop Grant, desiring a speedy resolution to the property dispute, was within his authority in refusing to approve further clothings or professions.

68 Maria Luddy, 'Religion, Philanthropy and the State in Eighteenth- and Early Nineteenth-Century Ireland' in Hugh Cunningham and Joanna Innes, eds, *Charity, Philanthropy and Reform from the 1690s to 1850* (London: Macmillan Press Ltd, 1998), pp. 148–67. Maria Luddy discusses how the 'careful negotiation' used to 'persuade' clerics and bishops masked the power of congregations.

members of religious institutions, they were lay rather than clerical, and were religious rather than secular. This was a space, though, in which they could and did exert their authority. Their religious commitment both empowered their lives and limited their activities. Women religious understood their authority to come from their religious identity and in turn from their relationship to their congregation. One important aspect of their authority stemmed from their rule and constitutions, which were legitimated by Rome. Their rule and constitutions were a daily part of their lives and tangible documents that could be utilised to achieve their ends. Congregation leaders such as Frances Taylor were concerned with issues of authority and educated their sisters as to their obligations and their rights according to the constitutions. Women religious also passed on strategies for resisting unjustified clerical and episcopal authority for other women religious to emulate. They exerted their own authority in matters pertaining to congregation objectives. At times, they appeared to act in a manner contrary to the obedient and docile Victorian model of womanhood. Women religious were encouraged by their religious identity to act with authority and responsible obedience despite the limitations placed on them by Victorian culture and the Roman Catholic Church. They readily complied with the Victorian ideals of a respectful and subservient womanhood and they, in theory, deferred to the authority of the Roman Catholic Church and its officials. However, by their actions, they firmly reminded bishops and clergy of their rights according to their constitutions.

# Conclusion

Religion was one of the major forces that shaped Victorian society. Piety, morality and philanthropy took on gendered characteristics and these were intrinsic in the definition of Victorian womanhood. Historians have alternately applauded religion for empowering women and demonised it for encouraging patriarchal attitudes and limiting women's sphere of activities. Philippa Levine has suggested that the evolving position of women and the deconstruction of masculinity and femininity owe a great debt to religion and sees the church offering women 'a role in spiritual life which at one and the same time empowered and confined them'.[1] This book argues that religious belief provided nineteenth-century Catholic women religious with the tools to transcend the normative boundaries of femininity and to redefine the parameters of womanhood. This is not to say that these redefined parameters were all empowering; women religious willingly accepted many of the strictures of the Roman Catholic Church that subjected them to its patriarchal structure and sometimes limited their actions. Yet women religious had more authority and were more empowered than has been acknowledged by historians. They were active agents in manipulating their world and shaping their individual future as well as the future of their congregations. The evangelical nature of their 'call' led them beyond the boundaries of their convent grounds; they were fervent evangelisers, spreading the Catholic faith to those they educated, nursed and cared for. The growth of the numbers of congregations and convents in the nineteenth century attests to their utility, their drive and their success as evangelists.

Part I of this book looked at the developing identities of women entering religious life. Women's religious congregations in England, as in other parts of the world, entered a period of dramatic growth in the nineteenth century. There were many women who had the 'same idea at the same

---

1 Philippa Levine, *Victorian Feminism 1850–1900* (London: Hutchinson, 1987), pp. 11–12.

time'. In England, this expansion of religious life was set in a unique framework in a country that was just dismantling repressive penal laws against Catholics. Moreover, until the nineteenth century, religious life for Catholic women had been primarily the province of the English gentry and aristocracy who could afford to send their Catholic daughters to English convents on the continent. The introduction of active simple-vowed religious congregations in England offered new opportunities to Catholic women. The demand for their services was greater than the supply; clerics and the laity were constantly making requests for 'a few sisters' to run a school, to visit parishioners and to nurse the sick. This form of life developed into a popular option for Catholic women.

Women became acquainted with religious life in many ways: kinship relationships, convent education, clerical recommendations and philan-thropic work all provided a means to assess conventual living. Serving God and improving the spiritual, educational and physical condition of the laity in a secure environment attracted all kinds of women. However, parents were not always so welcoming of this religious vocation. Many women overcame parental disapproval through the use of a religious ide-ology that promoted their vocation as the 'will of God' and thereby allowed them to choose religious live over the ubiquitous vocation of married life. Their vocation was tested in the postulancy and novitiate, where novices were immersed in the spirituality and the practical 'works of mercy' of the congregation. Identity formation in this training period included the inculcation of the ideals of obedience and humility: familiar principles of behaviour espoused by many Victorians. Despite this, women religious were expected to be strong: strong in their faith, strong physically and strong in their loyalty to the congregation.

Part II developed the working identities of women religious. The indi-vidual sister was a woman imbued with a sense of mission. Women's con-gregations were visible in the public sphere: in the institutions they built and in their interactions with students, patients, parishioners and civic and church leaders. These female-centred congregations largely directed their own activities in the public sphere and began the institution-building that was the hallmark of their philanthropic and evangelical efforts. Evangelisation was their objective. Nowhere was this more evident than in their efforts in education. Yet women religious also addressed the prac-tical realities of being educators. They actively sought and obtained formal training and certification, even creating Catholic teaching colleges to ensure that training could be obtained in a Catholic setting. Women religious consciously modelled themselves as professionals.

Part III examined the identity of women religious on a corporate level. As a congregation grew, and especially after a congregation's founder died, the need to maintain the spirit of the institute was addressed by creating a specific literature that recorded congregational history and, particularly, the founder's ideals and objectives. This literature reinforced a corporate identity that bound women together and separated them from the outside world. Despite the badge of corporate identity, differences existed, and differences of class and ethnicity were difficult to camouflage. Women religious were seen as 'belonging to a higher grade of society', yet women who entered nineteenth-century congregations came from varied backgrounds. Religious life appealed to women of limited means as well as to the wealthy elite. Prescriptive literature hinted at the class tensions that existed in congregations. Some congregations specifically attracted and encouraged women without dowries or formal education. Congregations also varied distinctively in the apostolic works they performed, in the people they served and in the women they attracted and accepted into religious life. To add to these complexities, the lay–choir dichotomy was inherent in the many active, simple-vowed congregations. Elaborate methods of separation and differentiation reinforced class differences despite the rhetoric of spiritual equality. Class and to a lesser extent ethnicity were important determiners of the place that women religious held in their congregation.

The authority of women religious stemmed from their religious identity and their relationship to their congregation. One important aspect of this authority for pontifical-rite congregations was derived from their constitutions, which were legitimated by Rome. A congregation's constitution was a daily part of its life and a tangible legal document that could be put to use to achieve the congregation's ends. Congregation leaders were conscious of issues of authority and educated their sisters as to their obligations and their rights according to the constitutions. This sometimes resulted in a tension between meeting the needs of bishops or clergy and keeping to the 'spirit of the institute'. Local superiors were instructed in the art of management, which included not only managing the convent, the sisters and philanthropic institutions under their purview, but also managing their relationship with bishops and clergy. The constitutions provided the authority to contest episcopal power and sometimes even challenge it. Women religious upheld the importance of their constitutions as the guiding force behind their own mission and authority.

Women religious held firm to their religious identity, which influenced their other identities: their corporate identity, their class and ethnic identity and their evangelising and professional identity. These identities merged to produce women who were both leaders and followers. Some women religious used their religious identity and the authority it implied to question episcopal and clerical demands. Others readily complied with episcopal and clerical authority. The great majority of women religious were the ordinary followers: teachers, nurses, administrators, cooks, portresses and domestic help. They are seldom seen or heard in the convent archives, but nonetheless it was also their energy and their drive which fuelled the growth of Catholic institutions in the nineteenth century.

This history of women religious has an important place in the construction of nineteenth-century gender history as it features women religious negotiating the boundaries of religious life. It was a contested identity – one that was obedient, docile and respectful of church authority – yet it was also an identity that had intrinsic authority and power, which women religious used to promote the goals of their congregations. Religious sisters prominently displayed their religious identity but also held professional identities, evangelising identities and corporate identities. The contested identity of women religious references the pluralities of their lives. It was not a simple life, but one filled with competing demands – the demands of their faith, the demands of their work, the demands of their congregation and the demands of church authority. Each individual assessed these demands and these identities differently. Contested identities meant consensus and acquiescence as well as conflict.

This contested identity both liberated and restricted women religious. Religion liberated women religious from one set of restrictions and limits. It gave them the ability to act, to commit themselves fully to the Roman Catholic cause and to become effective in the evangelisation of Catholics. Women religious conceived of their authority in terms of mission. Power was exercised in the convent, guided by an accepted organisational structure, often set down in writing and democratic in some ways. By the end of the nineteenth century, women's congregations were an organised, centralised, standardised, bureaucratic entity whose mission was focused, whose functions were regularised, and which had a specific place in English Catholic social life.

Yet women religious embodied the Victorian ideal of femininity. They believed and taught that women's place was in the home. They did not require a change in the patriarchal structure of the Roman Catholic Church. They rarely challenged their own subordination, which they deemed legitimate. Yet their actions often belied their rhetoric. Although they were often pious, self-abnegating and obedient women, they rejected the traditional role of motherhood in favour of a community life of service and action in the public sphere. While they conformed to the Victorian ideal of femininity, they lived life in a different space – a convent space which was created and maintained through women's leadership and power. These religious congregations inadvertently challenged the dominant values of society by creating an alternative lifestyle that was woman-centred. This was not, however, a counter-cultural movement. They used the cultural ideals of the family and the maternal aspects of femininity to move what was seen as private into the public space. They articulated their right to evangelise through the rhetoric of religious commitment.

This book has explored various identities of women religious in order to bring to the forefront the lives of women who established and managed significant Catholic educational, health care and social welfare institutions in England. These women have been generally excluded from historical texts, and their lives and work have lain hidden in the private archives of their congregations. By making them visible, by examining various facets of their identity, this book has shown how religious activism shaped the identity of active, simple-vowed Catholic women religious. Women religious, through their domestic ideology and their institution-building, legitimated their own incursion into the public sphere. Women's religious congregations empowered women from within and without the congregation and inadvertently stretched the gender boundaries that ascribed and proscribed the tenets of femininity in nineteenth-century England. Their religious activism was an important factor in understanding the consolidation of English Catholic culture in the nineteenth century. They were women who subtly challenged existing norms of behaviour. The history of women religious must be seen in the context of the society in which they lived. By examining their lives within a historical context, their vital contribution to the growth of Catholicism and the expansion of women's role in society is recovered. This analysis of women religious is part of a larger story of women who strove to overcome the proscribed limitations of their gender to legitimate their claims to autonomy and power.

# Appendix: sources and methods

The ten congregations listed in Table A1 were studied for most of the analysis performed in this book. They reflect the diversity of active simple-vowed religious life available to women in nineteenth-century England. No one congregation can be regarded as a representative congregation; it would be difficult to endorse any one or even a group of congregations as 'typical'. Each congregation had its own specific qualities and attributes. Some, like the Religious Sisters of Mercy and the Daughters of Charity of St Vincent de Paul, were large, fast-growing congregations. Others, such as the Daughters of the Heart of Mary or the Congregation of St Joseph of Peace, were much smaller and slow-growing in England. Some congregations were focused on one apostolate: Notre Dame de Namur and the Society of the Faithful Companions of Jesus were teaching congregations. Others had more varied apostolates: the Sisters of Charity of St Paul the Apostle managed orphanages, homes for workhouse boys and hospices for pilgrims and taught in mission schools, poor schools and middle-class boarding schools. Some of these congregations, such as the Society of the Holy Child Jesus and the Poor Servants of the Mother of God, were founded in England in the nineteenth century, whereas others, like the Congregation of St Joseph of Annecy, had a more ancient lineage. Some congregations had strict lay – class divisions and others, like the Poor Servants of the Mother of God, had no class divisions. Given such diversity, generalisations are difficult to make about religious life in England and Wales. However, the analysis offers quantifiable results to add to anecdotal observations.

The ten congregations hold in their archives the bulk of the rich sources that inform this book. Examined separately and together, the documents from these archives suggest some answers to the questions that this book asks about the identity of women who entered active simple-vowed congregations in nineteenth-century England and Wales. It is hoped that the inclusion of five of the ten largest nineteenth-century congregations will add some validity to the arguments made in this book.

Table A1 Congregations used in detailed analysis

| Congregation | Date congregation founded | Founded from | Date of first English foundation | Primary apostolate | Class division |
|---|---|---|---|---|---|
| Religious Sisters of Mercy | 1831 | Ireland | 1839 | Education | Lay–choir |
| Sisters of Charity of St Paul the Apostle | 1696 | France | 1847 | Assorted | None |
| Daughters of Charity of St Vincent de Paul | 1634 | France | 1857 | Assorted | None |
| Notre Dame de Namur | 1804 | Belgium | 1845 | Education | None |
| Faithful Companions of Jesus | 1820 | France | 1830 | Education | Lay–choir |
| Poor Servants of the Mother of God | 1869 | England | 1869 | Assorted | None |
| Society of the Holy Child Jesus | 1846 | England | 1846 | Education | Lay–choir |
| Daughters of the Heart of Mary | 1801 | France | 1846 | Assorted | None |
| St Joseph of Peace | 1884 | England | 1884 | Assorted | None |
| St Joseph of Annecy | 1650 | India | 1864 | Assorted | Lay–choir |

Yet the choice of these ten congregations, and the exclusion of the remaining sixty-nine, has no doubt influenced the tenor of these arguments. Including all seventy-nine simple-vowed congregations would have been unmanageable and virtually impossible given the difficulties in locating some of the congregation archives. Diminishing numbers of women entering religious life in the twenty-first century has meant the closure of convents; in some cases entire congregations that existed in the nineteenth century no longer exist in England today.

Three databases were developed from documents found in the archives and other sources. The institution database contains information on all active women's congregations in England and Wales. The convents database contains details of the individual convents making up each congregation. These two databases were used to analyse the growth of women's congregations in Chapter 1. The sisters database, the core of this book, contains demographic information on women who entered the ten congregations in England and Wales in the nineteenth century. The sections below will explain each database in more detail.

## Institutions database

The institutions database contains a list of all the orders and congregations in existence in England and Wales in the nineteenth century. It was created primarily from three texts, Francesca Steele's *The Convents of Great Britain* (1902), H. Hohn's *Vocations: Conditions for Admission etc., into the Convents* (1912) and Peter F. Anson's *The Religious Orders and Congregations of Great Britain and Ireland* (1949). The annual volumes of the *Catholic Directory*, a monthly publication entitled *The Harvest* and congregation histories also added to the data fields in the database. Some of my archive research, particularly in diocesan archives, has led me to include additional institutes in this database. For example, all three authors fail to mention the Congregation of the Infant Jesus, which arrived in England in 1845 and was merged into the Notre Dame de Namur congregation in 1851. The Congregation of the Infant Jesus does not appear in any of the three texts. However, it existed in the nineteenth century and should be included in the database for it to be complete.

In her text Francesca Steele identified each institute as 'active', 'mixed', 'contemplative' or 'educational'.[1] I have found Steele's definitions somewhat problematic. She has defined 'mixed' congregations as those that 'combine the active with the contemplative life'. The term 'educational'

---

1 Francesca M. Steele, *The Convents of Great Britain* (London: Sands, and Dublin: M.H. Gill, 1902), p. 8.

is also rather ambiguous. Some 'educational' orders such as the Religious of St Andrew were 'educational' but worked from inside the cloister, whereas others such as Sisters of Notre Dame de Namur were 'educational' and worked outside the cloister. She includes as 'mixed' (and not 'educational'), the Faithful Companions of Jesus, who were an educational institute and worked outside the cloister. This imprecision (at least for the purposes of this work) has caused me to revise these categorisations. I have used the vows that were taken in each institute as the differentiating feature. Women who took solemn vows were enclosed and were oftentimes contemplative. Some had 'active' apostolates, typically teaching, but this teaching was performed inside the cloister. Women who took simple vows were not enclosed and typically worked outside the cloister, either teaching or nursing. To provide focus and comparability, this book examines only simple-vowed congregations.

## Convents database

The convents database contains details of the individual convents founded by each of the ten congregations. This information was derived primarily from Francesca Steele's text, but also includes information from the ten congregation archives. The information from the congregation archives often differed from that found in Steele's text and included convents that had opened and closed during the course of the century. As Francesca Steele noted in her preface, she obtained much of the information directly from the institutes themselves, but some institutes were more generous with their information than others.

I have used the number of convents in a congregation, as indicated in Table A2, to determine its relative size. This methodology has a number of flaws. First, Steele's information may not be correct; and it is not possible to visit all institute archives to confirm her figures. Second, the average number of sisters per convent varies by congregations, so a congregation such as the Sisters of St Paul the Apostle, which has fifty-four convents, is deemed larger than the Daughters of Charity of St Vincent de Paul despite the fact that there are more sisters in the Daughters of Charity of St Vincent de Paul than there are in the Sisters of Charity of St Paul the Apostle. The number of convents reflects the particular expansion strategies of the congregations and the extent of the work each convent performed in a given location. Congregations such as the Sisters of Charity of St Paul the Apostle had fewer sisters in each convent than did the Faithful Companions of Jesus. The more precise measurement would be number of sisters. However, that information is not readily available for all religious institutes.

Both Barbara Walsh's *Roman Catholic Nuns in England and Wales,*

Table A2 Congregations used in detailed analysis

| Congregation | Date of English Foundation | Number of convents in 1900 | Number of sisters in 1900 | Number of sisters professed, 1830–1900 |
|---|---|---|---|---|
| Religious Sisters of Mercy | 1839 | 101 | 921 | 1,340 |
| Sisters of Charity of St Paul the Apostle | 1847 | 54 | 441 | 690 |
| Daughters of Charity of St Vincent de Paul | 1857 | 34 | 568 | 715 |
| Notre Dame de Namur | 1845 | 16 | 556 | 854 |
| Faithful Companions of Jesus | 1830 | 15 | 615 | 897 |
| Poor Servants of the Mother of God | 1869 | 10 | 163 | 276 |
| Society of the Holy Child Jesus | 1846 | 9 | 244 | 348 |
| Daughters of the Heart of Mary | 1846 | 12 | 93 | 138 |
| St Joseph of Peace | 1884 | 4 | 30 | 39 |
| St Joseph of Annecy | 1864 | 4 | 61 | 68 |

*1800–1937: A Social History* (2002) and Gloria McAdam's article in the *Women's History Review* entitled 'Willing Women and the Rise of Convents in Nineteenth-Century England' (1999) have published similar lists of institutes and convents using some of the same sources. These lists do not consistently agree with each other or with mine in details such as dates of foundation and numbers of convents. I have, as far as possible, corroborated my own databases with primary and secondary sources written by the institutes themselves in order to provide more accurate listings. Walsh has acknowledged that her convent figures are only 'broadly accurate' and that they could be underestimated. While Walsh's text does not give convent numbers for all institutes, she does note the number of convents for five congregations. Of these, three are in my sample. Her convent totals for 1897 differ from mine for 1900. Where she notes seventy-two Mercy convents, my sources give 101. Her sources indicated fifty-one convents of the Sisters of Charity of St Paul the Apostle, where mine give fifty-four. We are closest on the convents of the Daughters of Charity of St Vincent de Paul, where she notes thirty-five and I note thirty-four convents.[2] These variances are unfortunate, but are to be expected given the newness of this type of research and the time-consuming nature of visiting the archives of all institutes. No doubt, some of the difference lies in including convents that were opened and subsequently closed in the nineteenth century.

I have based my assumptions about the relative size of the congregations on the number of convents in existence in 1900. This information, again, comes primarily from the three texts noted above but also includes information from a selection of primary sources and secondary congregation histories. There are some significant variances from Francesca Steele's text. For example, documents in the various archives of the Sisters of Mercy indicate that 101 convents of the Sisters of Mercy existed in 1900; Francesca Steele lists only seventy-four. Wherever I was able to corroborate the number of convents with primary or more recent secondary sources, these figures were used.

When I began this work, I had intended to include a focus on religious life in Wales, in particular as the Catholic hierarchy instituted in 1850 was that of England and Wales. However, difficulties arose in gaining access to archives of women's religious congregations that were located specifically in Wales. The ten congregations in this work, many of them quite substantial in size, opened between them only four houses in Wales in the nineteenth century. Only thirty-five women who entered these ten congregations were born in Wales. Yet, as some congregations not included in my archival research did manage convents in Wales and as the formal Catholic Church hierarchy did include Wales, some of my statements reflect, by necessity, the includison of Wales, some of my statements reflect, by necessity, the inclusion of Wales. There is a great need for a better understanding of Catholicism and religious life in Wales in the nineteenth century.

### Sisters database

Profession registers were used to create a sisters database that includes demographic information on women who entered these ten congregations in England and Wales in the nineteenth century. These registers typically include each sister's birth name, religious name, date of birth, date of entry into the convent, date of profession and date of death. In some cases, registers include place of birth, parents' names and father's occupation. As the profession registers are not always complete, other sources, such as annals,

---

2 Barbara Walsh, *Roman Catholic Nuns in England and Wales, 1800–1937: A Social History* (Dublin: Irish Academic Press, 2002), p. 177.

necrologies, correspondence, subsidiary registers and even the census were used to fill in the gaps. The sisters database includes, as far as possible, all women who entered these ten congregations in the nineteenth century and worked, for at least part of their life, in England and Wales.

Much of the analysis throughout this text is done on 'professed' women religious. These are women who entered the novitiate in the nineteenth century and subsequently took their first vows. There were various types of vows, from temporary to perpetual. Temporary vows were taken for a period of time, from one to six years depending on the congregation. Typically, once the temporary vows had expired, women religious took perpetual vows, which were lifelong. Most registers include the dates when the first temporary vows were taken, and do not include the dates when perpetual vows were taken. These women were considered professed sisters despite the 'temporary' nature of their vows and were included in the analysis of professed sisters.

When the women religious included in these registers completed the novitiate, they were typically assigned to work in England or Wales. However, some were sent to convents abroad. These exceptions are few in number, and wherever known, these women religious have been removed from the database. More problematic were the Daughters of Charity of St Vincent de Paul, who included in their profession registers women who worked in convents in Ireland and Scotland, regions outside the parameters of this thesis. Women religious were assigned where they were needed, and it was possible for an English-born professed sister never to work in England or Wales. While this factor makes comparability more difficult, it has not altered my conclusions.

## Class and leadership analysis

The methodology used to calculate social class uses occupational groupings developed by the nineteenth-century social reformer Charles Booth. To address the problem of census comparability, he regrouped the occupations from the census into eleven industrial groupings with fifty-one occupational subcategories. Using the 1911 class distribution of occupational orders developed by the Registrar General, historian J.A. Banks has assigned social classes I to V to each of these industrial groupings, as can be seen in Table A3.[3] His is one of an assortment of schemes developed

3 J.A. Banks, 'The Social Structure of Nineteenth Century England as Seen through the Census', in Richard Lawton, ed., *The Census and Social Structure: An Interpretative Guide to Nineteenth Century Censuses for England and Wales* (London: Frank Cass, 1978), pp. 179–223.

**Table A3 Occupational groupings for class analysis**

|  | Occupational groupings | Class |
|---|---|---|
| Class I | Professional occupation | Upper class and middle class |
| Class II | Intermediate occupations | Middle class to working class |
| Class III | Skilled occupations | Working class |
| Class IV | Partly skilled occupations | Working class |
| Class V | Unskilled occupations | Working class |

*Source*: Banks, 1978, pp. 179–223.

by historians who use the census or the census enumerator's books for studies of urban or rural life.[4]

This methodology is not without some drawbacks. One of the major problems is that the Booth–Banks scheme assigns class to occupational classification, not individual occupations. Within some occupational groupings, more than one class can be assigned. For example, within the classification Public Services and Professional, the category Army is classified as containing occupations that can be either Class I or Class IV. Within this category are the occupations army officer, classified as Class I, and soldier, classified as Class IV. The second methodological drawback is one faced by all demographers: the occupation of farmer. The Booth–Banks classification scheme categorises farmers in Class II, but, one cannot differentiate between farmers and the sizes of their farms.

Despite these drawbacks, this method can be used to suggest explanations regarding questions of class within religious congregations. Two of the ten congregations researched recorded the father's occupation in the profession register: the Daughters of Charity of St Vincent de Paul and the Sisters of Charity of St Paul the Apostle. Each occupation was categorised by occupational grouping and its associated class. In addition, the Daughters of Charity of St Vincent de Paul listed in their register

4 W.A. Armstrong, 'The Use of Information about Occupation', in E.A. Wrigley, ed., *Nineteenth-Century Society: Essays in the Use of Quantitative Methods for the Study of Social Data* (Cambridge: Cambridge University Press, 1972), pp. 191–310; Joyce M. Bellamy, 'Occupation Statistics in the Nineteenth Century Census', in Richard Lawton, ed., *The Census and Social Structure: An Interpretative Guide to Nineteenth Century Censuses for England and Wales* (London: Frank Cass, 1978), pp. 165–78; D.R. Mills and K. Schurer, 'Employment and Occupations', in Dennis Mills and Kevin Schurer, eds, *Local Communities in the Victorian Census Enumerators' Books* (Oxford: Leopard's Head Press Limited, 1996), pp. 136–60.

information that could be collated to identify women who became sister servants, that is, women who acted as local superiors and managed a convent and the philanthropic works associated with the convent.

## Regional analysis

The regional analysis was based on the counties, regions and dioceses listed in Table A4. For the sake of consistency, I have used county boundaries as of the 1890s (Middlesex covers north London and Surrey covers south London) and diocesan boundaries based on the dioceses in existence in 1850.

**Table A4  Regions and dioceses by county**

| Region | County | Diocese |
|---|---|---|
| *London and the south-east* | Berkshire | Southwark |
| *London and the south-east* | Buckingham | Northampton |
| *London and the south-east* | Essex | Westminster |
| *London and the south-east* | Hampshire | Southwark |
| *London and the south-east* | Isle of Wight | Southwark |
| *London and the south-east* | Kent | Southwark |
| *London and the south-east* | Middlesex | Westminster |
| *London and the south-east* | Oxfordshire | Birmingham |
| *London and the south-east* | Surrey | Southwark |
| *London and the south-east* | Sussex | Southwark |
| *London and the south-east* | Guernsey | Southwark |
| *East Anglia* | Norfolk | Northampton |
| *East Anglia* | Suffolk | Northampton |
| *South-west* | Cornwall | Plymouth |
| *South-west* | Devonshire | Plymouth |
| *South-west* | Dorset | Plymouth |
| *South-west* | Gloucestershire | Clifton |
| *South-west* | Somersetshire | Clifton |
| *South-west* | Wiltshire | Clifton |
| *Midlands* | Derbyshire | Nottingham |
| *Midlands* | Herefordshire | Newport and Menevia |
| *Midlands* | Leicestershire | Nottingham |
| *Midlands* | Lincolnshire | Nottingham |
| *Midlands* | Northampton | Northampton |
| *Midlands* | Nottingham | Nottingham |
| *Midlands* | Rutland | Nottingham |
| *Midlands* | Shropshire | Shrewsbury |

| | | |
|---|---|---|
| *Midlands* | Stafford | Birmingham |
| *Midlands* | Warwick | Birmingham |
| *Midlands* | Worcester | Birmingham |
| *Wales* | Flintshire | Shrewsbury |
| *Wales* | Glamorgan | Newport and Menevia |
| *North-west* | Cheshire | Shrewsbury |
| *North-west* | Cumbria | Hexham |
| *North-west* | Lancashire | Salford |
| *North-west* | Westmorland | Hexham |
| *North-east* | Durham | Hexham |
| *North-east* | Northumberland | Hexham |
| *Yorkshire* | Yorkshire | Beverley |

# Select bibliography

## Congregation and diocesan archives

The archives used for this book are private archives and vary in the extent of their organisation, classification and cataloguing. Some archives have not classified or catalogued all their contents, so precise document reference numbers or descriptions are not available. In those cases, I have indicated a brief description of the item in place of a document reference number.

Dates of publication and authors are noted where known; however, many documents in the archives are not dated, nor are their authors noted. Much of the published material of the nineteenth century, such as books of necrologies, biographies, customaries and guides, was privately printed by an individual congregation and distributed within the congregation. This privately published material is included in this section of the bibliography, and does not include a publisher if privately published, or the date of publication if the date is not known.

## Archdiocesan Archives of Liverpool

Chancellors' Records, Series 8, III, Male & Female Religious Orders
Chancellors' Records, Series 8, IV, Male & Female Religious Orders
Female Orders & Convents – General
Female Orders & Convents – Specific Congregations
*Ceremonial for the Reception and Profession of the Religious Sisters of Mercy*
(Dublin: Browne & Noland, 1894)

## Archives of the Sisters of Mercy, Midhurst

Profession Register of the Sisters of Mercy
Annals

## Archives of the Sisters of Mercy, Sunderland

Profession Register of the Sisters of Mercy
Annals

## CSJP: *Archives of the Congregation of St Joseph of Peace*

Register of Professed Sisters
Columba Moran, 'History of the S.H. Convent'
'Lest We Forget'

Ferguson, Sr Catherine, 'Sisters of St Joseph of Peace: History of the Sacred Heart Province, 1884–1984', 1983
——'A Look at the Evidence: The Nun of Kenmare & Knock 1881–1883' (Dublin, 1991)
——'The Founding and Growth of the Sisters of St Joseph of Peace' (Leicester, 1984)
*Reflections and Counsels of Mother M. Evangelista to her Spiritual Children* (1963)

## DC: *Archives of the Daughters of Charity of St Vincent de Paul, Mill Hill, London*

Register of Sisters of the British Province

10: Personnel Records, 'Lives of Sisters'
11: House Records, 'Houses'
Box 1, no. 2: 'Seminary Remarks'
Box 1, no. 10: 'Seminary Particulars', 1889–1917

*Notes on Deceased Sisters*
'J.M.J. Rules of the Daughters of Charity Servants of the Poor Sick, Common Rules of the Daughters of Charity', 1920 (transcribed version of Règles Communes des filles de la Charité, 1867)
'Remarks on the Life of Sister Mary Langdale'
'Sr. Etheldreda Fitzalan Howard'
Pioneer Sisters of Charity of Saint Vincent de Paul in Great Britain and Ireland (1955)

## DHM: *Daughters of the Heart of Mary Archives, Wimbledon, London*

Register of Members of the Kensington Reunion and Wimbledon
C3 'Acts of Superior Authority 1858–1920'
C3 'London Diary: Clapham'
C3 'Provincial Council Meetings'
C4 'Death Notices English/Irish Provinces – Before 1900'
Special collection 'Old Letters and Documents'

*Annals*, vols I–IV
*Rule of Conduct for the Daughters of the Heart of Mary* (Roehampton: James Stanley, 1896)
*Constitutions des filles due coeur de Marie*
*Constitutions et Règlements de Conduite des Filles du Coeur de Marie*
Vaulk, Patricia, 'The Society of the Daughters of the Heart of Mary in England'

## Diocesan Archives of Northampton

A3.5 Collins MS
A3 Series Bishop Wareing, Convent Northampton
A6 Series Bishop Riddell's papers, women's congregations
F IV.5 Convent Book

## Diocese of Nottingham Archives

Box with rules and constitutions of various institutes
File cabinet contains files of various institutes

## FCJ: Faithful Companions of Jesus, Generalate Archives, Broadstairs, Kent

Tomes 1–3 Profession Register of the Faithful Companions of Jesus

A656 Annual Relation 1874
A731 Annals 1883
A740 Annals 1884
A923 'Gumley House Annal Letter'
A1205 Annals 1895
A1209 Annals 1896
A1210 Annals 1896
A1842 Annals 1897
A1850 Annals 1898
A1854 Annals Book 1 1899
A1856 Annals Book 2 1899

*Constitutions de la société des soeurs fidèles compagnes de jésus* (Vannes: Imprimerie Galles, 1879)
d'Houët, Marie Madeleine Victoire de Bengy de Bonnault, *The Early History of the Society of the Sisters Faithful Companions of Jesus as Related in the Memoirs of the Venerable Marie Madeleine Victoire de Bengy Viscountess de Bonnault d'Houët*, translated by Patricia Grogan FCJ (Margate: Martell Press, 1981)
McCarren FCJ, Mary Campion, *History of the Constitutions: Sisters, Faithful Companions of Jesus 1818–1985* (1993)
*Rules for the Coadjutrix Sisters* (Dublin: M.H. Gill & Son, 1882)
*Summary of the Constitutions* (Dublin: M.H. Gill & Son, 1882)

## Leeds Diocesan Archives, Headingley, Leeds

B/A John Briggs (1805–60) Correspondence
C/A Robert Cornthwaite (1837–90) Correspondence
File 20 Miscellaneous Religious Institutes

## Little Company of Mary, Provincial Archives

### RLR: *Sisters of La Retraite, Regional Archives, Streatham, London*

Mother Imelda, 'Sevenoaks', 20 November 1951 or 1957, pink two-ring binder
'Sevenoaks', 1882
Applegate, Catherine, 'La Retraite: Origins and Growth', 1979

'Constitutions of the Society of the Sacred Heart of Jesus', 1884

### RSM Bermondsey: *General Archives of the Institute of Our Lady of Mercy, Bermondsey*

Profession Register of the Sisters of Mercy
'Bermondsey Annals', 1839–1900
'Maxims of our Holy Foundress'
'Obituaries from Ursula O'Connor to Clare Arrowsmith'
200/3/3 'Rule and Constitutions of the Religious Sisters of Mercy of Our Blessed
   Lady of Mercy', [1835?], inscription dated 1844
'Some Lives of the Sisters of Mercy Bermondsey', 1840–74

*A Little Book of Practical Sayings, Advices and Prayers of Our Reverend Foundress*
   *Mother Mary Catharine [sic] McAuley*, compiled by Mary Clare (Georgiana)
   Moore (London: Burns, Oates & Co., 1868)

### RSM Dublin: *Mercy International Archives, Dublin*

Manuscript photocopy, Annals, Sisters of Mercy Limerick, 1838–59
Manuscript photocopy, Annals, Sisters of Mercy Limerick, 1859–75

### RSM Handsworth: *General Archives of the Union of the Sisters of Mercy of Great Britain, Handsworth*

Profession Register of the Sisters of Mercy

1/200/3/1 'Book of Customs', 1849, handwritten notes of 1849 meeting attended by
   Reverend Mother Juliana (Juliana Hardman) and Mother M. Aloysius (Mary
   Elizabeth Jackson)
1/200/4/4 'Instruction for Novice Mistress', no date but copied between 1848 and
   1884
1/200/9/1 'Handsworth Annals'
2/200/9/1 'Birmingham Annals'
4/300/2/3 'Documents Pertaining to St Anne's and St John's Convents'
5/200/9/1 'Coventry Annals'
7/200/9/2 'Chelsea Annals'

[Bridgeman, M. Francis, RSM], *Guide for the Religious Called Sisters of Mercy. Amplified by Quotations, Instructions, &c. Part I. & II.* (London: Robson and Son, 1866)
——, *Abridgment of a Guide for the Religious Called Sisters of Mercy* (London: Robson and Son, 1866)
*Sisters of Mercy Derby 1849–1999: A Sesquiennial Celebration* (1999)


### Salford Diocesan Archives, Burnley

A1825–A1877 Laity Directories, 1825–1877
A1877–A1900 Misc Documents

*Harvest* (1897–current)


### SCSP: Sisters of Charity of St Paul the Apostle Archives, Selly Park, Birmingham

Box 1 G. Dupuis, Personal Data, Early Letters
Box 4 Letters from Bishops
Box 26 'Registers of Postulants and Novices', 1847–1900
Box 80 Formation Notes

*Rules and Constitutions of the Sisters of Charity of St Paul in England* [1864]


### SHCJ: Society of the Holy Child Jesus Archives, Oxford

Clothing Register (1846–1900)
Choir Postulants' Register (1892–1921)
'Necrologies'

'Memoir of the Rev. Mother Angelica Croft, Second Superior General of the Society of the Holy Child Jesus', 1913
[Connelly, Cornelia], *Book of the Order of Studies in the Schools of the Holy Child Jesus* (1863)
[Connelly, Cornelia], *Manual for the Use of the Novices of the Holy Child Jesus* (St Leonard's-on-Sea, 1869)

Box 54 R24 'Constitutions of the Society of the Holy Child Jesus', 1887, printer's proofs
Beatification and Canonization of the Servant of God Cornelia Connelly Foundress of the Society of the Holy Child Jesus: Documentation Presented by the Historical Commission:
Vol. 42 Training Colleges and School Affairs 1864–79
Vol. 49 Community Affairs Defections Part II
Vol. 51 Affairs of Government 1857–69

Beatification and Canonization of the Servant of God Cornelia Connelly Foundress of the Society of the Holy Child Jesus: Writings of the Servant of God Cornelia Connelly:

Vol. VIII Letters of Members of the Society of the Holy Child Jesus
Vol. XIII Letters to Ecclesiastics Bishop Grant 1862–64
Vol. XVII Letters to Ecclesiastics Bishop Danell 1874–79

Forshaw, Helen, SHCJ, 'Choir and Lay: An Historical Perspective', in *History Society of the Holy Child Jesus: Ministries Part II* (2000), pp. 46–51
Mechtilde, S. Mary, SHCJ, *Mother Mary Walburga SHCJ whose Years of Labor in the Society were its Seed Time in America* (Rosemont, Pennsylvania, 1949)
Murphy, Anne, 'SHCJ and Ireland', in *History Society of the Holy Child Jesus: Beginnings* (1996), pp. 47–51


## SMG: *Central Congregational Archive of the Poor Servants of the Mother of God, Brentford, Middlesex*

I/A  Mother Magdalen's papers
I/B  'Annals'
I/C  Papers relating to the foundation of the congregation, early houses and missions
I/D  Personal accounts and narratives by Sisters
I/E  Correspondence with clergy and religious
I/F  Correspondence between Mother Magdalen and Lady Georgiana and Mr A.G. Fullerton
I/P  Letters from Mother Magdalen to Sisters from Paris
I/R  Letters from Mother Magdalen to Sisters from Rome

Profession Register of the Poor Servants of the Mother of God

'An Eight Days' Retreat for the Poor Servants of the Mother of God given by Mother Foundress (M. Mary Magdalen of the Sacred Heart, S.M.G.)'
'Instructions of Mother Foundress on Our Holy Rule on Confession, etc. Taken from her Letters, and from Sisters' Notes'
'Mother Foundress' Letters to the Institute (1877–1900)', 1957
'Mother as We Knew Her', 1957
'Necrology Book I: 1872–1945', 1956
'Notes of Conferences given to Local Superiors by Mother Foundress, Mother Mary Magdalen of the Sacred Heart Poor Servant of the Mother of God'

I/C *Rules & Constitutions of the Poor Servants of the Mother of God and the Poor* (1892)
I/C/1/4 'Constitutions SMG Vol 1st' and 'Constitutions SMG Vol 2nd'


## SND: *Notre Dame Archives, British Province, Liverpool*

Registers of Professed Sisters for the British Province (1845–1900)
Mission Database

Box 13 MPTC *A Voice* (1863–69)
BH2 Clapham CL.h/1 'Transcribed Letters from Clapham to Namur 1848–1850'
BX BB/1 in BH1 'Blackburn Annals', 1860–1913
BX BB/2 in BH1 F1 'Blackburn Community Matters'
BX BK/1 in BH1 'Birkdale Annals', 1878–1901
BX BS/1 in BH1 'Battersea Annals', 1892–1908
BX BS/4 in BH1 F1 'Battersea', 1869–1900
BX EV/1 in BH2 'Everton Annals'
BX PRV/1 – BX PRV/7 various documents
BX PRV/2 in BPND, box marked 'Province History 2: Notre Dame in England 1845–1850'
C3 'London Diary: Clapham', 1847–80
NH h/2 in BH3 'Northampton Annals', 1857–1900
NH h/3 in BH3 'Infant Jesus Documents'
PN.h/1 'English Translation of Letters to Namur'

*Book of the Instructions of Blessed Mère Julie* (1909)
*Règles et Constitutions des Soeurs de Notre-dame* (Namur, [1859])

## SSJ: Sisters of St Joseph of Annecy Archives, Llantanam Abbey

Professed Sisters Register

## Newspapers and periodicals

*Catholic Directory*
*Catholic Times*
*The Harvest*
*Laity's Directory*
*The Tablet*
*The Times*

## Other primary sources

A.J.S., 'On the Secondary Education of Catholic Women', *The Month* (May 1894), 26–33.
Arbuthnot, Mrs, 'The Danger of Conventual Education and the Importance of Home Training', in *Romanism and Ritualism in Great Britain and Ireland, A Report of the National Protestant Congress* (Edinburgh: R.W. Hunter, 1895).
Avis, Whyte, *The Catholic Girl in the World* (London: Burns & Oates, [1894]).
Bateson, Margaret, *Professional Women upon their Professions* (London: Horace Cox, 1895).
Bull, Paul, *The Missioner's Handbook: A Guide for Missioners, Evangelists, and Parish Priests* (London: Grant Richards, 1904).
*The Canons and Decrees of the Council of Trent* (London: Burns and Oates, 1848).
Casartelli, L.C., *Catholic Missions* (London: Catholic Truth Society, 1891).

Chambers, Mary Catharine Elizabeth and Henry James Coleridge, *The Life of Mary Ward (1585–1645)*, 2 vols (London: Burns and Oates, 1885).

Champneys, Basil, *Memoirs and Correspondence of Coventry Patmore* (London: George Bell and Sons, 1901).

Charlton, Barbara, *The Recollections of a Northumbrian Lady, 1815–1866: Being the Memoirs of Barbara Charlton (nee Tasburgh) Wife of William Henry Charlton of Hesleyside Northumbria*, ed. L.E.O. Charlton (London: Jonathan Cape, 1949).

Clarke, A.M., *The Life of the Hon. Mrs. Edward Petre (Laura Stafford-Jerningham) in Religion Sister Mary of St. Francis, of the Congregation of the Sisters of Notre-Dame de Namur* (London: Art and Book Company, 1899).

Connelly, Cornelia, *God Alone: An Anthology of Spiritual Writings of Cornelia Connelly, Foundress of the Society of the Holy Child Jesus* (London: Burns & Oates, 1959).

[Cusack, Margaret Anna], *Five Years in a Protestant Sisterhood and Ten Years in a Catholic Convent, an Autobiography* (London: Longmans, Green, 1869).

Cusack, M. Francis Clare, *Life Inside the Church of Rome* (London: Hodder and Stoughton, 1889).

——, *The Nun of Kenmare An Autobiography* (London: Josiah Child, 1889).

Cusack, M.F., *The Story of My Life* (London: Hodder & Stoughton, 1891).

De Paul, Vincent, *The Conferences of St Vincent De Paul to the Daughters of Charity* (London: Collins Liturgical Publications, 1979).

Deshon, George, *Guide for Catholic Young Women, Especially for those Who Earn Their Own Living* (New York: D. & J. Sadler & Co., 1863).

Devas, C.S., *Studies of Family Life: A Contribution to Social Science* (London: Burns and Oates, 1886).

Devine, Rev. Arthur, *Convent Life; Or, The Duties of Sisters Dedicated in Religion to the Service of God, intended chiefly for Superiors and Confessors* (London: The Passionists, 1889).

Ellis, Sarah Stickney, *The Women of England, their Social Duties, and Domestic Habits* (London: Fisher, Son & Co., 1839).

——, *The Wives of England, Their Relative Duties, Domestic Influence, & Social Obligations* (London: Fisher, Son, & Co., [1843]).

——, *The Daughters of England: Their Position in Society, Character and Responsibilities* (London: Fisher, Son & Co., 1845).

*The Foundations of the Sisters of Notre Dame in England and Scotland from 1845 to 1895* (Liverpool: Philip, Son & Nephew, 1895).

Gallwey, Father, SJ, *Convent Life and England in the 19th Century: Two Sermons Preached in the Church of the Immaculate Conception, Farm Street, Mid-Lent, March 7th 1869, On Occasion of an Appeal on Behalf of the Little Sisters of the Poor* (London: Burns, Oates & Co., 1869).

——, *The Committee on Convents. The Nun's Choice: Newgate or Newdegate. A Letter to a Barrister* (London: Burns, Oates, and Company, 1870).

Gordon-Gorman, W., *Converts to Rome: Since the Tractarian Movement to May 1899* (London: Swan Sonnenschein & Co., 1899).

Grant, Rev. Dr, *Meditations of the Sisters of Mercy Before Renewal of Vows* (London: Burns and Oates, 1874).

Grey, Mrs William, *Old Maids; A Lecture* (London: William Ridgway, 1875).

[Harnett, Mary Vincent], *The Life of Reverend Mother Catherine McAuley, Foundress of the Order of Mercy* (Dublin: John Fowler, 1864).

Hetherington, Rev. Dr., 'Sisters of Mercy; or, Popery and Poverty', *The Bulwark*, 1 (1867).

Hubbard, Louisa M., 'Statistics of Women's Work', in Baroness [Angela] Burdett-Coutts, ed., *Woman's Work* (London: Sampson Low, Marston & Company, 1893), pp. 361–6.

Jameson, [Anna], *Sisters of Charity Catholic and Protestant, Abroad and at Home* (London: Longman, Brown, Green, & Longmans, 1855).

Janes, Emily, 'On the Associated Work of Women in Religion and Philanthropy', in Baroness [Angela] Burdett-Coutts, ed., *Woman's Mission* (London: Sampson Low, Marston & Company, 1893), pp. 131–48.

Kerr, Amabel, 'Mother Margaret Hallahan', *The Catholic Magazine* (August 1896), 76–89.

——, *Sister Chatelain or Forty Years' Work in Westminster* (London: Catholic Truth Society, 1900).

[Lewis, Sarah], *Woman's Mission* (London: John W. Parker, 1839).

*The Life of Madame de Bonnault d'Houët: Foundress of the Society of the Faithful Companions of Jesus* (Dublin: M.H. Gill & Son, 1885).

*Liguori's Instructions on the Religious State*, ed. Giovanni Battista Pagani (Derby: Richardson and Son, 1848).

Manning, Henry Edward, *The Catholic Church and Modern Society* (London: Cecil Brooks & Co., 1880).

——, *Lost Sheep Found: An Appeal for the Convents of the Good Shepherd* (London: The Westminster Press, 1889).

Marshall, T.W.M., *Christian Missions: Their Agents, Their Method, and Their Results* (London: Burns and Lambert, 1862).

Martin, F. Abbé, *Vie de Madame de Bonnault D'Houët Fondatrice de la Société des Fidèles Compagnes de Jésus* (Paris: Librairie Saint-Joseph, 1863).

Murphy, John Nicholas, *Terra Incognita: or, The convents of the United Kingdom* (London, Longmans, Green & Co., 1873).

O'Reilly, Rev. Bernard LD, *The Mirror of True Womanhood: A Book of Instruction for Women in the World* (Dublin: M.H. Gill & Son, 1883).

Parliamentary Papers (1866), *First Report of the Royal Commission Appointed to Inquire into the Working of the Elementary Education Acts, England and Wales*, c.4863.

[Patmore, Coventry], *Angel in the House: The Betrothal* (London: John W. Parker and Son, 1854).

*Records of the Foundation and Progress of the Congregation of the Sisters of the Most Holy Cross and Passion: 1851–1911* (Dublin, 1911).

*Report on the Visitation of Females at their Own Homes in the City of Westminster* (1854).

Rowe, J.B., *Elementary Education and the Catholic Poor School Committee* (London: Burns and Oates, 1876).

Ruskin, John, *Sesame and Lilies. Two Lectures* (London: Smith, Elder & Co., 1865).

Scott, R.E., 'Convent Education', *The Month* (June 1894), 197–216.

Seymour, Rev. M. Hobart, *Convents or Nunneries. A Lecture in Reply to Cardinal*

Wiseman, delivered at the Assembly Rooms, Bath, on Monday, June 7, 1852 (Bath: R.E. Peach, 1852).

——, *On Convents. The Speech of the Rev. M. Hobart Seymour, at the Meeting of the Protestant Alliance, held in St James Hall, Piccadilly, On February 24th, 1865* (London: Protestant Alliance, 1865).

'The "Sisters of Peace" in the Dioceses of Nottingham', *The Tablet* (12 January 1884), 72.

Spurrell, James, *Miss Sellon and the 'Sisters of Mercy.' An Exposure of the Constitution, Rules, Religious Views, and Practical Working of their Society; Obtained through a 'Sister,' who has recently Seceded* (London: Thomas Hatchard, 1852).

Stanislaus, R.P., *Notice sur la vie, les vertues et les oeuvres de la Servante de Dieu Marie Madeleine Victoire de Bengy, Viscountesse de Bonnault d'Houët* (Paris, France: J. Mersch, 1895).

*The Synods in English: Being the Text of the Four Synods of Westminster*, ed. Robert E. Guy OSB (Stratford-on-Avon: St Gregory's Press, 1886).

Thomson, H. Byerley, *The Choice of a Profession: A Concise Account and Comparative Review of the English Professions* (London: Chapman and Hall, 1857).

Thurston, Herbert, 'Two Modern Dominicanesses', *The Month* (October 1895), 183–204.

Ullathorne, Bishop, *A Plea for the Rights and Liberties of Religious Women, with reference to the Bill proposed by Mr. Lacy* (London: Thomas Richardson and Son, 1851).

——, *A Letter addressed to Lord Edward Howard, on the Proposed Committee of Enquiry into Religious Communities* (London: Thomas Richardson and Son, 1854).

——, *Three Lectures on the Conventual Life* (London: Burns, Oates & Co., 1868).

Walker, Alexander, *Woman Physiologically Considered, as to Mind, Morals, Marriage, Matrimonial Slavery, Infidelity and Divorce* (London: A.H. Bailey & Co., 1839).

Ward, Mary, *Till God Will: Mary Ward through her Writings*, ed. M. Emmanuel Orchard IBVM (London: Darton, Longman & Todd, 1985).

'What of our Convent Schools?' *The Month* (April 1894), 517–26.

Wiseman, Nicholas, 'Froud's Remains', *Dublin Review*, 6 (May 1839), 416–35.

*Woman: As She Is, and As She Should be* (London: James Cochrane and Co., 1835).

## Unpublished theses

Adams, Pauline A., 'Converts to the Roman Catholic Church in England, circa. 1830–1870' (doctoral thesis, Somerville College, Oxford, 1977).

Barnhiser, Judith Anne, OSU, 'A Study of the Authority Structures of Three Nineteenth-Century Apostolic Communities of Religious Women in the United States' (doctoral thesis, Catholic University of America, 1975).

Barrus, Katherine DeMartini, '"Putting Her Hand to the Plough": Nuns and Sisters in Nineteenth-Century England' (doctoral thesis, University of Albany, State University of New York, 1999).

Edmunds, May P., 'But the Greatest of These is Chastity . . .' (doctoral thesis, Australian National University, 1986).

Jarrell, Lynn, OSU, 'The Development of Legal Structures for Women Religious between 1500 and 1900: A Study of Selected Institutes of Religious Life for Women' (doctoral thesis, Catholic University of America, 1984).

Kitching, Jack, 'Roman Catholic Education from 1700–1870: A Study of Roman Catholic Educational Endeavour from the Early Eighteenth Century to the Elementary Education Act of 1870' (doctoral thesis, University of Leeds, 1966).

Lannon, David, 'Bishop Turner and Educational Provision within the Salford Diocesan Area 1840–1870' (master's thesis, University of Hull, 1994).

Lowden, Kim, 'Spirited Sisters: Anglican and Catholic Contribution to Women's Teacher Training in the 19th Century' (doctoral thesis, Liverpool Hope University, 2000).

McAdam, Gloria, '"My Dear Sister . . .": An Analysis of 19th Century Documents Concerning the Founding of a Women's Religious Congregation' (doctoral thesis, University of Bradford, 1994).

Mangion, Carmen M., 'Centre of a Maelstrom: Anglican Sisterhoods in Victorian England' (master's thesis, Birkbeck College, University of London, 2000).

——, 'Contested Identities: Active Women Religious in Nineteenth-Century England and Wales' (doctoral thesis, Birkbeck College, University of London, 2005).

Marmion, John P., 'Cornelia Connelly's Work in Education, 1848–1879' (doctoral thesis, University of Manchester, 1984).

Stone, Hope Campbell Barton, 'Constraints on the Mother Foundresses: Contrasts in Anglican and Roman Catholic Religious Headship in Victorian England' (doctoral thesis, University of Leeds, 1993).

## Secondary sources

Acker, Sandra, 'Caring as Work for Women Educators', in Elizabeth Smyth, Sandra Acker, Sandra Bourne and Alison Prentice, eds, *Challenging Professions: Historical and Contemporary Perspectives on Women's Professional Work* (Toronto: University of Toronto Press, 1999), pp. 277–95.

Allen, Sheila, 'Identity: Feminist Perspectives on "Race", Ethnicity and Nationality', in Nickie Charles and Helen Hintjens, eds, *Gender, Ethnicity and Political Ideologies*, (London: Routledge, 1998), pp. 46–64.

Altholtz, J.L., 'The Political Behaviour of English Catholics, 1850–67', *Journal of British Studies*, 4 (1964), 89–103.

Anderson, Benedict, *Imagined Communities: Reflections on the Origin and Spread of Nationalism* (London: Verso, 1991).

Anson, Peter F., *The Religious Orders and Congregations of Great Britain and Ireland* (Worcester: Stanbrook Abbey, 1949).

Armstrong, W.A., 'The Use of Information about Occupation', in E.A. Wrigley, ed., *Nineteenth-Century Society: Essays in the use of Quantitative Methods for the Study of Social Data* (Cambridge: Cambridge University Press, 1972), pp. 191–310.

Arnstein, Walter L., *Protestant versus Catholic in Mid-Victorian England: Mr. Newdegate and the Nuns* (London: University of Missouri Press, 1982).

Atkin, Nicholas, 'The Politics of Legality: The Religious Orders in France, 1901–45', in Frank Tallett and Nicholas Atkin, eds, *Religion, Society and Politics in France since 1789* (London: The Hambledon Press, 1991), pp. 149–66.

Attwater, Donald, *The Catholic Church in Modern Wales: A Record of the Past History* (London: Burns Oates & Washbourne, 1935).

Augustine, P. Chas., OSB, DD, *A Commentary on the New Code of Canon Law*, 8 vols (London: B. Herder Book Co., 1918).

Bates, M. Rita, *Living his Theme Song: Virtues of Mother M. Evangelista Gaffney* (Paterson, New Jersey: St Anthony Guild Press, 1953).

Battersby, W.J., 'The Educational Work of the Religious Orders of Women: 1850–1950', in George Andrew Beck, ed., *The English Catholics, 1850–1950* (London: Burns Oates, 1950), pp. 337–64.

Bellenger, Dom Aidan, 'France and England: The English Female Religious from Reformation to World War', in Frank Tallett and Nicholas Atkin, eds, *Catholicism in Britain and France since 1789* (London: The Hambledon Press, 1996), pp. 3–11.

Bennett, John, 'The Care of the Poor', in George Andrew Beck, ed., *The English Catholics, 1850–1950* (London: Burns Oates, 1950), pp. 559–84.

Blake, Sister Ursula Blake, and Sister Annette Dawson, *Positio: Information for the Canonization Process of the Servant of God Cornelia Connelly (née Peacock) 1809–1879*, 3 vols (Rome: Sacred Congregation for the Causes of Saints, 1983).

Blott, K., *A Hundred Years: A History of the F.C.J.'s in Middlesbrough 1872–1972 with Particular Reference to the Growth of St Mary's Convent School* (Middlesbrough: H. & F. Stokeld Printers, 1972).

Bossy, John, *The English Catholic Community, 1570–1850* (London: Darton, Longman & Todd, 1975).

——, 'English Catholics after 1688', in Ole Peter Grell, Jonathan I. Israel and Nicholas Tyacke, eds, *From Persecution to Toleration: The Glorious Revolution and Religion in England* (Oxford: Clarendon Press, 1991), pp. 369–88.

Bowden, Caroline, 'Approaching Prosopographical Studies in the Early Modern Period: The Case of the English Convents', paper presented at conference entitled 'Consecrated Women: Towards the History of Women Religious of Britain and Ireland', Birkbeck College, London, 2003.

——, 'Community Space and Cultural Transmission: Formation and Schooling in English Enclosed Convents in the Seventeenth Century', *History of Education*, 34 (2005), 365–86.

Branca, Patricia, *Silent Sisterhood: Middle-Class Women in the Victorian Home* (London: Croom-Helm, 1975).

Bryant, Margaret, *The Unexpected Revolution: A Study in the History of the Education of Women and Girls in the Nineteenth Century* (London: University of London Institute of Education, 1979).

Burley, Stephanie, 'An Overview of the Historiography of Women Religious in Australia', *Journal of the Australian Catholic Historical Society*, 26 (2005), 43–60.

Burstyn, Joan N., *Victorian Education and the Ideal of Womanhood* (London: Croom Helm, 1980).

Callahan, Francis, *The Centralization of Government in Pontifical Institutes of Women with Simple Vows* (Rome: Gregorian University, 1948).

Casteras, Susan P., 'Virgin Vows: The Early Victorian Artists' Portrayal of Nuns and Novices', *Victorian Studies*, 24 (winter 1981), 157–84.

Chadwick, Owen, *The Spirit of the Oxford Movement* (Cambridge: Cambridge University Press, 1990).

Charles, Nickie, 'Feminist Practices: Identity, Difference, Power', in Nickie Charles and Felicia Hughes-Freeland, eds, *Practising Feminism: Identity, Difference, Power* (London: Routledge, 1996), pp. 1–37.

Clear, Caitriona, *Nuns in Nineteenth-Century Ireland* (Dublin: Gill and Macmillan, 1987).

——, 'Walls within Walls: Nuns in Nineteenth-Century Ireland', in Chris Curtin, ed., *Gender in Irish Society* (Galway: Galway University Press, 1987), pp. 134–51.

——, 'The Limits of Female Autonomy: Nuns in Nineteenth-Century Ireland', in Maria Luddy and Cliona Murphy, eds, *Women Surviving: Studies in Irish Women's History in the 19th and 20th Centuries* (Dublin: Poolpeg, 1990), pp. 15–50.

Coburn, Carol K. and Martha Smith, *Spirited Lives: How Nuns Shaped Catholic Culture and American Life, 1836–1920* (Chapel Hill and London: The University of North Carolina Press, 1999).

——, 'An Overview of the Historiography of Women Religious: A Twenty-Five-Year Retrospective', *U.S. Catholic Historian*, 22 (winter 2004), 1–26.

Copelman, Dina M., *London's Women Teachers: Gender, Class and Feminism 1870–1930* (London: Routledge, 1996).

Corfield, Penelope J., *Power and the Professions 1700–1850* (London: Routledge, 1995).

Cott, Nancy F., *The Bonds of Womanhood: 'Woman's Sphere' in New England, 1780–1835* (London: Yale University Press, 1977).

Cox, Jeffrey, 'Audience and Exclusion at the Margins of Imperial History', *Women's History Review*, 3 (1994), 501–14.

Crawford, Patricia, *Women and Religion in England 1500–1720* (London: Routledge, 1993).

——, 'Women, Religion and Social Action in England, 1500–1800', *Australian Feminist Studies*, 13 (1998), 269–80.

Cruise, Edward, 'Development of Religious Orders' in George Andrew Beck, ed., *The English Catholics, 1850–1950* (London: Burns Oates, 1950), pp. 442–74.

Cullen, Mary and Maria Luddy, *Women, Power and Consciousness in 19th Century Ireland* (Dublin: Attic Press, 1995).

Cunningham, Hugh and Joanna Innes, eds, *Charity, Philanthropy and Reform: from the 1690s to 1850* (Basingstoke: St Martin's Press, 1998).

Curtis, Sarah A., 'Lay Habits: Religious Teachers and the Secularization Crisis of 1901–1904', *French History*, 9 (1995), 478–98.

——, *Educating the Faithful: Religion, Schooling, and Society in Nineteenth-Century France* (Dekalb, Illinois: Northern Illinois Press, 2000).

Danylewycz, Marta, *Taking the Veil: An Alternative to Marriage, Motherhood, and Spinsterhood in Quebec, 1840–1920* (Toronto, Canada: McClelland and Stewart, 1987).

Daunton, Martin, *Charity, Self-Interest and Welfare in the English Past* (London: UCL Press, 1996).

Davidoff, Leonore, 'Where the Stranger Begins: The Question of Siblings in

Historical Analysis', in Leonore Davidoff, ed., *Worlds Between: Historical Perspectives on Gender and Class* (Cambridge: Polity Press, 1995), pp. 206–21.

Davidoff, Leonore, and Catherine Hall, *Family Fortunes: Men and Women of the English Middle Class, 1780–1850* (London: Hutchinson, 1987).

Davidoff, Leonore, Megan Doolittle, Janet Fink and Katherine Holden, *The Family Story: Blood, Contract and Intimacy, 1830–1960* (London: Longman, 1999).

*Decree on the Adaptation and Renewal of Religious Life, Perfectae caritatis* (28 October 1965), www.vatican.va/archive/hist_councils/ii_vatican_council/ [accessed 29 August 2006].

Devas, F.C., SJ, *Mother Mary Magdalen of the Sacred Heart (Fanny Margaret Taylor): Foundress of the Poor Servants of the Mother of God 1832–1900* (London: Burns, Oates & Washbourne, 1927).

Dewitt, Susan, CSJP, *A Great Love of Peace* (Bellevue, Washington: CSJP, 2000).

Digby, Anne and Peter Searby, *Children, School and Society in Nineteenth-Century England* (London: The Macmillan Press, 1981).

Diner, Hasia, *Erin's Daughters in America: Irish Immigrant Women in the Nineteenth Century* (Baltimore, Maryland, USA: The John Hopkins University Press, 1983).

Dougherty, Patrick, *Mother Mary Potter: Foundress of the Little Company of Mary (1847–1913)* (London: Sands & Co., Ltd., 1961).

Doyle, Peter, 'The Education and Training of Catholic Priests in Nineteenth-Century England', *Journal of Ecclesiastical History*, 35 (1984), 208–19.

——, 'Family and Marriage', in V. Alan McClelland and Michael Hodgetts, eds, *From Without the Flaminian Gate: 150 Years of Roman Catholicism in England and Wales 1850–2000* (London: Darton Longman & Todd, 1999), pp. 192–216.

Dyhouse, Carol, 'Mothers and Daughters in the Middle-Class Home, c. 1870–1914' in Jane Lewis, ed., *Labour & Love: Women's Experience of Home and Family 1850–1940* (Oxford: Basil Blackwell, 1986), pp. 27–48.

Ebaugh, Helen Rose, 'Patriarchal Bargains and Latent Avenues of Social Mobility: Nuns in the Roman Catholic Church', *Gender and Society* (September 1993), 400–14.

Edwards, Elizabeth, 'Educational Institutions or Extended Families? The Reconstruction of Gender in Women's Colleges in the Late Nineteenth and Early Twentieth Centuries', *Gender and Education*, 2 (1990), 17–35.

Engelhardt, Carol Marie, 'The Paradigmatic Angel in the House: The Virgin Mary and Victorian Anglicans', in Anne Hogan and Andrew Bradstock, eds, *Women of Faith in Victorian Culture: Reassessing the Angel in the House* (London: Macmillan Press Ltd., 1998), pp. 159–71.

Faderman, Lilian, *Surpassing the Love of Men: Romantic Friendship and Love between Women from the Renaissance to the Present* (London: The Women's Press, 1981).

Fahey, Tony, 'Nuns in the Catholic Church in Ireland in the Nineteenth Century', in Mary Cullen, ed., *Girls Don't Do Honours: Irish Women in Education in the 19th and 20th Centuries* (Dublin: Women's Education Bureau, 1987), pp. 7–30.

Fielding, Stephen, *Class and Ethnicity: Irish Catholics in England, 1880–1939* (Buckingham: Open University Press, 1993).

Fiorenza, Elisabeth Schussler, *In Memory of Her: A Feminist Theological Reconstruction of Christ Origins* (London: SCM Press, 1994).

Fitzgerald-Lombard, Charles, *English and Welsh Priests 1801–1914: A Working List* (Bath, England: Downside Abbey, 1993).

Fitzpatrick, David, 'A Curious Middle Place: The Irish in Britain, 1871–1921', in Roger Swift and Sheridan Gilley, eds, *The Irish in Britain 1815–1939* (London: Pinter Publishers, 1989), pp. 10–59.

Flaxman, Radegunde, *A Woman Styled Bold: The Life of Cornelia Connelly, 1809–1879* (London: Darton Longman & Todd, 1991).

Gibson, Ralph, 'The Christianisation of the Countryside in Western Europe in the Nineteenth century', in J.-P. Massaut and M.-E. Henneau, eds, *La christianisation de Campagnes* (Rome: Institut Historique Belge de Rome, 1996), pp. 485–509.

——, 'Female Religious Orders in Nineteenth-Century France', in Frank Tallett and Nicholas Atkin, eds, *Catholicism in Britain and France since 1789* (London: The Hambledon Press, 1996), pp. 105–13.

Giddens, Anthony, *Modernity and Self-Identity: Self and Society in the Late Modern Age* (Cambridge: Polity Press, 1991).

Gill, Sean, *Women and the Church of England from the Eighteenth-Century to the Present* (London: Society for Promoting Christian Knowledge, 1994).

——, 'Heroines of Missionary Adventure: The Portrayal of Victorian Women Missionaries in Popular Fiction and Biography', in A. Hogan and A. Bradstock, eds, *Women of Faith in Victorian Culture: Reassessing the Angel in the House* (Dublin: Macmillan Press Ltd, 1998), pp. 172–85.

Gilley, Sheridan, 'The Roman Catholic Mission to the Irish in London', *Recusant History*, 10 (1969–70), 123–45.

——, 'Protestant London, No-Popery and the Irish Poor: 1830–60 (Part I)', *Recusant History*, 10 (1969–70), 210–30.

——, 'Protestant London, No-Popery and the Irish Poor: 1850–60 (Part II)', *Recusant History*, 11 (1971–72), 21–46.

——, 'English Catholic Charity and the Irish Poor in London: Part I, 1700–1840', *Recusant History*, 11 (1971–72), 179–95.

——, 'English Catholic Charity and the Irish Poor in London: Part II, 1840–1870', *Recusant History*, 11 (1971–72), 253–69.

——, 'Papists, Protestants and the Irish in London, 1835–70', in G.J. Cuming and D. Baker, eds, *Popular Belief and Practice: Papers Read at the Ninth Summer Meeting and the Tenth Winter Meeting of the Ecclesiastical History Society* (Cambridge: University Press, 1972), pp. 259–76.

——, 'Roman Catholicism and the Irish in England', *Immigrants & Minorities [Great Britain]*, 18 (1999), 147–67.

——, 'The Years of Equipose, 1892–1943', in V. Alan McClelland and Michael Hodgetts, eds, *From without the Flaminian Gate: 150 Years of Roman Catholicism in England and Wales 1850–2000* (London: Darton Longman & Todd, 1999), pp. 21–61.

Gittins, Diana, 'Marital Status, Work and Kinship, 1850–1930', in Jane Lewis, ed., *Labour and Love: Women's Experience of Home and Family 1850–1940* (Oxford: Basil Blackwell, 1986), pp. 249–67.

——, *The Family in Question: Changing Households and Familiar Ideologies* (London: Macmillan, 1993).

Gleadle, Katherine, *The Early Feminists: Radical Unitarians and the Emergence of the Women's Rights Movement, 1831–1851* (London: Routledge, 1995).

Goddijn, H.P.M., 'The Sociology of Religious Orders and Congregations', *Social Compass*, 7 (1960), 431–47.

Gomersall, Meg, *Working-Class Girls in Nineteenth-Century England* (London: Macmillan Press, 1997).

[Gompertz, Mary Catherine], *Cornelia Connelly, 1809–1879: Foundress of the Society of the Holy Child Jesus* (London: Longmans, Green and Co., 1950).

Gordon, Eleanor and Gweneth Nair, 'The Myth of the Victorian Patriarchal Family', *The History of the Family*, 7 (2002), 125–38.

Gorham, Deborah, *The Victorian Girl and the Feminine Ideal* (London: Croom Helm, 1982).

Gove, Jennifer and Stuart Watt, 'Identity and Gender', in Kath Woodward, ed., *Questioning Identity: Gender, Class, Nation* (London: Open University Press, 2000), pp. 43–78.

Gwynn, Denis, 'Growth of the Catholic Community', in George Andrew Beck, ed., *The English Catholics, 1850–1950* (London: Burns Oates, 1950), pp. 410–42.

Gwynn, M.M. Xavier, SHCJ, *From Hunting Field to Cloister* (Dublin: Clonmore and Reynolds, 1946).

Hall, Catherine, 'The Early Formation of Victorian Domestic Ideology', in Sandra Burman, ed., *Fit Work for Women* (London: Croom Helm, 1979), pp. 15–32.

Hamer, Edna, *Elizabeth Prout, 1820–1864: A Religious Life for Industrial England* (Bath, England: Downside Abbey, 1994).

Heimann, Mary, *Catholic Devotion in Victorian England* (Oxford: Clarendon Press, 1995).

——, 'Devotional Stereotypes in English Catholicism, 1850–1914', in Frank Tallett and Nicholas Atkin, eds, *Catholicism in Britain and France since 1789* (London: The Hambledon Press, 1995), pp. 13–25.

Hexter, J.H., 'The Protestant Revival and the Catholic Question in England, 1778–1829', *The Journal of Modern History*, 8 (1936), 297–319.

Hickey, Daniel, *Hospitals in Ancien Regime France: Rationalization, Resistance, Renewal 1530–1789* (Montreal: McGill-Queen's University Press, 1997).

Hickman, Mary J., *Religion, Class and Identity: The State, the Catholic Church and the Education of the Irish in Britain* (Aldershot, England: Avebury, 1995).

——, 'Incorporating and Denationalizing the Irish in England: The Role of the Catholic Church', in Frank O'Sullivan, ed., *The Irish World Wide History, Heritage, Identity* (London: Leicester University Press, 1996), pp. 196–216.

Hilton, Mary and Pam Hirsch, eds, *Practical Visionaries: Women, Education and Social Progress, 1790–1930* (London: Longman, 2000).

Hogan, Anne, 'Angel or Eve?: Victorian Catholicism and the Angel in the House', in Anne Hogan and Andrew Bradstock, eds, *Women of Faith in Victorian Culture: Reassessing the Angel in the House* (London: Macmillan Press Ltd, 1998), pp. 91–100.

Hogan, Edmund M., *The Irish Missionary Movement: A Historical Survey 1830–1980* (Dublin: Gill and Macmillan, 1990).

Hohn, Rev. H[ermann], *Vocations: Conditions for Admission, etc., into the Convents, Congregations, Societies, Religious Institutes etc. According to Authentical Information and the Latest Regulations* (London: R & T Washbourne, 1912).

Holcombe, Lee, *Victorian Ladies at Work* (London: Archon Books, 1973).

Holmes, Geoffrey, *Augustan England: Profession, State and Society, 1680–1730* (London: George Allen & Unwin, 1982).

Holmes, J. Derek, *More Roman than Rome: English Catholicism in the Nineteenth Century* (London: Burns and Oates, 1978).

Holton, Sandra Stanley, Alison Mackinnon, and Margaret Allen, 'Introduction', *Women's History Review*, 7/2 (1998), 163–9.

Hoy, Suellen, 'The Journey Out: The Recruitment and Emigration of Irish Religious Women to the United States, 1812–1914', *Journal of Women's History*, 6/7 (1995), 64–98.

Hoy, Suellen and Margaret MacCurtain, *From Dublin to New Orleans: The Journey of Nora and Alice* (Dublin: Attic Press, 1994).

Hudson, George V., *Mother Geneviève Dupuis, Foundress of the English Congregation of the Sisters of Charity of St Paul the Apostle 1813–1903* (London: Sheed & Ward, 1929).

Hufton, Olwen, *Whatever Happened to the History of the Nun?* (Royal Holloway, University of London: Royal Holloway, 1999).

Hufton, Olwen and Frank Tallett, 'Communities of Women, the Religious Life and Public Service in Eighteenth-Century France', in Marilyn J. Boxer and Jean H. Quataert, eds, *Connecting Spheres: Women in the Western World, 1500 to the Present* (New York: Oxford University Press, 1984), pp. 75–85.

Hughes, Trystan O., *Winds of Change: The Roman Catholic Church and Society in Wales 1916–62* (Cardiff: University of Wales Press, 1999).

Jones, Colin, *The Charitable Imperative: Hospitals and Nursing in Ancient Regime and Revolutionary France* (London: Routledge, 1989).

——, 'Sisters of Charity and the Ailing Poor', *Social History of Medicine*, 2 (1989), 339–48.

Kanya-Forstner, Martha, 'Defining Womanhood: Irish Women and the Catholic Church in Victorian Liverpool', in Donald M. MacRaild, ed., *The Great Famine and Beyond: Irish Migrants in Britain in the Nineteenth and Twentieth Centuries* (Dublin: Irish Academic Press, 2000), pp. 168–88.

Keats-Rohan, KSB, 'Prosopography and Computing: A Marriage Made in Heaven?', *History and Computing*, 12 (2000), 1–13.

Kent, John, *Holding the Fort: Studies in Victorian Revivalism* (London: Epworth Press, 1978).

Kerr, Cecil, *Memoir of a Sister of Charity: Lady Etheldreda Fitzalan Howard* (London: Burns Oates & Washbourne, 1928).

Kerr, Cecil, *Edith Fielding Sister of Charity* (London: Sands & Company, 1933).

Kidd, Alan J., 'Philanthropy and the "Social History Paradigm"', *Social History*, 21 (1996), 180–92.

Kirkus, Sr M. Gregory, IBVM, *The Institute of the Blessed Virgin Mary: An Historical Sketch of the Institute in England* (1993).

Kirkus, Sr M. Gregory, *An I.B.V.M. Biographical Dictionary of the English Members and Major Benefactors* (London: Catholic Record Society, 2001).

Klaus, Robert J., *The Pope, the Protestants, and the Irish: Papal Aggression and Anti-Catholicism in Mid-Nineteenth Century England* (London: Garland Publishing, 1987).

Lancaster, Judith, *Cornelia Connelly and her Interpreters* (Oxford: The Way, 2004).

Langland, Elizabeth, *Nobody's Angels: Middle-Class Women and Domestic Ideology in Victorian Culture* (London: Cornell University Press, 1995).

Langlois, Claude, 'Les effectifs des congrégations féminines au XIXe siècle: de l'enquête statistique à l'histoire quantitative', *Revue d'Histoire de l'Eglise de France*, 60 (1974), 39–64.

Langlois, Claude, *Le catholicisme au féminin: les congrégations francaises à supérieure générale au XIXe siècle, histoire* (Paris: Les Editions du Cerf, 1984).

Lascelles, E.C.P., 'Charity', in G. M. Young, ed., *Early Victorian England, 1830–1865* (London, 1934), II, pp. 315–48.

Laslett, Peter, 'England: The Household over Three Centuries', in Peter Laslett and Richard Wall, eds, *Household and Family in Past Time: Comparative Studies in the Size and Structure of the Domestic Group over the Last Three Centuries in England, France, Serbia, Japan and Colonial North America, with Further Materials from Western Europe* (Cambridge: Cambridge University Press, 1972), pp. 125–58.

Lee, Joseph J., 'Women and the Church since the Famine', in Margaret MacCurtain and Donncha O Corrain, eds, *Women in Irish Society: The Historical Dimension* (Dublin: Arlen House, 1978), pp. 37–45.

Lees, Lynn Hollen, *Exiles of Erin: Irish Migrants in Victorian London* (Manchester: Manchester University Press, 1979).

Lewis, Jane, 'Introduction: Reconstructing Women's Experience of Home and Family', in Jane Lewis, ed., *Labour & Love: Women's Experience of Home and Family 1850–1940* (Oxford: Basil Blackwell, 1986), pp. 1–24.

——, 'Women and Late-Nineteenth-Century Social Work', in Carol Smart, ed., *Regulating Womanhood: Historical essays on Marriage, Motherhood and Sexuality* (London: Routledge, 1992), pp. 78–99.

Leys, M.D.R., *Catholics in England 1559–1829: A Social History* (London: Longmans, 1961).

Linscott, Mary, *Quiet Revolution: The Educational Experience of Blessed Julie Billiart and the Sisters of Notre Dame de Namur* (Glasgow: Burns, 1966).

——, 'The Experience of Women Religious', in Noel Timms and Kenneth Wilson, eds, *Governance and Authority in the Roman Catholic Church: Beginning a Conversation* (London: SPCK, 2000), pp. 70–90.

Lonergan, Margaret, 'The Archives of the Anglo-Scottish Province of the Little Sisters of the Assumption', *Catholic Archives Journal*, 11 (1991) 17–23.

Luddy, Maria, 'Women and Charitable Organisations in Nineteenth Century Ireland', *Women's Studies International Forum*, 11 (1988), 301–5.

——, 'An Agenda for Women's History in Ireland: 1800–1900', *Irish Historical Studies*, 28 (1992), 19–37.

——, 'An Outcast Community: The "Wrens" of the Curragh', *Women's History Review*, 1 (1992), 341–84.

——, *Women and Philanthropy in Nineteenth-Century Ireland* (Cambridge: Cambridge University Press, 1995).

——, '"Abandoned Women and Bad Characters": Prostitution in Nineteenth-Century Ireland', *Women's History Review*, 6 (1997), 485–505.

——, 'Religion, Philanthropy and the State in Eighteenth- and Early Nineteenth-Century Ireland', in Hugh Cunningham and Joanna Innes, eds, *Charity,*

*Philanthropy and Reform from the 1690s to 1850* (London: Macmillan Press Ltd, 1998), pp. 148–67.

McAdam, Gloria, 'Willing Women and the Rise of Convents in Nineteenth-Century England', *Women's History Review*, 8 (1999), 411–41.

McCarren, Mary Campion, FCJ, *Faithful Companion of Jesus: Venerable Marie Madeleine Victoire de Bengy, Viscountess de Bonnault d'Houët 1781–1858, Foundress of the Society of Sisters Faithful Companions of Jesus* (London: Catholic Truth Society, 1981).

McCarthy, Caritas, *The Spirituality of Cornelia Connelly: In God, For God, With God* (Lewiston, New York, USA: Edwin Mellen Press, 1986).

McClelland, Maria G., 'In Search of the Hull Mercy Nuns: An Archival Travelogue', *Catholic Archives Journal*, 16 (1996), 37–53.

——, *The Sisters of Mercy, Popular Politics and the Growth of the Roman Catholic Community in Hull, 1855–1930* (Lewiston, NY: Queenston, Lampeter: The Edwin Mellen Press, 2000).

McClelland, V. Alan, 'From Without the Flaminian Gate', in V. Alan McClelland and Michael Hodgetts, eds, *From without the Flaminian Gate: 150 Years of Roman Catholicism in England and Wales* (London: Darton Longman & Todd, 1999), pp. 1–20.

MacCurtain, Margaret, 'Towards an Appraisal of the Religious Image of Women', *The Crane Bag*, 4 (1980), 26–30.

——, 'Late in the Field: Catholic Sisters in Twentieth-Century Ireland and the New Religious History', in Mary O'Dowd and Sabine Wichert, eds, *Chattel, Servant or Citizen. Women's Status in Church, State and Society* (Belfast: The Institute of Irish Studies, 1995), pp. 34–44.

——, 'Godly Burdens: The Catholic Sisterhoods in Twentieth Century Ireland', in Anthony Bradley and Maryann Gialanella Valiulis, eds, *Gender and Sexuality in Modern Ireland* (Amherst: University of Massachusetts Press, 1997), pp. 245–56.

——, 'Catholic Sisterhoods in 20th-Century Ireland', *Religious Life Review*, 39 (2000), 19–31.

McDermott, M. Rosarii, *The Undivided Heart: The Life of Mother Evangelista First Mother General of the Sisters of St Joseph of Newark* (Newark, New Jersey: St Anthony Guild Press, 1961).

MacGinley, M.R., PBVM, *A Dynamic of Hope: Institutes of Women Religious in Australia* (Darlinghurst, New South Wales: Crossing Press, 2002).

McGrath, Madeleine Sophie, *These women? Women Religious in the History of Australia: The Sisters of Mercy Parramatta 1888–1988* (Kensington, New South Wales: New South Wales University Press, 1992).

McNamara, Jo Ann Kay, *Sisters in Arms: Catholic Nuns through Two Millennia* (London: Harvard University Press, 1996).

Magray, Mary Peckham, *The Transforming Power of the Nuns: Women, Religion, and Cultural Change in Ireland, 1750–1900* (Oxford: Oxford University Press, 1998).

Makowski, Elizabeth M., *Canon Law and Cloistered Women: Periculoso and its Commentators, 1298–1545* (Washington, DC: Catholic University of America Press, 1997).

Malmgreen, Gail, 'Introduction', in *Religion in the Lives of English Women, 1760–1930*, ed. by Gail Malmgreen (London & Sydney: Croom Helm, 1986), pp. 1–10.

——, 'Domestic Discords: Women and the Family in East Cheshire Methodism, 1750–1830', in Jim Okelkevich, Lyndal Roper and Raphael Samuel, eds, *Disciplines of Faith: Studies in Religion, Politics and Patriarchy* (London: Routledge, 1987), pp. 55–70.

Mangion, Carmen M., '"Good Teacher" or "Good Religious"?: The Professional Identity of Catholic Women Religious in nineteenth-century England and Wales', *Women's History Review*, 14 (2005), pp. 223–42.

——, 'Laying "good strong foundations": The Power of the Symbolic in the Formation of a Religious Sister', *Women's History Review*, 16 (2007), 403–15.

Mannard, Joseph G, '"A Kind of Noah's Ark": Vocations of Women Religious in the Archdiocese of Baltimore, 1790–1860', paper presented at conference entitled 'Triennial Meeting of the Conference for the History of Women Religious Through Multiple Lenses: Interdisciplinary Perspectives on the History of Women Religious', Loyola University, Lake Shore Campus, Chicago, Illinois, 1998.

Marks, Lynne, 'The "Hallelujah Lasses": Working-Class Women in the Salvation Army in English Canada, 1882–92', in Franca Iacovetta and Mariana Valverde, eds, *Gender Conflicts: New Essays in Women's History* (Toronto: University of Toronto Press, 1992), pp. 67–117.

Marmion, John P., 'The Beginnings of the Catholic Poor Schools in England', *Recusant History*, 17 (1984–85), 67–83.

*Mary Elizabeth Towneley (in religion Sister Marie des Saints Anges): Provincial of the English Province of The Sisters of Notre Dame of Namur: A Memoir* (London: Burns Oates and Washbourne, 1924).

Matchinske, Megan, *Writing, Gender and State in Early Modern England: Identity Formation and the Female Subject* (Cambridge: Cambridge University Press, 1998).

Mathew, David, 'Old Catholics and Converts', in George Andrew Beck, ed., *The English Catholics, 1850–1950* (London: Burns Oates, 1950), pp. 223–42.

Melnyk, Julie, ed., *Women's Theology in Nineteenth-Century Britain: Transfiguring the Faith of their Fathers* (London: Garland Publishing, 1998).

Milbank, Alison, 'Josephine Butler: Christianity, Feminism and Social Action', in Jim Obelkevich, Lynda Roper and Raphael Samuel, eds, *Disciplines of Faith: Studies in Religion, Politics and Patriarchy* (London: Routledge, 1987), pp. 154–64.

Mills, D.R. and K. Schurer, 'Employment and Occupations', in Dennis Mills and Kevin Schurer, eds, *Local Communities in the Victorian Census Enumerators' Books* (Oxford: Leopard's Head Press Limited, 1996), pp. 136–60.

Mills, Hazel, 'Negotiating the Divide: Women, Philanthropy and the "Public Sphere" in Nineteenth-Century France', in Frank Tallett and Nicholas Atkin, eds, *Religion, Society and Politics in France since 1789* (London: The Hambledon Press, 1991), pp. 29–54.

——, '"Saintes soeurs" and "femmes fortes": Alternative Accounts of the Route to Womanly Civic Virtue, and the History of French Feminism', in Clarissa Campbell Orr, ed., *Wollstonecraft's Daughters: Womanhood in England and France 1780–1920* (Manchester: Manchester University Press, 1996), pp. 135–50.

——, '"La Charité est une Mère": Catholic Women and Poor Relief in France, 1690–1850', in Hugh Cunningham and Joanna Innes, eds, *Charity, Philanthropy and Reform From the 1690s to 1850* (London: MacMillan Press Ltd, 1998), pp. 168–92.

Misner, Barbara, SCSC, *'Highly Respectable and Accomplished Ladies'*: *Catholic Women Religious in America 1790–1850* (London: Garland Publishing, 1988).

Moore, Judith, *A Zeal for Responsibility: The Struggle for Professional Nursing in Victorian England, 1868–1883* (Athens: University of Georgia Press, 1988).

Morgan, Susan, *A Passion for Purity: Ellice Hopkins and the Politics of Gender in the Late-Victorian Church* (Bristol: University of Bristol, 1999).

——, 'Faith, Sex and Purity: The Religio-Feminist theory of Ellice Hopkins', *Women's History Review*, 9 (2000), 13–34.

——, 'Review', *Gender & History*, 14 (2002), 163–5.

——, ed., *Women, Religion and Feminism in Britain, 1750–1900* (Basingstoke: Palgrave Macmillan, 2002).

Mort, Frank, *Dangerous Sexualities: Medico-Moral Politics in England since 1830* (London: Routledge & Kegan Paul, 1987).

Mullins, Daniel J., 'The Catholic Church in Wales', in V. Alan McClelland and Michael Hodgetts, eds, *From without the Flaminian Gate: 150 Years of Roman Catholicism in England and Wales 1850–2000* (London: Darton Longman & Todd, 1999), pp. 272–94.

Mumm, Susan, ' "Not Worse than Other Girls": The Convent-Based Rehabilitation of Fallen Women in Victorian Britain', *Journal of Social History*, 29 (1996), 527–46.

——, *Stolen Daughters, Virgin Mothers: Anglican Sisterhoods in Victorian Britain* (London: Leicester University Press, 1998).

——, ' "I Love my Sex": Two Late Victorian Pulpit Women', in Joan Bellamy, Anne Laurence and Gill Perry, eds, *Women, Scholarship and Criticism: Gender and Knowledge c. 1790–1900* (Manchester: Manchester University Press, 2000), pp. 204–21.

Murray, Janet, *Strong-Minded Women: And Other Lost Voices from Nineteenth-Century England* (London: Penguin Books, 1984).

Nelson, Claudia and Ann Sumner Holmes, 'Introduction', in Claudia Nelson and Ann Sumner Holmes, eds, *Maternal Instincts: Visions of Motherhood and Sexuality in Britain, 1875–1925* (London: Macmillan Press, 1997), pp. 1–12.

Nelson, Sioban, *Say Little, Do Much: Nurses, Nuns, and Hospitals in the Nineteenth Century* (Philadelphia: University of Pennsylvania Press, 2001).

Nolan, Janet A., *Ourselves Alone: Women's Emigration from Ireland, 1885–1920* (Lexington, Kentucky: University Press of Kentucky, 1989).

Norman, Edward R., *Anti-Catholicism in Victorian England, Historical Problems: Studies and Documents* (London: Allen and Unwin, 1968).

——, *The English Catholic Church in the Nineteenth Century* (Oxford: Oxford University Press, 1984).

O'Brien, Susan, 'A Transatlantic Community of Saints: The Great Awakening and the First Evangelical Network 1735–1755', *The American Historical Review*, 91 (1986), 811–32.

——, ' "Terra Incognita": The Nun in Nineteenth-Century England', *Past and Present*, 121 (1988), 110–40.

——, '10,000 Nuns: Working in Convent Archives', *Catholic Archives Journal*, 9 (1989), 26–33.

——, 'Lay-Sisters and Good Mothers: Working-Class Women in English Convents,

1840–1910', in W. J. Sheils and D. Wood, eds, *Women in the Church: Papers Read at the 1989 Summer Meeting and the 1990 Winter Meeting of the Ecclesiastical History Society*, Studies in Church History (Oxford: Ecclesiastical History Society, 1990), pp. 453–65.

——, 'Women of the English Catholic Community: Nuns and Pupils at the Bar Convent, York, 1680–1790', in Judith Loades, ed., *Monastic Studies: The Continuity of Tradition* (Bangor, Gwynedd: Headstart History, 1990), pp. 267–82.

——, 'Making Catholic Spaces: Women, Décor, and Devotion in the English Catholic Church, 1840–1900', in Diana Woods, ed., *The Church and the Arts* (Oxford: Blackwell Publishers, 1992), pp. 449–64.

——, 'Religious Life for Women', in V. Alan McClelland and Michael Hodgetts, eds, *From without the Flaminian Gate: 150 Years of Roman Catholicism in England and Wales 1850–2000* (London: Darton Longman & Todd, 1999), pp. 108–41.

——, 'A Survey of Research and Writing about Roman Catholic Women's Congregations in Great Britain and Ireland' in Jan de Maeyer, Sophie Leplaie and Joachim Schmiedl, eds, *Religious Institutes in Western Europe in the 19th and 20th Centuries* (Leuven, Belgium: Leuven University Press, 2004), pp. 91–116.

O'Connell, Marie, 'The Genesis of Convent Foundations and their Institutions in Ulster, 1840–1920', in Janice Holmes and Diane Urquhart, eds, *Coming into the Light: The Work, Politics and Religion of Women in Ulster 1840–1940* (Belfast: The Institute of Irish Studies, 1994), pp. 149–201.

O'Day, Rosemary, *The Professions in Early Modern England, 1450–1800: Servants of the Commonweal* (London: Longman, 2000).

O'Dowd, Mary and Maryann Gialanella Valiulis, eds, *Women and Irish History: Essays in Honour of Margaret MacCurtain* (Dublin: Wolfhound Press, 1997).

O'Leary, Paul, 'From the Cradle to the Grave: Popular Catholicism among the Irish in Wales', in Patrick O'Sullivan, ed., *Religion and Identity* (London: Leicester University Press, 1996), pp. 183–95.

Orth, Clement, *The Approbation of Religious Institutes* (Washington, DC: The Catholic University of America, 1931).

O'Sullivan, Patrick, 'Introduction to Volume 5: Religion and Identity', in Patrick O'Sullivan, ed., *Religion and Identity* (London: Leicester University Press, 1996), pp. 1–24.

——, 'Religion and Identity', in Patrick O'Sullivan, ed., *Religion and Identity* (London: Leicester University Press, 1996), pp. 183–95.

Patmore, Derek, *The Life and Times of Coventry Patmore* (London: Constable Publishers, 1949).

Paz, D.G., 'Anti-Catholicism, Anti-Irish Stereotyping, and Anti-Celtic Racism in Mid-Victorian Working-Class Periodicals', *Albion*, 18 (1986), 601–16.

Pearce, Joseph, 'The Catholic Literary Revival', in V. Alan McClelland and Michael Hodgetts, eds, *From without the Flaminian Gate: 150 Years of Roman Catholicism in England and Wales 1850–2000* (London: Darton Longman + Todd, 1999), pp. 295–319.

Perkin, Harold, *The Rise of Professional Society: England since 1880* (London: Routledge, 1989).

Perkin, Joan, *Women and Marriage in Nineteenth Century England* (London: Routledge, 1988).

Peterson, M. Jeanne, *The Medical Profession in Mid-Victorian London* (Berkeley: University of California Press, 1978).

Pinches, Sylvia, 'Church Charities in the Diocese of Birmingham, 1800–1918', *Catholic Ancestor*, 8 (2000), 28–36.

——, 'Lay Charities in the Diocese of Birmingham, 1800–1918', *Catholic Ancestor*, 8 (2000), 73–82.

Poole, Myra, *Prayer, Protest, Power: The Spirituality of Julie Billiart Today* (Norwich: Canterbury Press, 2001).

Pooley, Colin, 'Segregation or Integration? The Residential Experience of the Irish in Mid-Victorian Britain', in Roger Swift and Sheridan Gilley, eds, *The Irish in Britain 1815–1939* (London: Pinter Publishers, 1989), pp. 60–83.

Pope, Barbara Corrado, 'Immaculate and Powerful: The Marian Revival in the Nineteenth Century' in Clarissa W. Atkinson, Constance H. Buchanan and Margaret R. Miles, eds, *Immaculate and Powerful: The Female in Sacred Image and Social Reality* (Boston: Beacon Press, 1985), pp. 173–200.

Pope, Robert, 'Introduction', in Robert Pope, ed., *Religion and National Identity: Wales and Scotland c.1700–2000* (Cardiff: University of Wales Press, 2001), pp. 1–13.

Prest, Wilfrid, *The Professions in Early Modern England* (London: Croom Helm, 1987).

Prochaska, F.K., *Women and Philanthropy in Nineteenth-Century England* (Oxford: Clarendon Press, 1980).

Ranft, Patricia, *A Woman's Way: The Forgotten History of Women Spiritual Directors* (New York: Palgrave, 2000).

Rapley, Elizabeth, *The Dévotes: Women and the Church in Seventeenth-Century France* (London: McGill-Queen's University Press, 1990).

——, *A Social History of the Cloisters: Daily Life in the Teaching Monasteries of the Old Regime* (Montreal: McGill-Queen's University Press, 2001).

Raughter, Rosemary, 'A Discreet Benevolence: Female Philanthropy and the Catholic Resurgence in Eighteenth-Century Ireland', *Women's History Review*, 6 (1997), 465–84.

Raymond, Janice, *A Passion for Friends: Toward a Philosophy of Female Affection* (London: The Women's Press, 1991).

Rendall, Jane, *The Origins of Modern Feminism: Women in Britain, France and the United States 1780–1860* (London: Macmillan, 1985).

Reuther, Rosemary Radford, 'Catholic Women', in Rosemary Radford Ruether and Rosemary Skinner Keller, eds, *In Our Own Voices: Four Centuries of American Women's Religious Writing* (San Francisco: Harper San Francisco, 1995), pp. 17–60.

Rogers, Rebecca, 'Boarding Schools, Women Teachers and Domesticity: Reforming Girls' Secondary Education in the First Half of the Nineteenth Century', *French Historical Studies*, 19 (1995), 153–81.

——, 'Schools, Discipline, and Community: Diary-Writing and Schoolgirl Culture in Late Nineteenth-Century France', *Women's History Review*, 4 (1995), 525–54.

——, 'Retrograde or Modern? Unveiling the Teaching Nun in Nineteenth-Century France', *Social History*, 23 (1998), 146–64.

——, 'French Education for British Girls in the Nineteenth Century', *Women's History Magazine*, 42 (2002), 21–9.

Rowbotham, Judith, '"Soldiers of Christ"? Images of Female Missionaries', *Gender & History*, 12 (2001), 82–106.

——, 'Ministering Angels, not Ministers: Foreign Missionary Movement, c. 1860–1910' in S. Morgan, ed., *Women, Religion and Feminism in Britain, 1750–1900* (Houndmills: Palgrave Macmillan, 2002), pp. 179–96.

Rowlands, Marie B., 'Recusant Women, 1560–1640', in Mary Prior, ed., *Women in English Society, 1500–1800* (London and New York: Methuen, 1985), pp. 149–80.

Savage, Michael, 'Space, Networks and Class Formation' in Neville Kirk, ed., *Social Class and Marxism: Defences and Challenges* (Aldershot, England: Scolar Press, 1996), pp. 58–86.

Scarisbrick, J.J., *Selly Park and Beyond: The Story of Geneviève Dupuis and the Congregation of the Sisters of Charity of St Paul the Apostle* (Selly Park, England: Sisters of Charity of St Paul the Apostle, 1997).

Semple, Rhonda A., *Missionary Women: Gender, Professionalism and the Victorian Idea of Christian Mission* (Suffolk: Boydell & Brewer, 2003).

Sharp, John, 'Juvenile Holiness: Catholic Revivalism among Children in Victorian Britain', *Journal of Ecclesiastical History*, 35 (1984), 220–38.

——, *Reapers of the Harvest: The Redemptorists in Great Britain and Ireland, 1843–1898* (Dublin: Veritas, 1989).

Sheils, W.J., 'Catholicism from the Reformation to the Relief Acts', in Sheridan Gilley and W. J. Sheils, eds, *A History of Religion in Britain: Practice and Belief from Pre-Roman Times to the Present* (Oxford: Blackwell, 1994), pp. 234–51.

*Sister Mary of St. Philip (Frances Mary Lescher) 1825–1904* (London: Longmans, Green and Co., 1922).

Smith-Rosenberg, Carroll, 'The Female World of Love and Ritual: Relations between Women in Nineteenth-Century America', in Carroll Smith-Rosenberg, ed., *Disorderly Conduct: Visions of Gender in Victorian America* (Oxford: Oxford University Press, 1985), pp. 1–29.

Smyth, Elizabeth, ' "Writing Teaching Us Our Mysteries": Women Religious Recording and Writing History', in Beverly Boutilier and Alison Prentice, eds, *Creating Historical Memory: English-Canadian women and the Work of History* (Vancouver: UBC Press, 1997), pp. 101–28.

——, 'Professionalization among the Professed: The Case of Roman Catholic Women Religious', in Elizabeth Smyth, Sandra Acker, Sandra Bourne and Alison Prentice, eds, *Challenging Professions: Historical and Contemporary Perspectives on Women's Professional Work* (Toronto: University of Toronto, 1999), pp. 234–54.

——, 'Writing the History of Women Religious in Canada (1996–2001)', *International Journal of Canadian Studies*, 23 (spring 2001), 205–12.

Sneyd-Kynnersley, E.M., *H.M.I. Some Passages in the Life of One of H.M. Inspectors of Schools* (London: Macmillan and Co., 1908).

Stanislaus, F.M., *Life of the Viscountess de Bonnault D'Houët: Foundress of the Society of the Faithful Companions of Jesus 1781–1858* (London: Longmans, Green and Co., 1913).

Steele, Francesca M., *The Convents of Great Britain* (London: Sands, and Dublin: M.H. Gill, 1902).

——, *Monasteries and Religious Houses of Great Britain and Ireland* (London: R. & T. Washbourne, 1903).

——, *The Convents of Great Britain and Ireland* (London: Sands, 1924).

Stone, Judith F., 'Anticlericals and Bonnes Soeurs: The Rhetoric of the 1901 Law of Associations', *French Historical Studies*, 23 (2000), 103–28.

Stone, Lawrence, *The Past and the Present Revisited* (London: Routledge & Kegan Paul, 1981).

Suenens, Cardinal Leon Joseph, *The Nun in the World: New Dimension in the Modern Apostolate* (London: Burns & Oates, 1962).

Sullivan, Mary C., RSM, *Catherine McAuley and the Tradition of Mercy* (Dublin, Ireland: Four Courts Press, 1995).

—— ed., *The Correspondence of Catherine McAuley, 1818–1841* (Dublin, Ireland: Four Courts Press, 2004).

Summers, Anne, 'A Home from Home – Women's Philanthropic Work in the Nineteenth Century', in Sandra Burman, ed., *Fit Work for Women* (London: Croom Helm, 1979), pp. 33–63.

——, 'Hidden from History? The Home Care of the Sick in the Nineteenth Century', *History of Nursing Society Journal*, 4 (1992–23), 227–43.

Supple, Jennifer F., 'Ultramontanism in Yorkshire, 1850–1900', *Recusant History*, 17 (1985), 274–86.

Tallett, Frank and Nicholas Atkin, *Religion, Society and Politics in France since 1789* (London: Hambledon Press, 1991).

——, eds, *Catholicism in Britain and France since 1789* (London: The Hambledon Press, 1996).

Thompson, Margaret S., 'Women, Feminism, and the New Religious History: Catholic Sisters as a Case-study', in Philip R. Vandermeer and Robert R. Swierenga, eds, *Belief and Behaviour: Essays in New Religious History* (New Jersey: Rutgers University Press, 1991), pp. 136–63.

Thorne, Susan, 'Missionary-Imperial Feminism', in Mary Taylor Huber and Nancy C. Lutkehaus, eds, *Gendered Missions: Women and Men in Missionary Discourse and Practice* (Ann Arbor, Michigan: University of Michigan Press, 1999).

Tihon, André, 'Les religieuses en Belgique du XVIIIe au XXe siècle: approche statistique', *Revue Belge d'Histoire Contemporaine*, 7 (1976), 1–54.

Valenze, Deborah, *Prophetic Sons and Daughters: Female Preaching and Popular Religion in Industrial England* (Princeton, New Jersey: Princeton University Press, 1985).

Vicinus, Martha, *A Widening Sphere: Changing Roles of Victorian Women* (Bloomington and London: Indiana University Press, 1977).

——, 'Distance and Desire: English Boarding-School Friendships', *Signs*, 9 (1984), 600–22.

——, *Independent Women: Work and Community for Single Women, 1850–1920* (London: Virago Press, 1985).

Walker, Claire, *Gender and Politics in Seventeenth-Century English Convents: English Convents in France and the Low Countries* (Basingstoke: Palgrave Macmillan, 2003).

Wallis, Frank H., *Popular Anti-Catholicism in Mid-Victorian Britain* (Lewiston, New York: The Edwin Mellen Press, 1993).

Walsh, Barbara, *Roman Catholic Nuns in England and Wales, 1800–1937: A Social History* (Dublin: Irish Academic Press, 2002).

Walsh, Michael J., 'Catholics, Society and Popular Culture', in V. Alan McClelland and Michael Hodgetts, eds, *From without the Flaminian Gate: 150 Years of Roman Catholicism in England and Wales 1850–2000* (London: Darton Longman & Todd, 1999), pp. 346–70.

West, Elizabeth A., *One Woman's Journey: Mary Potter Founder – Little Company of Mary* (Richmond, Victoria, Australia: Spectrum Publications, 2000).

[Wheaton, Louise], *A Daughter of Coventry Patmore, Sister Mary Christina, SHCJ* (London: Longmans, Green and Co., 1924).

Whitehead, Maurice, '"Briefly, and in Confidence": Private Views of Her Majesty's Inspectors on English Catholic Elementary Schools, 1875', *Recusant History*, 20 (1991), 554–62.

Wilson, Linda, *Constrained by Zeal: Female Spirituality amongst Nonconformists, 1825–1875* (Carlisle, England: Paternoster Publishing, 2000).

Witz, Anne, *Professions and Patriarchy* (London: Routledge, 1992).

Woodward, Kath, ed., *Identity and Difference* (London: Sage, 1997).

——, *Questioning Identity: Gender, Class, Nation* (London: Open University Press, 2000).

Yeo, Eileen Janes, 'Social Motherhood and the Sexual Communion of Labour in British Social Science, 1850–1950', *Women's History Review*, 1 (1992), 63–88.

——, 'Some Contradictions of Social Motherhood', in Eileen Janes Yeo, ed., *Mary Wollstonecraft and 200 Years of Feminisms* (London: Rivers Oram Press, 1997), pp. 121–33.

——, 'Protestant Feminists and Catholic Saints in Victorian Britain', in Eileen Janes Yeo, ed., *Radical Femininity: Women's Self-representation in the Public Sphere* (Manchester: Manchester University Press, 1998), pp. 127–48.

——, 'The Creation of "Motherhood" and Women's Responses in Britain and France, 1750–1914', *Women's History Review*, 8 (1999), 201–18.

# Index